# THE CONSTITUTION OF IRAN

# THE CONSTITUTION OF IRAN

## Politics and the State
## in the Islamic Republic

---

ASGHAR SCHIRAZI

Translated by John O'Kane

I.B.Tauris Publishers
LONDON • NEW YORK

Published in 1997 by
I.B.Tauris & Co Ltd
Victoria House
Bloomsbury Square
London WC1B 4DZ

A full CIP record for this book is available from the British
Library

ISBN 1 86064 046 X

Set in Monotype Garamond by Philip Armstrong, Sheffield

Printed and bound in Great Britain by WBC Ltd, Bridgend,
Mid Glamorgan

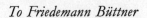

*To Friedemann Büttner*

# Contents

# Introduction

The Constitution of the Islamic Republic of Iran is full of contradictions which, viewed in their totality, reflect the extraordinary range of political forces involved in the Iranian revolution and the particular constellation of power that existed between these forces from the time the first preliminary draft of the document was produced in Paris between January and June 1978 until 15 November 1979 when, after much debate and revision, a final version was approved by an Assembly of Experts.

Among the many contradictions to emerge from this process two are fundamental and have had a decisive impact on the development of the Iranian state since the revolution. The first is the contradiction between the constitution's Islamic legalist and non-Islamic secular elements which flows largely from the claim that a state set up on the basis of Shi'i law and ruled by Islamic jurists (*foqaha*) is capable of offering solutions to all problems, not only in Iran, but throughout the world even though the constitution itself incorporates many non-Islamic and non-legalist elements. The second is the contradiction between its democratic and anti-democratic elements, arising chiefly from the conflict between the two notions of sovereignty embodied in the document: the sovereignty of the people on the one hand and of the Islamic jurists on the other, a sovereignty the jurists exercise as God's deputies. There is a third contradiction between those Islamic legalist elements in the constitution which support a hierocracy[1] and its Islamic anti-hierocratic elements. However, since the latter are based on a conception of Islam which has assimilated significantly greater democratic and secular attitudes, this contradiction can be seen as corresponding for the most part to the contradiction between the legalist and the democratic, secular elements.

These two major contradictions provide the central theme of this book which will examine the way they have found their way into the constitution and how, in a lengthy process of resolution, they have been eradicated under the Islamic Republic. The subject is of importance for two reasons. Firstly because, in revealing the inconsistency of a document which was meant to establish the principles of a model Islamic state and an exemplary Islamic society, the very existence of such contradictory elements raises questions about the external form of the constitution. And secondly because the process of resolution they necessarily set in motion from the moment the preliminary draft of the constitution was completed, before the revolution itself, has since been a key dynamic of political life in the Islamic Republic.

I

Part I of the book delineates the major contradictions of the constitution and examines the process that led to their incorporation into the document. The first chapter presents a detailed analysis of the text itself and makes it clear that, despite its commitment to establishing a legalist state, the constitution has been forced to incorporate many elements that are not in harmony with this goal. These elements appear alongside one another in the text, awaiting a resolution of the tension between them in everyday practice. The second and third chapters adopt a historical approach. They give an indication of the ideas and attitudes developed and articulated by strategic social and political forces during the debate that took place when the constitution was framed, provide a comparison of the constitution's final content from the point of view of what would have been required for it to be based on, or indeed to have fostered, consensus and help to explain why some ideas were, and others were not, incorporated into the final document.

The importance of the social forces considered in these chapters stems from their significance within Iran's socioeconomic structure, their preponderance in the intellectual-political movement which gathered force before and immediately after the revolution, and the part they played in bringing together the disparate groups that participated in the revolution. The influence such groups eventually exercised, for the most part as an opposition, in determining the political processes after the ratification of the constitution was an additional factor.

Parts II and III deal with the practical resolution of the contradictions of the constitution in the process of legislation and government – a process which has, in its turn, led to a form of Islamic state which was not thought possible even by many of the legalists. Part IV depicts some of the ways different Islamic circles have reacted to their experience of a 'real' Islamic state. While these reactions have occasionally taken the form of clinging to the existing system, they have also resulted, in some quarters, in doubts about the claim that Islamic law can solve all problems, and a rejection of outright Islamic legalism. The concluding section discusses the transformation that has taken place in Iran since the establishment of the Islamic Republic and the implications of that transformation. The constitution of 1979 was revised in 1989 and this revision and its consequences are discussed in various places in Parts II and III, as well as in the Conclusion.[2]

In Part 1 the forces that participated in the debate over the framing of the constitution are initially divided along general lines into secularists and Islamicists. But during the debates over the constitution the various secularist groupings did not behave in a uniform or consistent way, nor (often) in a way their political label would lead one to expect. Many gave their approval to the constitution out of tactical or strategic considerations. The divisions between the Islamicists, who were similarly represented by numerous political organisations or religious authorities, were also, at this point, shifting, varied and frequently obscure.

The committed hierocratic legalists are defined as those who advocated the mandate of the jurist (*velayat-e faqih*), in particular as understood by Khomeini. They supported the adoption of the *shari'a* as the juridical basis for the state, and held various orthodox positions on the adaption of this system to 'the demands of the times'. Many non-legalists also advocated the adoption of the *shari'a*, though with greater or lesser degrees of moderation. They are distinguished from the committed hierocratic legalists chiefly by their rejection of the concept of *velayat-e faqih* and in this somewhat arbitrary sense are categorised as non-legalists. A third group has rejected legalism in Khomeini's sense but on the question of applying the *shari'a* represents a position that is as, if not more orthodox, as that of the radical legalists. Further differentiation is certainly possible and would be an essential requirement in a more comprehensive study of this subject.

These divisions are valid for the period directly after the revolution when the struggle over the form the new constitution would take was at the centre of politics. For the period after the constitution was adopted, the book deals with those groupings and political organisations that were destroyed or reduced to opposition only to the extent that the elimination of the democratic elements of the constitution affected them. Its primary focus is on the forces and political divisions which manifested themselves within the jurist-dominated regime. Here a rough distinction is made between a conservative and a radical-populist grouping, to which is added a moderate element that began to manifest itself more obviously after the death of Khomeini.

The main sources used in Part 1 of the book are as follows:

1. The preliminary draft of the constitution as it was presented to the Assembly of Experts and the final text ratified by the Assembly of Experts.
2. More than 4,000 recorded statements on individual points of both the preliminary outline of the constitution and its final text.
3. Discussion and criticism that has appeared in the press or in books and brochures.
4. The minutes of the Assembly of Experts or Majles-e Khobregan (cited in the notes as MK).

These sources are not of equal importance and particular use has been made of those documents which express the opinions of powerful political organisations and influential individuals. Special attention has been given to a comparison of the constitution's preliminary outline with its final text,[3] since the preliminary outline not only represents the views of the non-legalist Islamicists but was also a version of the constitution which might have found approval with many liberal secularists. Had it been ratified, a constitution would have been adopted within whose framework a broader and a more stable social consensus might have been achieved.[4] The minutes of the Assembly of Experts provide an important contribution to understanding specific points in the constitution and to revealing the controversies that emerged amongst the members of the assembly during their debates.

Unfortunately, they only document the assembly's plenary sessions. This is an important point because many enlightening discussions and crucial compromises took place during sessions of the sub-committees.

These documents are supplemented in Part 1 by accounts of events that throw light on the political context in which the constitution was framed, and which contribute to a better understanding of particular questions with which it deals. Great attention is given to the process which led to the emergence of the preliminary outline of the constitution, as well as to the factors and arguments that shaped the Assembly of Experts' formulation of its final version. Close attention is also paid to the methods the clerical leadership of the revolution, which was by no means confident of achieving its ends, used to ensure that its particular conception of the constitution was victorious.

An important source used in Parts II and III is the press which, besides the general news, carried special reports, interviews, leaders, articles by outside contributors, and numerous discussions of policy and resolutions. Further documentation comes from the following sources:

1. The collections of laws, decrees, decisions of the Council of Ministers and recommendations issued by the Guardian Council, which were published each year by the Ministry of Justice (cited in the notes as LB).
2. The views of the Guardian Council which were collected, arranged and published first by J. Madani, and then by H. Mehrpur.
3. The minutes of parliamentary debates (*Surat-e Mozakerat-e Majles-e Showra-ye Islami*) published at regular intervals by the Publicity Department of Parliament (cited in the notes as MM).
4. The minutes of the Assembly for the Revision of the Constitution (Majles-e Baznegari-ye Qanun-e Asasi), also published by the Publicity Department of parliament (cited in the notes as MR).
5. Other documents published by the Publicity Department of parliament, such as the yearly activity reports of parliament.
6. Periodicals such as *Howzeh*, *Kayhan-e Andisheh*, *Kayhan-e Farhangi*, *Rahnamun* and *Kiyan*, in which members of the clergy and Islamic intellectuals have expressed their views on the reform of Islamic law, the present-day interpretation of Islam, etc. Articles on these topics were also published in the daily press, often in the form of ongoing series as in the case of Ayatollah Azari Qomi's articles in *Resalat*.

To these sources should be added books and pamphlets that deal with questions of Islamic law and politics. Extensive use has also been made of the author's interviews or conversations with politicians, academics and intellectuals. I must take this opportunity to express my warmest thanks to 'Abolhasan Bani-Sadr, Hasan Nazih, 'Abdolkarim Lahiji, Ahmad Salamatian, Naser Pakdaman, 'Ali Asghar Sadr Hajj Seyyed Javadi, Hasan Shari'at-madari and Ahmad 'Ali Baba'i. Others with whom I have had fruitful conversations reside in Iran.

Research for the book was undertaken with the support of the DFG (Deutsche Forschungsgemeinschaft) within the framework of the research project entitled: 'The Development of the Constitution of the Islamic Republic of Iran', directed by Professor Friedemann Büttner and Professor Baber Johansen. I wish here to thank the DFG for their generous support, and to express my gratitude to Professors Büttner and Johansen for the responsibility they have assumed in directing this project. I would also like to thank the FNK (Kommission für Forschung und Wissenschaftlichen Nachwuchs der Freien Universität Berlin) for meeting the costs of translating my book from German. Finally, I am especially indebted to Ilse Itscherenska, Houchang Chehabi and my editor, Anna Enayat, for their meticulous reading of my original typescript and the suggestions they have made for its revision.

## Notes

1 The term hierocracy is used here to mean the rule of a particular social class, the clergy. I will argue in the following chapters that in such a situation real religious issues recede into the background and serve almost exclusively as a means of legitimising political power.

2 On this subject see Pakdaman (1990); Tellenbach (1990); Schirazi (1991); and Milani (1992).

3 The texts of both these documents have been translated into German by S. Tellenbach (1985). A second translation of the constitution was commissioned by the Embassy of the Islamic Republic of Iran in Bonn. An English by Hamed Algar was published in 1980. For a commentary on the two German texts, particularly from a juridical point of view, see S. Tellenbach (1985) and F. Gisbert (1980).

4 It is noteworthy, for instance, that in an extensive criticism of the constitution's preliminar outline published by the Jebheh-e Melli (National Front), those stipulations which place legislation under the control of the *shari'a* were not rejected. See *Ayandegan*, 2/8/79. The same is true of the 'analytical' and 'critical' position adopted by the equally liberal Hezb-e Iran (Party of Iran) see: *Hezb-e Iran*, 1979. We will see in the next chapter that some secular left-wing organisations also abstained from criticising the Islamic character of the constitution.

# PART ONE

# Contradictions in the Constitution of the Islamic Republic

# ONE

# The Composition of the Constitution

This chapter sets out, and analyses, the points of conflict between the three major elements – Islamic legalist, secular and democratic – of the 1979 Constitution leaving the question of how and why they became such uncomfortable bedfellows to the next, which takes a close look at the historical and political dynamics that shaped the document.

## Islamic Legalist Elements

Islamic elements appear throughout the constitution, in the preamble as well as its 175 articles.[1] Generally speaking, they present the following character-istics:

1. They establish that the state and the revolution leading to the creation of that state are Islamic.
2. They define the tasks and the goals of the state in accordance with its Islamic character.
3. They bind legislation to the *shari'a*.
4. They ensure that positions of leadership will be reserved for Islamic jurists.
5. They place Islamically defined restrictions on the democratic rights of individuals, of the nation and of ethnic groups.
6. They set up institutions whose task it is to ensure the Islamic character of the state.

### The Islamic Definition of the State

The clauses of the constitution that define the state as Islamic begin in the preamble which brushes aside the multiple economic, social, cultural and political motives and goals which provided the driving force of the revolution and attributes a purely Islamic character to the event. 'The Islamic nature of the great Islamic revolution' expressed the will 'of the Islamic people' to establish the constitution 'on the basis of Islamic principles and guidelines'. 'The distinctive peculiarity of this revolution' lay in its 'ideological and Islamic character'. Indeed, it was this characteristic that guaranteed its victory, in contrast previous revolutions [In Iran] which, despite the clergy's participation in the leadership, had ultimately failed because they departed from 'noble Islamic positions'. 'The outline of an Islamic state based on the mandate of the jurists' set out by Imam Khomeini[2] provided the decisive co-ordinating impetus to the Islamic people's movement which in the end led to the foundation of the Islamic Republic.[3] So victorious a revolution could have no other outcome, endorsed by 98.2 per cent of the people who voted in the national referendum held on the 30–31 March 1979.

> Consequently, the Constitution of the Islamic Republic, as an expression of the political, social, cultural and economic relations and institutions of the community, must lead the way in consolidating the foundations of the Islamic state and propose a new blueprint for the form of state to be constructed on the ruins of the old despotic regime.

The official religion of the state is Islam as interpreted by the Ja'fari school of jurisprudence of the Twelver Shi'a. This religious definition of the state, in view of the eternal truth of Islam, can never be altered.[4] An additional distinguishing feature of the state's Islamic character is the national flag which bears as the special emblem of the Islamic Republic the inscription 'Allah-o Akbar'.[5] Two further points are that members of parliament and the president are required to swear an oath of allegiance exclusively to Islam [6] and high school students are obliged to study Arabic, the language of the Koran and the Islamic sciences.[7]

*The Principles, Goals and Tasks of the Islamic State*

An Islamic Republic is naturally based on principles which are defined by Islam and are in the main presented in Art. 2 of the constitution as follows:

1. There is only one God ... who by right is ruler and lawgiver, and man must submit to His command.
2. Divine revelation has a fundamental role to play in the promulgation of laws.
3. The resurrection plays an essential role in the process of man's development vis-à-vis God.
4. God's justice is inherent in His creation and His laws.
5. The Imamate will provide the leadership and will play a fundamental role in the progress of the Islamic revolution.
6. Man is endowed with nobility and elevated dignity. His freedom entails responsibility before God.

These principles are to stand as a guarantee that, by means of 'continual *ejtehad*[8] exercised by qualified[9] jurists on the basis of the Koran and the *sunna* (tradition) of those who are infallible (God's peace be upon them all)', along with certain more general, that is not specifically Islamic, requirements: 'justice as well as political, economic, social and cultural independence and national solidarity' will be achieved.

The Islamic character of the new state is defined both in the preamble and the main articles of the document. Among its goals are: the foundation

of 'an exemplary society' with the assistance of 'Islamic ideals', 'the realisation
of the movement's religious principles', 'the achievement of prerequisites'
on the basis of which man will be formed with the help of 'lofty and
universal Islamic values'. What is to be striven for, however, is not merely
the realisation of these goals for the Iranian people but for Muslims
throughout the world, and all those in the world who have been deprived of
their rights (*mostaz'afin*). What is to be striven for is 'smoothing the way to
establishing a single world-wide religious community'.[10]

The constitution assigns Islamic tasks to all the organs of state and the
state authorities. Thus, the 'ideologically oriented army' is not merely responsible for the defence of the nation's borders but must assume 'the burden of
the ideological mission, i.e. the Holy War (*jehad*) to spread the rule of God's
law throughout the world'.[11] This task belongs first and foremost to the
Revolutionary Guard, set up for this specific purpose.[12] Likewise, the mass
media 'must perform the service of disseminating Islamic culture as part of
the process of development of the Islamic revolution'.[13] And the judiciary
is to defend 'the rights of the people in the Islamic movement'. Finally, 'the
executive power must pave the way for the creation of an Islamic society'
and has 'a special significance in the task of putting into effect Islamic
regulations and prescriptions'.[14]

### Binding Legislation to the shari'a

The constitution binds legislative power to the *shari'a* as defined by Shi'i
Islam. The *shari'a* either forms the foundation on which legislation is based,
or defines the boundaries beyond which it may not proceed. The resolutions
passed by parliament must not contradict the *shari'a*. The stipulations of the
*shari'a* are designated in the text of the constitution by the following terms,
usually in the plural: ordinances (*ahkam*), regulations (*moqarrarat*), laws
(*qavanin*), principles (*osul* or *mabani*), criteria (*ma'ayir*), foundations (*asas*),
guidelines (*zavabet*) and standards (*mavazin*). In some cases the stipulations are
quite explicit as with the *hadd*-punishments or the prohibition of usury; in
other cases they determine the content of the relevant principles of the
constitution. The provisions that bind legislation to the *shari'a* are set out in
general terms in the preamble and in the chapter of the constitution which
deals with general principles, as well as in articles introduced elsewhere in the
document whenever it is deemed necessary to emphasise the *shari'a*'s authority.

Already in the preamble we read that 'legislation, which formulates the
guidelines for directing society' is to be based on the Koran and the *sunna*.
Consequently, the constitution is founded on 'the fundaments of Islamic
principles and guidelines'. Art. 2 binds legislation to the *shari'a* by representing
legislation as a power reserved for God and acknowledging that revelation
has a fundamental role in the promulgation of laws. Art. 4 states that 'all
laws and regulations ... must be based on Islamic principles'. Art. 72 forbids
'the Majles-e Showra-ye Melli' (the parliament) to pass laws which 'contradict

the principles and ordinances of the state religion of the land ...'. The same restriction is imposed on local councils whose resolutions must accord with 'Islamic principles' and the laws of the land based on the *shari'a*.[15] Art. 170 makes it incumbent on judges to refuse to implement government resolutions and decrees when these 'contravene Islamic laws and regulations'.

Explicit reference is made to Islamic ordinances in the following articles:

1. Art. 8, citing the authority of the Koran 9/71,[16] makes it the duty of the people and the government to 'enjoin upon one another what is just and forbid what is evil'.

2. Art. 11 binds foreign policy to the principle that 'all Muslims belong to a single community' and thus enjoins the government to strive for the unification of the Islamic peoples.[17]

3. Art. 12–14 reflect the Islamic conception of the position of religious minorities. This entails the recognition of the other four Islamic schools of jurisprudence and the three non-Islamic religions with a revealed Book, as well as the obligation of Muslims to behave properly towards non-Muslims and to respect their human rights.

4. Art. 10 sets limits on future laws, regulations and planning pertaining to the family – limits determined by the conception of 'the sanctity of the family' as grounded in Islamic law and 'Islamic ethics'. These are closely linked to Islamic conceptions of the position of women in society and their rights as a woman and mother which are set out in Art. 21. This article makes it the duty of the government to guarantee the rights of women 'in accordance with Islamic principles'. For instance, guardianship of a child is only conferred upon 'a worthy mother', 'when no legitimate male guardian is on hand'. This is a case where even the legal status of women is subject to the restrictions of Islamic principles.[18]

Likewise, the articles which describe the 'rights of the people in general and the democratic rights of the citizens in particular'[19] always include the precondition that these rights must be compatible with Islamic ideals and principles or simply with 'the law' (naturally, Islamic law is meant).

Art. 43 prohibits usury, hoarding and 'forbidden business activities'. Art. 49 also specifies certain business activities which, according to the *shari'a*, are forbidden and stipulates that wealth resulting from such activities is to be returned to its rightful owners or to the state. Art. 44 makes the protection of property in the state, private, or corporate sector, dependent on the condition that its possession is not in violation of 'the limits set by Islamic law'. Art. 45 puts into effect those Islamic ordinances which stipulate that certain assets occurring in a natural state, for example mineral resources or rivers, as well as 'inheritances without an heir' and 'material assets of unknown ownership', are to revert to the Islamic state. Art. 42 recognises the right to private property when the property in question has been acquired in a 'legal' fashion, i.e. in a manner that accords with the *shari'a*.

Chapter 5 bears the title 'The Sovereignty of the People and the Powers Thereby Conferred'. The first article[20] sets out the Islamic conception according to which absolute dominion is an exclusive prerogative of God. It follows from this that the sovereignty of the people is subject to restriction by the authorities who are considered to represent the dominion of God. Art. 91–98 describe the function of the authority entrusted with the task of examining the resolutions passed by the parliament. This authority is to establish whether the resolutions are contrary to Islamic principles and ordinances, and to declare them invalid if such is the case. Art. 5 as well as Art. 107–111 describe the office and the functions of 'the leader' (or 'the Leadership Council') who, as ruling authority, is concerned with maintaining the dominion of God, the Prophet and the Imams, and is responsible for 'the management and leadership of the community'. Art. 151 deals with conscription which, in view of the crisis confronting the Islamic state, is judged to be necessary and is legitimated by the Koran 8/60,[21] and specifies that military training be in accordance with Islamic principles.

Art. 156–174, which are concerned with the judiciary, frequently discuss the limits placed upon the judiciary's organisation and functions by the regulations of the *shari'a*. The preamble sets the scene for these articles by stating that the legal system of the Islamic Republic is founded on the basis of Islamic justice while according to Art. 61, judicial power is to be exercised by law courts which 'are to be set up following Islamic principles' and which, amongst other things, will ensure the application of 'divine *hadd*-punishments'.[22] Amongst the tasks attributed to the judiciary in Art. 156 is mentioned 'the enforcement of *hadd*-punishments and the relevant Islamic penal regulations'. Art. 163 stipulates that 'the characteristics and qualifications of judges' must be in accordance with Islamic law. Art. 167 gives judges the authority to judge disputes on the basis of authentic Islamic sources and legal rulings when pertinent laws are lacking. Art. 168 orders that criminal political acts be punished 'on the basis of Islamic principles'. Art. 171 makes judges who have caused wrongful harm to someone during the exercise of their function liable 'in accordance with Islamic principles'.

## *Assuring the Rule of the Islamic Jurists*

The constitution defines the Islamic Republic as a state ruled by Islamic jurists (*foqaha*). In accordance with verse 21/105 of the Koran[23] and 'on the basis of the trusteeship and the permanent Imamate', it is a state of jurists. On the other hand, the constitution states that only those jurists are entitled to rule who are 'upright, pious and committed experts on Islam' and recognised as such, and who 'are informed of the demands of the times' and are distinguished as 'God-fearing', 'brave' and 'qualified for leadership [of the state]'. They must hold the religious office of 'source of imitation' (*marja'-e taqlid*)[24] and be qualified to deliver independent judgements on general principles (*fatvas*). Chapter 1, where 'fundamental principles' are laid down, expresses this conception of the Islamic Republic in Art. 2 which defines 'continual *ejtehad* by qualified jurists' as a principle of the Islamic system of government. Likewise, Art. 5 stipulates that an individual jurist who is endowed with all the necessary qualities, or a council of jurists, has the right to rule and exercise leadership in the Islamic Republic as long as 'The Lord of Time', i.e. the Twelfth Imam of the Shi'a, remains in occultation. Art. 57 and 110 specify the exact extent of the ruling jurist's power. In Art. 57, it is stated in general terms that he is to have supervision over the three branches of the government. Art. 110 defines this supervisory authority in the following concrete terms:

1. He appoints the jurists to the Guardian Council.
2. He appoints the highest judicial authority in the country.
3. He holds supreme command over the armed forces by exercising the following functions: a) he appoints and dismisses the chief of the general staff; b) he appoints and dismisses the commander-in-chief of the The Guardians of the Islamic Revolution Corps (Sepah-e Pasdaran); c) He is in charge of setting up the Supreme Defence Council which consists of the president, the prime minister, the minister of defence, the chief of the general staff, the commander-in-chief of the Sepah-e Pasdaran and two advisers appointed by the leader; d) He appoints the commander-in-chief of the three branches of the armed forces on the recommendation of the Supreme Defence Council; e) On the recommendation of the Supreme Defence Council, he declares war and peace, and calls for a general mobilisation of the armed forces.
4. He signs the certificate of appointment of the president after the latter's election by the people.
5. In the national interest, he dismisses the president if the Supreme Court declares that the president has violated his legal duties or parliament (Majles-e Showra-ye Melli[25]) judges that he is politically incompetent.
6. On the recommendation of the Supreme Court, he grants amnesty or a reduction of sentence in accordance with Islamic principles.

These powers far exceed a simple supervisory role, and yet they do not amount to the plenipotentiary authority which is bestowed upon the leader according to the concept of *velayat-e faqih* in its absolute form (i.e. as interpreted by Khomeini) and certainly do not extend to the scale of power which Khomeini himself exercised in this capacity. For instance, it is nowhere stated in the constitution that the leader has a legislative function, or that he exercises direct judicial powers.

The constitution reserves not only the office of leader for Islamic jurists but also many other key government positions. For instance, the second most important government institution is the Guardian Council which has the right of veto over parliamentary resolutions and in practice occupies a dominant position in the legislature. Six of its 12 members must be jurists or *faqih*.[26] And these six alone have the right to vote on whether parliamentary resolutions are in conformity with the *shari'a*.[27] Likewise, the interpretation of the constitution,[28] supervision of presidential and parliamentary elections and of referendums, are all functions of the Guardian Council.[29]

Membership of the Assembly of Leadership Experts, as its name suggests, is similarly reserved for Islamic jurists, a precondition explicitly established in the election regulations that were adopted at a later date.[30] Moreover, the Assembly of Leadership Experts determines who will be the leader or members of the Leadership Council, and can dismiss them should they no longer be capable of fulfilling their duties or no longer possess the necessary qualifications for exercising the office of leadership.[31] Finally, the constitution reserves for jurists the five positions as judge in the Supreme Court[32] including the president of this court and the chief public prosecutor. Appointments to the latter two positions are made by the leader.[33]

All other offices mentioned in the constitution are reserved for Muslims, if not specifically for jurists, and this is the case even if the constitution is not explicit on the point. Similarly, according to Art. 144, the president can only be 'chosen from the circle of men of religious and political distinction'. And Art. 144 also stipulates that 'the army of the Islamic Republic 'must be an Islamic army', which means non-Muslims are not permitted to occupy leading military positions. This attitude is rigorously adhered to in practice, not only in the army but in all spheres of the government.

## Democratic Elements

### The Partial Recognition of the Sovereignty of the People

Non-democratic states are often set up with reference to some sort of democratic premise, usually by declaring that such an undertaking is in harmony with the will of the people. Without recognising the contradiction inherent in such a claim, or for that matter taking the question seriously, the authors of the Constitution of the Islamic Republic made an effort to emphasise that it was an expression of the will, i.e. the ideals, of the Iranian people. In general terms, the preamble puts forward the thesis 'that the state from the point of view of Islam ... is the crystallisation of a political ideal of a people who are united in religion and in their way of thinking.' At another point it states that the constitution, and its 'Islamic principles and guidelines', reflect 'the deepest wish of the Islamic community'. This wish, it is maintained, was clearly revealed by the people's active participation in the revolution.

Even if the people are not defined according to the democratic norms of pluralism but rather as a homogeneous community of like-minded individuals, this view of their will is still in contradiction with the concept of *velayat-e faqih*. According to this concept, political power emanates from God alone and is transferred from God to the Islamic jurists. It therefore in no way depends upon the voice of the people for its legitimisation. This contradiction is encountered in Section 5 of the constitution which bears the title 'The

Sovereignty of the People and the Powers Thereby Conferred'. There, in Art. 56, it is stated that God alone has 'the absolute right to rule over the world and all mankind' and that He delegates that right, not to the jurists, *foqaha*, but to 'men at large'. Accordingly, this 'God-given right' is to be 'exercised by the people', not by the jurists.

Likewise, Art. 1 explicitly traces the ultimate foundation of the Islamic Republic back to the will of the people. In accordance with this view, 98 per cent of the electorate expressed their choice of an Islamic Republic in the March 1979 referendum.[34] Art. 6 also recognises the sovereignty of the people, stating that 'in the Islamic Republic of Iran the administration of the country's affairs will be regulated by the will of the people'. That will is to be expressed in elections for the president and members of parliament, as well as for members of local councils, etc., or generally speaking through consultation with the people.

*Elections to Government Bodies*

According to Art. 7, the parliament, provincial councils, councils in district towns, and councils in cities, city neighbourhoods, provinces and villages, are all part of the decision-making and administrative bodies of the country. Members of these bodies, according to Art. 6, are chosen from amongst the people. The leader, however, is not elected, but as a political authority and a *marja'-e taqlid*, he is in a relationship of trust with the people: a relationship that is to be immediately dissolved if the leader ceases to have the qualifications that justify his holding office.[35] Art. 107 stipulates that after Khomeini there will be a Assembly of Leadership Experts (Majles-e Khobregan-e Rahbari)[36] whose task will be to choose an individual or a leadership council as Khomeini's successor. According to Art. 108, the Assembly of Leadership Experts will be elected by the people. This assembly will also have the right to dismiss the leader should he lose the people's trust. According to Art. 58 and 62, as well as Art. 6, members of parliament will be elected by the people by a direct and secret ballot. The same is true of members of local councils who will be elected by the inhabitants of the respective regions, as is stated in Art. 100. Art. 114 stipulates that the president of the republic is to be elected. According to Art. 59, 'in questions of grave import regarding economic, political, social and cultural matters' legislative power may be exercised by consultation with the people. In this context it is worth noting that the first Assembly of Experts (Majles-e Khobregan), whose task it was to frame the constitution, was an elected body – leaving aside how the election was manipulated in practice.

*The Powers of Parliament*

The powers of the parliament are seriously reduced in the constitution by the right of veto exercised by the Guardian Council. None the less, the parliament has other rights which make it an important decision-making organ of government. The most significant are specified in Art. 87–89 concerning the appointment of the Council of Ministers. The Council of Ministers cannot be constituted and the individual ministers cannot be chosen as long as parliament has not declared its confidence in them. Parliament can pose direct questions to the ministers and should it be dissatisfied with their work, can vote them out of office.[37] Further powers of parliament are established by Art. 76–83. Parliament has the right 'to undertake investigations and inquiries into all matters regarding the country'. 'Accords, contracts, treaties and international agreements' require parliament's approval. Decisions concerning any alteration of the nation's borders, as well as a declaration of a state of emergency, can only come about with the approval of parliament. The same is true for 'taking out a loan and granting credit or financial aid, whether domestic or foreign, that does not have to be paid back' and for granting economically important concessions to foreigners. Even the decision to employ foreign experts is reserved for parliament.

The powers of the local councils are not as great as was promised in Art. 7, but a loosely defined right of supervision of the administration of their respective parts of the country is accorded to them by Art. 100 . The Supreme Provincial Council is 'to draft bills as part of its regular task and present them before parliament, directly or through government channels'. Parliament 'must' review these bills.[38] Governors of provinces, cities and district towns are to be appointed by the government but according to Art. 103, they must 'take account of' the resolutions passed by the respective councils in the exercise of their powers.

The powers of the president are stipulated in Art. 57, 60, 113 and 124–129. The president is the link between the three separate branches of government, he is the head of the executive and he exercises executive power along with the Council of Ministers, whenever the powers in question are not reserved for the leader. He is responsible for implementing the constitution and he fulfils certain duties that have to do with official representation of the country.

If limiting the jurisdiction of the representative bodies of the people contradicts democratic norms, limiting the powers of the leader has exactly the opposite effect. Consequently, a democratic component of the constitution becomes visible when the powers of the leader, as stipulated in the constitution, are compared with the powers he has in practice. Indeed, the powers of the leader enumerated in Art. 57 and 110 fall far short of including all the rights which the concept of *velayat-e faqih* accords to him or indeed the actual practice of governing made possible for Khomeini during his lifetime.

## The Partial Recognition of Fundamental Rights

In order to delve further into the contradiction between the democratic and the Islamic legalistic components of the Islamic Republic's constitution, it is useful to observe how the democratic components were dealt with in practice by the government during the period directly after the revolution, and to note the ideological arguments which served to legitimate governmental practice. The same method may be applied to the case of democratic fundamental rights. Of course, the fundamental rights acknowledged in the constitution are permitted only if they do not contradict Islam, i.e. Islamic law and basic principles. But the mere fact that the constitution mentions fundamental rights may be seen as a concession to those forces who demanded such rights and had participated in the revolution for the sake of obtaining them.

The constitution devotes more articles to democratic fundamental rights (Art. 19–42) in a special section entitled 'The Rights of the People'. These rights include 'the equality of all Iranians, no matter what ethnic group or tribe they belong to', a prohibition on persecuting individuals for their opinions, freedom of the press, the freedom to form political parties and societies, respect of privacy, freedom in choosing a profession, freedom of assembly, legal protection, the prohibition of torture, and so on.

## Secular Elements

The legalist components of the constitution, as well as the political system they are designed to set up, are all based on the claim that the *shari'a*, because of its relation to the divine source of knowledge and its perfection, is endowed with universality and possesses the vitality to solve all humankind's social and personal problems in every time and place. For this reason, the *shari'a* provides the best of all possible foundations for government, in Iran and in the rest of the world. Consequently it makes sense that the state should be governed by people who are experts on the *shari'a* and who fulfil the other requirements for putting it into practice. This is the justification for the rule of the Islamic jurists, or at least those amongst them who possess the qualifications specified in Art. 5 and 109 of the constitution.

Of course, this claim is not expressed with a similar degree of clarity in any one place in the text of the constitution. Nevertheless, traces of it are visible in numerous passages. It is this belief which forms the basis for binding legislation and government to the *shari'a* and for making the leading positions in the state a monopoly of the jurists *foqaha*. The legalistically conceived principles and tasks of the Islamic state are founded on this claim, as is the ultimate goal it is meant to strive for. The 'model society' presented in the constitution as an ideal can only be brought about if government legislation conforms to the regulations and the principles laid down by the *shari'a*. If the Islamic revolution has been successful, if it has 'realised all the goals of the Iranian reform movements over the last century', for example destroying the machinations of imperialism with its attendant institutions and relationships, this has only been possible because the jurists' leadership of the revolutionary movement. The constitution takes upon itself the responsibility for opening the way to 'the ultimate goal' and 'the development of man's divine dimensions', because the Islamic state it outlines, and which provides standards of social behaviour, will be led by righteous experts on the *shari'a* and state legislation, and will thus be based on the Koran and tradition (*sunna*).

The fact that this claim is not explicitly set forth in the text of the constitution means that careful attention should be paid to its formulation in Khomeini's book *Velayat-e Faqih*. We read in Khomeini's book, for instance, that God the Beneficent, by means of His prophets, 'has sent down laws and customs concerning all things'. 'God has decreed laws that affect mankind from the time before man's embryo has formed until the day after his burial.' 'Just as God has established laws for religious practice', He has also laid down laws 'pertaining to the affairs of society and government' (p. 10). Other advocates of Islamic legalism have expressed this view with absolute clarity in the Assembly of Experts during the debates on the constitution, as well as on numerous other occasions over the last 15 years.

Despite this claim the Constitution of the Islamic Republic contains important elements which have been borrowed, not from the *shari'a*, but from Western secular sources and stand out as concepts that are alien to the *shari'a*. First and foremost among these is the very idea of a constitution (*qanun-e asasi*). One could also single out concepts such as: 'law' (*qanun*), 'sovereignty of the people' (*hakemiyat-e melli*), 'nation' (*mellat*), 'the rights of the nation' (*hoquq-e mellat*), 'the legislature' (*qovveh-e moqannaneh*), 'the judiciary' (*qovveh-e qaza'iyeh*), 'parliament' (*majles*), 'republic' (*jomhuri*), 'consultation of the people' (*hameh-porsi*), 'elections' (*entekhabat*). Less important concepts of the same kind would include: 'co-operatives' (*ta'avoni*), 'jurors' (*hey'at-e monsefeh*), 'public prosecutor' (*dadsetan*), 'mass media' (*resanehha-ye goruhi*), and so on.

Behind these concepts stands a whole complex of norms, values, institutions, procedural rules and organisations, as well as a range of established political and economic ideas unknown to the *shari'a*. The concept of 'the rights of the nation', for example, stems from a system of political values that is not recognised anywhere in Islamic law. Indeed the entire structure of the state – its separation into three separate branches with corresponding institutions, the division of each of these institutions into different councils, government offices and organisations, the rules regulating relations between these bodies as well as the clauses in the constitution allocating economic rights and functions to the state, the private and the co-operative sectors – had to be borrowed by the Assembly of Experts from foreign models. Many of the goals enshrined in numerous articles on economics, social policy, environmental protection, finances, foreign policy and so on are not even mentioned in the recent law-books written by the grand ayatollahs. A relevant example here is the four-volume work by Khomeini *Tahrir al-Vasila* which, amongst other things, deals with the so-called 'new matters' (*al-masa'el al-mostahdasa*) but where nothing is said about secular concepts of this kind.[39] Even in Khomeini's works dealing with the question of the *velayat-e faqih*, these subjects are not mentioned.[40] For example, in his book, *The Islamic*

*State,* the concept of a 'constitution' is only used in connection with the Constitutional Revolution of 1906–11.[41] Again, the MP Ayatollah 'Abbas 'Ali 'Amid Zanjani, who has written several books on 'political jurisprudence', enumerates the most common authentically Islamic politically relevant concepts: most of these do not appear in the constitution while 'Amid Zanjani, like Khomeini, completely ignores the secular notions that are actually used in the text.[42]

Modern ideas were absorbed into the political culture of Iran during the Constitutional Revolution of 1906–11 and the progressive movement that preceded it. That revolution produced a constitution which recognised the people as the source of political power and laid down for the first time a division of powers between the executive, legislature and judiciary. A portion of the clergy was influenced by the constitutional movement and took up some of its most important concepts in their writings. An example is the classic work on government written by Ayatollah Mohammad Hosein Na'ini in 1909, which to some extent uses a modern conceptual apparatus while adapting Shi'i law to modern forms of the state. But the advocates of *velayat-e faqih* in Khomeini's interpretation do not belong to the same tradition as Na'ini. They honour instead his opponent, Ayatollah Fazlollah Nuri, who rejected constitutionalism in favour of legalism, and condemned the separation of government powers, legislation, equality, freedom of the press, and so on as anti-Islamic.[43]

Furthermore, the secularist and legalist components of the Constitution of the Islamic Republic have not been adapted to one another in a harmonious way, but appear in one and the same text as elements that contradict and exclude one another. The sovereignty of the Islamic jurists negates the sovereignty of the people, the Islamic community is set over against the Iranian nation, Islamic regulations and principles limit the rights of the people, the Guardian Council deprives parliament of power, the leader suppresses the president, the concept of *velayat-e faqih* reduces the idea of a republic to an absurdity. The list could be extended.

Although these contradictions can exist alongside one another in the text of the constitution, such a state of affairs is impossible in the everyday reality of government where, one way or another, they must be removed. The text of the constitution and the attitude of the Assembly of Experts who framed it might give the impression that the contradictions will be eliminated to the advantage of legalism, but in practice another alternative has established itself. This will be discussed at some length in Part III.

## Notes

1 In the original text of the constitution, the word used to designate an article is principle (*asl*). This terminology accords with the ideological character of the document in which every article expresses a principle of government.

2 This is a reference to the publication of Khomeini's book, *Velayat-e Faqih* (The

Mandate of the Jurist) or *Hokumat-e Eslami* (The Islamic State) which appeared in 1971 but only reached a wide public after the revolution. This study will demonstrate that many Islamicists were themselves unwilling to adopt the particular form of Islamic state it presents.

3 'The impetus of the revolution and the secret of its victory was Islam', according to Khomeini in his message to the Council of Experts. *The Minutes of the Council of Experts* (hereafter referred to as M) 4/319.

4  Art. 12.

5  Art. 18.

6  Art. 67 and 121.

7  Art. 16.

8  *Ejtehad* is the exercise of independent effort by Islamic jurists in order to formulate new decisions in questions of law and faith on the basis of the sources of Islamic law, i.e. the Koran, the *sunna*, consensus and analogy, or reason.

9  'Qualified' is used in this book to render the expression in the constitution *jame' al-sharayet* – persons who have fulfilled all the 'relevant' requirements.

10  In this connection verse 21/92 of the Koran is cited: 'This is your community. It is the only community. And I am your Lord. Serve Me!' See Preamble.

11  Preamble, Art. 143 ff.

12  Art. 150.

13  Preamble.

14  Ibid.

15  Art. 105.

16  'The true believers, both men and women, are friends to one another. They enjoin what is just and forbid what is evil.'

17  This principle is based on a Koranic verse (21/92) cited earlier in this chapter.

18  Art. 20 states that the equality of the sexes before the law is subject to 'considerations of Islamic principles'.

19  Art. 19–42 and 175.

20  Art. 56.

21  'Muster against them all the men and cavalry at your disposal so that you may strike terror into the enemy of God and your enemy, and others besides that you know not; but God knows them.'

22  i.e. *'hodud-e elahi'*. From the debate over Art. 156 in the Assembly of Experts it is clear that what is meant here are the Islamic *hadd*-punishments. See M III/1579 ff.

23  '... that My righteous servants will one day inherit the earth.'

24  Grand ayatollahs (*marja'-e taqlid*) are designated as 'sources of imitation' whom the faithful may consult on questions of religion and jurisprudence. The faithful are free to choose for themselves the particular *marja'-e taqlid* they wish to follow.

25  Majles-e Showra-ye Melli or National Consultative Assembly is the term used in the 1979 constitution for parliament. Khomeini later ordered the name to be chaged to Majles-e Showra-ye Eslami or Islamic Consultative Assembly.

26  Art. 91.

27  Art. 96.

28  Art. 98.

29  Art. 99 and 118.

30  In the middle of July 1991, the Assembly of Experts even decided that the candidates for membership in this body would have to submit to an examination to establish that they were qualified *mojtaheds*. A *mojtahed* is a jurist qualified to exercise *ejtehad*. The examination is now administered by the Council of Guardians itself. See *Ettela'at*, 17/7/91.

31  Art. 107 and 111.

32  Art. 158.

33  Art. 156 and 162.

34  This is also mentioned in the preamble.

35  Art. 1, 107 and 111.

36  The term Assembly of Leadership Experts has been used in this book to distinguish this assembly from the Assembly of Experts that was responsible for framing the Constitution in 1979, .

37  Art. 88–9.

38  Art. 102.

39  Khomeini: 1987–90. This work deals with topics such as television, insurance and artificial insemination, but makes no mention of the constitution. In this regard see also Ayatollah Sadeq Ruhani (1978).

40  That is in *Hokumat-e Eslami* (The Islamic State) and certain chapters of *Kitab al-Bai'* which were published in a collection entitled *The Position and the Powers of the Ruling Jurists* (1986).

41  In *Hokumat-e Eslami* and *Kitab al-Bai'* the concept 'Islamic laws' (*qavanin-e eslami*) does not appear. The term *qavanin* (sing. *qanun*) here takes the place of the more authentic concept *ahkam* (ordinances) and should therefore be seen as an innovation. In Islamic discourse the term *qanun* properly designates special edicts which are issued by the government authorities in conformity with customary law (*'orf*). Cf. *Encyclopaedia of Islam*.

42  He deals with 'ordinance' (*hokm*), 'ruler' (*hakem, malek*), 'rule' (*hokumat*), 'the Imam' (*emam*), 'imamate' (*emamat*), 'caliphate' (*khelafat*), 'caliph' (*khalifeh*), 'guardian' (*ra'i*), 'protected subject' (*ra'iyat*), 'sultan' (*soltan*), 'land' (*molk*) and 'ruler of the age' (*vali-ye 'ahd*). 'Amid Zanjani: 1988–89, vol. I, p. 146f.

43  Nuri: 1983, vol. I, p. 55ff. and 102ff. For a discussion of Nuri's ideas see Nouraie: 1975; Martin: 1987; Hairi: 1977.

# TWO

# The Genesis of the Constitution

### The Preliminary Draft

The first attempt to draft a constitution began in Paris while Khomeini was preparing for his return to Iran. Hasan Habibi, who is now first deputy of the president, was charged with this task. At that time he resided in Paris and along with several other Islamic intellectuals was in close contact with Khomeini. Habibi's preliminary outline was completed on 22/1/79 and presented to Khomeini who took it to Tehran on 1/2/79. Shortly afterwards it was reworked by a commission made up of Habibi himself and five civil jurists,[1] and again delivered to Khomeini.[2] Further revisions were made by a commission chaired by Yadollah Sahabi, an advisory minister to the provisional government of Mehdi Bazargan.[3] Secular politicians such as Karim Sanjabi, a leading member of the Jebheh-e Melli (National Front),[4] also sat on this commission whose work lasted for three months.[5] The result was finally published on 14/6/79 as the official preliminary draft of the constitution.[6]

This document contains no reference to *velayat-e faqih*, nor does it reserve any special posts for Islamic jurists except on the Guardian Council. Even on this body the Islamic jurists are in a minority – five of them sitting with six civil jurists. According to the document, the Islamic jurists were to be chosen by parliament from an unspecified number of jurists to be proposed by the highest religious authorities, 'the sources of imitation'. The secular members of the council (three judges and three professors) were also to be chosen by parliament. The Guardian Council was not automatically to judge whether laws passed by parliament are in conformity with the *shari'a*, as it stands in the text of the constitution, but only on request. Such a request could be made by 'the sources of imitation', the president of the Republic, the president of the Supreme Court and the chief public prosecutor. The Islamic jurists, according to the preliminary draft, were to have no special rights – the resolutions of the Guardian Council were to be valid only if passed by a two-thirds majority and not, as in the final version of the constitution, by an absolute majority.[7] Should the council declare that any 'ordinary law' contradicts the constitution or 'the infallible principles of the *shari'a*', then parliament was to revise that law taking account of the objections raised by the council.[8] The emphasis on the infallibility of the principles of the *shari'a* was dropped from the final text. In the preliminary draft the office of leader was to be filled by the president. There was no question of his having to be from the circle of Islamic jurists.

The contrast between these two texts so far as the concept of *velayat-e faqih* is concerned, and its political significance, can only be properly grasped by tracing the process by which they were produced. Habibi's early draft[9] like the official preliminary draft, did not provide for the office of leader. The role of the jurists was confined to the Guardian Council which was to have 12 members, no more than four of whom would be *mojtaheds* appointed by 'the sources of imitation' not by the parliament. The Guardian Council could only intervene upon request (of the same officials mentioned in the preliminary draft). In matters relating to the *shari'a*, the *unanimous* decision of the four *mojtaheds* alone was to have validity: a provision not included in the preliminary draft but adopted in part in the final version of the constitution. In cases where unanimity could not be reached, the question under scrutiny was to be decided by 'a source of imitation.'[10] The highest government office was to be the president who was not required to be 'a man with religious or political authority'. His sole ideological qualifications were that he should not belong to 'a deviant school' of Shi'ism or sympathise with leftist or right-wing tendencies.[11] In addition, Habibi's draft does not accord any special status to the Islamic jurists in the judiciary.

Both Habibi's draft and the later official preliminary draft were revised in constant consultation with high-ranking Islamic jurists including 'the sources of imitation'.[12] Both, generally speaking, received Khomeini's approval. The few objections to these drafts that Khomeini actually voiced gave no indication that he would reject them, and certainly not because of their position on the concept of *velayat-e faqih*.[13] Bazargan and his party, the Nehzat-e Azadi-ye Iran (Liberation Movement of Iran or LMI), described Khomeini's corrections of the preliminary draft as 'insignificant'.[14] According to Sanjabi, Khomeini had no more than six or seven points of criticism, one of which related to 'the clergy's supervision of the laws and regulations'.[15] Bani-Sadr recounts in a book written in exile how Khomeini began to smile when he informed him in the presence of Ayatollah Mir Karim Musavi Ardebili that 'even the intellectuals' had agreed to the preliminary draft.[16] On more than one occasion Khomeini gave his approval publicly to that draft. For example, in a speech delivered to members of the Tehran Preachers' Society on 17/6/79, he twice said that the preliminary draft was, for the government, correct and that everyone would confirm it.[17] And he reiterated this point the following day before the Revolutionary Guards, declaring: 'We must support and confirm the constitution so that the constitution will be as Islam requires. It must be approved quickly. It is a blueprint made by the government and this blueprint is correct.' In the same speech he repeated the last sentence a second time.[18]

The preliminary draft also required the approval of the Revolutionary Council on which, alongside Ayatollah Mahmud Taleqani and Mohammad Reza Mahdavi-Kani, the leading members of the Hezb-e Jomhuri-ye Eslami

(Islamic Republican Party or IRP) sat at this time – namely the Ayatollahs and Hojjat al-Eslams Mohammad Beheshti, 'Ali Akbar Rafsanjani, 'Ali Khamene'i, Mohammad Bahonar and 'Abdolkarim Ardebili.[19] The Revolutionary Council examined the draft, approved of it unanimously and, in the form that it was published on 14/6/79, declared it to be the official preliminary draft of the Revolutionary Council.[20]

## Uncertainties before the First Referendum

Khomeini's overtly expressed approval of the preliminary draft was consistent with the position he customarily outlined in Paris when the international press asked him about the role of the clergy in the future Islamic Republic. On 26/10/78 Khomeini told a journalist from Reuters that: 'The *'ulama* themselves will not hold power in the government. They will exercise supervision over those who govern and give them guidance.'[21] To the question put to him on 7/11/78 by a reporter from Associated Press as to whether he himself would occupy a position in the new government, Khomeini replied: 'Neither my age nor my inclination and position would allow me to do something like that.'[22] A day later he gave virtually the same answer to a reporter from United Press and added that he had already stated this many times.[23] He repeated this position in several other interviews he gave in Paris.[24] Indeed in his interviews, speeches, messages and *fatvas* during this period there is not a single reference to *velayat-e faqih*. In many of these pronouncements he certainly referred to the 'Islamic state', but he never specified precisely what he meant by the term.[25]

Moreover, in conversations with his closest colleagues among the exiled intellectuals or with visitors to Paris from Tehran, Khomeini tried to give the impression that he had renounced the concept of the state he put forward in *The Islamic State*.[26] Bani-Sadr recalls that when he presented his objections to this concept, Khomeini accepted them.[27] Hasan Nazih, who after the revolution was put in charge of the oil industry, must have received the same impression when, as Taleqani's representative, he visited Khomeini in Paris. Khomeini gave him every assurance that he did not intend to take on any government functions. He wanted to be 'a spiritual leader of the nation.' The constitution would, he insisted, reflect the principles of the UN Charter for Human Rights. Fundamental rights would not be subject to any form of restriction as long as their claims did not have an adverse effect on the interests of the people.[28] Sadeq Qotbzadeh, who was later to become minister of foreign affairs, also held the same view expressed as follows in an interview with *Le Monde*: 'The Islamic state would not mean the rule of the clergy in the usual sense,[29] but rule based on divine laws and principles with the aim of establishing equality, justice, freedom and brotherhood.'

In the same vein, the National Front leader, Karim Sanjabi, declared two days after the change-over of power in February 1979 that the republic was called Islamic only because the majority of its citizens were Muslim. In the

Republic, Islamic principles of piety, comradeship, justice, equality and solidarity would be decisive in regulating social relations.[30] Three weeks later he went further and gave assurances that the bewilderment occasioned by the word 'Islamic' as applied to the future Republic was unfounded, declaring: 'The Islamic Republic is democratic.' According to Sanjabi, Khomeini and Kazem Shari'at-madari had stated that the clergy had no intention whatsoever of taking control of the government or setting up a hierocracy.[31] Sanjabi had acquired this impression, as he notes in his memoirs, on the basis of conversations with Khomeini in Paris.[32]

Even after his return to Iran Khomeini continued to give the impression that he had no interest in exercising government power. He had it announced everywhere that he would soon return to Qom to assume his work as a jurist. He took up residence in the city on 1/3/79 and the press reported that he intended to stay there.[33] The warnings of the radical-secularists that the clergy intended to set up a monopoly of state power for itself[34] were viewed by people like Bani-Sadr, who would later come to reject the clergy's monopoly, as exaggerated probably because Khomeini and his supporters had so frequently given assurances to the contrary.[35] There was, indeed, widespread belief in the truth of these statements, illustrated by the fact that the daily newspaper, *Ayandegan*, which viewed all the developments of the post-revolutionary period from a radical-secularist perspective, took it for granted in its 'Résumé of the Week' on 21/6/79 that Khomeini wanted the Assembly of Experts to pass the preliminary draft of the constitution in its published form. A further indication of the extent of this confidence is the earnest and zealous way secularist intellectuals and organisations in particular produced positive criticism of the preliminary draft of the constitution. This is attested by more than 4,000 proposals that were submitted for amending, replacing or correcting its contents.[36]

Similarly, the fact that Khomeini did not hold the first national referendum (that of 30–31 March 1979) on the issue of *velayat-e faqih* but rather on 'the Islamic Republic' must also have been taken by his supporters as proof that he had abandoned his former stance on this question. Although the designation 'Republic' did not originate with Khomeini,[37] by this time he had adopted it as his own. Thus, one month before the first national referendum, he declared that he would vote for an 'Islamic Republic' and that the people had everywhere supported this 'password'.[38] He repeated this several times in the days that followed, emphasising, however, that he did not wish to force his decision on anyone else: 'It is my intention to show the nation the way, but people are free to vote as they wish.'[39]

Likewise, repeated statements by leaders of the IRP that fundamental rights and individual freedoms would be guaranteed in the new constitution must have been reassuring. One of the leaders of the IRP was Hasan Ayat who said on 22/2/79: 'In Islam we know of no case, whether under the Prophet or the first caliphs or under the infallible Imams, where the people's free expression of opinions was suppressed ... Individuals and groups will be able to publish their own newspapers, found political parties and promote their own points of view.' The only requirement is that they undertake these activities openly, that is not under a false identity. 'If respect is maintained for such requirements, which are rooted in the principles and guidelines of democracy, not only will there be freedom of expression, of political parties and freedom of assembly, but the Islamic state itself will guarantee the security of the persons and groups involved.'[40] Ayatollah Beheshti confirmed these statements when, a few days later, he declared that in Islam 'a genuine and fundamental relationship' exists between 'freedom and religious belief'. This, he promised, would be maintained in the Islamic Republic.[41]

The reassuring effect of such statements was reinforced by promises given by influential religious authorities who genuinely did not aspire to holding direct government power. For instance, Ayatollah Taleqani held forth the prospect of a democracy that would be better than those of the West.[42] The Grand Ayatollah Shari'at-madari defined the function of 'the source of imitation' in the Islamic Republic as simply one of 'guidance' (*hedayat*) and 'supervision' (*moraqabat*).[43]

In addition, in the period before the referendum and the publication of the preliminary draft its authors, by attempting to gloss over matters, contributed to public disinformation about the character of the future constitution. For example, on 20/2/79, the daily newspaper *Kayhan*, in an article entitled 'The Chief Features of the Possible Constitution of the Democratic Islamic Republic', quoted one of this group who preferred to remain anonymous as saying that the constitution would 'be the most progressive in the world':

> It takes account of those freedoms that are based on the UN Charter of Human Rights and other international agreements and treaties. Nor does it allow any form of restriction of different viewpoints or the groups who represent those viewpoints ... In the Constitution of the Islamic Republic men and women enjoy the same rights and privileges. Women can hold the highest government offices.

> They can even become president. In this respect the Islamic Republic will in no way resemble Saudi Arabia. If the Republic is called Islamic that is simply because the official religion of the country is Shi'ism.

On 4/3/79, Ahmad Sadr Hajj Seyyed Javadi, the minister of the interior, endorsed this view adding that the constitution would reflect the Islamic view of God's sovereignty in a reasonable sense, declaring: 'Everything that reason stipulates is also stipulated by the *shari'a*. Therefore, Islamic stipulations are simultaneously the stipulations of reason.' [44]

The high point of this disinformation was reached when on Khomeini's instructions, three days before the first national referendum, the secretary to the Ministry of the Interior, Sadeq Tabataba'i, presented the people with certain information about the future constitution. Amongst other things, he stated:

In the new Constitution of Iran leadership is in the hands of the general public. As the representative of God, who is the true leader, the public will govern the state ... The constitution of our country will determine the form of the councils ... In the constitution the individual and collective rights of all persons and all parts of the nation will be taken into account, and the freedom of individuals and groups will be guaranteed ... The rights of the suppressed ethnic minorities will be restored. All political minorities will enjoy all political freedoms such as the right of free speech and freedom of assembly and coalition, and the right to be politically active ... The National Parliament will exercise other functions in addition to passing laws, functions such as monitoring the application of laws and supervision of the government.[45]

One day later 'Abbas Amir Entezam, a government spokesman, promised that in the future the clergy would no longer be involved in government affairs.[46]

Immersed in this flood of disinformation, which was partly a result of uncertainty over the public's acceptance of *velayat-e faqih* and partly a conscious effort at deception, at the end of March, scarcely two months after the transfer of power, the people voted in a national referendum. The voters were simply to decide 'whether the form of the future state would be the Islamic Republic or not.' There was no other possibility on offer. If an individual did not wish to vote for the continuance of the monarchy, which in any case had been overthrown, then there was no alternative to the Islamic Republic. The turn-out for the referendum was very high and 98.2 per cent of the participants said 'yes' to a form of government about which they were sadly misinformed.[47] Only a few democratic or communist organisations and individuals boycotted the referendum, including the National Democratic Front (Jebheh-e Demokratik-e Melli), the Organisation of the Feda'iyan-e Khalq and the Democratic Party of Kurdistan. Besides the Islamicists of different tendencies, among those who voted 'yes' were members of secularist organisations such as the National Front, the Party of the Iranian Nation, the Maoist faction of the former Confederation of Iranian Students, the pro-Soviet Tudeh Party and intellectuals such as 'Ali Asghar Sadr Hajj Seyyed Javadi. A few Islamic organisations such as the Mojahedin-e Khalq and the Hezb-e Jomhuri-ye Khalq-e Mosalman (Islamic People's Republican Party) voted 'yes' but made it clear that they would have preferred to have had the possibility of deciding between more than two alternatives.[48]

## A Constituent Assembly or an Assembly of Experts?

Once the idea of an Islamic state was accepted, it was possible to move towards what had been the real goal all along, namely pushing through the concept of *velayat-e faqih*. This meant creating a situation in which the preliminary draft of the constitution could be undermined and a new text substituted. The ease with which the referendum was won encouraged further action. Even proponents of the *velayat-e faqih* who had not dared to imagine that their goal might be realised[49] were now increasingly convinced that further steps were possible.

Originally, a Constituent Assembly (Majles-e Mo'assesan) had been promised in which hundreds of delegates would draw up the final version of the constitution. The decree of 4/2/79, in which Khomeini appointed Bazargan prime minister of the provisional government, charged him with the task of preparing forthwith for the election of this Constituent Assembly.[50] And during the months that immediately followed, Khomeini constantly reiterated his promise to summon the assembly, for example on 8/4/79 before a group of railway employees who visited him.[51] The modern Islamicists in particular attached great importance to the idea that the nation's new constitution should be approved by a body made up of as many representatives of the people as possible. In this way the assembly would win favour with the non-Islamic forces who also wanted the final working out of the new constitution to be undertaken by a Constituent Assembly, to which they hoped to be able to send their own representatives.[52]

Five days after the referendum the Ministry of the Interior announced that elections for the Constituent Assembly would be held in two months.[53] When Habibi's draft of the constitution was published in *Kayhan* on 28 and 29 April 1979 the formation of the Constituent Assembly was still under discussion. But once the official version of the preliminary draft was completed, the thought was circulated that the intervention of the Constituent Assembly was not really necessary in order to adopt the constitution; the people could give it their direct approval by means of a second referendum. Ultimately, Khomeini must have been behind this proposal. Bazargan has reported a meeting in Khomeini's house in Qom during which the matter was discussed and approved by those members of the Revolutionary Council who were present – all of them clergy. Other members of the Revolutionary Council and the Council of Ministers (who had not been present at Khomeini's meeting and who were mostly not clergy) continued to insist that the Constituent Assembly should be summoned.[54]

Those who supported 'direct consultation' with the people put forward various, seemingly plausible, arguments in favour of their position. These included: a) the need to speed up the process of normalisation which the government of Bazargan urgently required; b) fear that anti-revolutionary forces would exploit the current instability to launch a counter-offensive, and c) the urgent need to pass reform measures that would have the force of law. All these needs would be neglected for a considerable period of time if the endorsement of the preliminary draft were left to a Constituent Assembly. For the opponents of *velayat-e faqih* on the Revolutionary Council and the Council of Ministers the most interesting and perhaps the most convincing argument against an assembly was that which Rafsanjani is said to have put forward. He pointed to the great influence the clergy had exercised on the public a few months after the revolution and added that in the present situation the Constituent Assembly would consist of 'reactionary and fanatical members of the clergy who would absolutely refuse to give their approval to the preliminary draft of the constitution.'[55]

This warning must have dispelled any doubts that supporters of an Islamic Republic of the kind sketched in the preliminary draft of the constitution might have harboured about the intentions of Khomeini and the Islamic Republican Party to give approval to the document. As a result, the opponents of a second referendum were, in the end, prepared to enter into a compromise allegedly instigated by Ayatollah Taleqani. According to this compromise, instead of the Constituent Assembly the people would choose 'an assembly for the final examination of the constitution' which would check over the text of the preliminary draft and present it for final ratification in a national referendum.[56] This assembly would consist of just 40 delegates rather than the 'hundreds of representatives of the people' envisaged for the Constituent Assembly.[57] The reduced size, it was argued, would guarantee a speedy completion of business.

For the opponents of *velayat-e faqih* on the Revolutionary Council and the Council of Ministers the important point was that this smaller assembly, which was later to be unofficially renamed the 'Assembly of Experts',[58] should feel committed to the preliminary draft and basically do nothing besides approve it, at least in its main outline. Promises to this effect must have been given to them and the assumption was reinforced by the Bill for the Election of the Assembly for the Final Examination of the Constitution of the Islamic Republic of Iran passed by the Revolutionary Council on 5 July 1979. The first article of this bill stated that the task of the assembly would be 'to express its conclusive opinion on the text of the Constitution of the Islamic Republic of Iran which has already been reworked and checked over through several phases.'[59] The election of an assembly with such a brief would allow the opponents of a referendum to claim that they had, at least in part, fulfilled their promise to summon the Constituent Assembly.[60] They could also feel confidence in its work because they had been assured that the selection of candidates would be done in such a way that only one third of the representatives would be from the clergy.[61] Their confidence was further increased by a resolution that the proposed assembly would be required to complete its work within one month.[62] This stipulation was justified by the fact that the preliminary draft already existed and the assembly should therefore not need more time than that.

After the resolution in favour of the Assembly of Experts had been passed the argument about the urgency of the situation was still heard. But it was now increasingly accompanied by warnings to those who continued to insist on a Constituent Assembly and denounced the broken promises of the governing councils and prominent individuals. On 15/6/79, Khomeini went so far as to declare that the stubborn insistence on a Constituent Assembly should be considered as a conspiracy of counter-revolutionaries against Islam whose only purpose was to gain time.[63] Two days later he expressed the view that the supporters of the Constituent Assembly were either communists or misguided people who were unable to realise that the switch to a Assembly of Experts served to establish the order of the Koran.[64]

### The Public Propagation of *velayat-e faqih*

Once the resolution to scrap the Constituent Assembly had been successfully pushed through, it was possible to propagate the idea of *velayat-e faqih* in public.[65] This new phase began with a violent attack against those who criticised the monopolistic intentions of the clergy. At the same time, the preliminary draft of the constitution was subjected to a variety of criticisms formulated by legalists. Khomeini had already denounced his opponents on 26 May as having intentions to exclude the clergy from politics – a betrayal, he declared, whose purpose was the annihilation of Islam.[66] Whereas before this date Khomeini had dealt with the advocates of a Democratic Islamic Republic with relative caution, he now denounced them as enemies of Islam.[67] This was despite the fact that the prime minister belonged to this group, and that he was the first prime minister of a government which Khomeini himself had declared to be in conformity with the *shari'a*. A few days later Khomeini branded those who wished to bar the clergy from political power as communist supporters.[68] On 18 June, he declared that he disapproved of summoning a Constituent Assembly because 'we wish to create an Islamic constitution,' for which no 'Westernised jurists' were needed but only 'noble members of the clergy' and other knowers of Islam who were not clerics.[69] In accordance with this purpose, before the election of the Assembly of Experts he began to invite groups from different social backgrounds who visited him to give their vote to 'knowers of Islam'.[70]

However, Khomeini left the direct and more open propagation of *velayat-e faqih* to others. It is impossible to avoid the impression that there was a conscious delegation of tasks to circles below the level of Khomeini. A campaign was launched whose starting point may perhaps be seen as a speech Khomeini delivered on 20 June before a group of clergy in Khorasan in which he invited them to express publicly their views on the preliminary draft of the constitution.[71] On 23 June Ayatollah Hosein 'Ali Montazeri publicly criticised the preliminary draft and demanded that the president of the Islamic Republic should 'preferably be a Shi'i *mojtahed*'.[72] On 11 July he made it known that he was in favour of a 'pure' Islamic constitution which should be 'far removed from every Western principle'.[73] The Congress of Muslims for Examining the Preliminary Draft of the Constitution, which convened in Tehran towards the end of June, put forward the demand that the constitution take account of the fact that in Islam legislation is a prerogative of God. A legislature such as that provided for in the preliminary draft of did not stem from Islamic sources.[74]

On 27/6/79 *Kayhan* published a letter to Khomeini from a member of the clergy, Mohammad Hosein Hoseini Tehrani, in which he presented several proposals for amending the preliminary draft conceived on the basis of an absolute interpretation of legalism. He demanded, for instance, that the title 'Republic' should not have any influence on the character of the Islamic state. The right to rule should be accorded to 'the upright Islamic jurist' who as the first person in the state would exercise the function of president and in whose hands all three branches of government should be united. The author of a book on 'government systems of the world', Khosrow 'Alavizadeh, expressed the view that 'all the laws passed by parliament should require the approval of the Guardian Council in order to become valid laws.'[75] During the congress Hojjat al-Eslam Khamene'i, who was later to become Khomeini's successor, put forward the view that 'the principle of *velayat-e faqih*' must be included in the Islamic constitution.[76] On 9/7/79 a 'declaration of the excellent jurists of the religious Academy of Qom' appeared in *Kayhan* in which the inclusion in the constitution of the office of leader was demanded in almost the same form, and with the same function and absolute power, that the leader eventually came to have. Six days later, again in *Kayhan*, a declaration by the Grand Ayatollah 'Abdollah Shirazi appeared in which he demanded a right of veto for 'qualified jurists' with regard to framing the constitution, passing laws and filling all government posts, especially the office of president and prime minister. On 17 July, the Grand Ayatollah Sadeq Ruhani spoke out publicly and demanded that the Assembly of Experts should not be bound by the preliminary draft of the constitution because this draft was in no way compatible with Islam.[77]

## Engineering Elections to the Assembly of Experts

The abrupt abandonment of their promises over the preliminary draft by Khomeini and his like-minded advisers, and the massive propaganda campaign that followed in support of *velayat-e faqih*, made their goal in the elections for the Assembly of Experts – which finally took place on 3 August 1979 – perfectly clear. Not content with the influence they still exercised over the people, wherever they were able or felt it was necessary Khomeini's circle manipulated the elections. The opposition press reported on this with numerous concrete and convincingly documented examples and several pro-government newspapers recorded the massive protest against the way the elections were conducted. The irregularities included:

1. The dissemination of false information. For example, it was announced that the Grand Ayatollah Shari'at-madari had taken part in the elections, although it was known that he intended to boycott them.[78]
2. The falsification of results. For example, two Shi'i candidates won the election in Sunni Kurdish regions, which was generally seen as proof of a massive electoral falsification. In several provinces the votes counted and accepted as valid exceeded the number of people eligible to vote.
3. Acts of violence directed against unwanted candidates and their supporters.

4. The completion of ballot papers on behalf of the illiterate as the dominant clergy wished.
5. Informing voters that Khomeini and other important members of the clergy had declared it was a religious duty to vote for certain candidates.[79]

However, the biggest single advantage which the supporters of *velayat-e faqih* enjoyed in the election was that the voting regulations in some cases made whole provinces into single wards. In each province one delegate was chosen for every 500,000 voters. Had the electoral wards been drawn up on the basis of a division between city and countryside, many clerics, who were chiefly elected by the rural population, would not have been successful.[80] On the other hand, this division of the electoral wards was the logical consequence of replacing the Constituent Assembly with the Assembly of Experts, which drastically reduced the number of delegates to be elected.

Many participants in the election protested against these irregularities. A coalition of five Islamic radical organisations consisting of the Mojahedin-e Khalq, Jonbesh, JAMA (Revolutionary Organisation of the Muslim People of Iran), SASH (Islamic Organisation of Councils) and OMMAT (the Militant Muslims Movement) wrote an open letter to Khomeini.[81] The Grand Ayatollah Baha al-Din Qomi described electoral manipulation in the province of Khorasan as 'an unimaginable betrayal'[82] while the members of the Religious Academy of the City of Mashhad compared the elections to those held under the Shah's regime.[83] The Grand Ayatollah Shari'at-madari boycotted the proceedings and, along with the Islamic People's Republican Party that he was close to, demanded that they be annulled.[84] The Grand Ayatollah Hasan Mahallati also protested. The National Democratic Front, the National Front, several parties that represented the ethnic minorities and many other leftist-oriented organisations called for a boycott on the grounds that the formation of a Constituent Assembly had been blocked and the elections for the Assembly of Experts had been prepared and would be carried out by undemocratic means.[85]

The rigging meant that the election results were to the full satisfaction of Khomeini and the leaders of the IRP.[86] Out of 72 delegates whose election was officially recognised, 55 were clerics who, with few exceptions, followed the so-called 'line of the Imam'. This was also the case with most of the delegates who were not clergy. Indeed, the only elected delegate whose presence in the Assembly of Experts Khomeini would not tolerate was 'Abdolrahman Qasemlu, the leader of the Democratic Party of Iranian Kurdistan, who had been elected in West Azerbaijan where it was difficult for Khomeini's supporters to engineer the result. Qasemlu was obliged to stay well away from the assembly in order to avoid arrest.[87]

Even among Khomeini's supporters there were many who spoke of 'an assembly so uniformly composed' as a great insult to the whole of Iranian society. Fakhreddin Hejazi and Hojjat al-Eslam Ja'far Shojuni, who later both became members of the Islamic Parliament, declared: 'This irregular and discriminatory procedure will isolate the broad mass of capable and honest people who are the great capital resource for building up this country.'[88]

## The Inclusion of *velayat-e faqih* in the Constitution

The composition of the Assembly of Experts meant that it was now possible to include the principle of *velayat-e faqih* in the constitution. It was no longer necessary for the assembly to feel that it was bound to the preliminary draft. Whenever it was convenient the draft could be completely ignored. Indeed, Khomeini actually recommended such a procedure in his message to the assembly on the occasion of its inauguration:

> If the Islamic jurists present in the assembled body find contradictions to Islam in any of the articles of the preliminary draft or in the adopted amendments, they must declare this openly and not have any fear of the uproar this may cause in the press or amongst Westernised writers.

The task of the jurists was to ensure that the constitution and laws of the Islamic Republic conform totally to the requirements of Islam. Moreover, in the same message Khomeini defined the status the clergy were to hold in the assembly and consequently in the Islamic regime as follows: 'Determining whether [principles laid down in the constitution] are or are not in conformity with Islamic requirements is exclusively reserved for the revered jurists who, thanks to God, form a particular group in the assembly.' This task being a matter for experts, the other 'honourable delegates' who did not possess the necessary qualifications should not interfere. Khomeini also expressed the hope that delegates from two specific groups would not influence the constitution – those 'inclined to Western or East European schools of thought or influenced by deviant views' and 'persons who lack the capacity to understand Islamic regulations and sciences, and under the influence of deviant schools interpret the noble Koran and *hadith* texts according to their own wishes.'[89]

On the basis of these recommendations, from the very beginning the Assembly of Experts set aside the preliminary draft. Hojjat al-Eslam Khamene'i declared in the opening session that any procedural proposal that attempted to channel the work of the assembly should be rejected. The preliminary draft, he maintained, would 'restrict the range of thought and reflection.'[90] During the council's first working session, its president, Ayatollah Montazeri, stated that in his opinion the preliminary draft was not suitable as a basis for their work because 'if we were to take it as a standard [for our work], we would have to change many of its principles so that not much of the original would remain.'[91] Contempt for the preliminary draft went so far that during the 17th session the delegate Qahdarijani remarked that even when a particular principle was suitably formulated in the preliminary draft, the Assembly of Experts would ignore it, as if it was their duty to do so. 'The people now wondered what possible connection still existed between the principles adopted by the assembly and the principles laid down in the preliminary draft of the constitution.'[92]

Furthermore, statements made during these sessions make it is clear that from the outset other preliminary drafts had been prepared which took account of the concept of *velayat-e faqih* and therefore satisfied the majority in the Assembly of Experts.[93] Consequently these drafts, either as a whole or in single points, were given preferential consideration and exercised a greater influence on the constitution's final form than the 'official' preliminary draft which was nevertheless still presented as the only official draft of the text.[94]

In reality the delegates with dominant influence in the Assembly of Experts[95] paid no heed to the preliminary draft but saw to it that the clauses establishing *velayat-e faqih* were adopted in the final version of the constitution. The necessary proposals were put forward during debates on relevant articles or in speeches delivered at each plenary session before the assembly set about its work. As early as the third session, when the constitution was still being discussed in general terms, the delegate Kiavash demanded that *velayat-e faqih* be established 'in accordance with the command of God and the Prophet.'[96] During this same session, the delegate Heidari demanded that 'the principle of *velayat-e faqih* ... be fully recognised ... Control over the three branches of government and ultimate responsibility for their functions must be accorded to the ruler who possesses all the requirements to be a source of imitation and to exercise leadership in the Muslim community.'[97]

In these sessions the demand for the *velayat-e faqih* was always coupled with an indirect or explicit criticism of the preliminary draft which had disregarded this principle. For example, the delegate Hasan Taheri Khorram-abadi saw this neglect 'as a mistake of the preliminary draft of the constitu-tion.'[98] His colleague, Mohammad Karami, criticised the preliminary draft because it had completely ignored the divine character of government rule and the determining role of revelation in legislation. He attributed this omission to ignorance of 'the fundamental principles of Islam' on the part of those who had drawn it up: 'The preliminary draft of the constitution is full of divergences and scholarly errors.'[99] According to Khamene'i, the preliminary draft was based on Western sources and thus suitable for Europe but not 'for our Iranian and Islamic society' or 'for our revolution which is Islamic.'[100]

The actual process of including the *velayat-e faqih* in the constitution began during the ninth to the twelfth sessions of the assembly when Art. 2, which presents the doctrinal principles that form the basis of the Islamic Republic, was discussed. One of these principles, as we have already seen in Chapter 1, is 'continual *ejtehad* exercised by qualified jurists.' Those who, as 'Abdolrahim Rabbani Shirazi put it, can only translate the Koran with the help of a dictionary are not suited to such a task[101] which requires real experts. According to Beheshti, continual *ejtehad* is necessary because 'in a government system based on ideology all questions to do with legislation, arrangements for implementing regulations and establishing operational procedures' must be determined by ideological considerations. The primary source of knowledge for all ideological requirements is the Koran and the *sunna* which only the jurists understand fully. Likewise, when it comes to establishing regulations for new situations, there is a need for continual *ejtehad* which is a matter for the appropriate experts.[102]

The adoption of *velayat-e faqih* found its most unambiguous formulation in Art. 5. To avoid provoking an uproar, influential members of the assembly preferred to conduct the debates on this principle as far as possible out of public view, that is outside plenary sessions and instead in a general session of one of the several work committees. During a plenary session, only one advocate and one opponent of a motion under scrutiny were allowed to speak.[103] In this case, Beheshti, who had formulated Art. 5 himself, spoke as the advocate. He justified his proposal with the same arguments that he had put forward during the discussion of Art. 2. adding: 'In the present system the leadership and legislation cannot be left to the majority at any given moment. This would contradict the ideological character of the Islamic Republic.' He thus rejected democracy as un-Islamic on the grounds that the people could fall into error. In his view a state that had to take account of the voice of the people would have to submit to laws that were influenced by such errors.[104]

Art. 107–109 of the constitution are basically a further elaboration of Art. 5. They deal with the election of the leader or the Leadership Council, the formation of the council in charge of electing the leader, as well as the personal qualities which the leader or members of the Leadership Council should possess. In the debates on these articles the usual arguments in favour of *velayat-e faqih* were repeated. By way of emphasising its importance, the delegate Ayat, who was not a cleric, explained that he had only accepted election to the assembly so that he could use his influence to see that this principle would have validity in the constitution.[105]

The role the people should play in the election of a leader did not present a serious problem as far as the person of Khomeini was concerned. His position both as leader of the revolution and as a religious authority was unchallenged. The one question raised, though without too much insistence, had to do with the title of the office that Khomeini would hold in his capacity as ruling jurist. Should his function be that of president or should he have a position as leader over all the branches of government? Without lengthy discussion, the assembly voted for the second option. Numerous delegates were concerned to emphasise that as a result of the regulations they had adopted, the leader would be chosen by the people. This, they maintained, was an expression of the sovereignty of the people and demonstrated the importance of this concept in the Islamic Republic. Yet almost no one spoke out against the fact that the choice of the leader would be carried out indirectly, that is by the intervention of the Assembly of Leadership Experts. In anticipation of the later electoral regulations for this assembly, the delegate Fowzi declared that members chosen for the Assembly of Leadership Experts should consist exclusively of clergy with the rank of *mojtahed* and that persons wishing to present themselves as candidates should have their suitability confirmed by the religious authorities.[106] The special position of the Assembly of Experts was also underlined by the fact that the formulation of the rules for election to it, as well as the regulations governing its functions, were not entrusted to the representatives of the people, that is to parliament, but to the Guardian Council and to the Assembly of Leadership Experts itself. Two delegates protested against this ongoing accumulation of prerogatives. One of them was Bani-Sadr who felt obliged to warn the clergy that the path they were following could be taken as proof that 'they were out to appropriate everything for themselves.'[107]

As for the requirement formulated in Art. 109 that the leader or leaders must hold the position of 'sources of imitation' and must possess the necessary 'scholarly qualifications', the members of the Assembly of Experts were so like-minded that they needed only minutes to pass the motion without making any alterations to its text.[108] Although the question was raised[109] as to the relationship of the leader to the other 'sources of imitation',[110] no conclusions were reached. In the view of Ayatollah Mohammad Yazdi, the other *marja'* should retain their position as jurists, i.e. teach religious doctrine, issue *fatvas* and formulate regulations, but should not hold an official government office.[111] By way of preventing complications that might result from rivalry between 'the sources of imitation' the delegate Hojjati Kermani proposed that the office of leader be scrapped. Instead the functions of the leader should be integrated into the office of president. The president should be a jurist who is elected by the people. Imam Khomeini should be the first to fill this office. Thereafter, the president should be someone who is able to win the approval of 'the sources of imitation'. If this proposal were not adopted, the high-ranking members of the clergy who were not accepted on the Leadership Council would continue to play the same role they had played under the imperial government; they would simply go on opposing the political authorities.[112]

In the debate over the powers of the leader, the advocates of *velayat-e faqih* endeavoured to endow him with as many as they could. One particular proposal for inclusion in Art. 57, which deals with the relationship of the leader to the three branches of government, was based on the idea that there are in fact five branches of government, the role of the leader and the people being added to the familiar three. However, this unusual formulation was considered contradictory to the generally held conviction that the real source of all government power is God who has transferred His supreme power over the people and their representatives to the ruling jurists. In any case, the result of the debates was widespread agreement that all government departments should be under the supervision of the person who holds supreme command and the Imamate, i.e. the leader.[113]

The delegate Ayatollah Naser Makarem Shirazi declared that Art. 110 (see

Chapter 1) was of the greatest significance and would shape the destiny of Iran.[114] The most extreme, and yet the most logical, comment concerning this article was made by the delegate Ahmad Nurbakhsh who said that, according to the principle of *velayat-e faqih*, it was reserved for the Imam alone to decide on what his powers should be. Consequently, it was not certain that the Assembly of Experts really had the authority to make such a decision.[115] Whereas Nurbakhsh's remark was intended as an indirect criticism of *velayat-e faqih*, there were in fact several delegates who supported this view in the positive sense, delegates such as Mohammad Rashidian, Javad Fatehi and 'Abdolhosein Dastgheib. The latter declared: 'If the principle of *velayat-e faqih* is accepted, this will mean that the leader has the power to see that justice is done in all matters affecting the country.'[116] When the powers of the leader as commander-in-chief of the armed forces were discussed, the argument was put forward that certain technical questions would have to be decided by military experts. Ayat protested, claiming that this was an attempt to restrict the powers of the leader.[117]

On the question of the leader's powers vis-à-vis the president, many members of the assembly argued that they should not be restricted to dismissing the president. Heidari demanded that the leader should make the final decision over the president's appointment, after the latter had been elected by the majority of the people. Ayatollah Lotfollah Safi advocated that the leader himself should appoint the president. Ayatollah Montazeri made the following pronouncement: 'Even if the entire people has voted for the president, as far as I am concerned this has no real validity as long as he is not confirmed by the ruling jurist.'[118]

In the debate over the leader's powers, the question was often raised as to how the relationship between *velayat-e faqih* and the sovereignty of the people, which was also to be adopted in the constitution, should be understood.[119] Many delegates attempted to deny the contradiction between these two principles. Mohammad Fowzi put forward the thesis that whereas, on the one hand, God had bestowed the sovereignty of the people on every member of the nation, on the other hand, He had bestowed it on 'special individuals' with 'special qualities' – namely 'the qualified jurists'. 'The people exercise their right by choosing a single jurist or a group of jurists to be the leader. In so doing, however, they do not decide whether this or that particular jurist possesses the [necessary] qualifications'. Instead, that decision is made by experts who have been chosen by the people. Thus, the people exercise their sovereignty by choosing the experts who in turn determine who will be the leader. In this case 'determine' does not mean that the experts grant to the leader the powers which are his due, but that they simply establish the suitability of candidates for the position. Fowzi's colleague, 'Ali Tehrani, saw no contradiction between the two principles because the people, he argued, had given their approval to *velayat-e faqih*. In all questions, even in the choice of one's religion and the choice of the leader, the people had the right to choose. On the basis of this right, the people had decided in favour of *velayat-e faqih*. Ayatollah Yazdi resolved the contradiction by declaring that the people, through their free choice of religion and the *shari'a*, had decided in favour of the regulations that issue from these sources – which restrict their freedoms. They were now free within the limits set by the *shari'a*. And the principle of *velayat-e faqih* also belongs to the regulations of the *shari'a*.[120]

However, this method of resolving the problem did not go unchallenged. Ayatollah Montazeri declared:

> The people's right of self-determination with regard to their destiny means that they choose whom they wish. But when it comes to *velayat-e faqih*, this does not apply. It is more correct to say that 'the people honour *velayat-e faqih*'. They simply choose the ruling jurist, directly or through the experts.

Ayatollah Dastgheib presented a more original interpretation of the relationship between *velayat-e faqih* and the people. The reason that the jurists had not ruled in earlier centuries, he argued, was because the majority of the people were not ready to approve of such a system and would not submit to the jurists' authority. The sovereignty of the jurists only became a commandment once the people were ready to accept it. 'In any case, the right to rule belongs to the upright jurist. And this is one of the principles of our religion.' Another rather original interpretation was put forward by Ja'far Sobhani who saw the *velayat-e faqih* as the means of securing the sovereignty of the people. He justified this thesis by noting that 'whenever in the past, as now in the present, there was a strong jurist, this had truly proved to be to the benefit of the people's freedoms. The jurist had prevented dictatorship, either in part or, in some cases, completely.'[121]

## Notes

1 The five civil jurists were: Ahmad Sadr Hajj Seyyed Javadi, Naser Katuzian, Mohammad Ja'fari Langarudi, 'Abdolkarim Lahiji and 'Abbas Minachi. This information is taken from an interview Habibi gave in *Kayhan* 1/9/79, and the author's interview with Lahiji.

2 Reported on the same day by *Kayhan* and confirmed by Naser Mianchi, the minister of information and propaganda.

3 As a minister Sahabi later assumed responsibility for the so-called 'Revolutionary Project'.

4 See Sanjabi: 1989, p. 331.

5 See the interview with Sahabi in *Kayhan* 16/6/79.

6 See *Kayhan* 14/6/79, and *Ettela'at* 16/2/79.

7 According to the final version of the constitution, a two-thirds majority is required only if a question of interpretation arises.

8 Preliminary draft, Art. 142–7.

9 Habibi's early draft was published in *Kayhan* on 28/4/79 and 29/4/79. According to Sahabi, the purpose of publication was to steer the discussion about the Constitution in the desired direction.

10 Art. 78 and 151–6.

11 Art. 90.

12 See Sahabi's statements in *Kayhan*, 12/5/79 and 16/6/79, and Habibi's remarks in *Kayhan*, 2/9/79.

13 'A. Lahiji, interview with the author.

14 'The Imam and a few of the grand ayatollahs had seen it, read it and approved of it, despite their wishing to make a few insignificant improvements.' *Nehzat-e Azadi*: 1983, p. 35.

15 Sanjabi: 1989, p. 321. In the newspaper *Enqelab-e Eslami* (23/8/79) published by Abolhasan Bani-Sadr, Khomeini's objection to the possibility that women might hold the office of president or occupy the position of a judge is mentioned(see Bakhash: 1985, p. 74). A further alteration to the text which Khomeini requested was that in matters concerning the *shari'a* the agreement of the majority of the clerics on the Guardian Council should be sufficient to decide an issue (author's interview with Bani-Sadr). Khomeini also insisted that judges should be chosen from the ranks of the *mojtaheds*. Moreover, supposedly out of consideration for the other 'sources of imitation', he supported the demand that the national religion be officially referred to as Twelver Shi'ism instead of Islam (author's interview with Salamatian).

16 Bani-Sadr: 1982, p. 386. In a lead article published in *Enqelab-e Eslami* on 20/6/79, Bani-Sadr also reported that Khomeini 'only felt it necessary to make a few insignificant corrections ... [which] would not result in any real alteration of the Constitution.' See Bani-Sadr: 1980, p. 6. Sahabi told *Ayandegan* on 19/6/79 that Khomeini, who had received a copy of the preliminary draft five days before, had returned it to the Ruling Council without making any changes and had stated that he would give his opinion of the draft within the one month deadline allowed to the rest of the population. This statement was taken to mean that Khomeini did not wish to have any special rights bestowed upon him. However, this view does not tally with the reports about the actual changes that Khomeini had demanded. It is therefore to be assumed that Sahabi issued this statement with an eye to its effect on the public.

17 *Kayhan*, 18/6/79.

18 *Kayhan*, 19/6/79.

19 This party and its leaders were, along with Khomeini, the key players in the adaptation of the preliminary draft into the final version of the constitution.

20 See Sahabi in *Kayhan*, 16/3/79; Nehzat-e Azadi: 1983, p. 35. Also confirmed in author's interviews with Bani-Sadr and Salamatian.

21 *Tali'eh-e Enqelab-e Eslami* (a collection of interviews given by Khomeini in Najaf, Paris and Qom): 1983, p. 30.

22 Ibid., p. 64.

23 Ibid., p. 81.

24 Ibid., p. 85, 142, 145, ff.

25 This assertion is based on a book entitled *A Collection of Writings, Speeches, Messages and Fatvas of the Imam Khomeini from the Second Half of the Year 1341 up to his Exile in Paris (14/7/1357)*, Tehran 1982. This collection does not contain Khomeini's book on the Islamic state, or his other writings on the subject of Islamic law such as *Kitab al-Bai'*. which at this time appeared in Arabic and partially deal with *velayat-e faqih*..

26 Certainly the willingness of Khomeini's audience to believe in assurances of this kind contributed to his achieving his purpose.

27 Bani-Sadr: 1982, p. 330. According to Bani-Sadr, when he visited Khomeini in Najaf directly after the publication of *Velayat-e Faqih* and informed him of the negative response the book had evoked from the public, Khomeini replied that his only purpose had been to launch a discussion of the subject. Now it was up to Bani-Sadr and Motahhari to draw up an outline of an Islamic state. Bani-Sadr then went on to write his book *The Essential Features and Guidelines of the Islamic State*, which Khomeini praised and which contains no

mention of *velayat-e faqih*. Bani-Sadr also reported that after Sadeqi (later the president of a congress which examined and criticised the preliminary draft of the Constitution) came out in favour of *velayat-e faqih* in a public speech in Paris, Khomeini refused to receive him (interview of the author with Bani-Sadr).

28 See interview with Nazih in *Kayhan*, 1/2/79. In an interview he gave on 21/2/79 Nazih said: 'On the basis of the interviews and statements of His Excellency the Grand Ayatollah Khomeini, one may conclude that in the Islamic Republic it will be the Iranian people who decide over their own destiny' (published the same day in *Kayhan*).

29 Later Qotbzadeh was to fight against the Islamic state once it had established itself 'in the usual sense'. In so doing he lost his life. The interview referred to was reproduced in *Kayhan* on 4/2/79.

30 *Kayhan*, 13/2/79.

31 *Kayhan*, 4/3/79. On 28/5/79, by way of giving his approval to the still unpublished preliminary draft, Sanjabi told *Ettela'at*: 'The constitution would be based on democratic principles and the application of Islamic principles of justice, virtue, equality and solidarity.'

32 Sanjabi: 1989, p. 434. According to Salamatian (a confidant of Sanjabi and a member of the 1st Majles, Khomeini gave assurances in these conversations that, amongst other things, the *qesas* punishments would not be put into effect since such decisions were the prerogative of 'the Infallible One'. When a few months later it appeared that they would be applied, on 15/6/81 the National Front appealed to the population to demonstrate against this decision. Khomeini threatened to declare that the leaders of that organisation were apostates if they didn't withdraw their appeal (interview of the author with Salamatian). According to Islamic law, apostasy is punishable by deaths.

33 *Kayhan*, 2/3/79.

34 It must have been at the instigation of these circles that on 9/1/79, i.e. before Khomeini actually returned to Iran, an article signed 'Imam Khomeini' appeared in *Kayhan* with the title 'The Islamic State and the Necessary Qualifications of its Leader'. The article consisted of the first part of Chapter 2 of Khomeini's book on the *velayat-e faqih* but the impression was given that it had been recently written.

35 See the lead article in *Enqelab-e Eslami* 15/7/79, and Khomeini's speech to Islamic students in the Hedayat Mosque, Tehran. Also in Bani-Sadr: 1980, p. 53 ff. and p. 315 ff.

36 MK IV/3 and 307. See also the daily press of this period. The most consistent criticism was voiced during the seminar held by the League of Jurists in June of that year.

37 In both *The Islamic State* (1983 edition, p.47) and *Kitab al-Bai'* (Tehran 1987, p. 20) Khomeini emphasised that the Islamic state would be different from all presently existing forms of government, including a republic (1983 edition, p. 47). Khomeini first spoke in favour of a republic in Paris, e.g. during interviews with Austrian television and the *Guardian* on 1/11/78. See Khomeini: 1983, p. 35 and p. 40.

38 *Kayhan*, 19/2/79. On this occasion, however, Khomeini declared that he was against the new state being called a 'Democratic Islamic Republic' as Bazargan and his party had proposed (*Kayhan*, 24/2/79). Thus he refused to approve the Revolutionary Council's statutes, the first article of which employed this designation. See Bazargan: 1983, p. 42.

39 *Kayhan*, 7 and 10/3/79.

40 *Kayhan* 22/2/79.

41 *Kayhan*, 6/3/79. On 24/1/79, *Kayhan* quoted Beheshti as saying: 'Islam is the religion of freedom.' See also his speech published in *Ettela'at* on 19/3/79 concerning 'the most fundamental principles of the Islamic Republic' which makes no mention of *velayat-e faqih*. Khomeini made similar promises while in Paris: 'In an Islamic state there is no dictatorship ... Parties and all individuals are free, except for parties that work against the interest of the state and the people' (*Kayhan*, 22/1/79). 'Women are just as free as men and decide over their own destiny' (*Kayhan*, 16/1/79). Similar statements are found in Khomeini: 1984.

42 See his press conference of 5/2/79, reported by *Kayhan* on 6/2/79. See also his interview in *Kayhan*, 17/3/79. The religious leader of the Sunni Kurds, Ahmad 'Allameh Moftizadeh, made similar promises. See *Kayhan*, 11/3/79.

43 *Kayhan*, 24/2/79 and 11/3/79. On the other hand, the Grand Ayatollah Sadeq Ruhani wanted the clergy to be given the right of veto with regard to legislation in the Islamic Republic (interview in *Ettela'at*, 4/6/79).

44 Published in *Kayhan* that same day.

45 *Kayhan*, 27/3/79; *Ayandegan*, 28/3/79.

46 *Ayandegan*, 31/3/79.

47 Ibid., 3/4/79.

48 Sazman-e Mojahedin-e Khalq: 1979; *Ayandegan*, *Kayhan* and other daily newspapers, on 18/3/79 and the days that immediately followed, published reports on the attitude of individual organisations vis-à-vis the referendum.

49 Bani-Sadr reported that Khomeini, at the beginning of his sojourn in Paris, believed it was impossible to overthrow the Shah's regime, and Bazargan thought any such idea was insane (interview of the author with Bani-Sadr). Several years later Ayatollah Mahdavi-Kani, Secretary of the League of Militant Clergy, described Khomeini's practical success in pushing through the concept of *velayat-e faqih* as a miracle. 'The majority of the *foqaha*', so he recalls, 'supported the *velayat-e faqih* but they did not believe they could ever achieve this right that was their due' (*Resalat*, 17/3/92).

50 Nehzat-e Azadi: (n.d.), *Moshkelat*, p. 1. Khomeini, in a statement to the press in Paris on 16/1/79, promised to summon a constituent assembly which would work out the final version of the constitution. See Khomeini: 1984, p. 341.

51 *Ayandegan* 9/4/79. That same day *Ettela'at* reported on a speech which Khomeini gave before the employees of a steel factory in Isfahan and in which he invited them to elect suitable representatives for the Constituent Assembly.

52 See the article: 'It's Not a Question of Numbers', published on 1/8/79 in *Azadi*, the organ of the National Democratic Front.

53 *Kayhan*, 5/4/79. The government worked out the electoral regulations and had the Revolutionary Council approve them. Accordingly, one representative would be chosen for every 100,000 voters. See the *Open Letter of the National Front to the Iranian Nation*, Jebheh-e Melli: 1979, p. 3.

54 Qotbzadeh and Morteza Katira'i, both laymen, were also in favour of Khomeini's proposal, whereas Bazargan, Sahabi, Ahmad Sadr Hajj Seyyed Javadi, Hashem Sabbaghian and Bani-Sadr were against it. The meeting in question took place on 22/5/79. Newspapers reported on it without giving any details. On 23/5/79, Taleqani reported simply that the Constitution and the nature of the Constituent Assembly were discussed during the meeting. Details were to be made known within a week: *Ayandegan* 24/5/79. See also Nehzat-e Azadi: 1983, p. 35; Bani-Sadr: 1982, p. 316 f.; Sanjabi: 1989, p. 324. According to Lahiji, the proposal was supposedly put forward from different sides as early as March 1979 (author's interview with Lahiji).

55 Bani-Sadr: 1982, p. 386. According to Salamatian, Ayatollah Beheshti argued along the same lines. Sanjabi is meant to have gone along with the idea of consulting the people for the same reason (author's interview with Salamatian). This last statement of Salamatian is corroborated by Sanjabi himself in his memoirs: 1989, p. 333. Likewise, Ahmad 'Ali Alibaba'i, a personal confidant of Ayatollah Taleqani, in a conversation with the present author, confirmed that Beheshti had warned Bazargan in the same terms. Alibaba'i learned of this from A. Ha'eri who had been present when Beheshti and Bazargan met, and had heard the warning.

56 Nehzat-e Azadi: 1983, p. 35. Bani-Sadr explained that he also rejected this proposal. He had compared the assembly to the Council of the Catholic Church and pointed out

that the proposal would give the impression of a return to the Middle Ages (interview by author with Bani-Sadr).

57 When protests were voiced against this provision, the number of experts to be elected was raised to 73. The daily press and the organs of the opposition reported in detail on these protests. The protesters included the National Democratic Front, the National Front, the Islamic People's Republican Party which was closely linked to the Grand Ayatollah Shari'at-madari, associations of writers, journalists, jurists and university professors, and numerous well-known intellectuals. See: *Ayandegan* 27, 28, 31/5/79 and 4, 10, 31/6/79.

58 Ayatollah Beheshti is cited as the originator of this change of the council's title. See Nehzat-e Azadi: 1988, p. 12. We shall see how the new name gives a better description of the composition of this institution.

59 LB: 1978/1979, p. 52. Similarly, the standing orders of the Assembly of Experts, which had been worked out by the Revolutionary Council, stipulated that the Assembly of Experts would carry out its task on the basis of the preliminary draft of the Constitution. On this point see Madani: 1986–90, p. 70.

60 This claim hardly satisfied the radical democrats and leftist organisations already in opposition. They insisted that now, as before, the constitution should be worked out by the Constituent Assembly. On this point see, for instance, the *Open Letter of the National Front to the Iranian Nation* (Jebheh-e Melli: 1979, p. 4). See also *Azadi*, Nr. 19, 1/8/79.

61 Bani-Sadr: 1982, p. 387. Ayatollah Taleqani, in putting forward his compromise solution, did so on the understanding that the proposed assembly 'would consist of civil jurists, intellectuals, writers, journalists and people who had had previous experience in framing laws' (author's interview with Hasan Nazih). This provision was meant to be an implicit answer to the question of how, if a large assembly of several hundred delegates could be dominated by 'the reactionary clergy', this could be avoided in a considerably smaller assembly.

62 Madani: 1986–90, vol. I, p. 66.

63 *Kayhan*, 16/6/79.

64 *Kayhan*, 18/6/79. On this occasion Khomeini calculated that if the text of the constitution were to be written by the Constituent Assembly, it would take one to two years to complete the task.

65 This does not mean that there was no earlier public advocacy of *velayat-e faqih*, merely that it had only happened sporadically.

66 Published in *Kayhan* the same day.

67 Ibid.

68 *Kayhan* 3/6/79.

69 Published in *Kayhan* the same day.

70 *Kayhan*, 18/6/79, and 4, 12, 26/7/79, as well as in the issues that followed.

71 *Kayhan*, 21/6/79. This is not meant to imply that all subsequent criticism of the preliminary draft expressed by legalists was the result of Khomeini's delegating the task. It should also be noted that the viewpoints cited here only represent a small selection of the many expressed.

72 Published in *Kayhan* the same day. One day before the elections to the Assembly of Experts, Khomeini stated that the preliminary draft was more influenced by the West than by the *shari'a*. He demanded that the concept of *velayat-e faqih* be included in the constitution and that the Guardian Council should have the right of veto (*Jomhuri-ye Eslami*, 2/8/79).

73 Published in *Kayhan* the same day.

74 *Kayhan*, 26/6/79.

75 Ibid., 28/6/79.

76 Ibid., 2/7/79.

77 Published in *Kayhan* the same day.

78 See *Khalq-e Mosalman*, the organ of the Islamic People's Republican Party, on 1 and 16/8/79. Further information about these manipulations is presented by this newspaper as well as by *Azadi* on 8/8/79, *Neda-ye Azadi* on 12/8/79, *Ettehad-e Chap*, the organ of the leftist-oriented organisation of the same name, on 11/8/79, *Kar*, the organ of the Feda'iyan-e Khalq, on 6/8/79, and *Ayandegan* from 24/7/79 to 7/8/79.

79 For instance, in Tehran polling station posters were put up that said: 'At the order of the Imam, the Islamic groups have formed a coalition and are presenting their candidates for the Assembly of Experts in this manner.' There then followed the list of candidates and the names of the amalgamated organisations, such as the League of Militant Clergy of the City of Tehran, the Teachers of the Religious Academy of Qom, etc. See, for example, *Kar* on 6/8/79.

80 Author's interview with Salamatian.

81 Sazman-e Mojahedin: 1979, Supplement.

82 *Kayhan*, 7/8/79; *Khalq-e Mosalman*, 19/8/79.

83 They wrote in their telegram to the prime minister: 'You have surely been informed of the crimes that have been perpetrated during the elections ...' A list followed that enumerated some of the concrete cases 'of crime'. *Kayhan*, 7/8/79.

84 *Khalq-e Mosalman*, 11/5/79 and 21/10/79.

85 See *Ayandegan*, 2/8/79 and Bakhash: 1986, p. 80.

86 The number of votes cast only amounted to 10.7 million (based on M. B. Hakim: 1988, p. 270). The public was in fact never officially given figures for the turn-out.

87 On 14/9/79, Khomeini himself told leaders of the IRP that he intended to have Qasemlu arrested if he came to Tehran. *Kayhan*, 16/9/79.

88 Nehzat-e Azadi: 1983, p. 37; reprinted in *Kayhan*, 11/8/79.

89 MK IV/319 f.

90 MK I/13.

91 MK I/38.

92 MK I/434.

93 Amongst them was the preliminary outline of the Sazman-e Mojahedin-e Enqelab-e Eslami. The delegate Qoreishi proposed that this outline be adopted as the basis for the Council's work (MK I/73). Bani-Sadr has mentioned another such outline put forward by Hasan Ayat in which *velayat-e faqih* is included and, indeed, is accorded more far-reaching powers than those finally decided upon in Art. 110. The latter version was known as 'the American outline' because Ayat was closely linked with Dr Mozaffar Baqa'i who as leader of the Hezb-e Zahmatkeshan (Working People's Party) had approved the CIA-organised 1953 putsch against Mosaddeq's government. (Interview with Bani-Sadr)

94 And that is the reason why it appears in vol. IV of the minutes of the Assembly of Experts.

95 Ayatollah Beheshti was the dominant figure in the Assembly of Experts. Although he was the deputy of the assembly's president, he presided over most of its sessions and also exercised a powerful influence outside the plenary sessions.

96 MK I/49.

97 MK I/51, 58, 61, 65, 73.

98 MK I/64.

99 MK I/39.

100 MK I/53.

101 MK I/209.

102 MK I/261.

103 This procedure was adopted with Khomeini's approval. When during a plenary session Mohammad Javad Hojjati Kermani requested that the debate be prolonged, Beheshti

announced that 'the Iranian people and our excellent leader' were against such a proposal (MK I/383).

104  MK I/379 f.

105  MK II/1092.

106  MK II/1084.

107  MK II/1103.

108  This requirement was contested during a later revision of the constitution and the article was changed. Decisive in this regard was the fact that after Khomeini's death no other 'source of imitation' was considered a suitable to successor him. See Schirazi: 1991.

109  The question was put by Bani-Sadr; MK II/1066.

110  There were at the time several 'sources of imitation' besides Khomeini including Shari'at-madari, Mar'ashi, Golpaygani, Kho'i, Khonsari, Qomi, Mahallati, Ruhani, Hakim, Shirazi, etc.

111  MK II/1069.

112  MK II/1124.

113  The actual debate over this article was conducted outside the plenary session because it was clear that no agreement could be reached within a plenary session. Following the controlled 'official' debate it passed in a matter of minutes. (MK I/537 ff.; III/1697)

114  MK II/113.

115  MK II/972; 1192.

116  MK II/1065; 1115; 1158.

117  MK II/1112.

118  MK II/1119; 1141; 1161.

119  Chapter 5 bears the title: 'The Sovereignty of the People and the Powers Thereby Conferred'.

120  MK I/510; 512; 517.

121  MK II/1158; 1163.

THREE

# The Clash over *velayat-e faqih*

### Criticism in the Assembly of Experts

Given its composition, it was not to be expected that the Assembly of Experts would subject the principle of *velayat-e faqih* to intense criticism. Indeed, the relevant articles were all adopted in the constitution with a large majority.[1] For various reasons, even the delegates who were fundamentally against *velayat-e faqih* did not voice consistent criticism of the principle. Some simply cautioned the assembly not to show so great a disregard for the mood prevalent outside its meeting rooms and not to proceed in too rash and radical a manner. In anticipation of such a danger, Hashem Sabbaghian, the minister of the interior, in his address to the opening session of the assembly demanded that the constitution reflect 'the national unity' of all social classes and all individuals. Furthermore, he expressed the hope that 'monopolistic claims and factional tendencies' would not find a place in the constitution. Before this, Prime Minister Bazargan had addressed the assembly similarly expressing hope that it would work out a constitution all Muslims could look upon as their own.[2] During the negotiations over Art. 2, the delegate 'Ezzatollah Sahabi advocated the position which had been adopted in the preliminary draft. He declared that he was in favour of *velayat-e faqih*, as far as that meant that regulations would be worked out on the basis of the *shari'a*: 'However, *velayat-e faqih* does not mean that the jurist necessarily assumes an active, or even a supervisory, role in politics and exercises political power directly.' On the same occasion Bani-Sadr observed that, with the exception of Khomeini, no jurist was in the position to exercise the function of a ruler. Consequently, 'the authorised agents in the various branches of the government in their totality must be conceived of as the qualified jurist' and in this capacity they should run the government.[3]

During the debate on Art. 5 Rahmatollah Maraghe'i objected to the fact that those directing the Assembly of Experts had replaced Art. 2 of the preliminary draft, in which the will of the people was designated as the basis of sovereignty, with Art. 5 which had a completely different meaning. Such a procedure was beneath the dignity of the assembly. He was not, he declared, fundamentally against *velayat-e faqih*, if this were taken to mean the sovereignty of Islam, but he rejected outright the idea that 'a special social class should make a monopoly out of Islam for itself'. In support of his position, he quoted the following words of Ayatollah Taleqani: 'The Prophet set as a goal

45

for himself establishing the freedom of men at large, freedom from discrimination based on class ... freedom from regulations and laws which were
imposed on others in order to further the advantage of one group or class.'
Despite this bold critique, in the sessions that followed Maraghe'i felt himself
under such stress that he either remained silent or dressed his criticism in
language so opaque that his audience could scarcely understand him.[4]

Nurbakhsh, in a speech to the 22nd session of the assembly, expressed
his concern that if *velayat-e faqih* were to fail, people would turn their back
on Islam forever, and that *velayat-e faqih* could be transformed into a 'Yazid-
like'[5] government. He attempted to draw attention to the fact that 'the primary
reason that the leader of the revolution had achieved victory was that he had
relied upon the people.' Therefore, it was imperative that power be turned
over to the people: 'Not the clergy, but all the social classes together must
decide on political matters.' In the plenary session he stressed that not all the
*'ulama* advocated *velayat-e faqih*.[6] But eventually he began to have doubts about
the effect of his criticism and decided to stay away from the assembly.[7]

Only Hamidollah Mir Morad Zahi, the delegate from Sistan and Baluch-
istan, openly rejected every aspect of *velayat-e faqih*. He was not allowed to
justify his view because the chairman of the session in which he chose to
speak declared that the debate on the subject was closed.[8] Ayatollah Taleqani
was also opposed to the particular form of *velayat-e faqih* which the assembly
sought to adopt and is said to have voted against Art. 5 when it was discussed
outside the plenary session.[9] In any case, he was unhappy about his participation in the assembly and viewed it as something that had been forced upon
him. He had come to believe that working out a constitution at this time was
premature,[10] a position which Ayatollah Shari'at-madari and others had voiced
before him. Bani-Sadr quotes a conversation he had with Taleqani in which
the latter expressed his dissatisfaction over the clergy's apparent desire to
take control of everything themselves: 'Now, based on their own measure-
ments, they want to tailor-make the constitution like a suit of clothes.'[11]

When the Assembly of Experts was engaged in establishing the powers
of the leader during the negotiations over Art. 110, two delegates felt obliged
to warn their colleagues not to go too far. Ayatollah Makarem Shirazi
expressed the view that the supreme command of the armed forces should
not be granted to the leader but to the president. He pointed to the
impression that this principle would make on 'the world at large':

> Bear in mind that our domestic and foreign enemies will accuse us of dictatorship
> and hostility to the sovereignty of the people ... They will say that a small
> handful of religious scholars have gathered together in the Assembly of Experts
> and framed a constitution which establishes their own dominion. By God, see
> that you do not do this ...! It is possible that the people will remain silent today,
> but tomorrow they will abolish the constitution.[12]

In his turn, Hojjat al-Eslam Hojjati Kermani advised that account should be
taken of possible reactions in society to adopting *velayat-e faqih* in the
constitution:

Signs of a negative reaction in society have already appeared ... Rumours
concerning the dictatorship of the mullahs and the despotism of the clergy
have been spread throughout the country ... With this constitution we are
provoking dissatisfaction among many intellectuals ... Tomorrow the mass of
the homeless, the unemployed, the hungry and the discontent will join with the
disgruntled intellectuals.

This could only lead to undesirable consequences which, Kermani proposed,
might be avoided if the office of leader were combined with the presidency
so that the shift to *velayat-e faqih* would not ignore the effects of 'sociological
and mass-psychological mechanisms'.[13]

## Opposition outside the Assembly of Experts

The warning sounded by Hojjati Kermani was in response to growing protest
at the way the Assembly of Experts was dealing with the preliminary draft,
and its adoption, despite its earlier promises, of *velayat-e faqih*. The wave of
protest persuaded the Council of Ministers to take action. In mid-October
the great majority of ministers voted to dissolve the Assembly of Experts[14]
on the grounds that it had exceeded the deadline by which it was to have
completed its work,[15] and that it had overstepped its authority because it was
engaged in rewriting the text of the constitution, instead of making
adjustments to the preliminary draft.[16]

On the assumption that Khomeini would be against their resolution and
would prevent Bazargan from implementing it, the Council of Ministers
decided to release it to the press immediately. But Bazargan insisted that the
ministers should first travel to Qom to brief Khomeini who was, predictably,
enraged.[17] The resolution was quietly dropped. The public learned of these
events indirectly through newspaper reports of a speech given by Khomeini
on 22/10/79 to the clergy of Tehran's West District in which he violently
attacked those who advocated the council's dissolution characterising them
as 'unworthy human beings' and 'deviants' who were out to lead the people
astray and 'to suppress our movement'.[18]

From the Islamic point of view, the most significant protests against the
procedure of the Assembly of Experts and the particular form of *velayat-e
faqih* it wanted came from Ayatollah Reza Zanjani and the Grand Ayatollahs
Shari'at-madari and Qomi. Ayatollah Zanjani, who also enjoyed respect within
secularist circles, argued that the assembly's procedure 'would entail tumultuous consequences'. He held the position that:

According to the unanimous opinion of the Imami Koranic interpreters and
theologians, *velayat-e faqih* in an unrestricted form based upon the Koranic verse
about the *ulu al-amr*[19] is exclusively reserved for the rightly-guided Imams (peace
be upon them!). For it does not stand to reason that God, the All-wise, would
bestow the powers of the infallible Imam upon fallible human beings.

Zanjani advocated *velayat-e faqih* as it is defined in Art. 2 of the Supplement
to the 1906/7 Constitution which, at least in principle, had been in force up

to the revolution. According to this definition, a commission consisting of five *mojtahed*s would have the right to veto any laws passed by parliament if those laws were not in conformity with the *shari'a*. The commission was to be elected by parliament from a group of 20 *mojtahed*s.[20] Consequently, Zanjani considered the Assembly of Experts to be superfluous and harmful because it would only cause further disagreements and rifts within the ranks of the revolutionaries. He maintained it would be better for the time being to keep the 1906/7 Constitution in effect with the condition that the provisions pertinent to the monarchy be struck from the text.[21]

The Grand Ayatollah Shari'at-madari, who had played an important role in the revolution, argued along similar lines. In his opinion, the principle of *velayat-e faqih* applied only in cases where the *shari'a* had not provided an authorised agent, and then only when it was a matter of dealing with unavoidable issues.[22] Otherwise, 'power and sovereignty are rooted in the people.' This was proven by the fact that recourse had been made to a national referendum in order to give legitimacy to the Islamic Republic. The election of the Assembly of Experts by the people was another proof of the sovereignty of the people. Therefore, the members of the Assembly of Experts could not approve any principle which would put in question the sovereignty of the people.[23] Shari'at-madari questioned the authenticity of the formula '*velayat-e amr* and *emamat-e ommat*' which is used in Art. 5 of the constitution:[24] 'It is not clear what this formula means and where anything like this occurs in Islamic jurisprudence or in the concept of *velayat-e faqih*.' It lacks 'any fixed meaning and any juridical definition'.[25] Naturally, Shari'at-madari did not go so far as to accord the people the power to question the validity of those Islamic laws which should and would be applied.[26] He held the view that there should be no haste in working out a new constitution. In the meantime, the Islamic Republic could temporarily be governed on the basis of the old constitution along with Art. 2 of the Constitutional Supplement and without the parts of the text that pertain to the monarchy.[27] The Grand Ayatollah Qomi, for his part, rejected the underlying thesis of the far-reaching form of *velayat-e faqih*, according to which the jurists dispose over the same full powers as the Prophet and the Imams. Toward the beginning of October, he expressed this view in a letter to the public which was published in the daily press.[28]

Amongst the Islamic organisations, the Islamic People's Republican Party (Hezb-e Jomhuri-ye Khalq-e Mosalman) declared itself in the clearest and most consistent manner to be against the hierocratic interpretation of *velayat-e faqih*, as it was being adopted by the Assembly of Experts. As early as April 1979, the party's leading members stated that they would not recognise the authority of 'the sources of imitation' in politics. They would do no more than consider the clergy's advice on political matters. Only in questions of *feqh* would the clergy's opinion be decisive.[29] They also rejected the replacement of the Constituent Assembly by the Assembly of Experts.[30] They kept away from the elections for the Assembly of Experts and held public gatherings every week in their headquarters in the centre of Tehran during which opponents of *velayat-e faqih* presented their arguments.

This party's views reached a wide audience through its weekly publication, *Khalq-e Mosalman*. In a final evaluation of the Assembly of Experts' work, Hadi Esma'ilzadeh, a member of the party's Committee of Jurists, wrote: 'The Assembly of Experts has approved the setting up of a dictatorial regime.' He compared the result of the assembly's work to poisonous nourishment for a tree, a tree that represented the sovereignty of the people. He went on to describe the assembly as 'a miscarriage', and to criticise in detail the outcome of its work contrasting it with true democratic principles.[31] The consistency of this party's position is demonstrated by its boycott of the referendum held on 3 December 1979 on the constitution framed by the Assembly of Experts. It would, it said, only participate if the text of the constitution was revised to guarantee the sovereignty of the people, which demand was of course rejected. Its declaration on this issue states: 'Although there is a chapter in the constitution's text which is outwardly devoted to the sovereignty of the people, that sovereignty is in practice undermined by the powers accorded to the leader or the Leadership Council.'[32]

The leftist-oriented Islamic organisations voiced a more indirect criticism of *velayat-e faqih*. The communiqué issued by the five allied organisations referred to in the last chapter makes no reference whatsoever to *velayat-e faqih*. Instead, in their statement they emphasise their proposal for 'a system of councils' (*nezam-e showra'i*) as 'the form of the Islamic state'.[33] The leaders of the Mojahedin-e Khalq adopted the same position in speeches and interviews in which they also expressed themselves independently of the four other groups.[34] Shortly before the referendum they felt it necessary to announce that they would condemn any form of disturbance during the proceedings of the referendum.[35] In a speech on 16 October, 40 days after the death of Taleqani, Dr Habibollah Peiman, the leader of one of these five organisations, stated the view that *velayat-e faqih* could only function as long as Khomeini held the position of ruler. After Khomeini a situation of hopelessness could only be avoided if the people themselves were to exercise sovereignty.[36] Yet a few days before the referendum, despite certain reservations, he announced his approval of the text of the constitution justifying his position on the grounds that it was necessary for the stability of the revolution given 'our struggle against imperialism and … intense internal conflicts'. In such circumstances, the haste to ratify the constitution had to be accepted, even if this meant that the document contained errors which would have to be rectified at a later date. He felt that the constitution did make some provision for the 'system of councils' because it established a Leadership Council. He was disturbed, however, by the fact that the leader was to be designated by the Assembly of Leadership Experts and stated that it would be better if parliament were to carry out this function.[37]

The justification formulated by Peiman for conditional approval of the constitution and participation in the referendum, based on the priority of the 'anti-imperialist struggle', was typical of many radical Islamic organisations at that time. This 'anti-imperialist struggle', which reached its climax with the occupation of the American Embassy on 4 November 1979, caused not only the radical Islamic organisations to put aside their previous demands but also several non-Islamic leftist-oriented parties such as the Tudeh Party and its Maoist offshoot of the 1960s, the Revolutionary Organisation. Khomeini's strategy of linking his fight against the USA, which he described as 'the Great Satan', with a domestic political programme phrased in radical language contributed substantially to the response of these groups to his policy. They ended up participating in the December referendum and voting for the constitution and therefore *velayat-e faqih*.[38] None the less, the contradiction between the form of government they actually wanted and *velayat-e faqih* could neither be resolved nor repressed for an indefinite period. It was bound to re-emerge with even greater force once the radical promises of the ruling jurists proved to be no more than lip-service to leftist ideals. The result was a sense of indignation and disillusionment in leftist circles. The attitude of many of these groups towards the constitution is vividly illustrated by a letter which one group of radical Islamicists wrote to Khomeini on 3/12/79:

> In a situation in which everyone is either intimidated or caught up in a spirit of enthusiasm, we feel we have no other choice but to approve of the referendum proposed by the leadership. In giving our approval we wish to guarantee that our right to exist in this society is not taken away. But this does not mean that we agree with this bill which abounds in contradictions, [disregards] the sovereignty of the people – that quintessence of God's representation by means of human beings – exposes the revolutionary heritage of Islam after so many centuries to the danger of decline and deterioration and jeopardises the attraction of an ideology which, over the last eight decades, as if by a miracle has confronted other ideologies with its own modern concepts, demonstrated its superiority and protected the youth from hopelessness and error by showing them the straight path of Islam. We foresee with absolute certainty the outbreak of powerful antagonisms between various groups and classes in the not too distant future. And we foresee the outbreak of these antagonisms not only amongst the ordinary people but within the state apparatus itself, which has now become the bearer of *velayat-e faqih*.[39]

The position set out in this letter was that not only of the radical but also of moderate Islamicists such as Bazargan and his party, the Liberation Movement of Iran (Nehzat-e Azadi-ye Iran). On 26 November, 'in a call to participate in the national referendum' the latter organisation justified its position by invoking the need 'to guarantee achieving the goals that have been set, for the sake of the continuance of the revolution and to assure the stability of the Islamic Republic.' At the same time, it stated that the constitution displayed many omissions and mistakes, and 'from a juridical and practical point of view contained contradictions'. However, it was hoped that the law could be changed since it was not the word of God or a form of sacred revelation.[40]

During the three and a half month period between the convening of the Assembly of Experts and the referendum a series of momentous events took place which exercised a direct or indirect influence on the course of the assembly's deliberations and on the result of the referendum. Indeed, to some extent these events were staged precisely for that purpose. Perhaps the most important was the armed confrontation between the autonomous Kurdish movement and the central government which continued for a long time after the referendum. The leaders of this movement correctly perceived the contradiction between their demands for autonomy and the centralised authoritarian orientation implicit in the principle of *velayat-e faqih* which they logically rejected.[41] In this connection, other autonomous movements must also be mentioned, in the province of Khuzestan and in the Turkmen regions of the province of Mazandaran.

Another movement that opposed Khomeini's autocratic rule and rejected *velayat-e faqih* was that concentrated primarily around Azerbayjan and promoted by the supporters of the Grand Ayatollah Shari'at-madari. Amongst other things, demonstrations on 18 September and 16 October served to strengthen the position represented by this 'source of imitation' vis-à-vis the constitution.[42]

With the death of Taleqani on 9 September, the modernist Islamicists lost an extremely popular man whom they had hoped would act as an effective counter-balance against the monopolistic desires of the host of clergy gathered around Khomeini. His death occurred shortly before the passing of Art. 5 in the Assembly of Experts, the article which established the principle of *velayat-e faqih* and against which Taleqani had previously voted.[43]

Because of the occupation of the US Embassy and the taking hostage of its American employees, many members of radical circles came to believe that it was necessary to submit completely to Khomeini's leadership and not to oppose his campaign in favour of the constitution. The resignation of Bazargan's government on 6 November helped to strengthen their conviction. In radical circles Bazargan was perceived as the representative of reprehensible liberalism or capitalism, as well as an advocate of a friendly foreign policy towards the US. Consequently, they celebrated his resignation as a victory for radicalism achieved under Khomeini's leadership.

During these three and a half months, attacks against the democratic rights of the opposition were continued, and can in part be traced to the period preceding the change of power in February 1979. On 7 August *Ayandegan*, the daily newspaper with the widest circulation, which had agitated against *velayat-e faqih*, was prohibited. Then, immediately after the Assembly of Experts began its deliberations, there followed the prohibition of a series of other newspapers and periodicals. Over the first three days after *Ayandegan* was closed, 41 newspapers and periodicals were prohibited.[44] On the day the Assembly of Experts was convened Khomeini personally forbade the Democratic Party of Kurdistan to engage in any activity whatsoever. Three days later, the property of Hedayatollah Matin-Daftari, a leader of the

National Democratic Front, was confiscated.[45] On the same day, on the orders of the public prosecutor of the revolutionary courts, the Revolutionary Guards shut down the headquarters of the Mojahedin-e Khalq.[46]

At the same time there was much activity directly pertinent to the work of the Assembly of Experts and its position on the *velayat-e faqih*. This included formal declarations, the collection of signatures and the composition of tracts and articles published in the daily press or by other means, all of which expressed views for or against *velayat-e faqih*. All this was reflected in the speeches given by members of the Assembly of Experts who reacted strongly to criticism and were delighted whenever they could announce declarations of sympathy.

The Assembly of Experts brought their work to an end on 15 November, after their original deadline of one month had been extended three times. The national referendum on the constitution the Assembly of Experts had worked out took place on the 2–3 December 1979. The official claim is that 15,758,956 voters out of an electorate of 21 million took part. There were supposedly 15,680,339 votes for and 78,516 against the constitution.[47] Great numbers of those who opposed the constitution abstained. If these figures are compared with the 20,439,908 votes that are said to have been cast in the first national referendum at the end of March 1979, at least an approximate idea can be gained of how many people Khomeini was no longer able to mobilise after only nine months.

## The Exponents of Absolute *velayat-e faqih*

The discussions about *velayat-e faqih* inside as well as outside the Assembly of Experts, revealed a group of people who were unwilling to accept even the somewhat limited restrictions which the text of the constitution imposed on the power of the ruling jurists. These people also expressed their displeasure with such 'new-fangled' institutions as parliament, especially when these were granted powers which they preferred to see reserved for the jurists. They demanded an absolute form of *velayat-e faqih* with the same full authority as the Prophet had exercised as God's deputy on earth. As mentioned earlier, the delegate Rashidiyan raised objections to the fact that it was the Assembly of Experts that defined the leader's jurisdiction.[48] His colleague Karami considered any kind of legislation other than that laid down by the *shari'a* as apostasy.[49] Ayatollah Khadami insisted on absolute obedience to the ruling jurists,[50] and Taheri Khorramabadi represented the view that in the Islamic Republic the constitution would be nothing less than the authentic Islamic system of jurisprudence.[51]

Contradictions which appeared because of the adoption of foreign elements into the constitution were addressed and criticised time and again during sessions of the Assembly of Experts. When the assembly was debating the sovereignty of the people, the delegate Farsi wished to know where the sovereignty of the people was to be found in the system of Islamic law and what Koranic verse or tradition of the Prophet would support this concept. Kiavash drew attention to the fact that there was no connection whatsoever between this principle and *velayat-e faqih*. Ayatollah Beheshti, however, saw no problem in this respect. Islam must be allowed to react in an adequate manner to problems and questions which arise in human culture.[52]

Similarly, the foreign origin of parliament was discussed in the Assembly of Experts. The delegate 'Abdollah Ziya'i-Niya declared: 'We all know that parliament was forcibly imposed on the *shari'a* ... It has no legal foundation in the *shari'a*.' According to Islam, legislation, which is the function of parliament, lies in the hands of God. Ziya'i-Niya did not, however, reject parliament completely. It should be made up of a small number of representatives whose function would be to conform to the law of God.[53]

Contradictions to the *shari'a* that concerned less fundamental issues were also pointed out and addressed. During the discussion of Art. 21 which deals with the rights of women, the delegate Ayatollah Safi, citing the relevant Islamic regulations, characterised as un-Islamic the stipulation that the protection of the family was a matter for the courts. This was solely a matter for a *mojtahed* who should be consulted in each individual case. Likewise, in the question of legal guardianship the state should not intervene because here too the decision rests with a *mojtahed*. Furthermore, the permanence and the institutionalisation of the courts lacks any basis in the *shari'a*, which conceives of courts as being of temporary duration. Ayatollah Montazeri also considered it false that guardianship be handed over to the mother in the absence of another legal guardian because it was possible that a competent *mojtahed* might be of the view that someone else could fulfil this duty better.[54]

The articles of the constitution which dealt with the judiciary caused further problems because of many stipulations that are alien to the *shari'a*. On the question of juries which, according to Art. 168, should be present at courts competent to judge political crimes and crimes violating the press laws, the delegate Khamene'i raised a protest, pointing out that according to the *shari'a* a *mojtahed* should pass sentence. It was not required that a *mojtahed* accept any other body as a participant in reaching a judgement, unless that body merely had an advisory function.[55]

The public character of court proceedings, as stipulated by Art. 165 and 168, was also contested in the Assembly of Experts. The delegate Hosein 'Ali Rahmani asked the assembly to consider the fact that this regulation was neither approved in the Koran nor in *feqh*. His colleague Ziya'i-Niya, however, replied that it was not decisive whether previous approval existed, but whether the *shari'a* explicitly prohibited the regulation. Islamic jurisprudence was based on establishing what is permitted, not on prohibitions. Moreover, the courts which were convened by the Prophet himself did not exclude the public.[56]

Similar questions also arose when the assembly dealt with issues such as forbidding torture, the decision over military training for women, regulations for the system of taxation in the Islamic Republic, giving concessions to foreign citizens, deciding on the salary of judges, establishing that the leader must be of Iranian nationality, and in other such cases.[57]

The disagreements which emerged around the question of the Guardian Council amongst the different Islamic organisations had less to do with the decision to create a council loyal to the *shari'a* that would exercise supervision over legislation than with the composition and the powers of that body. There were, however, voices in the Assembly of Experts that wanted to make the Guardian Council even stronger in terms of absolute legalism than was the case in the final version of the constitution. For instance, Hojjat al-Eslam Khamene'i, who after Khomeini's death became leader, did not agree that civil jurists should also be represented in the Guardian Council. He justified his position by arguing that with the fall of the shah the legal system of the former regime, which was primarily based on the French system, was now superfluous. Consequently, the experts on this system no longer had a function in the Islamic Republic. Ayatollah Safi stated that the presence of civil jurists in the Guardian Council 'could give the impression that Islam was deficient and that there were problems which could only be solved by turning to a system of jurisprudence other than the Islamic one'.[58]

A power of veto for the Guardian Council over parliament's resolutions was in conformity with the prevailing view in the Assembly of Experts that according to Islam legislation is the sole prerogative of God and God has transferred this right to the *foqaha*. Viewed from this perspective, parliament does not actually possess legislative rights. Hence the delegate Jalaleddin Farsi advocated two parliaments, one made up of Islamic jurists who would formulate, codify and pass laws on the basis of the *shari'a*, and another composed of practical experts whose task would be to draw up plans for ministries and to choose officials for government administration and the executive.[59] According to Mohammad Mehdi Rabbani Amlashi, parliament should be granted an advisory function which would be at the disposal of the ruling jurists. Such a parliament would be made up of well informed good advisers, who also had the capacity 'to derive relevant present-day laws from Islamic law'.[60]

Different variations on these views were heard outside the Assembly of Experts, especially during the period between the publication of the preliminary draft of the constitution and the formation of the Assembly of Experts. In a lengthy letter to the editor of *Ayandegan*, the lawyer Gholam Hosein Rezanezhad wrote that in the Islamic Republic he considered parliament as an institution to be sheer nonsense and rejected the idea of sovereignty of the people as un-Islamic. He argued that the Koranic passages quoted in the preliminary draft of the constitution by way of sanctioning *showras* did not apply to matters of government but only to private affairs: 'If sovereignty belongs to the people, then it doesn't belong to God, and if it belongs to God, then what right do the people have to choose representatives who will pass laws that have authority over the Muslims?'[61] The leader of the Congress of Muslims Critical of the Constitution, Mohammad Sadeqi, demanded amongst other things that parliament's only function should be the practical application of God's laws. For this reason, it should be made up of jurists and representatives of the 'sources of imitation'.[62] In his open letter to Khomeini, the cleric, Hoseini Tehrani, spoke out against a republic because a republic had its support in the approval of the majority, whereas the Islamic state was based on divine right (*haqq*). The right to rule in an Islamic state belonged exclusively to the most prominent, wise, intelligent and pious jurist who was to be chosen by a commission of wise men (*ahl-e hall va 'aqd*) for the duration of his life or for as long as he possessed the necessary qualifications for his office. Parliament's function was merely that of consultation. The results of parliament's consultations should be presented to the wise jurist who was free of lust and passion, and who would base his judgement on the Koran and the *sunna* and, having considered the circumstances and the demands of the time, would take the necessary decisions and issue the appropriate decrees.[63]

If the actual wording of the text of the constitution does not establish *velayat-e faqih* with this degree of purity, it is nevertheless clear that the pervading spirit of the document expresses the concept of an absolute hierocracy.[64] This form of *velayat-e faqih* corresponds to the image sketched in Khomeini's book on the subject which appeared a decade before the revolution. In that book, the power of the ruling jurist is also absolute. On behalf of his people he exercises the function of a legal guardian, a protector and a liberator. The people are not active subjects of the state but the state's objects. Furthermore, given the alleged perfection of the *shari'a*, there is no need for a legislature. Parliament is not to function as a legislative body, but merely as an 'institution for planning'.[65]

## Notes

1 Art. 2 was passed by 60 out of 66 votes (2 abstentions), Art. 5 with 53 out of 65 votes (4 abstentions), Art. 57 with 51 out of 56 votes (4 abstentions) and Art. 110 with 57 out of 61 votes (4 abstentions). The votes of the four representatives of the religious minorities were no doubt amongst the hostile votes and the abstentions. During the assembly's entire existence when a motion was put to the vote, on the average out of 66 votes cast there were 2 hostile votes and 4 abstentions (MK IV/281).

2 MK I/7 f.

3 MK I/91; 93.

4 MK I/375; 545; II/1067; 1100.

5 Yazid, the son of Mo'aviya, was the second caliph of the Umayyad Dynasty. The Shi'a hold him responsible for the martyrdom of the third Imam, Hosein, in the year 680.

6 MK I/382.

7 He no longer attended sessions of the assembly during the morning, but when he also wished to stop coming in the afternoon 'the Imam' obliged him to attend (MK II/1086).

8 MK I/382.

9 *Khalq-e Mosalman*, 23/9/79.

10 See his conversation with Dr 'Ali Golzadeh Ghafuri in *Kayhan*, 25/8/79.

11  Bani-Sadr: 1980, p. 199 ff.

12  He was not an opponent of *velayat-e faqih* and saw no contradiction between this concept and the sovereignty of the people (MK II/1114 f.). In *The Islamic State* (1979), he defines *velayat-e faqih* as a system of supervision to guarantee that the laws and their application are Islamic. However, he did not take the concept to mean rule by the clergy (p. 70 f.).

13  MK II/1122. Bani-Sadr has described a meeting during which opponents and critics of *velayat-e faqih* in the Assembly of Experts discussed the possibility of a concerted effort against adopting the concept in the constitution. Amongst other things, those present considered the option of handing in their resignation. They finally decided to continue to attend the assembly in order to carry on 'their common, though fruitless' fight against *velayat-e faqih*. Not everyone, however, held to their agreement, though Bani-Sadr himself did maintain an unflagging resistance.

14  See Nehzat-e Azadi: 1983, p. 36. Of the 22 members of the Council of Ministers, 17 voted for this decision. *Kayhan*, 30/6/79.

15  The Assembly of Experts was set a one-month deadline to complete its work. By this date it had already had two extensions.

16  This information is chiefly based on a letter which Ayatollah Mohammad Sadduqi, the Chief Public Prosecutor of the Revolutionary Courts, handed over to the press on 29/6/80. This letter, which Sadduqi attributed to 'Abbas Amir Entezam, who had formerly been the Spokesman for Bazargan's government and was in prison at the time describes how the decision in question was reached. See *Kayhan*, 30/6/80. The author's interviews with Hasan Nazih and 'Abdolkarim Lahiji have also confirmed these points. See also Nehzat-e Azadi: 1983, p. 36. As punishment for his involvement in this initiative, Amir Entezam is still in prison at the time of writing and suffers extremely harsh treatment. See *Enqelab-e Eslami*, No. 334–5, 1994.

17  Hasan Nazih recounted how Khomeini threatened Bazargan, saying he would 'give him a punch in the mouth'(author's interview with Hasan Nazih).

18  *Kayhan*, 23/10/79. In an address to the people on 7/11/79 considered to be his farewell speech, Bazargan reacted to these unfriendly words, while expressing his concern at how the Assembly of Experts was dealing with the preliminary draft of the constitution. Amongst other things, he said: 'As I take leave of you, I am greatly troubled that, once this constitution has been ratified, the country will remain in a state of anarchy and lack any orientation, while the sovereignty of the people, who are God's deputies on earth ... will disappear and be replaced by a form of class rule ... even if that class is made up of members of the clergy...' See Nehzat-e Azadi: (n.d.) *Moshkelat*, p. 288 f.

19  Koran 4/59: 'Oh believers! Obey God and the Messenger and those in authority amongst you.'

20  On the 1906 constitution see Rahimi: 1978.

21  *Khalq-e Mosalman*, 28/10/79.

22  In an interview with the *Tehran Times*, as an example of an 'unavoidable issue' Shari'at-madari referred to Khomeini's appointment of a provisional government after the revolution, when there was no legal authority capable of taking such a measure. Once parliament was elected, however, the jurist lost his right to act this way, since it was then possible for the sovereignty of the people to be exercised through their representatives.(*Khalq-e Mosalman*, 18/10/79.)

23  *Khalq-e Mosalman*, 23/9/79. 'No one should declare the voice of the people to be invalid, and maintain that ... the jurist is everything.' Ibid., 20/10/79.

24  The concepts *'velayat'* and *'emamat'* can also be translated as 'the office of leadership' or 'the leadership command' or 'the authority for leadership'.

25  Ibid., 21/10/79.

26 Interview in *Ayandegan*, 9/4/79.

27 *Khalq-e Mosalman*, 7 and 14/10/79. Shari'at-madari presented his views on *velayat-e faqih* in a series of lectures in Mashhad before the elections for the Assembly of Experts. In these he declared that Khomeini's interpretation of *velayat-e faqih* was untenable. Tape recordings of these lectures exist. (Based on author's interview with Shari'at-madari's son, Hasan Shari'at-madari.)

28 *Khalq-e Mosalman*, 7/10/79. Sheikh 'Ezzeddin Hoseini, a leading Sunni Islamic scholar, rejected *velayat-e faqih* and demanded that the Assembly of Experts be dissolved. Ibid., 11/11/79.

29 See report of the party's press conference in *Ayandegan*, 26/4/79.

30 'Without the Constituent Assembly, the rights of the people will be violated' (*Ayandegan*, 31/5/79). The party adopted this position despite the fact that Shari'at-madari had been talked into giving his assent to the Assembly of Experts. On the shift in Shari'at-madari's attitude see *Ayandegan*, 10/6/79 (against the assembly) and 20/6/79 (in favour of it).

31 *Khalq-e Mosalman*, 18/11/79.

32 Ibid., 25/11/79.

33 Sazman-e Mojahedin: 1979, Appendix.

34 A collection of these texts has been published by Sazman-e Mojahedin: 1979. In an open letter which the Mojahedin wrote to the Revolutionary Council one week before the Assembly of Experts completed its work, there is likewise no mention of *velayat-e faqih*. On the other hand, they once more stress that the system of councils is the desirable form of Islamic government. See *Kayhan*, 8/11/79.

35 *Kayhan*, 25/11/79. However, they did not take part themselves in the referendum (*Khalq-e Mosalman*, 4/12/79).

36 *Kayhan*, 21/10/79.

37 *Kayhan*, 25/11/79. See also the declaration of his organisation OMMAT (Militant Muslims Movement) in which it announces its participation and invites its supporters to vote for the Constitution (ibid.). OMMAT approved of the replacement of the Constituent Assembly by the Assembly of Experts with the same reference to urgency in the fight against imperialism and the counter-revolution. See the party organ, *Ommat* (reprinted in *Ayandegan*, 26/6/79).

38 For the list of those who voted for and against, see *Khalq-e Mosalman*, 4/12/79.

39 Hojjat al-Eslam Shojuni was a signatory of this letter. See Nehzat-e Azadi: 1983, p. 37 f.

40 Nehzat-e Azadi: 1983a, p. 218 ff.

41 See Drögemüller (1983) for a good eye-witness account of these events.

42 Hundreds of thousands are supposed to have participated in these demonstrations. The immediate cause of this particular demonstration was the unsuccessful attempt on Shari'at-madari's life. See *Khalq-e Mosalman*, 9/9/79 and 21/10/79.

43 Taleqani preferred not to express his rejection of *velayat-e faqih* and the claim to monopolistic government rule by the clergy gathered around Khomeini. Insiders see as the reason for this caution his fear of persecution or even worse punishment. He considered the kidnapping of his sons by the Revolutionary Committee a few months after the revolution as a warning which was aimed directly at himself. (Authors interviews with Nazih and Lahiji.) On the kidnapping and the reaction it provoked, see *Ayandegan* and *Peygham-e Emruz* on 14/4/79 and in subsequent issues.

44 *Kayhan*, 20/8/79 and 21/8/79.

45 *Kayhan*, 22/8/79.

46 *Kayhan*, 23/8/79.

47 MK IV/307.

48  MK II/1065.

49  MK I/39.

50  MK II/943.

51  MK I/400.

52  MK I/518, 519, 524.

53  MK III/1668.

54  MK III/1738, 1741.

55  MK III/1677.

56  MK III/1620 ff.

57  MK I/777, III/1402, 1413, 1494 ff., 1591 ff., 1733 ff.

58  MK II/948, 951.

59  MK I/77.

60  MK I/62.

61  *Ayandegan*, 3/7/79. See also his articles in *Ayandegan*, 19 and 30/7/79.

62  *Ayandegan*, 27/6/79.

63  *Kayhan*, 27/6/79.

64  To my knowledge, it was Azari Qomi who in *Resalat* (6/6/89) for the first time spoke out against the spirit of the constitution supporting the absolute power of the ruling jurist.

65  Khomeini: 1982, p. 34 ff.

# PART TWO

# The Suppression of the Democratic Elements

# FOUR

# The Power of the Leader

The history of the Islamic Republic can in a certain sense be characterised as one in which power has – for most of the time – been increasingly concentrated in the hands of the leader, a process which went far beyond even the restrictions laid down in the constitution. The high point of this process was reached at the beginning of January 1988 when Khomeini declared the rule of *velayat-e faqih* to be absolute. It continued until the Khomeini's death but was subsequently interrupted because his successor could not claim to possess the qualifications to be accorded absolute power. In these circumstances, the absolute power of the leader had to be transferred to a collective body which will be discussed below in greater detail.

## Khomeini's Power before the Advent of Parliament

Power had already begun to concentrate in Khomeini's hands before the revolution. While residing in Paris he used his dominant position to decide many questions concerning the leadership of the revolution itself and the formation of the future government. If other leaders of the revolution wished to participate in decision-making, they were obliged to do so through the person of Khomeini. This process continued after Khomeini's return to Iran and to the time of his death. He exercised dictatorial powers both when he imposed his will on different branches of the government and when he took decisions without consulting these authorities.

The Revolutionary Council was established in Paris – with Khomeini's 'permission'. Khomeini not only decided that the council should be set up, but also on its powers, its composition and even – throughout the period until parliament was inaugurated – when it would convene.[1] Similarly, the appointment of Bazargan as the first prime minister and the definition of the tasks his provisional government was to perform bore Khomeini's signature.[2] At a later date Bazargan wrote on his government's relationship to Khomeini: 'He determined the main political lines and the general goals pursued by the government. Whenever important and fundamental questions were being dealt with, he was asked to give his command.'[3]

In this period members of the government, as well as the Revolutionary Council, would visit Khomeini at least once a week in Qom to listen to his instructions and report on events. The prime minister and Council of Ministers met with him more frequently. When legislation was drafted he would be consulted whenever questions of a religious nature arose. Bazargan gives the following examples of issues over which direct consultation with Khomeini took place: the question of interest, nationalisation of the banks, confiscations, the procedure of revolutionary courts and committees, a possible general amnesty, relations with the superpowers and neighbouring countries, questions of land ownership, the shaping of domestic policy and sensitive military matters.[4]

Even if preliminary decisions in preparation for a resolution were taken by the Council of Ministers or the Revolutionary Council, the final decision in all matters of importance was reserved for Khomeini. Likewise, it was frequently Khomeini who would have the last word on tactical and strategic procedures to push through resolutions, as he did during the process of framing the constitution. Even when Khomeini was not visibly involved in a fundamental decision, the final outcome was always in accordance with his wishes. In certain cases he preferred to remain in the background and to delegate decision-making to one of his trusted subordinates. Such cases often involved religious law or politically ambivalent questions, such as land-ownership, where he felt it would not be opportune to adopt an unambiguous position.[5]

Although Khomeini quite often preferred to delegate decision-making to others or to have the government or the Revolutionary Council express their opinion, it was more usual for him to make a decision and have it implemented without consulting anyone. A good example is the way he created the revolutionary courts immediately after the fall of the old regime, appointing their judges himself and according the courts absolute powers.[6]

There were also cases in which it appeared that Khomeini was not the initiator of a particular decision taken by those close to him but only subsequently gave his approval. Most of the time, however, these were actions for which Khomeini had long since provided the inspiration and concerning which his wishes were perfectly clear to the actual initiators. The hostage-taking at the American Embassy in Tehran (4/11/79) may be seen as one example of such an operation. Even though this action, which was carried out against the will of the provisional government,[7] was not launched under direct orders from Khomeini,[8] he had no hesitation about giving it his approval. On the evening of that same day, he is alleged to have assured the hostage-takers through his son that they did not have to worry about his support. Indeed, they were encouraged not to abandon the embassy premises.[9] Furthermore, Khomeini made his attitude clear to opponents of this action in different ways as, for example, in a speech he delivered two days later to officials of the insurance company.[10] Six days before the occupation, he had declared to 'the students who follow the line of the Imam' that 'all our problems come from the USA'.[11]

The closure of universities, which preceded the so-called cultural revolution and represented the first step towards the Islamicisation of culture and the educational system, also took place with Khomeini's approval,[12] even if in this case as well the concrete preparatory actions were carried out by other subordinate organs.[13] These organisations acted in accordance with Khomeini's wishes and in the full knowledge that he would approve of their actions. Khomeini had prepared the ground long before, drawing his supporters' attention to the dangers emanating from universities which, in his view, directly threatened the Islamic revolution. The day before the forces of order occupied the universities, Khomeini had accused them of dependency on foreign countries, of Westernising the students and of allowing themselves to become the arena of the propaganda war carried out by the left-wing students.[14]

Generally speaking, whatever methods Khomeini adopted to implement his own decisions or however great his influence on others, it was always clear that any decision stood a better chance of being implemented if it could be said to have originated with him. Therefore, measures adopted by government organisations were always presented in the name of the Imam; some, we can be sure, Khomeini had not wished to initiate.[15]

## Khomeini's Supremacy over the Constitution

That Khomeini functioned as the highest legislative power until parliament began passing laws in August 1980 did not appear as a blatant contradiction of the sovereignty of the people because a majority of the people had accorded him this power. However, once the country's legislative institutions – parliament and the Guardian Council – began their work, the contradiction became that much greater. During this period the most important decisions concerning both the legislature itself and legislation were still significantly influenced by Khomeini. Indeed his influence was so great that it brought about changes in the powers conferred on parliament and the Guardian Council, including revisions of the text of the constitution in ways the constitution itself does not sanction, and the establishment of a council to undertake such revisions.

The first decision aimed at changing the powers of the two legislative institutions gave parliament full authority, in an emergency, to pass laws with an absolute majority that contradicted the *shari'a* and the primary Islamic ordinances (*ahkam-e avvaliyeh*). The immediate occasion for this was a measure taken by the Revolutionary Council and later by parliament to restrict private ownership of agricultural and communal lands. Because they contradicted the *shari'a*, these measures were rejected by some of the high-ranking clergy and later by the Guardian Council. However, the government of the Islamic Republic deemed them indispensable and so in October 1981 Khomeini bestowed upon parliament the power to pass them. The relevant decree was Khomeini's answer to a letter written to him by the president of parliament, Rafsanjani, on 11 October 1981 in which he asked Khomeini to make use of the powers accorded to the most eminent jurist and leader with regard to several resolutions passed by parliament – in other words to decide how this contradiction could be resolved.[16] We see, by the way, how in this letter it is openly acknowledged that the leader exercises supremacy over the legislature.

Since Khomeini's response did not succeed in breaking the opposition of the Guardian Council, which found other ways to thwart resolutions of parliament, he issued another decree on 6 April 1984 in which he declared that the relevant resolutions of parliament must depend on a two-thirds majority but that such resolutions would no longer need the approval of the Guardian Council.

When this solution could not resolve problems resulting from a contradiction between the *shari'a* and the demands of modern legislation, and when recourse to other regulations based on adapting the *shari'a*[17] proved equally unsuccessful, Khomeini intervened again with a very far-reaching measure. In January 1988 he declared that an Islamic state had the right to disregard Islamic ordinances when passing resolutions and framing laws. The only principle to be followed was 'what is in the interest (*maslahat*) of maintaining [the ruling] order'. In the relevant decree issued on 7 January 1988, Khomeini announced that government rule was 'derived from the absolute dominion of the Prophet of God'. This was 'the most important of God's ordinances (*ahkam-e elahi*)' and stood above 'all ordinances that were derived or directly commanded by Allah'. If a measure was in the interest of the state and Islam, it could annul all other Islamic ordinances, even prayer, fasting and the pilgrimage to Mecca.[18]

On 6 February 1988 Khomeini set up a body with the task of assessing what was in the interest of the state. This body was known as the 'Council for Assessing what is in the Interest of [the Ruling] Order', and will be referred to in this book as the Assessment Council. The members of this council[19] were chosen by Khomeini, as were their tasks and powers. So that legislation would not be blocked because of disagreement between parliament and the Guardian Council, the Assessment Council was given the power to make a final decision in disputed cases. Moreover, the new council actually had permission to frame legislation on its own initiative apart from parliament and the Guardian Council.[20]

Of course no provision was made in the Constitution of the Islamic Republic for any such council. Khomeini's decisions of this kind were based solely on the principle that the rule of the jurists, in this case represented by the person of Khomeini, is unrestricted. According to this principle, Khomeini not only had the power to issue government decrees independently of parliament and the Guardian Council, but to issue decrees that ignored the constitution if, in his opinion, they were in the interest of the Islamic state.

Yet it was thought improper, or perhaps merely inexpedient, to disregard the constitution in the longer term. Therefore, it was decided to anchor the Assessment Council in the constitution. This task was carried out by the Assembly for Revising the Constitution which began its work in April 1989 and finished in August of the same year. Amongst other things, this Assembly saw to it that the Assessment Council was provided for in the text of the constitution. Its formation was legitimated by an appeal to the spirit of the constitution – that is, once again, to the notion of the absolute power accorded to the ruling jurists. With the usual consistency, appointments to the council were decided by Khomeini himself. Thus, the Islamic Republic now had one more constitutionally-sanctioned institution with legislative powers whose members were not chosen by the people but by the leader (Art. 112).

The Assessment Council was not the only body which Khomeini endowed with the power to pass legislation independently of parliament and the Guardian Council, and outside the framework of the constitution. Another was the Supreme Council of the Cultural Revolution formed in 1980 shortly after the universities were closed. This Council, whose members were ap-pointed by Khomeini, was instructed to transform the education system in universities and schools on the basis of Islamic culture.[21] In January 1987, at the request of President Khamene'i, Khomeini conferred on it the right to formulate 'guidelines and rules' (*zavabet va qava'ed*) independently of parliament.[22]

Similarly, Khomeini conferred legislative powers on the Supreme Council for Supporting the War (Showra-ye 'Ali-ye Poshtibani-ye Jang) and the Supreme Council for Reconstruction (Showra-ye 'Ali-ye Bazsazi). The latter council was established in September 1988 in order to draw up plans for the reconstruction of the country after the war had ended, the former had been set up several years earlier in order to mobilise the country's potential for waging war.[23] In contrast to the Council of the Cultural Revolution, which still exists today, these other two councils were of short duration.

On Khomeini's authority, the Council of Ministers and the Supreme Council of Justice also came to enjoy legislative powers. For the first of these, the high point of its authority came in 1987 when Khomeini conferred on it the right to impose discretionary punishments (*ta'zirat*) on persons convicted of hoarding and conspiring to drive up prices.[24] Similar efforts on the part of parliament had previously failed because of opposition from the Guardian Council.[25] As Rafsanjani stated in a session of the Assembly for Revising the Constitution, the president of the Supreme Council of Justice, Ayatollah Musavi Ardebili, 'over the last ten years was repeatedly given the authority to resolve the problems of his office'.[26] Rafsanjani was referring to the numerous resolutions passed by this council which would normally only be passed by parliament and the Guardian Council.

## Khomeini's Legislative Powers

Khomeini frequently exercised legislative powers without consulting the constitutional organs of government, or those legislative bodies he himself had set up. We will refer here only to a few representative cases.

How often cases of this kind occurred in connection with the judicial system is clear from a remark made by the then president of the judiciary, Ayatollah Yazdi, during a speech delivered to the Eighth Conference of

Islamic Thought in Tehran. They were so common, he said, that he could not attempt to enumerate them all, although he did mention the following specific cases:

1. The standardisation of sentences involving discretionary punishments, a problem that parliament, the Guardian Council and the judiciary could not agree upon.
2. Allowing insufficiently educated judges (*qazi-ye ma'zun*)[27] to practice in the courts; according to Art. 162 of the constitution only *mojtaheds* were qualified to hold such posts.
3. Determining those cases in which discretionary punishments involving whipping or flogging were appropriate.
4. Deciding whether justice should be dispensed by single judges or by several judges, and whether this should be after separate consultation or jointly.
5. Determining under which circumstances appeals could be allowed after a legal judgement has been delivered.
6. Clarification on the issue of whether smugglers, like 'hypocrites' (*monafeqin*, by which was meant members of the Mojahedin-e Khalq or their sympathisers), should be tried singly or in their quality as members of a group which has already been condemned as 'insurgents against God' or 'perpetrators of corruption on earth'.[28]

Among other striking cases relating to the system of justice, was Khomeini's decision that the Supreme Council of Justice should not function as a council but that tasks should be divided among its members upon whom greater individual responsibility was conferred.[29] This decision was directed against Art. 157 and 158 of the constitution. Another example is the famous decree of the Imam issued in December 1982 which consisted of eight separate points, many of them relevant to the justice system. For instance, the decree made it illegal to arrest and subpoena persons without a proper court order and to search homes without a warrant.[30] Finally, one may mention the creation of the Special Court for the Clergy (Dadgah-e Vizheh-e Ruhaniyat) which had been decreed by Khomeini immediately after the change-over of power and signed by the leader Khamene'i.[31]

When it came to regulating issues of private ownership of land, which played a decisive role in bringing about changes in the powers of the legislative institutions and the creation of the Assessment Council, Khomeini not only played the principle role in that he determined the actual contents of the relevant legislation, he also had the final word on the implementation of such laws. In November 1980, he issued a decree blocking the implementation of a law concerning the amount of arable land a person was allowed to own, which had been passed by the Revolutionary Council in April of that year. Likewise, each year he re-issued permission for the farmers who had illegally occupied estates during the first years after the revolution to retain and work those lands until such time as the legislature should enact a final resolution on this question.[32]

Khomeini determined the content of the highly disputed Labour Law by deciding to bypass the *shari'a* and to have it formulated as a modern law, rather than on the basis of Islamic laws governing tenant farming, as the Guardian Council had wished.[33] Then there was the issue of whether foreign trade would become a monopoly of the state, as stipulated by Art. 43 of the constitution, or whether, in accordance with the wishes of the Guardian Council, it would remain in private hands. Khomeini, who was asked to resolve this question, decided that private individuals should be allowed to participate in foreign trade [34] although it took several years for the government to put this decision into practice.

In dealing with a moot point of religious law – whether the Islamic state had the right to oblige citizens to pay taxes – Khomeini drew the attention of the conservative members of the clergy to the fact that the war with Iraq, for example, could not possibly be financed by the *sahm-e emam* (the portion of *khoms* – i.e. the Shi'i one-fifth tax – contributed to the Imam).[35] He consequently concluded that the state, in its quality as 'a primary Islamic ordinance (*hokm-e avvaliyeh*)', does have the fundamental right to impose taxes.[36] This interpretation, however, releases the faithful from the obligation of paying the *khoms* as well, which is a tax that primarily benefits the clergy.[37]

Similarly, it was necessary for Khomeini to issue a *fatva* in order to resolve, at least to some extent, the conflict over the right of ownership of mineral resources. The *fatva* in question stipulates that 'oil, natural gas and mineral resources, when they exceed in quantity the limits of private ownership established by customary law, are not subject to the regulations concerning land ownership.' Oil and natural gas are basically national property. The Islamic state has the right to extract these resources but it must pay the landowners rent for their land or a purchase price, though that price is not to be based on the mineral wealth contained in the land.[38] A *fatva* Khomeini had already issued in 1982 is relevant in this connection. In that *fatva*, Khomeini had confirmed the assumption made by the chairman of the Central Bank that the Islamic state is the sole owner of all foreign currency acquired through the sale of oil, which it is to spend on 'governing the country and protecting the interests of the nation'.[39]

Several questions to do with art and sports were also resolved by Khomeini. When, for example, ultra-conservative members of the clergy pointed out that on television domestic films were shown in which women did not fully comply with Islamic dress rules or athletes – male or female – appeared half-naked, the authorities responsible for running the radio and television turned to Khomeini and asked him for specific instructions. Khomeini's response was:

> Viewing films or theatrical productions of this kind is, from the point of view of the *shari'a*, not reprehensible ... Likewise, most of the musical performances are not reprehensible ... but two points must be taken into account: firstly, the make-up artists must be *mahram*[40] ... and secondly the spectator must not watch these films with lustful intentions.[41]

In another *fatva*, Khomeini declared it permissible to listen to music produced by instruments that can be used for licit as well as illicit music (*alat-e moshtarakeh*). The same *fatva* gave permission to play chess if it is only done for the fun of the game.[42]

Also of interest is Khomeini's intervention in the conflict over the tedious question as to whether the consumption of caviar is permissible. Because foreign currency earnings from the export of caviar were so high it was impossible to support the religious objection against this commodity. The solution lay in engaging experts to declare that sturgeon belongs to the category of fish that bears some form of scales somewhere on its body, which enabled Khomeini to issue a *fatva* declaring that it could be eaten.[43] Similarly, Khomeini's intervention was requested to check violations of the traffic regulations by chauffeurs working for the authorities. His *fatva* on this question states: 'Violation of the traffic regulations is not permitted under any circumstances.'[44]

The *fatvas* issued by Khomeini that can be counted a direct intervention in the process of legislation are too numerous to be listed here. We should note, however, that they were recognised as laws, and even after his death were enforced as such – a point affirmed by a member of the Parliamentary Committee for Legal Affairs, Hojjat al-Eslam Asadollah Bayat in November 1990. However, in order to give them the formal character of laws, the *fatvas* were worked over in parliament before being passed on to the courts.

Khomeini's direct influence on legislation was also felt through his books, in particular the *Tahrir al-Vasila*, which provided the two legislative bodies, as well as the courts, with a basis for taking decisions on many questions of law.[45] Thus the Guardian Council, in its legal ruling No. 6782 (20/11/82), declared that any law that contradicted Khomeini's *Tahrir al-Vasila* and his *Towzih al-Masa'el* would not be permissible.[46] In 1982, the Supreme Court ruled that until the pre-revolutionary laws had been replaced by Islamic laws, judges should base their decisions on *fatvas* that would be issued by such sources as the relevant bureau in Khomeini's house.[47]

## Khomeini's Supremacy over the Executive

Khomeini's supremacy over the executive can be clearly demonstrated in connection with the most important decisions undertaken by that branch of government. There were also occasions when his influence can be noted on the level of small details.

Khomeini decided both the general guidelines for foreign policy, which found expression in particular slogans, as well as specific steps which were taken in order to put these slogans into practice.[48] 'Neither West nor East!', 'Export the revolution and the Islamic Republic!', ' War, war until victory!', 'War against international superpower!' and 'Disavowal of unbelief!' were amongst Khomeini's guidelines, as was his declaration that the world powers were devils of varying degrees of evil. The denunciation of 'the great Satan', by which was meant the USA, was just as much his contriving as was the decision to negotiate with the same 'Satan' in order to purchase weapons.

The foreign policy pursued by Khomeini was rooted in his conception of an Islamic state and the role he envisaged for it on the level of world politics. Having proclaimed the universality of Islam, the newly created Islamic state was obliged to set as its goal the world-wide spread of the faith. Furthermore, as a power that wished to pursue international policies with this kind of a vision, Iran could not orient itself towards the West or towards Eastern Europe. To Khomeini the slogan 'Neither West nor East!' meant more than the principle of a foreign policy of independence; it was also an expression of his long-term ambition to establish rule over all the world powers. His call to the Muslims of the world to disavow unbelief (*bara'at az moshrekin*) can only be understood in this sense.

These visions often found their clearest expression in the speeches and announcements which Khomeini made to his supporters. The following are a few quotations from such sources:

> Muslims of the world must make hostility and cunning towards the great powers into a principle.[49]

> It is clear to the whole and to those who bear official responsibility that the survival and the consolidation of the Islamic Republic of Iran depends on a policy which rejects both the East and the West. Disavowal of such a policy amounts to betrayal of Islam and the Muslims, and will lead to the degradation of the dignity, the independence and the reputation of the land and the nation of Iran ... God grant that the brave people of Iran gather their revolutionary hate and anger and direct the flames of their wrath – which will annihilate all forms of oppression – against the criminal Soviet Union and the world-devouring USA, as well as against the henchmen of these two powers, so that, through the grace of God, the flag of the true Mohammadan Islam will be raised over the whole world, and those deprived of their rights, along with the barefoot and the virtuous, will become lords over the earth.[50]

> We have often proclaimed this truth in our domestic and foreign policy, namely that we have set as our goal the world-wide spread of the influence of Islam and the suppression of the rule of the world conquerors ... We wish to cause the corrupt roots of Zionism, capitalism and Communism to wither throughout the world. We wish, as does God almighty, to destroy the systems which are based on these three foundations, and to promote the Islamic order of the Prophet ... in the world of arrogance.[51]

> Establishing the Islamic state world-wide belongs to the great goals of the revolution.[52]

Khomeini's most important decisions in the field of foreign policy had to do with the war against Iraq and relations with Israel, as well as relations with the United States and the Soviet Union. Immediately after the revolution, he ordered the government to break off its diplomatic relations with Israel whose destruction, he declared, was one of the most urgent goals of the Islamic Republic. None the less, Khomeini was aware that Israel could be very useful to Iran in its war against Iraq. With or without the approval of the USA, Israel could deliver the weapons Iran so desperately needed at that time. He thus did his best to exploit this possibility, while making every effort to maintain secrecy. When in November 1986 information about these relations was made public through the scandal known as the Iran-Contra affair, eight MPs demanded an explanation. Khomeini, who was incensed at the disclosures, vented his anger against them and condemned their demand as an act that would only serve Iran's enemies. Thereupon, the eight MPs wrote a letter to the president of parliament in which they apologised for their behaviour, declaring:

> The question which we put to the minister of foreign affairs was based on the belief that discussion of these problems in parliament would be in the interest of the revolution and would meet with the approval of the Imam. Now that we have learned the wishes of the Imam and been instructed as to the interests of the nation, we are aware that there is no longer any reason for our question.

During the same session in which this letter was read out, the president of parliament added his own apology and declared that MPs almost unanimously disavowed this behaviour.[53]

Outwardly, Khomeini delegated the settling of the hostage affair to parliament and his own negotiator, the minister Behzad Nabavi. In reality, however, he personally retained a tight control over matters. It would seem that his reason for placing others in the foreground was the fact that the foreign policy benefits of this action were not likely to offer any grounds for pride.[54] The benefits, of which Hojjat al-Eslam Musavi Kho'iniha, the leader of the action, was later to speak with satisfaction, were more of a domestic political nature. But since the action was officially justified as being against the USA, it was not possible to claim credit for its positive effect on the level of domestic politics.[55]

As information that has subsequently emerged clearly shows, the continuation of the war against Iraq after Iraqi troops had been driven from Iranian territory in the summer of 1982 and victory over the invaders was assured, could only have been decided with Khomeini's approval. The decision was consistent with the great significance that this war had for achieving the goals of his world-wide mission: 'Our war is not aimed solely against Saddam, but against all unbelief.' Khomeini conceived of this war as 'a blessing', 'a form of worship', 'an essential element in the Islamic revolution' and 'its philosophy of human existence'.[56] He gave up only when it became clear that Iran could not win and economists had forecast that continuing the war would bring about a catastrophe in the country.[57] When he finally announced his readiness to end the war, in his own words 'to drink the cup of poison', which was what it meant to him to conform to Resolution 598 of the UN Security Council, parliament found itself confronted with a wholly unexpected situation. Indeed, parliament, 'inspired by the guidance of the Imam', had resolved, only two weeks earlier, to declare the continuation of the war until the victory of 'the strategy of the Islamic Republic'.[58] As if by way of apologising for this big surprise, the president of parliament, Rafsanjani, stated: 'It will take time before we come to understand in the future the decision which the Imam has taken and why he has suddenly launched this immense movement, which, viewed outwardly, appears to contradict the movement we have been engaged in up until now.' [59]

Although the constitution confers on the leader the power to declare war and make peace, it stipulates that he is to make such decisions on the advice of the Supreme Defence Council.[60] In practice, however, Khomeini's powers were not subject to any limits of this kind. Thus, when Khamene'i was asked in 1988 whether it would not have been better to have ended the war after the liberation of the border city Khorramshahr, he replied: 'Permission to end the war or the refusal to give such permission belong to the powers of leadership based on *velayat-e faqih*.' [61] Indeed Khomeini's authority to pursue the war was so undisputed that one of the leading functionaries from amongst the conservative legalists felt moved to say: 'The goal of the war was to obey the Imam.'[62]

In the realm of domestic policy, the guidelines laid down by Khomeini were primarily concerned with establishing a firm foundation for hierocracy, effectively concentrating power in his own hands and maintaining a balance of power between the rival camps amongst his followers.[63] Consequently, his intervention in domestic political questions was just as extensive as in the area of foreign policy. He concerned himself with questions ranging from the hiring of personnel to the decision to distribute gifts amongst his loyal supporters.[64]

Khomeini's decisions to appoint or dismiss leading functionaries went far beyond the powers conferred on him by Art. 110 of the constitution. His most important interventions of this kind included the dismissal of Bani-Sadr from the office of president, the rejection of Ayatollah Montazeri as his designated successor, and helping Mir Hosein Musavi to consolidate his position as prime minister in the face of his many opponents in parliament.

Although parliament, in accordance with the constitution, played a role in dismissing Bani-Sadr, the problem, as Musavi later stated before the Assembly for Revising the Constitution, 'was not solved by parliament but by the Imam'.[65] Khomeini took this decision once he realised that the president's immoderate self-confidence would prevent him from completely subordinating himself to the leader.[66] The actual charges made against Bani-Sadr in parliament and used to justify his dismissal were opposition to the Imam and a lack of belief in the principle of *velayat-e faqih*.[67]

Another factor behind Bani-Sadr's dismissal was that he opposed the will of the Islamic Republican Party in his choice of prime minister and the Council of Ministers. This question was resolved by Khomeini at the request of several people, including Bani-Sadr himself.[68] Although Khamene'i disagreed with the prime minister appointed at this stage, Mir Hosein Musavi, he had to put up with him, despite this being contrary to the stipulations of the constitution, because Musavi was under Khomeini's protection.[69] Khomeini was fully aware of the deficiencies of Musavi's populist, state-oriented Cabinet, but he continually supported it in face of the opposition of the powerful minority in parliament that favoured the private sector. In October 1985, he even informed the opponents of the Cabinet in writing that he considered the Cabinet's dismissal inappropriate 'at present'.[70]

When, however, on the occasion of the subsequent vote of confidence, 73 MPs voted against the prime minister and 26 abstained, a storm of indignation broke at this disregard of the will of the Imam. Khomeini himself likewise expressed his anger at the situation.[71] The recalcitrant MPs apologised, stating that they had understood the Imam's intervention on behalf of the Cabinet as an advisory ordinance (*hokm-e ershadi*) and not as a mandatory ordinance (*hokm-e mowla'i*).[72] In March 1987, Khomeini declared that support of the government was a commandment of the *shari'a*, and once again scolded its opponents.[73] When in September 1988 the prime minister gave in to his critics and announced that he would step down, Khomeini wrote him a letter full of recriminations and ordered him to withdraw his resignation. Musavi obeyed saying that Khomeini knew best what was in the interest of the government.[74] Khomeini did not simply demand several times that MPs support Musavi's government, but forbade them to make almost any criticism of it whatsoever.[75] The opponents of the government, despite their reluctance, declared: 'On the order of the Imam, we will be silent.' [76]

Khomeini also intervened in the appointment of ministers whenever he felt such action was necessary.[77] This was the case with Akbar Velayati, the minister of foreign affairs, who obtained his post at the wish of the Imam. By the same token, MPs who refused to declare their confidence in the prime minister in 1985 repeatedly experienced difficulties during later parliamentary sessions when parliament subjected their mandates to examination.[78]

The dismissal of Montazeri from his position as designated successor of the leader came in March 1989 after a two-year period of tense argument between himself and Khomeini. In a letter Khomeini wrote to parliament concerning this matter, two facts clearly emerge: firstly, that parliament had not been informed of the process that led to Montazeri's dismissal, and secondly that Khomeini had dismissed Montazeri (that is told him to resign)– although the official position was that Montazeri had resigned on his own initiative. In this letter, dated 15/4/89, Khomeini writes:

> I have heard that you have not been informed concerning the revered Montazeri and do not know how matters have turned out … My religious duty has obliged me to make the necessary decision in order to safeguard Islam and the government. Therefore, it is with a bleeding heart that I have dismissed the fruit of my heart [the phrase he used to describe his student Montazeri] in the interest of the government and Islam. In the future my brothers and sisters will learn more concerning my decision, if God is willing.[79]

In this case as well, Khomeini unambiguously acted in violation of the procedures laid down in the constitution which stipulates that dismissal of the leader is a matter for the Assembly of Leadership Experts (Art. 107), i.e. the same assembly that had designated Montazeri as Khomeini's successor during its sessions of 16–19 November 1985.[80] Although Montazeri's dismissal took place shortly before Khomeini's death, there was time enough for Khomeini to determine who would be his successor. By writing a letter to the president of the Assembly for Revising the Constitution, which was in session at the time, Khomeini made the necessary arrangements to designate Khamene'i, a low-ranking member of the clergy. Specifically, this involved eliminating Art. 109 from the constitution which required that the leader be 'a source of imitation' (*marja'-e taqlid*). Likewise Khomeini personally assured Rafsanjani and Emami Kashani of Khamene'i's suitability for holding this office.[81]

## The Representatives of the Imam

Although the constitution confers only supervisory powers over the government on the leader, in practice the whole of the state apparatus was geared to carry out his orders. Hojjat al-Eslam Hadi Khamene'i, when he was a member of the Assembly for Revising the Constitution, remarked that although Khomeini's office consisted of only one room,[82] his hands reached into the most distant corners of state administration. His representatives amongst the government authorities were in fact his special assistants. Officially, the representatives of the Imam only exercised a supervisory function, but in practice, as Bazargan writes, they decided on everything in the government agency where they were posted.[83] The fact that there is no mention of these representatives in the constitution caused, at least in the Guardian Council, many headaches, and the council insisted that they be legally recognised in the revision of the constitution. It was clearly inappropriate that so influential an apparatus of power not be based on legality.[84]

The intervention of the representatives of the Imam in the work of the government authorities, and the disturbance and resentment which this caused, was from another point of view a reason for not making their office a legal institution. If they acquired a legal status, according to Prime Minister Musavi, this would paralyse the government. To justify his point Musavi described how the heads of different government organisations feared the representatives of the Imam and how this fear impeded their work. If their position were to be legalised, the representatives of the Imam would be subject to no limits whatsoever and would interfere in everything. 'This would mean the breakdown of the executive apparatus of the government.'[85]

Rafsanjani and other members of the assembly expressed similar objections to giving institutional status to the representatives of the Imam.[86] One form of argument against the proposal ran: the leader already exercises power over the whole state apparatus and so there is no need of creating a government office for his representatives. Likewise, the ministers are for all practical purposes his representatives.[87] It is clear from the whole debate over this proposal that the representatives of the executive had no objections to the plenipotentiary powers of the Imam, but they preferred to be his representatives themselves and felt the state apparatus should not be disturbed by new institutions.

The proposal to institutionalise, and thereby to legalise, the Imam's representatives did not obtain a majority in the Assembly for Revising the Constitution. It was not difficult to reject the proposal because it was made at a time when Khomeini's death was expected, which gave rise to the hope that the Imam's representatives could be eliminated. In the end their role was not formalised, but the representatives remained. They now represent Khomeini's successor.

In addition to the influence of his representatives, Khomeini intervened directly in government matters through the so-called 'revolutionary institutions' such as the Foundation for the Disinherited and the War-Disabled, the Foundation of Martyrs, the Committee of the Imam, and so on.

Up to this point we have attempted to present the actual powers Khomeini exercised in specific cases. All these different powers, however, may be summed up in one sentence: over and above his functions as a religious authority, Khomeini held in his hands the reins of all branches of government. In his person were united the legislature, the executive, the judiciary and all other powers necessary to run a government. As leader and *marja'-e taqlid*, he could intervene in all matters of government whenever he wished or was asked to do so. In accordance with his wide-ranging powers, he kept himself informed on all questions to do with domestic and foreign policy. With this purpose in mind, he read relevant reports, listened to foreign and domestic broadcasts, followed several TV programmes and granted audiences to functionaries and delegates of the people in order to listen to their requests.

## The Veneration of *velayat-e faqih*

With the concentration of all power in the hands of Khomeini, the sovereignty of the people was for all practical purposes abolished. If this did not correspond to the actual wording of the constitution, it was none the less consistent with the spirit of that document and with the concept of *velayat-e faqih* as set out in Khomeini's book on the subject. That this was due to the circumstances under which the text was formulated was often referred to at a later date. For instance, Ayatollah Ebrahim Amini in the Assembly for Revising the Constitution explained it as a result of 'the then prevailing atmosphere' and 'the special subjective attitude that then existed towards the *marja'iyat* [the office of 'source of imitation'] and the leadership.' In reality, he went on to add, the leader, like the Prophet and his successor 'Ali, did not exercise a supervisory function, but was nevertheless the ruler. Amini then stated his delight at the fact that the leader, due to his special personality, had carried out 'his work' with the same plenipotentiary powers that the Prophet had enjoyed.[88] Ayatollah Ahmad Azari Qomi, another member of the assembly, announced a few days after Khomeini's death: 'We are aware of the Imam's view that *velayat-e faqih*, because of the circumstances of the time, was not mentioned in its proper form in the constitution and that appropriate notice was not taken of the absolute power [of the *faqih*].'[89] Ayatollah Mohammad Mo'men referred to the urgency of the times as the reason why this had happened. It had been imperative to draw up the constitution and to pass it quickly.[90] Hojjat al-Eslam Bayat felt that the fault with the constitution was that it viewed *velayat-e faqih* as something parallel to the government or wholly outside it. 'But the truth is that it is the foundation of our ideology, our system and the ruling system of the Islamic Republic.' When defining the task which was to be carried out in this connection by the Assembly for Revising the Constitution, he went as far as to say: 'We are not conferring power on the ruling jurist. He has that power. When we exercise any function in the Islamic Republic, when parliament passes resolutions or the executive apparatus performs its work and the justice system applies Islamic legal ordinances, the basis for the legitimacy of all these activities lies in the concept of *velayat-e faqih*.' [91]

Bayat made this statement while he was vice-president of parliament and it reflected the view of the other MPs. When MPs displayed their devotion to the Imam, they strove to surpass one another in formulating their support for his absolute powers as the following examples show:

The source of legitimacy for our intervention[in the process of legislation] is the will of the Imam. We have obtained the right to power, ideologically speaking, from the leader.(Rafsanjani)[92]

If it were not for the confirmation on the part of the Imam ... parliament, as well as the government and the justice system, would lose their legitimacy. They would automatically cease to exist.(Mohammad Rabbani Amlashi)[93]

It is firmly established for every Shi'a that it is the duty of every single Muslim to obey the Imam, to stand at his side, to submit to him and at every crossroad to follow the Imam's decision.(Hosein Soltani)[94]

The principle of leadership is the most important principle in Islam. The acceptance of all worship by God depends on submission to the leader (*bey'at*). Submission means subordinating to the leader your own person, your wealth, your life, your opinions and your will. Whoever sets out on a different road than this, as if to display his own capacities, not only has no capacities but is travelling the road of destruction. That person has called down upon himself the curse of God. (Mohammad 'Alavi-Tabar)[95]

Submission alone has no effect. After submission, obedience must follow. (Hashem Hejazifar)[96]

The legitimacy of our government is based on the existence of *velayat-e faqih*. And our constitution also acquires its legitimacy because the great leader of the revolution has signed it.(Mohammad Reza Bahonar)[97]

Similar statements, taken from speeches in which MPs make their lack of power into a principle, could be quoted for many pages. Nor were MPs alone in voicing this kind of acclamation. Other influential functionaries –

ministers, imams of congregational mosques, experts on constitutional law and government ideologues – expressed such views with exactly the same enthusiasm. For example, Khamene'i attributed the status of religious legal ordinances to orders issued by the Imam.[98] And the former minister of labour, Tavakkoli, described the three branches of government as 'instruments for the exercise of *velayat* [-*e faqih*].'[99] In the eyes of Jalaleddin Madani, the separation of government powers was foreign to Islam: 'If the constitution accepts this kind of new verbal expression, this does not mean that it accepts the reality of such ideas.'[100]

The plenipotentiary powers of Khomeini were finally so thoroughly established as a principle that belief in them became the standard for loyal profession of the true Islam. Whoever did not accept his exercise of such powers was either no longer a Muslim or was an adherent of so-called 'American Islam'. Consequently, opposing camps among the ruling Islamicists regularly reproached one another for not believing in this principle. This tendency went so far that the idea was publicly aired as to whether it was actually necessary to retain the concept of republic in the name of the Islamic state. Prime Minister Musavi stated in the Assembly for Revising the Constitution that there was no cause for fear if anyone wished to express openly the view that the state should no longer be called a republic.[101] At this point, only a few elements in the populist state-oriented camp amongst the legalists professed support for the republican component of the constitution. During the elections for the 4th Majles in 1992, the main issue revolved around these republican sympathies. The conservative and moderate legalists entered into an alliance and did everything in their power to hinder the state-oriented populists from winning seats in parliament.

Although the concentration of power in the hands of Khomeini is consistent with the application of the theory of *velayat-e faqih*, the reason for it is not to be found solely in the desire to make the theory into a reality. The whole system of hierocracy was under pressure to move in this direction because there was no other way to resolve the internal contradictions that led to legislative bottlenecks. There had to be resort to an overriding authority recognised by all sides. As these kinds of conflicts and contradictions multiplied, ever more frequent recourse was made to the leader for a solution. Increasingly requested to decide on issues, Khomeini was more and more given the necessary powers to resolve conflicts. We have referred to this development earlier and will go into the question more fully in Part III.

## Khamene'i's Power as Leader

The concentration of power in Khomeini's hands depended to a great extent on his charismatic qualities. Proof that personal qualities were necessary to exercise such a degree of power is provided by Khomeini's successor who, while attempting to follow in his footsteps, has not achieved comparable success.

The first demonstration of Khamene'i's lack of influence took place in the Assembly for Revising the Constitution. Despite the fact that Khomeini had exercised absolute power, the assembly refused to conform to the spirit of the constitution and to confer greater power on the office of leader by revising Art. 110. This occurred even though, during the debate on the deficiencies of the constitution, this point had been stressed and relevant proposals had been made before a plenary session of the assembly.[102] But these proposals had been put forward in the plenary session a few days after Khomeini's death when it was already established who in an emergency would be appointed as his successor.

Influential functionaries of the government spoke out in the assembly against these proposals. Ayatollah Mehdi Karrubi was of the opinion that the explicit mention of greater powers for Khomeini's successor would be harmful, for obviously the gap between Khomeini and anyone who followed him would be great.[103] Ayatollah Ahmad Jannati felt that mention in the constitution of the absolute power that belonged to the *faqih* would be against the interests of Islam and the Muslims. 'For indeed the revered Imam was endowed with merits which I cannot imagine any other person will soon attain.' He added that the destiny of a community and a nation must not be placed in the hands of a single person, especially in such harsh times so full of contradictions and conflicts. Indeed, he actually went so far as to request that the power of the *faqih* be restricted on the grounds that otherwise the result would be anarchy, lawlessness and mistrust.[104] Rafsanjani also spoke out against giving the leader complete power to determine policies, for in such a case: 'The government and parliament would not be able to do anything.'[105] The prime minister felt that organising something of this nature would pose numerous problems.[106] With somewhat greater subtlety, Ayatollah Yazdi advised the future leader that he ought only to intervene in government affairs within the framework of the laws, the three branches of the government and the constitution. Then there would be no further opposition to his absolute power.[107] On one occasion, outside the assembly, Ayatollah Jannati even stated that the articles of the constitution dealing with the office of leader could not be adhered to in the long run.[108]

The opposition which emerged to revising the constitution to comply with the spirit of the document, at a time when Khomeini was no longer alive and his successor was perceived to be at most one among equals, proved sufficient to stop the undertaking. The advocates of the revision succeeded only in reformulating part of Art. 57 so that the text referred to 'absolute general trusteeship' when describing the official supervisory role of the leader vis-à-vis the three branches of government. On the other hand, the condition was more or less placed upon the leader that he must decide on the general policies of the country 'in consultation with' the Assessment Council. Likewise, he was obliged to try to resolve 'the problems of government by the mediation' of that body, if such problems could not be resolved through the usual channels (the revised formulation of Art. 110).

Of course it is true that, according to the revised constitution, the members of this council were to be appointed by the leader, but this had been added as a mere formality because the assembly assumed that Khomeini had already decided who would be in this council. This consideration emerges clearly in the debate on the question in the Assembly for Revising the Constitution.

After his election, Khamene'i made every effort to emulate his predecessor's role as an authority positioned above all branches of the government which could balance the rival camps amongst the legalists. However, the more he failed in this attempt, the more pressure he came under to seek support from forces which shared his attitudes, had been successful in the struggle for a share in power and, because of their position in the religious academies, were able to guarantee support for him in those circles. Since these forces belonged to the camp of the conservative legalists, Khamene'i was more and more forced to give up the role of mediator and become a partisan of the conservative legalists.

In exchange for adopting this position, he obtained a corresponding degree of protection from this camp. Already in the Assembly for Revising the Constitution, Azari Qomi, for instance, took sides with him during the debates over the powers to be accorded to the leader. He spoke out against adopting the above mentioned proposals but with the argument that enumerating the leader's powers in the constitution would give the impression that they wished to set limits on them. 'In an Islamic state the concept of the ruler, the leader, and the Imam, means basically that no restrictions can be set upon him.'[109] In his daily, *Resalat*, Azari Qomi, along with numerous other conservative clerics, continued his campaign to support Khamene'i. The fact that Khamene'i was not 'a source of imitation' must not be taken to mean – so he argued in one of his many articles on this subject – that Khamene'i's powers should be limited. It was even the absolute duty of 'the source of imitation' to obey him.[110] Even Khomeini's decrees only had validity if they were confirmed by Khamene'i.[111]

The de facto refusal by various authorities to attribute the same plenipotentiary powers to Khamene'i as his predecessor had enjoyed would, of course, be in opposition to *velayat-e faqih* if such a refusal were stated openly. But no one was prepared to adopt that form of opposition. Consequently, even the radical legalists did not express a clear opinion on this question. The result is that the conservatives reproach them all the more vigorously as being opponents of *velayat-e faqih*.

One of Khamene'i's chief handicaps has been his relatively low rank in the system of religious authority. This weakness affects the credibility of his claims to power even amongst the supporters of the regime. Amongst the clergy his position is especially disputed, in particular when he attempts to impose his authority on the power-conscious ayatollahs and grand ayatollahs. In practice, the latter make all such attempts difficult for him, especially in those cases where certain ayatollahs feel they themselves have a rightful claim to be the leader.[112]

During the period that he has held the office of leader of the Islamic Republic, Khamene'i has attempted many times to obtain the position of *marja'-e taqlid*, to issue *fatvas*, to intervene in legislation, to dominate the executive and to exercise judicial functions. On 20/2/92, it was announced that he declared it permissible to use the organs of brain-dead persons for transplantation.[113] On 27/10/92, *Salam* reported that the Supreme Court had asked him for a *fatva* concerning a criminal offence. However, the court had simultaneously made the same request of the Grand Ayatollah Golpaygani. On 17/7/93, *Resalat* reported that Khamene'i had approved the bill to provide legal protection to the Basijis (militia) who were employed to fight against immorality. On 17/1/94, he published a *fatva* in which, at the request of the customs officials at the Iranian–Armenian border, he pronounced on what should be the relations of these officials with their non-Muslim Armenian counterparts.[114] In a *fatva* published on 24/2/92, he declared to the chairman of the National Bureau of Social Welfare (Sazman-e Behzisti-ye Keshvar) that the faithful should place their alms-tax at the disposal of this bureau to help families without a father.[115] On 28/5/94 he declared that the use of a dish-antenna to receive foreign TV broadcasts was permissible as long as it 'caused no harm' although a few days earlier the dishes had been declared forbidden by the Grand Ayatollah Araki.[116] This contradiction was in accordance with Khamene'i's intensified efforts to obtain recognition as 'a source of imitation'. It appears that the last obstacle to his ambition was the white-haired Grand Ayatollah Araki whose imminent demise Khamene'i was apparently expecting.[117] The lectures which Khamene'i gave in his Tehran home for select students on subjects usually reserved for advanced seminars could also be interpreted as a preparation for obtaining the position.[118]

Khamene'i has also made efforts to intervene in decisions which would strengthen and consolidate his position as an individual, as well as a representative of the camp that supports him. This is made clear by his attempt to control the armed forces,[119] his insistence on determining foreign policy[120] and his prominent role in establishing the principles of policies for economic development and planning.[121] When, on 14/2/94, he dissolved the Board of Directors of the radio and television he was violating Art. 175 of the constitution – his first attempt to place himself above the constitution.[122] There have been other cases where Khamene'i has intervened in the various spheres of government but these have not been frequent enough to conclude that he has behaved like his predecessor.

Yet these observations should not lead to the conclusion that Khomeini's successor wields no power at all. What can be said is that, by contrast with Khomeini, the power he has at his disposal falls far short of the power he would wield were he to be regarded as the embodiment of the spirit of the constitution or in a position to exercise the absolute power of the ruling jurist. After the death of Khomeini, representation of the spirit of the constitution was not transferred to his official successor but to the totality of influential members of the clergy who held various top positions in the government or who controlled life in the religious academies in Qom and elsewhere. On the other hand, it is clear that Khomeini's death did not have the effect of restoring sovereignty to the people. The absolute power of the ruling jurists prevails throughout the whole country now as before, even if that power is not wielded solely by the leader.

## The Limits of Obedience to Khomeini

Even in Khomeini's case, the supremacy of the leader over the state was not sufficient to obtain absolute obedience from his followers or to ensure that his orders were always carried out in full. Apart from the fact that many of his orders were intended to appease the people and could not be carried out in practice,[123] in several cases his commands went against the interests of functionaries who had a share in government power. These officials applied great cunning in their attempts to avoid putting orders into practice, or even worked against them. Moreover, although Khomeini's policies were aimed at maintaining a balance between rival camps in order to retain power in his own hands, there were times when he was obliged to make substantial concessions in the interest of one camp or another. Meanwhile, these mutually hostile camps constantly endeavoured to make use of any possibility of interpreting Khomeini's decisions to their own advantage, to manipulate them for their own ends, or to hinder their having a real effect.

It was not easy to oppose Khomeini's decisions openly or to work against their enforcement, but it was always possible to achieve partial success through subterfuge or the use of cunning legal ruses. The best example of this was the refusal of 99 MPs to give their approval to the Cabinet of Musavi, although Khomeini had publicly demanded that they do so. The ideological justification for this disregard of the principle of absolute obedience was, as we saw earlier, the division of Khomeini's decrees into decrees with mandatory force and decrees with advisory force. The faithful were free to obey or to refrain from obeying advisory decrees. Ayatollah Azari Qomi, who undertook to differentiate between these two categories, enumerated a series of other merely advisory decrees that Khomeini had issued. Moreover, he referred to several cases where the government authorities had not carried out Khomeini's orders. According to Qomi, such cases included the creation of a Ministry for Enjoining the Good and Forbidding the Evil, free water and electricity, the construction of houses for everyone, the annihilation of Israel, the appointment of a chief authority over the radio and television by the presidents of the three branches of the government, turning over agriculture, industry and trade to the private sector and interrupting the broadcast of speeches in parliament if they contradicted the constitution. Furthermore, he noted that the Imam had given orders in secret to many MPs which they had not carried out.[124]

The occasional refusal to obey Khomeini's orders in no way meant that the sovereignty of the people had been reinstated. Those who refused to carry out an order often came from the ranks of government functionaries, who did not in any sense represent the people, and they did not necessarily justify their refusal as serving the interest of the people. As members of the ruling class or participants in the hierocracy, they had sufficient grounds of their own for their attitude. That is to say, their primary concern was to ensure that their interests were fully considered in decisions that determined the distribution of power and privileges. If such decisions did not meet with their approval they might refuse to accept the situation in whatever manner was open to them. While they viewed the absolute power of Khomeini as identical with their own, they were only willing to submit to his power when it was clearly to their own advantage. Their occasional refusal did not constitute a break in the process of concentrating power in the hands of a few. It merely illustrates the fact that the concentration of power was not viewed as exclusively on behalf of one person but rather as the interest of the whole state class and, more particularly, the government leadership.

## Notes

1 On the formation and the development of the Revolutionary Council see Bazargan: 1983.

2 Ibid., p. 53.

3 Ibid., p. 53.

4 Ibid., pp. 27 and 45.

5 See Schirazi: 1993.

6 Hojjat al-Eslam Sadeq Khalkhali, the most famous of these judges, repeatedly referred to the fact that Khomeini had given him in writing full authority to impose the death sentence on opponents of the regime. During a session of parliament on 30/3/90, he read out this letter to his colleagues. See MM, p. 19 and *Kayhan*, 22/5/79. Up to the time of the resignation of Bazargan's government in November 1979, the revolutionary courts sanctioned the execution of 550 people. See Bakhash: 1986, p. 59 ff.

7 See Bazargan's last radio and television speech published by Nehzat-e Azadi: 1988, p. 277 ff.

8 According to 'Abbas 'Abdi, who was one of the student operatives involved, Khomeini had not previously been informed of this action. See *Salam*, 3/11/91. However, Asgharzadeh, another participant who was later to become an MM, stated in an interview with *Bayan* (5/6/90, p. 14) that Khomeini had been 'briefly' (*ejmalan*) informed by Hojjat al-Eslam Mohammad Kho'iniha.

9 Asgharzadeh, op. cit.

10 *Kayhan*, 6/11/79.

11 *Kayhan*, 29/10/79.

12 The decision for this was taken by the Revolutionary Council, after it received Khomeini's permission. *Kayhan*, 20/4/80.

13 Bani-Sadr (1982, p. 127 ff.) holds the IRP responsible for this. See also Bazargan: 1984, p. 106 ff.

14 *Kayhan*, 2/2/80.

15 For example, when it was announced: 'At the order of the Imam, the provincial and communal councils will be formed.' *Ayandegan*, 21/4/79.

16 Majles-e Showra-ye Eslami: 1982, p. 66.

17 See Chapters 9 to 12.

18  See Khomeini's letter to President Khamene'i, published in *Kayhan*, 7/1/88. More on the subject is found in Chapters 11 and 12.

19  This council consisted of six clerics from the Guardian Council, the president, the prime minister, the president of the Council of Justice, the public prosecutor and one alternating minister. Khomeini's son represented his father.

20  MR II/846, 856. According to statements made by Ayatollahs Musavi Ardebili and Mo'men in the Assembly for the Revision of the Constitution, Khomeini revoked this power in a letter addressed to the Assessment Council on 29/12/89. p. 846.

21  See Bazargan: 1984, p. 107 f.

22  In a letter dated 1/1/87 Khamene'i had asked Khomeini to decree that 'the resolutions of this council be accorded the force of laws'. Khomeini's answer was: 'The guidelines and rules laid down by the honourable Council of the Cultural Revolution must be adhered to.' See LB: 1986/87, p. 509.

23  See Hojjat al-Eslam Bayat in MR I/225; *Kayhan*, 4/18 and 21/8/88.

24  *Kayhan*, 22/7/87.

25  On this point see Madani: 1986–90, vol. VI, p. 379 ff. For more on this subject see Chapter 11.

26  MR I/246.

27  This was the term applied to judges who had not attained the rank of *mojtahed*. In contradiction to Art. 162 of the constitution, Khomeini allowed them to hold posts because there were not enough properly qualified judges available.

28  *Ettela'at*, 30/5/90.

29  MR I/241. The corresponding changes in the constitution were only written into the document during the 1989 revision.

30  *Kayhan*, 11/12/82.

31  See the statements of the chief state prosecutor and the state prosecutor of this court published in *Resalat* on 12/9 and 16/10/90. For further information see *Kayhan*, 7/7/87 and 3/10/91. Setting up this court contradicts the constitution in so far as it is a violation of the principle of equality established in the constitution.

32  See Chapter 9; for further details Schirazi: 1993.

33  For further information see Chapter 11.

34  MR I/243. See also Khomeini's speech to the Council of Ministers published in *Jomhuri-ye Eslami*, 27/8/84, and Kooroshy: 1990, p. 182 ff.

35  See *Howzeh*: 1990, No. 37/38, p. 12.

36  See Ayatollah Mohammad Yazdi's series of articles on interpreting the Constitution in *Resalat*: Part 152, 5/10/86, as well as Bayat: 1986, p. 299. According to Ayatollah Azari Qomi, taxation is only a secondary ordinance. See his series of articles on the subject of *hokm-e hokumati* (state ordinance) in *Resalat*: Part 31, 28/10/87, and *Resalat*, 13/8/91.

37  See the relevant *fatva* in *Pasdar-e Eslam*, Nr. 2 (1981), p. 38. Also see Chapter 13.

38  *Resalat*, 26/10/87.

39  *Kayhan*, 30/11/82.

40  Meaning that they must belong to the immediate family of the woman in question.

41  *Resalat*, 22/12/87. The *fatva* in question was issued on 19/4/87.

42  See Khomeini's refutation of the objections Hojjat al-Eslam Mohammad Hasan Qadiri raised against this *fatva* in *Howzeh*, No. 28 (1988), p. 2 f. See also Chapter 12.

43  See *Pasdar-e Eslam*, No. 26 (1983), p. 66 ff. In the next two issues of the magazine, Ayatollah Karimi presented a discussion of the problems involved from the point of view of religious law.

44  *Pasdar-e Eslam*, No. 52 (1986), p. 6.

45  *Kayhan*, 14/11/90.

46  See Madani: 1986–90, vol. IV, p. 299. *Towzih al-Masa'el* is in fact a shortened version of *Tahrir al-Vasila*.

47  *Kayhan*, 24/8/82.

48  Sa'id Raja'i Khorasani, who had formerly been Iran's representative at the UN, commented on this state of affairs: 'Our departed Imam exercised supervision over all aspects of the country's foreign policy with energy and attentiveness ... from the outer appearance of the embassy buildings to the manner with which the embassy staff members behaved'.(MM 12/11/90). Khamene'i has said that Khomeini's permission had to be obtained even to invite important foreign personalities to visit Iran, See Yazdi: 1987, p. 22.

49  *Bayan*, No. 17/18 (1991), p. 7.

50  Op. cit.

51  *Bayan*, No. 4 (1990), p. 8.

52  *Resalat*, 25/3/88.

53  MM 23/11/86. On this subject see Bani-Sadr: 1992, vol. III.

54  According to Raja'i Khorasani, during the negotiations in Algiers which resolved the problem, Behzad Nabavi 'caused' a loss to Iran of 4 to 12 billion dollars (*Kayhan*, 12/9/88). Although these figures do not appear to be precise, they give an idea of how the officials of the Islamic regime themselves judged the results of this action. Obviously, all that Khomeini had been able to gain was an offer to deliver weapons to Iran if the hostages were released before the US presidential elections.

55  On this subject see Bani-Sadr: 1991, and Bakhash: 1986, as well as MM 14–17/9/80, 1/11/80 and 14/1/81.

56  *Payam-e Enqelab*, No. 93 (1983), p. 12 ff.

57  Rafsanjani, *Resalat*, 10/8/91.

58  MM 6/7/88.

59  MM 21/8/88, p. 21.

60  When the Constitution was revised, this clause was dropped from the text. However, in practice this only happened after the death of Khomeini.

61  *Resalat*, 7/12/88.

62  *Resalat*, 14/1/89.

63  Ayatollah Musavi Ardebili said on this point: 'If those in charge do not agree on a particular question, they bring the matter before the Imam and resolve the problem on the basis of his guidance'(*Kayhan*, 20/9/88). According to Rafsanjani, whenever the balance of power between Parliament, the Guardian Council and the government was disturbed, Khomeini would intervene on behalf of the disadvantaged party and thus restore the balance (*Kayhan*, 23/5/84).

64  An example of this was when Khomeini presented the stocking factory 'Star Light' to Hojjat al-Eslam Hadi Ghaffari because, amongst other things, he had by organised armed raids against the opposition. On this subject see the revelations which appeared in *Resalat*, 23 and 24/4/82, and 24/5/90.

65  MR I/267. On 21/6/81, parliament formally declared that Bani-Sadr was no longer worthy of holding office.

66  Bani-Sadr rejected Khomeini's repeated invitations to do so. See *Betrayal of Hope*, p. 19 ff.

67  MM 20/6/81, p. 30 f.

68  On 6/5/80, Bani-Sadr in a letter suggested to Khomeini that the prime minister should be appointed with Khomeini's permission. Khomeini followed this suggestion in his answer (*Kayhan*, 10/5/80).

69  In 1985, Khamene'i proposed him as prime minister before parliament with one brief matter-of-fact sentence, which was contrary to customary practice. (MM 10/7/85, p. 26). See also *Enqelab-e Eslami*, Nos. 109 and 110 (1985).

70  *Enqelab-e Eslami*, No. 109 (1985).

71  *Kayhan*, 17/10/85 and *Salam*, 3/3/92.

84 THE SUPPRESSION OF DEMOCRATIC ELEMENTS

72 The first form of decree is more of a recommendation, whereas the second has the authority of a command. On the difference between the two see Azari Qomi in *Resalat*, 14/5/91.

73 *Kayhan*, 15/3/87.

74 *Resalat*, 8/9/88.

75 In 1987, Khomeini declared that any opposition to the government or the prime minister, as well as to the army and the Revolutionary Guard, was the work of the devil (*Kayhan*, 5/3/87).

76 These were the words of Habibollah 'Askarowladi, published in *Resalat*, 28/8/86. In 1992, Morteza Nabavi, the chief editor of *Resalat*, stated that his newspaper had not criticised Musavi's government because: 'It was more important to obey the Imam than to exercise the right to criticise'(*Salam*, 10/5/92). However, this statement was not always true of all the followers of the Imam.

77 The prime minister made this clear in the Assembly for Revising the Constitution (MR I/260 f.).

78 This was the case, for example, of Maryam Behruzi (*Resalat*, 23/4/90) and Ahmad Zeidabad (*Resalat*, 4/7/88). The election of members was only valid if parliament did not raise any objection against it. On this point see Chapter 5.

79 For more on this subject see Schirazi: 1991, *passim*.

80 On this subject see Mohammad Mohammadi Reishahri's political memoirs (1990) which describe the whole process from the point of view of an employee in the security service. See also Schirazi: 1991.

81 The latter have both confirmed this (*Kayhan*, 10 and 18/6/89).

82 MR I/286.

83 Bazargan: 1984, p. 122.

84 This was how Ayatollah Mo'men, a member of the Guardian Council, argued in the Assembly for Revising the Constitution in defence of his suggestion that the representatives of the Imam be adopted in the Constitution (MR II/698 ff.).

85 MR II/692.

86 MR II/654, 680, 687.

87 This remark was made by the Prime Minister Musavi (MR II/692).

88 MR I/296 f.

89 Op. cit., II/673.

90 Op. cit., p. 651.

91 Op. cit., p. 661 f.

92 MM 10/6/86, p. 20.

93 MM 17/10/85, p. 18.

94 MM 22/10/85, p. 18.

95 Op. cit., p. 19.

96 MM 17/12/89, p. 18.

97 MM 1/11/88, p. 20.

98 *Kayhan*, 28/10/82.

99 *Resalat*, 6/1/88.

100 Madani: 1986–90, vol. II, p.136.

101 MR I/270.

102 The spokesman for the committee in question in the assembly related that his committee was making an effort to extend the powers of the leader enumerated in Art. 110 of the constitution (MR II/642 ff.). The rejection of the proposal to adopt the office of the representatives of the Imam in the constitution or give the leader the power to dissolve parliament were further demonstrations of this attitude on the part of the assembly.

103 MR II/653.

104  MR II/676 f.

105  MR II/679.

106  MR II/691 f.

107  MR II/694.

108  *Kayhan*, 13/5/89. Azari Qomi reported on several occasions that there were people who felt that the office of Leader was superfluous. The Guardian Council was sufficient to carry out all the functions of that office (*Resalat*, 6 and 10/5/89).

109  MR II/673 f., and *Ettela'at*, 30/6/89.

110  *Resalat*, 3/7/89.

111  *Resalat*, 21/5/91.

112  In particular, the Grand Ayatollah Golpaygani must have felt he had a rightful claim to be the leader.

113  *Salam*, 20/2/92

114  He stated that it was permissible for both groups to shake hands and to invite one another to dinner, as long as the ritual purity of dishes containing meat was clearly established (*Salam* 17/1/94).

115  *Salam*, 24/2/92

116  Based on a fax published by the Bureau of Public Relations for Radio and Television on 28/5/94. Typically, all the *fatvas* of Khamene'i published in newspapers are in response to questions put to him by different government offices.

117  After the death of Golpaygani, the ruling clergy automatically addressed the question of whom they should acknowledge as 'a source of imitation'. Since other grand ayatollahs could not be considered for the position because of their political stance, it was decided to appoint the only suitable candidate who was available, i.e. Araki (*Resalat*, 15/12/93). It appeared to many that the time was not yet right to choose Khamene'i. More than anyone else, Ayatollah Yazdi stood up for Khamene'i by attesting to the latter's qualifications for the office of *marja'-e taqlid* (*Resalat*, 12/12/93). One of the reasons why recognition of Khamene'i as a *marja'* met with opposition even among supporters of the regime could be their fear that once he held this rank, they would lose influence over him. After Araki's death in November 1994 the 'state' clerics did in fact recognise Khamene'i as a *marja'* but only as one among a number of officially recognised *marja's* (*Salam*, 3/12/94). On 14 December Khamene'i announced that he regarded his own *marja'iyat* valid for the Shi'i community outside Iran and not within the country (*Salam*, 15/12/94).

118  In the terminology of the religious academies, these are called *dars-e kharej*, i.e. extra-curricular instruction which is only given by recognised scholars. As if on command, a demand was put forward by 'students and professors' of the religious academy of Qom that the instruction given by the leader be broadcast on radio and television, so that they might also benefit from it (*Resalat*, 12/4/94).

119  In particular, by filling the positions of command with persons devoted to himself.

120  In a recent press conference, Nateq Nuri, the president of parliament, said that the leader 'has closed the door on negotiations with the United States'. No one was to undertake any initiatives without Khamene'i's permission (*Resalat*, 25/5/94).

121  In this regard, Khamene'i emphasised that the second forthcoming five-year plan should not contradict 'the promulgations of *feqh* (*Salam*, 21/12/93).

122  Art. 175 provides for a board of directors made up of two representatives from each of the three branches of government.

123  For example, the order of 1/3/79 that stipulated that every family should be given a house (*Kayhan*, 3/3/79).

124  *Resalat*, 14/5/91. Hojjat al-Eslam Rasul Montakhab-Niya once stated before students that during the second parliament several members had, in more than 10 cases, directly or indirectly opposed the views of the Imam (*Kayhan*, 8/11/87).

# FIVE

# The Impotence of the People

The sovereignty of the people was eliminated from the constitution not only as a result of the concentration of power in the hands of the leader but also because the institutions set up by the constitution to represent the people (parliament, the presidency and the Assembly of Leadership Experts) either lost their representative character as a result of rigged elections or ceded their powers to other state organs not chosen by the people. Another contributing factor was the government's refusal to create the system of elected local councils provided for in the constitution.

## The Erosion of Parliament's Representative Function

The constitution itself had already deprived parliament of its role through restrictions which greatly reduced its legislative powers. But in addition to this, more and more people, whether by formal or informal means, were in practise divested of their right to elect their representatives.

### Restrictions on the Eligibility of Political Candidates

The constitution left the organisation of parliamentary elections to the legislative institutions themselves (Art. 62). The first regulations were decided upon by the Revolutionary Council and regulations for elections to the 1st Majles were issued on 6/2/80.[1] Already in these, the eligibility of candidates depended on a series of conditions that were open to arbitrary interpretation and set in order to prevent unwanted people from being elected or even running as a candidate. For instance, a candidate must not be 'suspected of dishonesty or moral depravity' and his 'allegiance to the government of the Islamic Republic' must not be in doubt. In addition, numerous officials who had held government posts in the pre-revolutionary period, right down to the level of municipal councils, were forbidden to present themselves as candidates.

Later amendments placed yet more drastic restrictions on parliamentary candidates. Thus an amendment passed on 28/2/84, required them to have made 'a practical commitment' or 'an authentic religious profession and commitment to Islam'. Large landowners who had had barren lands registered in their name, people condemned by the courts as apostates or sentenced to hadd-punishments and whose repentance had not been confirmed, or anyone who fell under the sanctions stipulated by Art. 49 of the constitution,[2] were according to this amendment disqualified from standing in an election. Although even stricter conditions, formulated by the parliamentary committee and in part passed by parliament, were vetoed by the Guardian Council, such proposals are themselves an indication of the methods of exclusion that were in practice being adopted. The parliamentary committee's proposal was that candidates' suitability should be tested on the basis of their 'political and social views'.[3] Parliament resolved that even those who had been members of village councils, village mayors and members of houses of arbitration *(khanehha-ye ensaf)* before the revolution should be excluded.[4]

Towards the end of the 3rd Majles an effort was made to make these restrictions less stringent since it had become clear that, in the coming elections to the 4th Majles (1992–96), they might be directed against the state-oriented populists, who comprised the majority in the 3rd Majles. A few members proposed that parliament 'drop the requirement of practical commitment to the principles of Islam'. By way of justification, they pointed out that this requirement could be misused in various ways. Hojjat al-Eslam Khalkhali went a step further and concluded that it meant that many jurists would not be eligible to stand for election because they did not accept the concept of *velayat-e faqih*. 'Certainly, we cannot say they are not practising Muslims.'[5] However, this proposal was so contradictory to current practice that it soon had to be withdrawn. The author of a leading article in *Kayhan* compared the MP who put the proposal to someone busily sawing off the branch of the tree he is sitting on (14/1/91). The Society of Teachers of the Religious Academy of Qom stated that it would clear the way for liberals, as well as shameless perpetrators of wickedness, opponents of *velayat-e faqih*, counter-revolutionaries and people who would gladly facilitate the penetration of the country by the USA.[6]

Recourse to requirements of suitability made it possible, even before the elections for the 1st Majles (1980–84), to subject a whole range of unwanted candidates to procedures of exclusion. Marxists were forbidden from standing on the grounds that they could not profess faith in Islam.[7] During the elections for the 2nd Majles (1984–88), it was the turn of the liberal-Islamicists of the Liberation Movement. Although they had been represented in the 1st Majles, this time they preferred to stay away from the elections. It is certain that they would have been accused of merely paying lip-service to *velayat-e faqih* and on these grounds been declared unsuitable as candidates.[8]

Consequently, only 'true' supporters of *velayat-e faqih* still had seats in the 2nd Majles. But the process of exclusion had by no means reached its peak and was now applied to supporters of the system. For this purpose the existing requirements for suitability were no longer adequate and others were introduced on an informal basis. The Guardian Council, which was dominated by a majority of conservative clerics, decided, at first indirectly but then directly, on the form and character the new requirements would take. On the one hand these requirements, to which we will return time and again, were dictated by the demands of the outright struggle for power by different influential groups within the system and, on the other hand, by representatives of the interests of the conservative camp in the area of the economy and law. And yet, as long as Khomeini was still alive, the Guardian Council was not able to make the most of this power. Thus only a few candidates who were classified as left-wing extremists were excluded from the elections to the 3rd Majles (1988–92).[9]

Exclusion from the elections for the 4th Majles, which took place three years after Khomeini's death, was practised on a much greater scale. This was a time when the conservatives, in alliance with the moderates gathered around Rafsanjani, had already succeeded in suppressing the radical-populists in many different areas of power. Out of 3,150 persons who applied for permission to present themselves as candidates, 1,110 were deemed unsuitable by the Guardian Council.[10] Amongst their number were almost all the leading spokesmen of the radical populists, including 45 members of the 3rd Majles, some of whom had been members since 1980. Moreover, there were a few former ministers from previous governments including Hojjat al-Eslam Mohtashami and Behzad Nabavi. In the elections to the 5th Majles the council accepted the credentials of only 3,276 of the 5,365 people who registered as candidates.[11] Again there were, among the rejected candidates, a large number of state functionaries, members of the official and unofficial opposition and even members of the 4th Majles.

The Guardian Council has gone about the business of rejecting unwanted candidates so autocratically that it feels no obligation to give any reason for its decisions – even to the candidates themselves let alone the public. However, statements by other spokesmen for the conservative camp make it clear that, to the council, if a person represents a position contrary to that of the conservatives and the moderates, it is sufficient to reject him as unsuitable. In the elections to the 4th Majles anyone who opposed one particular slogan proclaimed by the conservatives – obedience to the leadership and support of the government – was guilty in advance. Hojjat al-Eslam Ruhani, who was later to become vice-president of parliament, referred to this slogan when, a few months before the elections, he said that the members of the 4th Majles must obey the leader and give their absolute support to the government.[12] The leader himself made it clear that opponents of the regime should stay away from parliament.[13] In order to keep the protest of rejected candidates from becoming too loud, the authorities reminded the latter of files which documented offences they had committed, financial or otherwise, and which were sufficient to bring them before the courts. A member of the Guardian Council, Ayatollah Jannati, expressed his astonishment that persons concerning whom the courts were in possession of incriminating files would still attempt to present themselves as candidates for political office.[14]

The Guardian Council, by interpreting the constitution in the appropriate manner, first secured for itself the right to examine directly the suitability of candidates for the 4th Majles. Art. 99 of the constitution includes amongst the powers of the Guardian Council supervision of elections to parliament, to the Assembly of Leadership Experts, for the president and of national referendums. But it is not clear what exactly is meant by supervision. According to the two bills which until 1991 had governed the way this article was put into practice, the examination of prospective candidates was the task of the Ministry of the Interior. However, the Guardian Council could annul the decisions of this ministry.[15] Out of fear of the imminent exclusion of the radicals, the majority in the 3rd Majles made an attempt at the end of 1991 to restrict the supervisory activity of the Guardian Council to the phase after candidates had been selected. Although the pertinent resolution was passed by a majority in parliament, as might be expected it was vetoed by the Guardian Council.[16] In reaction to this initiative, the Guardian Council itself put forward its own interpretation of the constitutional article in question and resolved that 'supervision' (*nezarat*) in the constitution meant 'giving approval' (*nezarat-e estesvabi*).[17] The vehement protests of the majority in parliament and of their allies against this arbitrary interpretation were of no avail. Once the proposal had been approved by Khamene'i[18] and had found additional support in that quarter it became the legal basis for the massive rejection of unwanted candidates in the elections for the 4th Majles.[19]

The massive application of this measure, the reasons the regime found acceptable for rejecting opposition candidates, together with the deep sense of the loss of their rights felt by those who were excluded, prompted the newspaper *Salam*, which sympathised with the radical-populist camp, to conclude that eligibility to stand for parliament was no longer a right but a privilege. In fact, this conclusion had been justifiable ever since the elections to the 1st Majles. 'Does this not amount to the transformation of the fundamental rights of citizens into privileges, if for whatever reasons the general eligibility ... is so restricted that the greater part of society is unable to find the persons it wishes amongst the candidates?'[20]

Further means were used to restrict the eligibility of candidates and thus indirectly the rights of the voter. One of these was to annul the elections in localities which produced undesirable results. This included a refusal to hold elections in particular places, often on the pretext that they would lead to civil unrest. During the elections to the 1st Majles, the results for 30 cities were annulled.[21] In the case of the 2nd Majles, an opposition boycott meant that the field was left free for supporters of the *velayat-e faqih* and there were only 12 annulments, all due to irregularities such as faulty counts.[22] According to the magazine *Bayan*, which was published by the minister of the interior, Mohtashami, the Guardian Council had planned to carry out numerous annulments during the elections to the 3rd Majles but was prevented by Khomeini. Thanks to his intervention, the results were scrapped in only 15 wards.[23] In connection with the elections for the 4th Majles, annulments only occurred in three cases.[24] Because of the strong control exercised over the whole voting procedure by the Guardian Council and because exclusions had already been effected at the stage of establishing the suitability of candidates, there was less need to use this method of sifting out unwanted rivals. In the elections to the 5th Majles annulments were declared for 14 constituencies.[25]

In Chapter 2 we identified other methods of influencing election results in connection with the elections for the Assembly of Experts. The same methods were also employed during the parliamentary elections. Hojjat al-Eslam Montakhab-Niya has listed ten ways in which the results of the elections to the 4th Majles were influenced. These include denunciation of candidates, monopolistic use of the media to promote a particular party, partisan control of the supervisory commission and outright manipulation during the count. The conclusion he drew was the same as that of the opposition abroad: that extensive manipulation meant that the outcome of the elections was clear before they took place.[26] Another MP said of the elections in his ward (Borujan) that before even one-third of the votes had been counted the number of votes had exceeded the total number of persons entitled to vote. When the citizens protested against this obvious electoral fraud, they were fired upon with machine guns and a great number of them were massacred.[27]

A further obstacle to becoming an MP is to be found within parliament itself. Once a candidate has dealt with the hindrances to establishing his suitability and the vote rigging, he still requires a vote of accreditation from his colleagues in the plenary session of the new parliament. This procedure often involves subjecting opposition candidates once again to a thorough examination of their biography, political career and ideological orientation to find grounds to justify denying them a vote of confidence. In the 1st Majles, 12 elected candidates were denied a vote of confidence. Amongst them was Ahmad Madani, who had actually won more than four million votes as a candidate in the first presidential elections.[28] During the 2nd, 3rd and 4th parliaments, this process of exclusion was less frequently employed for the reasons already mentioned – two, three and two people were denied accreditation in each of these respectively.[29] In the 5th Majles no credentials have, at the time of writing, been rejected.[30]

In this connection mention should also be made of the number of MPs who decided to resign from parliament because of political pressure or as a protest against the government, or who were expelled from their seat. Several of those who resigned went immediately into exile or were arrested. In the 1st Majles, five such cases are known, including Salamatian and Ghazanfarpur, both colleagues of Bani-Sadr.[31] In the 2nd Majles, there were three expulsions,[32] and in the third there was at least one.[33] We also know of two other members of the 3rd Majles who spent some time in prison for political reasons.[34]

Those who manage to take up a seat in parliament after this gruelling selection process generally speaking tend to operate within the limits set by the principles that dominate the selection process. Within such limits, if an MP can count on the support of an influential power group, he or she has a certain degree of freedom to criticise the government or the opposition camp. But should they, even involuntarily, disregard the relevant principles – which are defined by the absolute power of those who actually rule the Islamic Republic, the leader and those influential persons ensconced in its higher institutions – they will be reprimanded by colleagues, or even subjected to physical violence in parliament itself. Furthermore, outside parliament they will have to reckon with the threat of reprisals in their electoral ward by the Revolutionary Court, the Special Court for the Clergy or the Hezbollah. The atmosphere of fear which prevails in parliament has been described by Mehdi Bazargan, who sat as a member during the 1st Majles, in the following words:

> In the Islamic Majles, intimidation, slander, oppression and similar methods intended to uphold a monopoly of power take such proportions that members of the minority [faction], who originally numbered 40 to 50 persons, and the neutrals who have been virtually forbidden to organise themselves, do not dare to utter their views or to express opposition and thereby overstep the boundaries of what is permitted. Should they do so, they will be confronted with threats and slander in their electoral wards. In parliament itself an atmosphere of such hostility, harassment and aggression prevails that it is impossible for opposition MPs to speak and express an opinion or to voice protest and criticism.[35]

In subsequent parliaments there were no members opposed to the *velayat-e faqih*, and yet an identical atmosphere prevailed. A witness to this fact is Prime Minister Musavi, who declared in the Assembly for Revising the Constitution that six months after the end of the 1st Majles: 'It is easy to arrange things in such a way that MPs who do not obey the leadership can never set foot in their electoral ward.' As an example he mentioned the MPs who had disagreed with the dismissal of Bani-Sadr. They remained 'in fact in Tehran and did not visit their electoral wards for two years, being prisoners within the four walls of parliament.'[36] During the 2nd Majles, the MP 'Abd-e Khoda'i complained of the lack of freedom in parliament.[37] Nateq Nuri, who at this time was president of the parliament, once mentioned in a sermon that there was a discrepancy of 40 to 50 votes between voting procedures that were secret and those carried out in the open.[38] By this remark he meant to illustrate the opportunism that flourished in parliament but his remark also illustrates the level of fear that prevailed amongst MPs. Finally, on the opening day of the 5th Majles, Hezbollah, in a letter to MPs, threatened to search out any 'liberals' among them, drag them into the streets and there bring them before a revolutionary court.[39] Exactly the same threat had been made by President Khamene'i a few weeks earlier.[40] This is the same parliament that Rafsanjani had declared in 1989 to be the freest in world history.[41]

## The Restriction of Parliament's Legislative Power

The stipulations of the constitution mean that the power of parliament is greatly limited by the Guardian Council. But the extent of these restrictions can only be fully appreciated if account is taken of how legislation is carried out in practice. This is best understood by analysing the power of veto which the Guardian Council is able to exercise over all parliament's resolutions in the name of the *shari'a* and the constitution. During the 1st Majles, the Guardian Council raised objections to 102 out of 370 (i.e. 27.5 per cent) of the bills or proposals approved by parliament, and sent them back to be amended. During the 2nd Majles, this figure rose 118 out of 316 (37.3 per cent) and during the 3rd Majles to 96 out of 245 (39.9 per cent). This practice was continued with enthusiasm during the 4th Majles in which 128 bills were returned for revision.[42] Moreover, a large number of parliamentary resolutions were repeatedly rejected by the Guardian Council, in some cases as often as five times.[43] The formation of the Assessment Council kept the number of repeated rejections from increasing further. Rejection of a parliamentary resolution meant that the bill was either dropped altogether or altered according to the wishes of the Guardian Council. Since the Assessment Council has come into existence, it makes the final decision on resolutions which parliament and the Guardian Council cannot agree upon.

Sometimes the contradiction to the *shari'a* or the constitution established by the Guardian Council involves the whole content of a parliamentary resolution, but more often it has to do with individual articles and paragraphs.[44] If one were to count the number of articles, paragraphs and sentences to which the Guardian Council has objected, the percentage rejection of parliamentary initiatives would turn out to be much higher. As a rule the parliamentary resolutions which the Guardian Council objects to are of greater importance in terms of their influence on social life in the Islamic Republic than the resolutions which do not encounter opposition. Mohsen Alef, himself a member of the Guardian Council, has described the former category of resolutions as 'fundamental'. According to a report which he published in *Resalat* (6–18/6/87), out of 64 parliamentary resolutions of fundamental importance 31 were rejected by the Guardian Council. These included resolutions that dealt with foreign trade, landownership, industrial law and the co-operative system.

When examining resolutions the Guardian Council adopts an attitude of dominance towards parliament which any observer can easily note. Consequently, the council rarely feels obliged to inform parliament of the reasons for its decisions. In its rulings (*nazariyeh*) it usually confines itself to stating than that a particular resolution is contrary to the *shari'a* or to one or another of the articles of the constitution. For the most part parliament's requests that the reasons for such decisions be given meet with a negative response.[45] Occasionally the council does include a few words indicating the area in which the alterations it requires should be undertaken. And in a few exceptional cases, when there has been great pressure from outside, a member of the council has appeared in public to explain a particular decision.[46]

Already during the 1st Majles, representatives and MPs voiced their resentment at how the Guardian Council dealt with parliament's resolutions.

The then president of parliament, Rafsanjani, accused the council of over-stepping its limits when it rejected a bill approved by parliament concerning buying and selling merchandise.[47] He was of the opinion that, if things continued in the same way, the power of veto of the Guardian Council would in practice lead to the disempowerment of parliament.[48] On another occasion, he described the procedure adopted by the Guardian Council as 'extremely dangerous' and demanded that it should only exercise its powers on request.[49] He also said that, as matters stood, the Guardian Council could decide tomorrow to dismiss the Cabinet, the president or the Supreme Council of Justice, or even undertake something of this kind together with the leader.[50] Others inside and outside parliament followed Rafsanjani's line of criticism with sharper or with more moderate words. The secretary of the ministry of the interior once complained that the Guardian Council had virtually paralysed the government for the last seven years.[51] In connection with the elections for the 4th Majles, Hosein Mehrpur, a member of the Guardian Council, complained that criticism of the council had degenerated to a level of mockery and abuse which threatened the very basis of the council's existence.[52]

Criticism of the Guardian Council came chiefly from the radical-populist camp amongst the ruling legalists. The stronger their representatives grew in parliament, the more violent the conflict between the two legislative institutions became. Accordingly, tension was at its highest during the 3rd Majles in which the radical populists were strong, and continued to mount as it became clear that the conservative camp intended, with the help of the Guardian Council, to prevent the radicals from participating in the next elections. In one sense the tension between the radical legalists and the Guardian Council can be seen as a struggle between different camps in the state class to occupy positions of power. In another sense it can be seen as a conflict between parties supporting different interpretations of the *shari'a*. Basing itself on the classical conservative conception of the *shari'a* which holds private property to be sacred, the Guardian Council has rejected every resolution of parliament which threatens to restrict the private sector or the rights of property holders. Those who justified such resolutions put forward more modernist interpretations of the Islamic legal sources and supported their views by referring to the requirements of government, which could not always be reconciled with the primary Islamic ordinances. In 1982, Rafsanjani, adopting a somewhat conciliatory tone, described the conflict in the following terms: parliament based itself on secondary Islamic ordinances that were legitimate in face of the present need to solve day-to-day problems, whereas the Guardian Council saw as its task the protection of the *shari'a* and the application of the primary Islamic ordinances, even if they did not meet the needs of everyday policies.[53]

Protests against the Guardian Council by the radical-populist camp have been aimed not at the institution *per se*, but rather at its individual members and the conservative position they support. None the less, apologists for the

Guardian Council, while attesting to the integrity, competence and sense of justice of its members,[54] accuse its critics of wishing to question the very institution and emphasise its importance to the continuance and the very essence of the Islamic state. 'Amid Zanjani writes the following in his book on Islamic jurisprudence: 'If the Guardian Council were eliminated from the political system of the Islamic Republic, this system would lose its divine legitimacy, its character as the representative of divine legislative authority and ... the very justification for its existence.'[55] M. Alef has demanded that parliament should adopt 'an attitude of obedience, humility and submission' towards the council.[56] The MP 'Abd-e Khoda'i went so far as to say that the Guardian Council was the highest institution in the Islamic Republic.[57] In 1990, Rafsanjani, now speaking as president and an ally of the regime's conservative camp, described the council as 'a blessing for parliament' and warned of the error of thinking that parliament would be able to achieve great successes if the Guardian Council did not exist.[58] The most effective support for the Guardian Council, however, always came from Khomeini. He repeatedly called on parliament to formulate its resolutions in such a way that the council would not have to reject them. At the same time, he asked the council to take account of the needs of the times when attempting to institute the primary Islamic ordinances.[59]

The Guardian Council's intervention in the legislative system of the Islamic Republic has not been limited to laws and legal initiatives but has also extended to statutory instruments (a'in-nameh-e ejra'i) approved by the Council of Ministers and other executive institutions, decrees of the Council of Ministers (tasvib-nameh), treaties (qarardad) and statutes (asas-nameh). This extension of powers does not correspond to the actual wording of the constitution but is based on the particular interpretation given to that document by the Guardian Council itself.[60] When it examines decisions which have religious relevance the council feels all the more obliged to judge whether they are in accordance with the shari'a. For example, the statutory instruments of the laws on landownership which were approved by the Council of Ministers are clearly thought to belong to this category.[61] In many cases, the Guardian Council has also taken it upon itself to interpret laws, although Art. 73 of the constitution stipulates unambiguously that this is the exclusive right of parliament. The influence of the Guardian Council even extends to the Court of Administrative Justice (Divan-e 'Edalat-e Edari). Mehrpur reports that the council has examined and judged 56 of the cases dealt with by this court.[62]

Another power reserved to the Guardian Council is specifically stated in the constitution – namely the right to interpret the constitution. The council has made use of this right in hundreds of cases, particularly during the early years of the Islamic Republic.[63] If they are passed by a three-quarters majority, the council's rulings on the constitution, as Madani has stressed, have the same validity as the constitution itself. Otherwise, they have the force of advisory judgements (ray-e mashvarati) and are not compulsory.[64] According to its own statutes, the council is to interpret the constitution when requested to do so by the leadership of parliament, the Supreme Court, the Council of Ministers or the president.[65] In practice the council also acts in this capacity at the request of lower government authorities. Most of the rulings on the constitution issued by the Guardian Council concern the relationship between the separate branches of government or between individual authorities within each branch of government. Through its frequent rulings on such issues, the Guardian Council has succeeded in influencing the content of the constitution in a direction which has pleased the conservative camp.[66]

There are other institutions besides the leader and the Guardian Council which participate in legislation but were not set up in order to represent the people. The most powerful of these is the Council for Assessing the Interest of [the State] Order (Majma'-e Tashkhis-e Maslahat-e Nezam), or in abbreviated form, the Assessment Council. This operates on the basis of statutes which it approved itself on 24/10/89 and which Khomeini approved on 12/12/89. Yet when it deems it necessary, the Assessment Council is prepared to violate these statutes and to pass laws without reference to a request by parliament or the Guardian Council. Out of the 50 decisions taken by the Assessment Council since the autumn of 1992, only 14 were because parliament and the Guardian Council could not come to an agreement over them. The remaining 36 decisions were contrary to the council's statutes.[67] At the same time, according to Mehrpur, 10 to 12 per cent of parliament's resolutions are still placed before the Assessment Council for a final decision – a sign of how often parliament and the Guardian Council cannot agree.[68] The Assessment Council is free to formulate its decisions either by agreeing with the position of the Guardian Council or that of parliament. However, it can also decide a question by adopting a wholly independent position of its own.

In practice, the Assessment Council has existed since 1981 as an authority that can go over the head of the official government and decide on the most important questions of policy. Members of the council can therefore be counted among the most influential functionaries of the Islamic Republic. From time to time this fact has been alluded to by government officials.[69] Obviously MPs have been far from pleased with the restriction of parliament's rights by this council. But they only voiced their protests publicly once the Assessment Council became publicly visible and its legislative powers were extended. It was because of these protests that Khomeini decided to withdraw the permission he had given the council to legislate independently. In practice, however, this decision had no real effect. The Assessment Council has continued to overstep its authority and, consequently, MPs have continued their protests against it. On 17/11/91, for instance, the MP Qasem Sho'leh-e Sa'di objected that the Assessment Council was changing out of all recognition even those parts of parliamentary resolutions which the Guardian Council had not queried.[70] Another MP wanted to know on what legal basis the Assessment Council made its decisions. He added that the council was violating the rights of parliament and demanded the restoration of this body's legislative function. 'Legislation', he declared, 'is the right of parliament.'[71] A third MP said that the Assessment Council, by interfering in the process of legislation, was acting in violation of the constitution and enumerated several cases in which it had arbitrarily overstepped its powers.[72]

MPs levelled similar protests against other institutions that intervened in legislation. Amongst these is the National Security Council (Showra-ye Amniyat-e Melli) which was formed on the instructions of the Assembly for Revising the Constitution and charged with the task of looking after 'the national interests and watching over the Islamic revolution, as well as the territorial integrity and the national sovereignty of the country.' The National Security Council's functions are formulated in Art. 176 of the constitution as follows:

1. Determining the country's policies concerning defence and security within the framework of general government policy.
2. Co-ordinating political, social, cultural and economic activities that affect security, together with the general measures adopted for defence and security within the country.
3. Making use of all the country's material and spiritual resources in order to mobilise resistance against domestic and foreign threats.

The National Security Council is composed of the presidents of the three branches of government, the chief of the General Staff of the armed forces, the functionary responsible for matters of planning and the budget, two deputies appointed by the leader, the minister for foreign affairs, the minister of the interior, and the minister for security. Also included in the council is whichever minister has authority over the problem being dealt with at a given moment, and the highest ranking officers of the army and the Revolutionary Guards. The president of the Islamic Republic presides over the council. Moreover, the council's decisions are binding once they have been confirmed by the leader.

The Security Council is yet another institution which existed long before it was legally recognised. It has been capable of going over the head of official government functionaries and deciding key questions of government policy.[73] Whereas in a certain sense the Assessment Council is the highest legislative authority, the Security Council can be described as a kind of super-government. It makes decisions about a whole range of matters which should, at the very least, be supervised by parliament. In fact, its decisions are an outright infringement upon the powers of the legislature. And yet, parliament generally learns of these decisions only after they are made. In some cases the council's decisions contradict those of parliament.[74] Furthermore, the Security Council often makes decisions or intervenes in matters which lie far beyond the limits of authority set out for it in the constitution. As the president of the judiciary Ayatollah Yazdi, reports, the council draws up plans for fighting against 'the cultural invasion instigated by the West and its allies within the country' and restraining 'social immorality'.[75] It is chiefly in this council that foreign policy is decided. According to the president of parliament, Hojjat al-Eslam Nateq Nuri, the Ministry of Foreign Affairs only carries out the preparatory phase for these decisions. 'Consequently, parliament does not play an important role in connection with foreign policy.'[76] The Security Council's intervention in areas which are not normally defined as defence or security should not occasion surprise, for in authoritarian states every event becomes a matter of security for the regime, whether it be the publication of a political caricature in a magazine or the protest of poor people against increases in prices.

The Supreme Council for the Cultural Revolution, as we saw in Chapter 4, is another institution with legislative powers which was not elected by the people. The council's goals and tasks are defined in its statutes which were drafted by Khomeini himself in 1986. They clearly demonstrate the extent of this council's activity in areas which in a democratic system would normally be dealt with by parliament. Amongst its tasks are 'working out the principles for cultural policies under the government of the Islamic Republic, and defining the goals and the direction of plans for culture, education and research' as well as 'the spread and reinforcement of the influence of Islamic culture in all areas of society, and the intensification of the cultural revolution and the development of general culture.'[77] The resolutions passed by this council have regularly appeared since 1986 in a separate part of the statute-books published annually by the Ministry of Justice. They are referred to as 'operational regulations', 'statutes', 'orders' and so on but in reality they have the character of laws.

In order to illustrate the legislative activity of the judiciary it is sufficient to quote from a 1983 article, 'Where is the Judiciary Headed?' by the MP Mohammad Khamene'i:

> The judiciary ... has entered the dangerous abyss of overstepping the law and has usurped the position which is exclusively reserved for parliament. Although the resolutions undertaken by the Ministry of Justice without consulting with parliament or receiving parliament's permission are never called *qanun* (laws) but are referred to as *bakhshnameh* (circulars) or *tasvibnameh* (resolutions), they are beyond any shadow of a doubt nothing less than laws, if one considers their real significance and effect.

To corroborate his view, Khamene'i goes on to cite a series of examples which include the annulment of 10 articles of the civil code.[78]

But to appreciate the full extent of intervention in legislation by non-elected institutions, it is also necessary to mention the Supreme Administrative Council (Showra-ye 'Ali-ye Edari), the Supreme Council for Supporting the War (Showra-ye 'Ali-ye Poshtibani-ye Jang) and a few other economic institutions which are responsible to the leader alone. In addition to these councils mention must also be made of mayors who, in the municipalities, make a series of decisions affecting taxation, urban development and other such matters, for which they have no legal authority. The oppressive and arbitrary character of these decisions at times reaches such proportions that the citizens have no other recourse but to rebel and organise demonstrations against them.[79]

### The Relationship between Government and Parliament

The Constitution of the Islamic Republic confers on parliament a series of powers in addition to its legislative function, but these too are restricted by government institutions with higher authority. The most important of these powers consists of the government's dependence on a vote of confidence from parliament (Art. 87, 133, 135 and 136). According to the constitution, government officials are accountable to parliament, both as individuals and collectively, and parliament can question them, remind them of their duty and formally withdraw its confidence from them (Art. 70, 88, 89, 135 and 137).

Parliament has repeatedly made use of these powers. During every parliament the number of inquiries has been high. For instance, during the 1st and 2nd Majles 24 and 25 inquiries respectively were held.[80] Although interpellations (estizah) have occurred less often, there have been some cases in every parliament and they have occasionally led to the dismissal of the minister in question. During the 1st Majles, two interpellations took place without resulting in a dismissal. During the 2nd Majles, one interpellation occurred, but the hearings were not actually held until the 3rd Majles. During this latter period, there were three interpellations and one of them led to the dismissal of a minister. Finally, during the 4th Majles a minister was forced to resign, in part because of the pressure parliament brought to bear. A second minister only managed to survive the interpellation proceedings with the help of the Guardian Council.[81] In the 4th Majles proceedings were brought against the minister of commerce but MPs passed a vote of confidence for him and in at least two other cases the president of parliament prevented interpellation proceedings.[82]

In each parliament there have been ministers proposed by the prime minister and the president who did not succeed in winning a vote of confidence. The 1st Majles refused to declare its confidence in two prime ministers proposed by the president[83] while six ministers fell because parliament did not give them a vote of confidence. In the 2nd Majles eight ministers fell from office and three fell in the 3rd Majles. In the 4th Majles, the president, after being re-elected to his office, had to fill seven ministerial posts with new candidates in order to obtain parliament's vote of confidence.[84]

The subjection of ministers to parliamentary questioning or interpellations, or the refusal of a vote of confidence to government ministers should not be interpreted as proof of the independence and power of parliament vis-à-vis the executive. Rather these incidents should be seen as a clear sign of the power struggle which is going on at all levels amongst those persons, groups, client networks and political camps that have some share in government power. Parliament is only one of the several arenas where this struggle takes place. Neither parliament nor the government can be characterised as wielding state power independently of these other agents. Of course, some of the most influential powers-that-be occupy positions in both these organs of state but their power does not stem chiefly from the fact that they are members of these institutions. As long as Khomeini was still alive he, and not parliament, had the final word on the composition of the government. Musavi's government survived as long as it did despite its incompetence – which even Khomeini admitted – because Khomeini wanted it that way. The government formed after Khomeini's death during the 3rd Majles did not correspond to the will of its radical-populist majority. But they approved many bills drafted by this government because they had to obey certain forces which were beyond their control. In fact, it was these very forces which in the end saw to it that the radical-populist MPs did not obtain seats in the 4th Majles.

The submission of MPs to outside forces which determined the function of parliament was, of course, partly due to their recognition of the general interest of the regime, which in turn was also of benefit to individual MPs. However, fear of unpleasant consequences also played a role in shaping their attitude. When analysing parliament's behaviour towards the government, it is of key importance to consider what meaning individual refusals may have had and against whom they were directed. With regard to the government as a whole or explosive issues of domestic and foreign policy, MPs were less daring in the way they expressed themselves publicly. In fact, issues of this nature were scarcely discussed or decided on in parliament. On the other hand, when it came to a vote of confidence for individual ministers or to dealing with questions the government had left to parliament to decide, then the MPs had ample opportunity to exercise their abilities.

This form of relative independence on the part of parliament is illustrated most clearly by its rejection of bills (*layeheh-e qanuni*) brought before it by the government. The 1st Majles rejected 44, the second 19 and the third 26 of the bills presented to them. Up to April 1995 the 4th Majles had rejected 28 legislative initiatives and 21 bills.[85] However, it is interesting that, with the exception of the 1st Majles, the number of rejected legislative initiatives (*tarh-e qanuni*) put forward by MPs themselves was greater than that of the rejected bills, namely 22, 55 and 102, respectively.[86] Especially during the 3rd Majles when the majority of MPs were not in agreement with the government, instead of expressing their opposition directly they preferred to express it in the form of legislative initiatives. These initiatives were usually contrary to government policy. But interestingly, before being sent on to be rejected by the Guardian Council, they were voted down in parliament itself. The more radical these initiatives were in departing from government policy, the greater the tendency of parliament to withhold its approval.

In this connection we should mention legislation which parliament on several occasions obliged the government to draw up and which it viewed as absolutely essential and extremely urgent. An example is the Bill on Self-Sufficiency in Agricultural Products of Strategic Importance which in 1985 parliament demanded that the government frame. Seven resolutions of this kind were passed during the 1st Majles, and two during the 2nd. But on 22/12/88, the Guardian Council took this right away from parliament, declaring on the basis of Art. 75 of the constitution that the framing of bills was a matter exclusively reserved for the government.[87]

The government's relation to parliament is also formally defined by the latter's right of supervision over the government's activities. This entails the right of parliament to examine whether and to what extent the government has put into practice parliamentary resolutions or deviated from them. By deviation is meant not only the failure to put laws into practice but also the improper formulation of statutory instruments, as well as contrary government resolutions and regulations. The MP Majid Ansari described this practice in the following words:

> It is quite common to observe that the Council of Ministers or the council's subordinate commissions formulate executive orders in such a way that they are for all practical purposes contrary to the law passed by parliament. Sometimes one may observe that a particular situation is rejected in a bill passed by parliament, but the executive orders are formulated in such a way that the rejected situation can still be maintained.'[88]

In order to prevent this practice the Assembly for Revising the Constitution changed Art. 138 and made it obligatory for the government to inform parliament when it drew up statutory instruments and government resolutions so that if these were contradictory to the laws in question, parliament could return them to the Council of Ministers for revision. This addition to the older wording of the pertinent article of the constitution confirmed that there had been a violation of parliament's right, which is what parliament some time earlier had set out to establish. The corresponding law obliged the government to inform parliament, its commissions and its president concerning governmental resolutions, circular letters, regulations and ordinary as well as secret agreements.[89]

Parliament's general right of supervision is also guaranteed by Art. 76 and 90 of the constitution. According to Art. 76, parliament has the right 'to undertake investigations and inquiries on all matters concerning the country'. Art. 90 declares that parliament is a kind of supreme authority for the people's complaints which it has the duty to examine and on the basis of which it has the right to prosecute. What happens in practice, however, contradicts this specific and general right of supervision. A clear proof of the people's representatives are ignored is the fact that they were scarcely informed about the government's decisions during the war. We saw earlier what happened to the eight MPs who asked to be informed about the Iran-Contra affair.

Likewise, the relationship of the government authorities to the so-called Commission of Article 90, which was set up by parliament, highlights the failure to implement parliament's right of supervision. The commission in question was established in 1981. After that date, all government officials were obliged to give prompt answers in a detailed and convincing manner to all the commission's questions concerning complaints.[90] Since government officials refused to carry out this duty, parliament passed a law on 25/4/85 which made such refusal a punishable offence.[91] It later proved necessary to make the penalty provided by this law more severe, since the threat of punishment as it stood was evidently not having the desired effect.[92] But the threat of tougher punishments proved to be of little avail. For this reason, the vice-president of parliament described the legislature's right of supervision as 'colourless and ineffective'.[93] In 1994 MPs were still complaining that the mayor of Tehran, for example, did not respond to the subpoenas issued by the commission.[94]

The government's refusal to be supervised by parliament and to conform to parliamentary resolutions forms part of a more general relationship that prevails between the government, that is to say, the leadership of the regime, and parliament, and which the MPs characterise as disregard for the law. It shows, on the one hand, how little respect there is for parliament among powerful officials and, on the other hand, the far-reaching independence of the bureaucrats on very low levels of the power structure.

A selection of the repeated complaints of MPs and others will help to illustrate this point. Rasul Hoseini Kuhestani, for example, believes that 'a great part of the problems the country faces stem from not putting laws and resolutions into practice'.[95] The president of the 3rd Majles, Ayatollah Mehdi Karrubi, by way of illustrating how the government authorities ignore the law mentions the failure to apply the legislation to prevent price rises.[96] The former minister of labour, Ahmad Tavakkoli, cites the report of the Auditor-General's Office for the first six months of 1370 (1991–92) which states that 1,152 legal violations by the Organisation of National Industries (Sazman-e Sana'i-ye Melli) were recorded, 604 by the Foundation for the Disinherited (Bonyad-e Mostaz'afin) and 461 by the Industrial and Mining Bank (Bank-e Sana'at va Ma'dan).[97] A striking example of this attitude is the former minister of the interior, Hojjat al-Eslam Mohtashami, who openly justified disregarding the law by explaining that the goals and ideals of the revolution were more important than the law.[98]

This disregard for laws passed by parliament is often explained as a consequence of the fact that in Iran not norms (*zabetehha*) but personal relationships (*rabetehha*) provide the basis for behaviour.[99] The MP Ebrahim Mir Ghaffari described 'the flight from the law' (*qanun-gorizi*) as a characteristic of Iran's government administration which he compared to 'a sick and dangerous monster'.[100]

A parliament whose powers are restricted in this manner on all sides and which is held in contempt can find small consolation in the fact that from time to time it is flattered by a leading politician or official. This occurs chiefly with the help of quotations from Khomeini. In accordance with his tactics of maintaining a balance of power or other such considerations, Khomeini had occasionally described parliament in high-sounding phrases which he certainly did not believe himself. The following are a few examples: 'The Islamic parliament is the sole centre which all must obey.' 'Parliament is the starting point for whatever happens in the state.' 'Submission to the parliament means submission to Islam.' 'The parliament stands above all other institutions.' 'Parliament is the embodiment of the people and the very crystallisation of the people in one particular place.'[101]

In his book *The Islamic State*, on the other hand, the only function Khomeini attributes to parliament is planning. There is no question of parliament undertaking legislation which is a matter for God and for the jurists who guard over the *shari'a*. In a speech delivered in 1985 to MPs, Khomeini described parliament as 'a consultative Islamic assembly'.[102] But even in this capacity parliament's real role in the Islamic Republic is a subordinate one. Consultation over the most important issues takes place on other levels of state – in the Assessment Council, the Guardian Council, the Security Council, or on the level of councils which represent the most influential jurists. If a few MPs have some say in these councils, this is because of their personal position and not their official function as representatives of parliament.

Of course, parliament is a consultative assembly in so far as its actual function is to participate in the formulation and framing of laws. This function is generally described as one of applying 'know-how' (*kar-shenasi*). But parliament must share even this function with government ministries where the most important steps in formulating bills are carried out. In addition, generally speaking only a few MPs actually possess special abilities that would qualify as 'know-how'. The level of education of the majority attests to their lack of suitability for such work. Out of the 261 to 268 MPs who sat in the four parliaments, those with a doctorate numbered 9, 37, 18 and 38, in the 1st, 2nd, 3rd and 4th parliaments respectively, 20, 25, 15 and 83 MPs had a state diploma, 45, 52, 85 and 83 had a bachelors degree and the rest were at most high-school graduates. A large number of MPs (though they are on the decrease) had attended religious academies where the main subject of study is religious law and teaching methods are traditional and which do not prepare their students to govern a modern state. The number of MPs with this kind of education in the 1st to the 4th Majles was 143, 120, 84 and 65.[103] In other words, the number of MPs trained in Islamic law is decreasing, although parliament is meant to be an Islamic institution charged with the task of helping to bring about the general application of Islamic law.

For much of the period since the revolution, parliament has functioned as a forum for debate between power blocs, political camps and interest groups within the Islamic state. Close observation of the way it has fulfilled this task provides much information about the power struggle and ideological debates that have taken place within the regime. In the 4th Majles, however, the dominance of the conservative camp meant far less debate, although the relative calm that prevailed through much of this legislative period was upset in its closing months by intensified conflict between power blocs in the state. Another function of parliament – the delivery of sycophantic speeches in its plenary sessions, usually in praise of the leader or the president of the republic – illustrates the weakness of its position vis-à-vis the real powers in the state.

Several MPs have given quite accurate descriptions of parliament. The vice-president of the 3rd Majles, Hojjat al-Eslam Bayat, is worth quoting on this subject. He stated that parliament is 'helpless' (*bi-chareh*) and 'ineffective' (*bi-khassiyat*). In his opinion, it could only reveal its anger during negotiations about the national budget, in other words raise questions annoying to the government. But, as he saw it, parliament cannot discuss the restrictions placed on its powers. 'The Imam made it clear that this is not permitted. This means we do not have the right to discuss the restrictions imposed on parliament's powers.'[104]

## The People's Indifference to Parliament

An additional reason why parliament is less representative of the people than might appear at first sight is the fact that only a limited percentage of the population takes part in the parliamentary elections, although, as the first national referendum demonstrated, a far higher turn-out is attainable when the electorate is properly motivated.

It is virtually impossible to determine with accuracy the number of voters who have participated in elections. The official statistics are not a reliable source although the figures published by the leaders of the Islamic Republic are not comparable to those given out by other authoritarian states where participation is regularly recorded as well over 90 per cent. Even so, there is no reason to assume that Iran's more differentiated official statistics actually correspond to reality.[105] Moreover, when assessing the level of electoral participation, it should be borne in mind that an incalculable number of voters go to the ballot-box out of fear of reprisals. Indeed, participation in elections is regularly recorded by stamping a person's identity card. People who not have such a stamp must, when dealing with the authorities, worry about being classified as opponents of the regime.

Be that as it may, even the official statistics indicate a relatively low level of electoral participation. Let us take as an example the elections for the 4th Majles in the city of Tehran. In the first round 1,701,292 voters participated. According to the government, this figure represents 53 per cent of the electorate; according to the newspaper *Salam*, it represents 35.7 per cent. The government's calculation is based on a total electorate of 3.2 million, whereas *Salam* puts the figure at 4.5 million. In the second round of the elections, the number of participants dropped to 1,025,629, i.e. 32 per cent or (according to *Salam*) 22.7 per cent of the electorate. Interestingly, in the first round of the elections only 2 out of 30 approved candidates obtained the necessary majority of 33 per cent of the votes cast, with one receiving 55.1 per cent and the other 39.5 per cent. In the second round, only 3 out of 28 candidates received over 50 per cent of the votes cast. The lowest on the list of those elected only received 32.6 per cent of the votes. This figure (334,817 votes in concrete terms) represents 7.4 per cent of the total electorate as calculated by *Salam*, or 10.4 per cent according to the government. The then president of parliament failed to be elected in the first round but succeeded in the second round with votes that amounted to 10.8 per cent or 15.2 per cent of the total electorate.[106]

The turn out in the elections to the 5th Majles was ( according to official figures) only marginally better. In the first round in Tehran only about 2.1 million of a total electorate of 4.5 million (54.3 per cent) cast their votes and only two candidates succeeded in getting a seat in this round with 35.9 and 34.8 per cent of the vote respectively – that is the votes of 19.5 and 18.9 per cent of the electorate. In the second round the number of participants fell to 1.4 million and the last on the list of elected candidates took their seat in parliament on the basis of votes cast by only 8.9 per cent of the total electorate.[107]

These electoral results, to the extent that they may be trusted, make it clear how far the representatives of the hierocracy have distanced themselves from the people. The point is underlined by the fact that the top functionaries of the different political camps received the lowest number of votes despite their appearance as candidates on two separate electoral lists. The turn-out of the electorate was low, despite repeated declarations by many ayatollahs and the leader, Khamene'i, that it was the religious duty of the faithful to participate and that abstaining from the elections was a reprehensible act according to Islam.[108] The Grand Ayatollahs Golpaygani and Araki had both urged the people to cast their vote.[109] Ayatollah Emami Kashani had hoped to raise the level of electoral participation by stating that 'the propaganda apparatus of the world powers is attempting to hinder the people's participation in the elections.'[110] The presidential elections which took place one year later confirmed the trend of lower levels of participation.

## Other Restrictions on the Sovereignty of the People

### *Electing the President*

The direct election of the president is another recognised opportunity for the people to participate in government through their representatives. According to Art. 113 of the constitution, the president occupies 'the highest official post in the country after that of the leader' and 'he bears responsibility for putting the constitution into practice and directing the executive branch of government, aside from those matters which directly concern the leader'.[111] According to Art. 114 of the constitution, he is to be elected directly by the people for a four-year term of office. But the people's electoral rights have, in this case as well, been greatly restricted.

The first restriction comes in the constitution itself. The president must be (a male) religious or political personality, he must profess loyalty to the principles of the Islamic Republic and the official religion of the country (Art. 115). Sunni Muslims, those of different religious faiths or atheists are consequently excluded in advance from this office. Although the electoral regulations passed in 1981 and amended in 1985 imposed no other conditions on candidates for this office,[112] it soon became evident that professing belief in *velayat-e faqih* in the absolute sense and willingness to submit to Khomeini's wishes were further requirements.

In practice there was only one elected president who did not fulfil this last requirement – the first president, Bani-Sadr, who for this reason soon lost his office despite the fact that, according to official sources, he had received 10.7 million votes from the people. Aside from the brief presidency of the layman Mohammad 'Ali Raja'i,[113] all the presidents after Bani-Sadr not only fulfilled the formal conditions laid down in the constitution but also, as members of the clergy, were the embodiment of the principle of *velayat-e faqih*. The extent of the suppression of the democratic principle of eligibility and freedom to vote in presidential elections is amply illustrated by the number of candidates whose suitability was examined by the Guardian Council and rejected. The following table makes this clear:

| Electoral Year | Examined Candidates | Approved Candidates |
|---|---|---|
| 1980 | 124 | 8 |
| 1981 | 71 | 4 |
| 1981 | 45 | 4 |
| 1985 | 50 | 3 |
| 1989 | 80 | 2 |
| 1993 | 128 | 4 |

Source: Menashri, 1990; *Kayhan* 9/7/87; *Salam*, 15/5/93.

Amongst the candidates excluded in 1980, along with a group of religious political personalities, was Mas'ud Rajavi, the leader of the People's Mojahedin. At Khomeini's request he was for all practical purposes forced to withdraw his candidacy. Amongst the candidates rejected at a later date were Mehdi Bazargan, the first prime minister of the Islamic Republic, Hojjat al-Eslam Kho'iniha, the former public prosecutor, and Mohammad Mehdi 'Abd-e Khoda'i, the general secretary of the Feda'iyan-e Eslam Party.[114] In all these cases, despite the candidates' request, the reason for their rejection was never announced.

As long as Khomeini was still alive, all the presidents, with the sole exception of Bani-Sadr, made every effort to display their loyalty and submission to Khomeini. Although they stood at the head of the executive, their subordinates in the government received their directives from Khomeini. Before the revision of the constitution, which eliminated the office of prime minister, the latter, conceiving of himself as the head of the executive, opposed the president. During the presidency of Khamene'i, Rafsanjani exercised a great amount of executive power, not in his capacity as president of parliament, but on the basis of his personal position in the regime. Indeed, in practice he, and not the president, was the second-in-command after the leader.

After Khomeini's death, Rafsanjani became the president. As such, during his first years in office he disposed over more power than Khamene'i, who had succeeded Khomeini as leader. But more recently Rafsanjani has been losing this power to the dominant conservative camp which has increasingly reinforced Khamene'i's powers as leader. However, these shifts in the power structure have little to do with the people who exercise less and less influence on the government leadership. For this reason, popular indifference towards the presidential elections has been growing. Official figures, show that only 57 per cent of the electorate took part in the elections of June 1993. The opposition within the regime calculated that participation was around 50 per cent.[115] At 16.7 million, the number of participants was even lower than the 16.8 million who had voted in the third presidential election in 1981, although the size of the electorate had in the meantime risen by 10 million.

## The People's Restricted Role in the Designation of the Leader

Art. 5 and 107 of the constitution in its earlier form stipulated that the leader, though not directly elected by the people, is to be directly recognised by them. Accordingly, 'the task of leadership and its concomitant powers' are to be reserved for 'the honest, God-fearing jurist who is brave, capable of leadership and well-informed about present-day requirements', as long as he is recognised and accepted as leader by the majority of the people. Only if no jurist is able to obtain the approval of the majority will an individual or a council of jurists be appointed. In such a case, the Assembly of Leadership Experts, which is elected by the people, will determine who is to be the leader or who are to be the members of the Leadership Council. Furthermore, since Art. 107 and 109 stipulate that holding the rank of *marja'* is a condition for becoming leader, a direct connection is thereby established between electing the leader and the will of the people. For a *marja'* is a person who is recognised as such by the people.

However, since the revision of the constitution the people can only influence on the choice of the leader through the Assembly of Leadership Experts. The annulment of the people's right to elect the leader directly was the result of dropping the *marja'iyat* as a requirement for holding the office of leader.[116] The immediate cause for scrapping both these requirements was the fact that during the revision of the constitution, which was still going on when Khomeini died, there was no *marja'* available whom the ruling mullahs could appoint as leader without creating problems. Ayatollah Montazeri, who had been designated as Khomeini's successor in 1982 and for this reason had been promoted to the rank of grand ayatollah, had in the meantime fallen into disfavour.[117] Other grand ayatollahs, who were numerous enough at this time, did not fit in with the power politics of the masters of the hierocracy. So there was no other solution but to do away with the requirement of *marja'iyat*.

Various arguments were put forward, inside and outside the Assembly for Revising the Constitution, to justify this act which affected the very essence of the theory of *velayat-e faqih*. The least credible of these was the assertion that the *marja'iyat* had never really been a requirement for holding the office of leader. Khomeini is supposed to have written a letter to the Chairman of the Assembly of Leadership Experts on 29/4/89 in which he emphasised that he had always been of the opinion that the *marja'iyat* was not a require-ment for the office of leader. Indeed, it would be sufficient if the leader were an honest *mojtahed*.[118] This assertion contradicts the relevant passages in Khomeini's book on the Islamic state. There (p. 52) it is maintained that 'the ruler must possess the highest scholarly rank (*afzaliyat-e 'elmi*)', which amounts to making the *marja'iyat* a necessary requirement. Moreover, Khomeini put his signature to the constitution in 1979 without raising any objections to the expressly mentioned requirement of the *marja'iyat* in Art. 107 and 109. Again, this is consistent with Rafsanjani's remark during the fifth session of the Assembly for Revising the Constitution when Khomeini, having then con-sidered the actual situation and the fact that 'being a *marja'* was not at present a necessary requirement for the leadership', came out in favour of separating these two functions. Rafsanjani declared: 'This was a statement which I had never heard before from the Imam. This was something completely new. In other words, this was the latest word I heard from him.'[119] Precisely because of the great importance of the *marja'iyat*, attempts were made in the years before the revision of the constitution to confer the rank of *marja'* on Montazeri. Another fact which indicates the untenable nature of this assertion is that, in the first law of 1980 concerning the election of the Assembly of Experts, the ability 'to establish a person's qualifications for the *marja'iyat* and the leadership' was made a necessary requirement for the suitability of candidates for membership on this assembly.[120] But the most important point in this connection is the fact that the requirement of *marja'iyat* for holding the office of leader is a logical consequence of the theory of *velayat-e faqih*, according to which government rule is the exclusive right of the expert on Islamic law. Accordingly, the most learned of the experts – in other words one of the *marja's* – would have the greatest right to hold this office.[121]

Just how artificial the arguments justifying the inevitable renunciation of this requirement could become is illustrated by Ayatollah Amini's assertion that what is required of a candidate to be leader is not that he actually be a *marja'*. It is enough if he has the potential to become a *marja'*.[122] Ayatollah Azari Qomi felt he had found a solution to the problem when he stated that, as an assembly of legal experts, the Assembly of Experts itself could confer the rank of *marja'* on the leader.[123] This of course represents a reversal of the relationship of leader and *marja'*. The rank of *marja'* is not a requirement for becoming leader, but the leader may, and is potentially qualified to become, a *marja'*. Ayatollah Yazdi was coming a lot closer to the true reason for dropping the requirement of *marja'iyat* when he said a person could be a *marja'* without being the leader. 'Being the leader is one thing and articulating God's ordinances is another.'[124] Rafsanjani pointed out that normally jurists attain the level of *marja'iyat* at an age when they can no longer fulfil the requirements of government leadership. Therefore, these two functions, at least under present circumstances, should be separated.[125] Ayatollah Amini drew attention to the fact that the institution of *marja'iyat* could be abused. Ambitious supporters of a particular *marja'*, disregarding his lack of leadership abilities, but desiring to further their own power through him, could push him forward.[126] Ayatollah Mo'men used the same argument in connection with the right of the people to elect the leader. There might be those who would abuse this right for their own purposes with the help of riots, demonstrations and manipulations.[127]

Of course, several members of the Assembly for Revising the Constitution were aware of problems posed by this annulment. It was possible that someone besides the leader might become popular with the people, that the people might not accept the leader as a *marja'*, or that conflict might arise between the leader and the *marja'*, and the people might give priority to the decision of the *marja'*.[128] In an attempt to prevent this from happening, the Assembly for Revising the Constitution resolved that the Assembly of Leadership Experts should, to the best of its ability, choose for the post of leader the most popular and most learned from amongst the available candidates.[129]

Despite the solemn interpretations in the Assembly for Revising the Constitution, the election of the leader by the Assembly of Leadership Experts means that the leader is not even elected indirectly by the people.[130] It is true that the members of the assembly are elected by the people, but the electoral rights of the people are greatly restricted in this case as well by the requirements for eligibility placed upon candidates. Whatever power bloc is dominant at a given moment determines these requirements in accordance with its own interests. In practice this means excluding opponents and rivals as much as possible from government power.

This monopolising trend already manifested itself in the first law governing the elections for the Assembly of Leadership Experts (1980). According to this law, only those could be elected who, amongst other things, disposed of 'the fullest knowledge of the principles of *ejtehad*' and had acquired this ability through study at the best religious academies, and who were thus capable of 'recognising persons who were suitable for the *marja'iyat* and leadership'. Moreover, the candidate must enjoy a reputation for piety and have an irreproachable political past. Whether the candidate fulfilled these requirements or not was to be decided on the basis of testimony from three 'well-known professors at religious academies who teach on the highest level of the curriculum'.[131] In the statutory instruments accompanying this law, the right was also given to the leader to establish the suitability of candidates for the rank of *mojtahed*. Moreover, members of the clergy who were known as *mojtaheds* in learned circles or amongst the *'ulama* in the provinces, were exempt from having to present such testimony.[132] This restriction on eligibility was justified by the assertion that only *mojtaheds* were in the position to judge whether candidates for the office of leader were suitable in terms of their knowledge of the religious law. Even academics and experts in other disciplines would not possess this ability.[133]

The first Assembly of Leadership Experts was elected under this law. When the second assembly was elected in 1990, the conditions of eligibility were even more restrictive and the circle of those examining the suitability of candidates was even more exclusive. This election took place at the height of the competition between opposing camps for leadership positions which intensified after Khomeini's death. The tightening of procedures regulating the election under these circumstances had direct implications in this struggle. Since the conservatives and moderates proved to be more successful in the conflict, they were able for the most part to exclude their rivals and opponents from this assembly as well.

The first step towards achieving this goal was the transference of the right to examine the candidates to the Guardian Council.[134] The Assembly of Leadership Experts, which was chiefly composed of conservative members of the clergy, took this decision before its term of office ran out. Thus, the possibility of providing testimony of suitability on behalf of unwanted candidates was taken away[135] from those ayatollahs and grand ayatollahs who were deemed 'naive' or even 'counter-revolutionary'.[136]

The second step was to tighten up the requirements for eligibility. Whereas in 1980 it was possible for members of the clergy who had some knowledge of the principles of *ejtehad* to stand as candidates, now proof was required that a candidate had attained 'the scholarly rank of *mojtahed*'. Testimonies or other circumstantial evidence would not suffice for this purpose. Instead, candidates must undergo an oral and a written examination which was administered by certain *'ulama* on the Guardian Council. On the basis of a final screening of the results of this exam, the Guardian Council decided whether candidates were suitable to present themselves in the election for membership in the Assembly of Leadership Experts. Only candidates whose aptitude was personally confirmed by the leader were exempt from this examination procedure.[137]

These requirements meant that in the elections for the second Assembly of Leadership Experts almost every candidate from the radical camp was eliminated at the stage of the aptitude test. Yet they had for years borne the title of ayatollah or hojjat al-eslam, and been amongst the closest colleagues of Khomeini. Some had been members of the first Assembly of Leadership Experts and the Assembly of Experts for Framing the Constitution and had functioned as MPs, in some cases from the very beginning. There had been 178 applicants who wanted to stand for 76 positions. Of these 62 failed the examination while seven preferred to stay away from it. This meant that only

109 candidates remained and that voters in several constituencies did not even have a choice of candidates.[138]

The protests against this procedure of exclusion, especially from the radical camp, were so violent that Rafsanjani describing the situation, said: 'Matters almost reached the point of becoming a war in the streets.'[139] But the protests changed nothing. The assembly set up by this procedure did not even represent the whole hierocratic spectrum, much less the other political currents in Iranian society. The level of participation in the elections also reflected this state of affairs. The turn-out of 11.6 million, if the official figures can be believed, was 6 million less than in the elections for the first Assembly of Leadership Experts in 1982. This was only slightly above one-third of the total electorate. And yet even those prominent personalities who had been excluded from presenting themselves as candidates had urged the population to participate in the elections. Since during earlier elections they had always maintained that participation was a religious duty, they could scarcely avoid urging participation on this occasion. Another example of this low-key approach is to be found in the bye-elections to the Assembly of Leadership Experts held in Tehran and Mazanderan at the same time as elections to the 5th Majles. The matter was kept so quiet that few voters knew anything of them until they entered the polling booths. Fourteen people had initially presented themselves as candidates and of these the Guardian Council approved the credentials of only five. The winner took his seat in the assembly with the votes of only 14.4 per cent of the electorate.[140]

*The Restriction of the Representation of the People by the Assembly for Revising the Constitution.*

The Assembly for Revising the Constitution provides another example of disregard for the sovereignty of the people. Although the constitution of 1979 had made no provisions for its own revision, on 24/4/89 Khomeini established by decree an assembly which he entrusted with the task of undertaking such revisions as were, at that time, considered urgent. After the dismissal of Montazeri as Khomeini's designated successor, it was especially urgent to drop some of the requirements for holding the office of leader. Similarly, it was necessary to set aside certain organisational hindrances to the leader by doing away with the office of prime minister and some other less important changes. Finally, regulations were to be drafted for setting up an Assembly for Revising the Constitution in the future.

The members of the Assembly for Revising the Constitution, which began its work in June 1989, were chosen by Khomeini. Itself established by decree, the regulations this assembly issued for the setting up of a future Assembly for Revising the Constitution ignored the representation of the people. Its members were not to be elected by the people but were determined by the leader who appointed 10 out of 66 members or by Art. 177 which stipulated that all the members of the Guardian Council, the permanent members of the Assessment Council, three government ministers, three members of the judiciary and three representatives from the universities, would be appointed to the assembly. The only members who could be said to have been (indirectly) elected by the people were 10 MPs, the five members of the Assembly of Leadership Experts and the president.

Although an amendment to Art. 177 stipulates that changed and enlarged parts of the constitution must be approved by the people in a national referendum, the democratic credentials of this kind of referendum may be seriously doubted given that the people are requested to vote yes or no to a quantity of articles, paragraphs, etc. which they can scarcely examine effectively. As if the authors of Art. 177 did not trust the carefully screened members of the Assembly for Revising the Constitution, they included a provision stating that the assembly had no right to undertake any changes affecting the Islamic character of the state or the linking of government laws and ordinances to Islamic principles and the Islamic faith.

## The System of Councils and its Suspension

The notion of *showras* or councils – in the sense of local administrative autonomy throughout the country – had, by the time of the revolution, been favoured by many politically-oriented people in Iran for several decades and was especially popular amongst members of the different ethnic minorities. Almost all the political groups which took part in the revolution spoke about *showras* although they by no means meant the same thing by the term, and certainly not everybody said openly what he or she meant. Furthermore, the revolution was itself partially organised on the basis of councils formed in various industries and in city neighbourhoods. These councils continued to exist after the fall of the old regime and they insisted on being recognised or established as institutions. In the Kurdish and the Turkmen regions in particular, the *showra* movement had acquired popularity, both in the cities and in the villages. In many cases these councils were set up or were dominated by left-wing organisations or groups representing autonomous movements.

The pressure exerted at this time by the *showra* movement was so great that the Revolutionary Council felt obliged by the end of June 1979, that is shortly after the publication of the preliminary draft of the constitution, to pass a law providing that the regional administration of the country, from the village level to the level of province, would be under the authority of *showras* that were to be elected.[141] Already on 20/4/79, Ayatollah Taleqani had announced that 'at the command of Imam Khomeini the local councils will soon be formed'.[142] And while the Assembly of Experts was still working out the pertinent articles of the constitution, the first and, for some time to come, the only attempt at electing councils was introduced and partially carried out.[143] On 6/10/79, the prime minister issued a decree which announced that councils would be set up in government administration and in certain industries.[144]

In these circumstances, it apparently seemed opportune to members of the Assembly of Experts to reserve a place for *showras* in the constitution.[145] They therefore followed the preliminary draft[146] in providing for regional councils. The councils were to undertake their duties 'with consideration for national unity and the territorial integrity of the country' and 'within the framework of their powers'. It is noteworthy that the Assembly of Experts was prepared to go a step further than the preliminary draft, even though the system of councils was not reconcilable with the concept of *velayat-e faqih*, by promising to set up councils in industries, educational facilities, administrative offices and the public service sector. Hence the Assembly of Experts, in accordance with its populist orientation and tactical considerations, complied with the vociferous demands put forward by political groups outside it. However, it emphasised that 'the decisions of the *showras* must be in conformity with Islamic principles and the laws of the country' (Art. 105).

None the less, even at this early date there was scepticism about the real intentions of the ruling jurists. Three days before his death, Ayatollah Taleqani, the most outspoken advocate of *showras* amongst the clergy, expressed doubt that they would ever be set up, arguing that the rulers were afraid they would no longer have decision-making power once councils were created.[147] His prediction has, to the time of writing, proved to be true. Over the intervening years there have been a series of delays in framing the laws and statutory instruments needed to set up *showras*; in the relevant legal texts, restrictions have been imposed on their powers; the government has refused to allow elections for the *showras* to be held and it has consistently dissociated itself from the idea of *showras* in theoretical and legal discussions. The final result is that the whole question has been transformed into one that arouses heated polemical debate inside and outside parliament. All the while, however, the government has promised that elections for the *showras* will soon take place.

The bill passed by the Revolutionary Council in June 1979 concerning local councils has led to no tangible results. In November 1982, that is 29 months later, parliament passed the Law on the Government Organisation of Islamic Councils, which ordered the founding of councils on every level of Iran's administration.[148] This law, which received approval from the Guardian Council eight days later, stipulated amongst other things that the Ministry of the Interior was to frame an election law and present it to parliament within two months (Art. 2, note 2). Moreover, it stipulated that, two months after the approval of statutory instruments, the elections were to be held (Art. 4). However, the law in question was only presented to parliament in October 1983.[149] Together with the law of November 1982, it then, without ever being put into effect, became the subject of a lengthy debate between the opponents and the supporters of *showras* which lasted until the spring of 1986. It underwent minor alterations in a first and second reading during the 2nd Majles, which in no way justified the lengthy postponement of its application. On 23/7/86, the amended law, along with its relevant electoral regulations, was approved by the Guardian Council,[150] and sent nine days later to the Ministry of the Interior for implementation.[151] All that was still required so that the elections for councils could take place was the framing and approval of the law's statutory instruments by the government. But the public waited for 18 months before the press finally reported that an assembly of provincial governors was discussing the matter. In this assembly the prime minister announced that he was dissatisfied with the law and demanded that it either be altered or replaced by a new one.[152]

The changes in question were only decided upon by parliament and the Guardian Council at the beginning of 1990.[153] This decision had scarcely been taken when some MPs remarked that the regulations affecting the composition of the central commission that would supervise the elections were drawn up in such a way as to give advantages to their opponents. They voiced their wish for changes which parliament took until 23/4/91 to decide upon. The law, as it now stood, stipulated that the Ministry of the Interior was to work out the relevant statutory instruments within one month and carry out the elections.[154] But although shortly before the approval of the latest changes by parliament in April 1991 the secretary of the Ministry of the Interior, Haqiqi, had declared that his ministry had made all the preparations for the elections for councils,[155] the elections were postponed until immediately after the parliamentary elections scheduled for May of the following year.

What actually happened after the parliamentary elections was an attempt on the part of the government to change this tiresome law yet again. This occurred after parliament, on its own initiative, had undertaken to find a substitute for the law, only to find it vetoed by the Guardian Council. According to this substitute, until councils were elected, the administration of cities was to be given over to a commission made up of representatives of the three branches of government and local persons of trustworthy reputation.[156] Parliament took this initiative after civil unrest of varying degrees of intensity, triggered by the excesses of the municipal administration against the poorer strata of the population, broke out in Mashhad, Arak, Tehran and a few other cities. The government's endeavour to alter the law concerning councils resulted in a bill published in *Resalat* on 15/5/93 which imposed far-reaching restrictions on the administrative jurisdiction of local councils and which highlighted the fact that the government had all along been set on refusing to put the relevant provisions of the constitution into practice.

Whereas the earlier additions and changes to the 1979 law chiefly consisted of further restrictions to the powers of councils, a recent government bill, which received its first reading on 24/5/94, stipulates that councils will only be set up on the level of villages, district towns and cities. The administration of the provinces and chief district cities, as before, is to remain in the hands of the central government. Likewise, even the Supreme Provincial Council, which had been stipulated in Art. 101 and 102 of the constitution, was scrapped. Under this bill, the councils have scarcely any decision-making powers. Their function consists chiefly in what the bill describes as co-operation with the authorities, as well as with the forces of order, in supervising the task of local community administration and encouraging the population to undertake self-help. City councils, however, have the power to decide on the budget of the municipal administration and those institutions connected to it, as well as to determine the taxes which citizens are to pay to them and to nominate a mayor. Only if their nomination is approved by the minister of the interior or the governor of the province and the city, is the mayor then elected. The city councils can also dismiss their mayor in cases where they approve the motion with a two-thirds majority. Finally, the bill stipulates that the councils must be elected, at the latest, two years after the law has been put into effect.[157]

The earlier changes to the law more or less tended in the same direction and strove for the same goal. According to the law of 1979, the village and city councils were to elect their mayors themselves. The executive institutions on all levels of the regional administration were obliged to implement the decisions of the councils in question. The councils had the right to work out the 'executive orders' concerning matters of culture, education, the economy, finance and the justice system within the framework of the policies determined by the central government. Moreover, they were allowed to supervise the work of the executive branch of government.

In the texts of the laws passed in 1982 and 1986, these powers were subjected to rather far-reaching restrictions. Except for the mayors of cities, the responsible officials on every other level of regional administration were to be appointed by the central government. The councils were to serve the local and central institutions of regional administration as transmitters of information, complaints, proposals, reports and opinions, as well as mediators with regard to the co-operative contributions of the regional population in carrying out construction projects. Provincial governors were only obliged 'to take note of' decisions of the councils, decisions which were to remain within the jurisdictional limits set by the constitution. The *showras*, as of now, bore the adjective Islamic. Members of the councils had to be persons who were known to be practising and committed Muslims, who were loyal to the constitution and showed no 'sympathising tendency' towards parties, organisa-tions or groups that were illegal or based on 'eclectic or atheistic attitudes'. In the 1990 amendment it was stated that: 'The appointment and dismissal of mayors for the city of Tehran and other provincial capitals would be based on a proposal from the city councils and the decision of the Ministry of the Interior.' This same condition also applied to the election and the dismissal of mayors of other cities but was not formulated in so unambiguous a sentence.

The reasons for the obvious refusal to put into effect the law concerning local councils lie first and foremost in the contradiction between an auto-nomous, participatory administration in the regions and the authoritarian, hierocratic state of the jurists. This has been true no matter which of the known legalist camps has made up the government. On the whole, the legalists are far too authoritarian and élitist to allow the people to participate in the process of decision-making, as would be the case in a system of regional administration based on *showras*. Ayatollah Taleqani had already pointed this out in the Assembly of Experts for Framing the Constitution in 1979. Later on several other government officials went on record as holding the same point of view.

In an interview with the periodical *Bayan*, Hojjat al-Eslam Mohammad Ashrafi, the chairman of the Parliamentary Committee for Internal Affairs during the 3rd Majles, expressed himself on this question more candidly than anyone else. In a somewhat cautious but quite unambiguous manner, he stated: 'I believe it is quite probable that several persons in the government do not agree with the idea of *showras*. They never have, and most likely never will, give their approval to elections for Islamic local councils, because they do not believe in councils.' Referring to the resolutions against *showras* as an institution, which were passed by the Assembly for Revising the Constitution, he continued: 'The government is disposed to doing away with the councils, just as councils have been done away with by the revision of the constitution.' He then quoted a provincial governor who had openly admitted his rejection of the *showras* because he felt he had already had enough difficulty in dealing with the three MPs for his province. 'But tomorrow it will not be three but three hundred representatives that I have to deal with ... That's why I'm against *showras*.' Ashrafi summed up his comments in the following words: 'The lack of belief in the principles of real participation of the people is the basic reason why establishing councils and holding elections have been hindered up until now.'[158]

It was the opinion of the majority of the Assembly of Experts that Islamic principles do not allow a system of councils based on a democratic interpretation, any more than they allow the sovereignty of the people. This contradiction came out quite clearly during the debate over the *showras*. Ayatollah Beheshti declared that the concept *showra*, which is derived from the Arabic word *showr* (to advise), can in no way be taken to mean a system of participation by council members in decision-making, in any case not with regard to those matters where the *shari'a* has reserved the decision for the jurists. The concept in Islam expressed rather the idea of offering advice, which meaning is attested by verses in the Koran. In this regard, he gave the example of an authoritative body which had a *showra* attached to it so that they might offer help to the presiding individual in reaching a decision on the issue at hand. He made the distinction between the will of the people and a system of *showras*, a distinction which he maintained was based on quite different 'philosophies'.[159] He rejected the system of councils. The will of the people had the function of serving as a support for government power and providing the government with legitimacy. The state must be able to find support through the people. The state must be accepted and approved by the people on all levels of government administration. But this does not mean that the will of the people should also take part in all government decisions. Beheshti only accorded participation in decision-making to the people within the limits which are set by the *shari'a* and the concept of *velayat-e faqih*.[160]

However, the constitution is not clear on this point. By the concept *showr* (to advise) can be understood *showra* (councils). A further reason for rejecting the *showras* lies in a particular interpretation of Islamic legal sources according to which the concept *showr* in the Koran and the *hadith* is not understood to mean an institution which discusses and then takes decisions on matters. All that the concept entails is that when decisions are to be made, people are recommended to take suitable advice. In the debates over the relevant laws, as well as in the press in general, this interpretation of the Islamic sources was repeatedly referred to and supported with quotations from the Koran and traditions (the *sunna*). Here are some examples:

During the debate over the law of 1982, Hojjat al-Eslam Farajollah Va'ezi expressed the view that the concept of *showras* as an institution was not based on the text of the Koran but on the attitudes of the socialists.[161] In the daily *Ettela'at*, one jurist expressed the opinion that the *showras* were contrary to the Koran because their decisions were based on the majority, whereas Islam does not give value to the voice of the majority when that voice contradicts the ordinances of God and the decisions of those who are infallible.[162] Hojjat al-Eslam Soltani uses the same argument in his series of articles entitled 'Voting from the Viewpoint of Islam and the Constitution'. Ayatollah Montazeri maintained in his book *The Juridical Foundations of the Islamic State* that the ruler is not bound to follow the judgement of persons whose advice he seeks. He alone must make the final decisions.[163] When interpreting the articles of the constitution concerning the *showras*, Madani emphasised that *showras* can only be established in connection with the Imamate and in its service. He was of the view that most advocates of the *showras* were not proper Muslims or intended to adapt Islam in an eclectic way to other ideologies.[164]

Although not all statements made about *showras* after the adoption of the constitution necessarily referred to local councils, the statements were so categorical in their rejection of *showras* as an institution for decision-making that the rejection could, without hesitation, be extended to the local councils. Another occasion on which this fundamental position became manifest was when the Assembly for Revising the Constitution went to work to abolish *showras* in connection with the office of leader, the justice system and the organisations for TV and radio. The possibility provided for in the original constitution that the office of leader be fulfilled by a council was now abolished (Art. 107), the Supreme Court ceded its position as the highest institution of the judiciary to 'an upright *mojtahed*', and it was resolved that the organisations for TV and radio were to be presided over by a chairman whom the leader would appoint (Art. 175). The arguments put forward to justify these decisions were the same as those we have already become acquainted with.[165]

However, in the radical-populist camp there are spokesmen for the regime who are advocates of *showras*. They believe that a system of *showras* can be brought into harmony with *velayat-e faqih*. This would be possible, according to Hojjat al-Eslam Khalkhali, if *showras* possessed rights for decision-making within the framework of Islamic ordinances and the rule of the jurists.[166] A system of *showras*, conceived in this fashion, would revolve around the axis of the Imamate, according to Hojjat al-Eslam Morteza Razavi. They would serve as the mediator between the Imam and the *'umma*, as an institution for planning and implementation. They would not have legislative powers because such powers belong exclusively to God and the Prophet.[167] Hojjat al-Eslam 'Ali Musavi, who has written a book against religious despotism, sees in *showras* a means which people can employ to fight against religious despotism. He believes that with the help of the *showras* those deprived of their rights would be able, in social matters, to take their destiny into their own hands. He defends the *showras* with the same enthusiasm as he defends *velayat-e faqih*. *Showras* do not contradict *velayat-e faqih* because the latter is itself opposed to religious despotism. Religious despotism is not based on *velayat-e faqih* but on government rule established through violence by hypocrites in religious dress.[168]

## Notes

1 See LB: 1979/80, p. 497 ff.

2 LB: 1983/84, p. 497 ff. Art. 49 lists the businesses and activities which the *shari'a* declares are forbidden.

3 MM 24/1/84, p. 21.

4 MM 29/1/84, p. 32. See also MM 28 to 31/12/83. The Guardian Council ruled that by this resolution parliament, on improper grounds, had 'excluded people from their natural right to be elected' (Madani: 1986–90, vol. IV, p. 330).

5 MM 8/2/91, p. 21 ff.

6 *Resalat*, 27/2/91.

7 The view of the minister of the interior (*Kayhan*, 6/2/80).

8 See LMI's statement in *Enqelab-e Eslami*, 18/4/84.

9 They were the following candidates: Karimi, Razavi, Soltani, Rahimi and Asadi-Niya. For information on the elections to this parliament see *Bayan*, Nos. 14–18 (1991–92) and *Resalat*, 13 and 16/4/88.

10 *Kayhan*, 5/4/92. According to the minister of the interior, in the end only came to 795 candidates were rejected. In some cases, the Guardian Council, which only had five days to check the suitability of more than 3,000 applicants, withdrew its decision; 232 applicants withdrew anticipating rejection by the council.

11 *Ruznameh-e Rasmi-ye Jomhuri-ye Islami*, 24/6/96.

12 *Kayhan*, 24/2/92. The then president of parliament mentioned three requirements: loyalty to the line of the Imam, obedience to the leadership and support of Rafsanjani's government (*Resalat*, 3/3/92). The radical-populist majority in the 4th Majles did not always comply with this slogan.

13 *Kayhan*, 30/3/92.

14  *Kayhan*, 5/4/92. *Resalat* reported that the candidature of Hojjat al-Eslam Hadi Ghaffari was rejected because the Special Court for the Clergy had once sentenced him to 15 strokes of the whip (21/4/92).

15  On this point see LB: 1980/81, p. 545 ff., and LB: 1986/87, p. 231 ff.

16  On the debate over this law see MM 29/12/91, p. 32 f., and 9/1/92, p. 21 ff. Concerning its rejection see *Salam*, 3/2/92.

17  According to *Resalat* (25/7/91), this is different from *nezarat-e estetla'i* (informative supervision) and means that the person exercising supervision must give his approval for an undertaking to be legitimate.

18  The minister of the interior, 'Abdollah Nuri, informed the press about this (*Kayhan*, 10/2/92).

19  On 12/7/95 parliament declared that the Guardian Council's right to *nezarat-e estesvabi* would include all stages of the elections. MM 12/7/96.

20  *Salam*, 9/3/92.

21  Statement to parliament by Mir Salam, secretary of the ministry of the interior, on 25/5/80 (*Kayhan*). The cities included: Isfahan, Darreh Gaz, Kermanshah, Dehloran, Mehran, Darreh Shahr, Nurabad, Saveh, Bahar, Rudsar and Faridan. See *Kayhan*, 31/3/80, 21–22/4/80, and 21/5/80 and 29/5/80. In Darreh Gaz, 'Abolfazl Qasemi was elected, and in Kermanshah, Karim Sanjabi, both were leading members of the National Front. Sanjabi: 1989, p. 338 f.

22  Nevertheless *Enqelab-e Eslami*, which was published abroad, maintained that political considerations were responsible for these annulments. It meant the conflict between hostile camps within the regime itself. See also Krüger: 1988, p. 10 f.

23  Nos. 17 and 18 (1992). The magazine describes in detail the annulments of the elections in Tehran. See also *Khabarnameh* for May and June 1988, a bulletin published by the League for the Defence of the Freedom and Sovereignty of the Iranian Nation.

24  See report of the minister of the interior (*Resalat*, 15/4/92).

25  *Ruznameh-e Resami-ye Jomhuri-ye Islami*, 24/6/96.

26  *Salam*, 16/4/92.

27  *Salam*, 15/4/92.

28  MM 7/6/80, 6–13/7/80 and 17/8/80.

29  See MM 25/11/86, 5/3/89, 28/6/92 and 11/8/92.

30  *Ruznameh-e Rasmi-ye Jomhuri-ye Islami*, 24/6/96.

31  Majles-e Shura-ye Eslami: 1986, p. 83.

32  Op. cit.: 1990, p. 65. The MPs were taken straight from parliament to prison.

33  Fazel Hamadani, the MP for Kabutar Ahang, resigned in protest against the arbitrary use of power by the governor of Hamadan province(*Resalat*, 22/4/91).

34  Saleh Abadi was sentenced by the Revolutionary Court to two years imprisonment (*Resalat*, 21/10/92). On the imprisonment of Asgharzadeh see *Salam*, 22/8/92.

35  Bazargan: 1984, p. 136 f.

36  MR II/654 f.

37  *Resalat*, 14/9/87.

38  *Salam*, 20/2/91.

39  *Resalat*, 1/6/96.

40  *Jomhuri-ye Islami* 17/4/96.

41  *Resalat*, 5/4/89.

42  Majles-e Showra-ye Eslami: 1986 and 1990. Our source for the 3rd Majles is information provided by its president (*Salam*, 4/5/92) and MM. For the 4th Majles see MM.

43  During the Ist Majles, 17 resolutions were rejected twice and five were rejected three times. During the 2nd Majles eight were rejected twice and only one was rejected

three times. The Labour Law was sent back and forth between parliament and the Guardian Council five times. See Madani: 1986–90, vol. IV, and M. Alef in *Resalat*, 6 and 7/6/87. In the case of the 4th Majles 18 bills were rejected more than once. See MM.

44 Madani: 1986–90, vol. VI, pp. 435 and 455 ff.

45 See the letter of the president of parliament dated 27/12/84 and the reaction to it by the Guardian Council in Madani: 1988–90. In response to an MP's request the Guardian Council wrote: 'Establishing whether laws are or are not contradictory to Islamic principles takes place in the form of *fatva*s and is the task of the *foqaha* of the Guardian Council.' Madani: op. cit., p. 451.

46 See the explanations of Ayatollah Mahdavi-Kani on the bill concerning foreign trade in Madani: op. cit., p. 234 f. See also the above mentioned series of articles by M. Alef in *Resalat* and the speech of Ayatollah Emami Kashani on the attitude of the Guardian Council towards parliamentary resolutions concerning landownership (*Resalat*, 9/6/87).

47 *Kayhan*, 13–15/8/84. See also Chapter 13.

48 *Kayhan*, 21/10/85.

49 *Kayhan*, 14/8/84.

50 *Kayhan*, 15/8/84.

51 *Enqelab-e Eslami*, 11/2/87.

52 *Salam*, 2/10/91. Zavvare'i, who was for a time an MP, compiled a collection of the complaints against the Guardian Council published them in *Resalat* 14 to 27/8/86.

53 MM 27/9/82.

54 Referring to the Guardian Council, Khamene'i stated: 'I see you, from the standpoint of ethics and learning, as upright, intelligent and honest men' (*Kayhan*, 23/2/92).

55 'Amid Zanjani: 1988–9, vol. I, p. 417.

56 Ibid.

57 *Resalat*, 4/10/86.

58 *Resalat*, 29/5/90.

59 *Jomhuri-ye Eslami*, 25/1/82 and 12/2/82, *Kayhan*, 1/1/88, and MR II/846 f.

60 The Guardian Council justifies its interpretation by referring to Art. 4 of the constitution which requires that all laws and regulations should be based on Islamic principles. See 'Amid Zanjani: 1988–89, vol. I, p. 398.

61 For other examples of intervention by the Guardian Council in matters of this kind see Madani: 1986–90, vol. IV, pp. 329, 405, 426, 429, 432, 436, etc.

62 *Resalat*, 23/2/92.

63 Mehrpur in *Resalat*, 23/2/92. According to Madani's compilation of these cases (Madani: 1986–90, vol. IV, p. 399 ff.) 90% occurred before 1985.

64 Op. cit., p. 68.

65 Madani, op. cit., p. 67.

66 Mallat (1992) points out in his comparison of the powers of the Guardian Council with those of the French Conseil Constitutionnel and the American Supreme Court that the area of jurisdiction of the Guardian Council is far greater. He sees in its prerogatives a sign of the supremacy of the judiciary over the legislature.

67 These figures are based on Mehrpur's report in *Resalat*, 29/12/92. In what looked like an attempt to resolve this contradiction, the vice-president of parliament, Hojjat al-Eslam Ruhani, said in an interview with *Resalat* (30/5/94) that these were cases which the leader had asked the Assessment Council to decide. Ruhani is apparently referring to Art. 112 of the revised constitution which, however, only has to do with the leader receiving advice from the Assessment Council. There is no provision in this article for the Assessment Council to undertake its own legislative activity.

68 *Resalat*, 23/2/92. During the 4th Majles there was a marked decline in this practice, a further indication of the purge the Guardian Council carried out before the elections. In

the 4th Majles 3 bills were sent to the Assessment Council for a inal ruling. See MM, 4th Majlis.

69  For example, the political secretary of the Ministry of the Interior remarked that the decision not to implement the law concerning parties while the war lasted must have been made by a council 'like the Assessment Council'. He added that this council had existed since 1981. *Kayhan*, 27/12/88.

70  See MM.

71  The MP in question was Abolhasan Ha'erizadeh. See MM 12/5/91, p. 20.

72  This was how Yadollah Eslami expressed himself. See MM 3/12/91, p. 20 f.

73  In this connection, former minister of the interior, Hojjat al-Eslam Nuri, mentions the following institutions: the Council for Co-ordinating Information, the Supreme Policy Council, which is made up of the presidents of the three branches of the government, 'as well as other councils' (MR III/1468).

74  Although parliament made the resumption of diplomatic relations with the UK conditional on that country presenting an apology to the Iranian people (LB: 1988/89, p. 780), the Security Council resolved that relations could be resumed without this condition being fulfilled.

75  *Resalat*, 19/10/90 and 20/11/91.

76  *Kayhan*, 8/2/92.

77  LB: 1986/87, p. 510 f.

78  See the periodical *Masa'el-e Jomhuri-ye Eslami-ye Iran*, 23/10/83, pp. 10 f., 59 f. and 64.

79  The massive revolts of 1992 in the cities of Mashhad and Arak, and the small-scale demonstrations in Tehran and other cities, were directed against this usurpation of power. See the report of the parliamentary commission which investigated the events in Mashhad in *Salam* 11/8/93. Information on the illegal measures of oppression adopted by the mayor of Tehran can be found, for example, in *Kayhan* 11/6/93, *Resalat* 16/6/93 and in both newspapers on subsequent days and years.

80  During the first two years of the 4th Majles there were 10 such formal inquiries. See the supplement to *Resalat*, 30/5/94.

81  121 MPs voted for the minister and 121 against him. In this case the Guardian Council interpreted the constitution in his favour. The minister was not bound to present proof that he was worthy of confidence; it was the job of parliament to prove the contrary. See *Salam*, 24/2/93 and 10/3/93.

82  These were against Ganji, the minister of education and Besharati, the minister of the interior. *Resalat*, 27/4/94; *Salam* 14/2/96.

83  Mir Salim was nominated by Bani-Sadr and Velayati by Khamene'i.

84  The conservatives, who were in the ascendant both inside and outside parliament, demanded that at least 12 ministerial posts be occupied by new incumbents (*Resalat*, 29/7/93). After hard negotiations, Rafsanjani managed to reduce this number to six. Surprisingly, however, a seventh candidate, Mohsen Nurbakhsh, who as minister for the economy and finance was one of the most important members of Rafsanjani's Cabinet, did not obtain the agreed vote of confidence from parliament. See *Salam*, 18/8/83. Parliament's refusal to give votes of confidence to Rafsanjani's ministers and the arguments over this problem, which went on for months, reveal how weak Rafsanjani's position was at that time.

85  *Salam*, 4/4/96.

86  For the 4th Majles the data available do not indicate this distinction. According to the supplement to *Resalat* on 30/5/94, during its first two years the 4th Majles rejected a total of 34 draft bills and legislative initiatives. The president of the 3rd Majles announced in May that 85 initiatives had been rejected (*Salam*, 4/5/92). According to our own reckoning, by the beginning of February 1992 these amounted to 102.

87  Madani: 1986–90, vol. VI, p. 427. Art. 74 stipulates: 'Bills passed in the Council of Ministers shall then be brought before parliament.'

88  MM 16/1/90, p. 19.

89  Passed on 17/11/87 and confirmed by the Guardian Council one week later. See Majles-e Showra-ye Eslami: 1990a, p. 587. The law passed by parliament on 16/1/90 limited the authorities who had to be informed to the president of parliament (LB: 1989/90, p. 711).

90  Majles-e Showra-ye Eslami: 1988, p. 9.

91  The penalty involved could be imprisonment from 3 to 12 months, and suspension from office for 6 to 12 months. The offences in question were to be punished by courts in a summary trial. See Majles-e Showra-ye Eslami: 1990a, p. 150 f.

92  Op. cit., p. 342 f. Hojjat al-Eslam 'Ali Movahhedi Savoji, a member of the Commission of Article 90, stated that officials persisted in their refusal to respond to the commission (*Resalat*, 12/10/88).

93  MR I/226.

94  *Resalat*, 12/1/94. In connection with the disputes between the moderate and the conservative camps, the 4th Majles managed in a few cases to apply its supervisory function more effectively. The clearest example was over the management of the radio and television broadcasting services which for years were controlled by Rafsanjani's brother and which were consequently seen as the domain of the president. A detailed report of the Parliamentary Commission for Islamic Guidance and Culture, which dealt with abuses in these organisations led in February 1994 to the dismissal of Rafsanjani's brother by the leader. See *Resalat*, 14/2/94 and the supplement to the issue of 30/5/94.

95  MM 15/1/89.

96  *Resalat*, 2/6/87.

97  *Resalat*, 2/6/92.

98  *Kayhan*, 21/1/89.

99  *Kayhan*, 22/9/90.

100  *Kayhan*, 12/10/91.

101  These quotations come from *Sahifeh-e Nur* cited in M. Arezumand 'Elections and Parliament in the Words of the Imam' in *Ettela'at*, 3/4/92.

102  *Kayhan*, 17/10/85.

103  Majles-e Showra-ye Eslami: 1981, 1985, 1989 and 1993.

104  MR I/226.

105  The figures may simply be the result of a more clever public relations policy. The opposition maintains fundamental doubts about the government's statistics on electoral participation. As *Enqelab-e Eslami* would have it 'on the basis of well informed sources' the published figures for the June 1993 last presidential elections were two to three times higher than the reality (15/8/93). However, claims of this kind from the opposition can be doubted just as much as the government's claims.

106  *Salam*, 20/4/92 and 12/5/92; *Ettela'at*, 21/4/92.

107  *Ruznameh-e Rasmi-ye Jomhuri-ye Islami*, 24/6/96 and Mohammad Maleki, 'Tahlili az Entekhabat-e Panjomin Dowreh-e Majles-e Showra-ye Islami dar Tehran,' *Iran-e Farda*, No. 25, 1996 pp. 12–15; *Enqelab-e Islami* puts the total number of eligible voters in Tehran at 6.7 million. (No. 381, April 1996, p. 7).

108  *Resalat*, 28/3/92 and 9/4/92.

109  *Resalat*, 11/4/92.

110  Op. cit.

111  The regulation of relationships between the three branches of government was a power of the president before the revision of the constitution.

112  See LB: 1981/82, p. 44 ff.; LB: 1985/86, p. 174 ff.

113  He was elected on 24/7/81 and a month later on 30/8/81 murdered in a bomb attack.

114  See Menashri: 1988; *Kayhan*, 9/7/87; *Salam*, 15/5/93.

115  *Salam*, 21, 24 and 26/6/93. Again the discrepancy between the two sets of statistics is based on different estimates of the total electorate.

116  The revised form of Art. 109 makes the possession of 'the scholarly capacity to issue *fatvas*' the sole requirement. Thus previously specified virtues have been dropped in favour, simply, of the capacity of the leader to issue *fatvas* within the framework 'of basic divisions of *feqh*'. According to the new version of Art. 107, the office of leader can only be held by a single person.

117  On this point and on the revision of the constitution see Schirazi: 1991.

118  *Ettela'at*, 10/6/89.

119  MR I/196 f.

120  LB: 1980/81, p. 542. The same requirement appears in the statutory instruments for this law (LB: 1982/83, p. 92).

121  This is also the view of interpreters of the Constitution such as Hojjat al-Eslam 'Amid Zanjani (1988–89, vol. I, p. 263) and Madani (1986–90, vol. II, p. 157 f.). Madani writes: 'Certainly the leader or a member of the Leadership Council must come from amongst the *marja's*.'

122  MR I/176.

123  *Resalat*, 1/5/89. This contradicts the thesis, which Ayatollah Azari Qomi also subscribed to, that the Assembly of Experts does not determine who is leader but simply recognises him as such. The leader is leader by virtue of his own capacities – including his qualification as a *marja'* .

124  MR I/181.

125  Op. cit., p. 196 f.

126  MR II/656.

127  Op. cit., p. 705.

128  These concerns were expressed by Ayatollah Mahmud Mohammadi Gilani (op. cit., p. 684).

129  This criterion, however, was not applied in the case of Khamene'i.

130  According to Ayatollah Yazdi: 'Since the Experts are chosen by the people, the leader is also chosen by the people.'

131  LB: 1980/81, p. 542. 'The highest level of the curriculum' is a translation of '*dars-e kharej*', the courses offered to students who have completed their preliminary (*moqaddamat*) and intermediate studies (*sath*).

132  LB: 1982/83, p. 92.

133  Prime Minister Musavi's proposal to extend eligibility to experts in other scholarly and scientific disciplines was rejected with this argument in the Assembly for Revising the Constitution (MR II/691).

134  *Ettela'at*, 16/7/90.

135  Ayatollah Azari Qomi admitted openly that the decision was taken in order to stop 'unwanted elements from infiltrating' the Assembly of Leadership Experts (*Resalat*, 26/7/90).

136  The terms employed by Azari Qomi in *Resalat*, 28/7/90.

137  See the explanations given by Ayatollah Emami Kashani in *Kayhan*, 15/8/90.

138  *Resalat* and *Kayhan*, 7/10/90. On this point see also *Bayan*, Nos. 5 and 6 (1990), p. 19 ff.

139  *Resalat*, 13/10/90.

140  *Salam*, 20/5/96.

141  See the Local Councils Law in LB: 1979/80, p. 48 ff.

142 *Ayandegan*, 21/4/79.

143 On 12/10/79, elections for city councils were held in 140 cities. However, the preparation and organisation were so inadequate that they either produced no results or the results could not be recognised. The minister of the interior, however, saw as the cause of this failure the low level of participation of the electorate. See *Kayhan*, 15/10/79. Some councils, on a trial basis and under immediate pressure, had actually been elected previously, for instance in Kurdistan.

144 Published in *Kayhan* the same day.

145 Art. 6, 7, and 100–6.

146 Art. 3 and 74.

147 M. Taleqani: 1983, p. 63.

148 LB: 1982/83, p. 102 ff.

149 *Kayhan*, 11/5/85.

150 LB: 1986/87, p. 191 ff.

151 *Kayhan*, 2/8/86.

152 *Resalat*, 4/9/88.

153 LB: 1990/91, p. 588 ff.

154 LB: 1991/92, p. 47 ff.

155 *Kayhan*, 22/4/91.

156 MM 26/8/92, 30/8/92 and 1/9/92.

157 *Salam*, 24/5/94. The bill received a 2nd reading on 23 April 1995 but was rejected by the Guardian Council. On 22 April 1996 parliament began the process of revision but so far there is no sign that this has been completed.

158 No. 10 (1991), p. 12 ff. One should not forget that *Bayan*, which conducted the interview and published it with approval, was edited by former minister of the interior, Hojjat al-Eslam 'Ali Akbar Mohtashami, who during his time in office took no visible steps towards holding elections for the *showra*s. The secretary for social affairs in the Ministry of the Interior was far more candid when as early as 1/5/85 he admitted that the law concerning the *showra*s would not be implemented because it did not correspond to the system of government of the Islamic Republic. See *Kayhan*, 1/5/85.

159 According to Beheshti, all disagreements over the nature of councils could be explained in terms of the importance attached to the will of the people. M I/359.

160 M 327, 330, 400.

161 MM 20/7/82.

162 23/8/89. The Shi'a recognise 14 persons as infallible: the Prophet Mohammad, his daughter Fatima and the 12 Imams.

163 Montazeri: 1988–92, vol. III, p. 77 ff. He is here indulging in self-criticism because in the Assembly of Experts he voted in favour of government based on *showra*s. 'As it appears, the system of *showra*s is contrary to the path that wise men and jurists have followed. The country and the people cannot be ruled that way.'

164 Madani: 1986–90, vol. III, p. 152. There are too many contributions to cite them all here. On this point see the detailed statements of Ayatollah Kazem Ha'eri: 1985, p. 85 ff., and 'Amid Zanjani: 1989, 454 f.

165 MR I/231,321; II/656,707. The order for these changes was given by Khomeini (MR II/548).

166 *Kayhan*, 14/5/86.

167 *Kayhan*, 19/5/86.

168 Musavi: 1982, p. 87 ff.

# SIX

# The Suppression of Fundamental Rights

The attempt to make the constitution conform in practice to the absolute *velayat-e faqih* and to suppress the sovereignty of the people entails a further extension of the restrictions its text already places upon democratic rights in the name of 'Islamic principles'. The requirements of the hierocracy were what defined 'Islamic principles' both in passing laws and putting them into effect, and what determined the level of tolerance of fundamental rights.

In order to judge the extent of the restrictions that have been placed on democratic rights, it is necessary to look briefly at how the Islamic state has dealt with the fundamental rights of its citizens. This will at the same time provide an opportunity to become acquainted with the arguments employed to justify these restrictions. We begin with an examination of the way democratic rights have been treated in the Islamic Republic concentrating on the manner with which the hierocrats dealt with political parties and the press.

## The Ban on Political Parties

Art. 28 of the constitution states that: 'Parties, societies, political and corporate associations, as well as Islamic organisations and organisations of the recognised religious minorities, are free', as long as they do not harm 'the foundations of the country's independence, freedom, national unity', or 'Islamic principles and the foundations of the Islamic Republic'. The explicit intention of Art. 28 (ignoring the qualifications it contains) corresponds to an established tendency that has grown over the last few decades for citizens in the urban areas of Iran to form political and corporate organisations whenever the regime in power has allowed such activity or has not been in a position to hinder it. This was the case during the revolutionary period of 1978 and 1979, when virtually all currents of political thought took advantage of the prevailing freedom to found organisations of varying size and importance. In the wake of almost three decades of dictatorship a great many groups of this kind came in to being and in the first few months after the revolution their number exceeded 100.[1]

But the freedom which made it possible to form these organisations did not last for long. The legalists began their assault even before they had secured government power for themselves. Before the revolution they attempted, through repressive methods, to exclude the leaders of the non-

Islamic groups from directing revolutionary actions; afterwards, they put aside all restraint and went about suppressing the political organisations which they found unacceptable.

The high point of the initial phase of this development was reached on 12/8/79 when the National Democratic Front (Jebheh-e Demokratik-e Melli), along with many other left-wing organisations, led a demonstration in Tehran involving several hundred thousand people against the prohibition of the daily newspaper *Ayandegan*. The reaction to the demonstration reached a climax when, six days later, Khomeini delivered a speech to a group of supporters in Qom expressing his regret that he had not acted 'in a revolutionary manner' from the beginning. He had made the mistake of giving 'the wicked elements' of the population the opportunity to push their way to the front.

> Had we acted in a revolutionary manner from the beginning ... and broken the pen of all the hireling organs of the press, forbidden all the wicked periodicals and newspapers, brought their chief editors before the courts, forbidden the indecent parties, punished their party leaders, set up the gallows on the public squares and wiped out the wicked perpetrators, these problems would never have arisen ... Had we been revolutionaries, we would never have allowed these wicked perpetrators to appear. We would have forbidden all parties and front-movements.[2] We would have founded a single party, namely the Party of God, the party of those who have been deprived of their rights.

Khomeini promised that from that moment he would act 'in a revolutionary manner'. He demanded that the Revolutionary Public Prosecutor forbid all 'subversive periodicals' which were 'directed against the people' and that their editors be brought before the courts along with people who 'have founded conspiratorial parties and form their leadership'.[3]

Four days later the public prosecutor, Ayatollah Azari Qomi, complied with Khomeini's demands and ordered the arrest of the secretary of the National Democratic Front, Hedayatollah Matin-Daftari, and the confiscation of his property.[4] This was a prelude to outlawing the organisation. In addition, the day after Khomeini's speech the Revolutionary Council decided to outlaw the Democratic Party of Kurdistan.

Although Khomeini's attitude towards parties was perfectly clear,[5] action against them could only be taken one step at a time. At first only the most recalcitrant were dealt with and further prohibitions were postponed for tactical and organisational reasons. However, from the date of Khomeini's speech to early March 1981 when parliament began discussing the law concerning political parties, other parties were declared illegal. Amongst them was the Islamic People's Republican Party (Hezb-e Jomhuri-ye Khalq-e Mosalman), which was prohibited in January 1981.[6]

Looking at the actions taken against political parties before and after parliament's discussion and approval of the law on parties (March to July 1981), it is difficult to avoid the conclusion that the purpose of this law was primarily to sanction the status quo ante. And if the actual proceedings against parties went much further than the law allowed, this is explained by the fact that the law was passed at a time when it was still not possible to formulate legislation in such a way that it corresponded in full to reality.

The Law on the Activities of Parties, Societies, Political and Corporate Organisations, Islamic Associations and Associations Founded by Recognised Religious Minorities made the formation of parties dependent on a permit from the Ministry of the Interior (Art. 8). The permit is issued by a commission of the ministry composed of one representative of the chief public prosecutor, one from the Supreme Court, one from the Ministry of the Interior and two representatives of parliament. This commission also exercises supervision over the activities of approved parties and organisations (Art. 10). Should it find that the activities of any party are contrary to the law, it can withdraw its permit and propose before the courts that the party be dissolved (Art. 15 and 17). Ten loosely defined offences provide justification for requesting that a party be dissolved. These include activities 'which exploit the existing religious, racial and cultural diversity in Iranian society in order to stir up or intensify conflict within the ranks of the Iranian nation ... which harm the Islamic principles and foundations of the Islamic Republic ... which promote anti-Islamic propaganda', as well as those which involve 'the distribution of books and other publications that lead people astray', or undermine the independence of the country (Art. 16).

This list of offences reflects the recriminations that the leaders of the Islamic Republic had from the beginning made against the political parties which were repeated by the regime's supporters during the parliamentary debate over the law. Hosein Harati felt that the spirit of the constitution had found expression in the law and warned against imitating a Western model of political parties. The Islamic Republic, he went on to stress, was itself a model worthy of imitation. 'We do not want democracy but a republic which is under the supervision of *velayat-e faqih*.' He characterised 'the small political groups' that had emerged after the revolution as 'products of Russian or American origin' and confirmed that the law had been created to stop their activities.[7] His colleague, Mohammad Taqi Besharat, declared that the law would guarantee the freedom only of those who pursued the same goal as *velayat-e faqih*. He described the opponents of the regime as 'microbes in the body of society' and said that 'measures of hygiene' should be applied in a society that was thus afflicted.[8]

During its second reading, MPs put forward proposals to make the bill more stringent. Movahhedi Savoji proposed that groups whose political programme was suspect should simply be refused a permit – there was no need to wait until they contravened the law.[9] To prevent the fomenting of conspiracy by parties, Ayat proposed that they be obliged to divulge the names of their members to the commission provided for in Art. 10.[10] However, a proposal to define offences cited in the law as political which, in accordance with Art. 168 of the constitution, would have meant that they would be tried before a jury, was rejected. The spokesman for the Ministry of the Interior in parliament, Zavvare'i, contested the political character of such offences and cited, by way of confirmation, the case of Qasemlu, first secretary of the Democratic Party of Kurdistan, who in his opinion was guilty of attempting to violate the territorial integrity of Iran.[11] Many MPs condemned the bill because it was not strict enough, remarking that it was adequate neither for the ideology of the Party of God nor for the needs of the people.[12]

The opposition declared itself to be against the bill. Mohammad Mohammadi, for example, maintained that it was permeated with the spirit of dictatorship. Mohammad Mojtahed Shabestari pointed out that it was contrary to the constitution which did not stipulate that parties could only be founded if they received permission from the government authorities.[13]

By the time the law was finally passed and approved by the Guardian Council even Bani-Sadr, whose term of office was meant to run to June 1981, was in exile. Indeed, the only political organisations that were still tolerated were the Tudeh Party and the majority faction of the Feda'iyan-e Khalq which was close to the Tudeh. Both these groups had put the full weight of their support behind the regime, partly out of conviction and partly for opportunistic reasons, and had even accepted some of the dirty work of policing on its behalf. But even they were only tolerated until February 1983, when they were accused of treason, espionage and conspiracy and disbanded. On 5/9/81 two weeks before the law on political parties was approved by parliament, the chief public prosecutor announced that 'the Islamic ordinances would be applied to the small groups'. 'Small groups' was the contemptuous term used by spokesmen of the regime to designate opposition organisations, in particular the radical organisations. Whoever was found guilty of one of the five offences enumerated in this announcement was labelled a perpetrator of evil (*mofsed*) and an armed insurgent (*mohareb*), and threatened with the severest punishments. The offences in question were: active work as a member or sympathiser in one of 'the small groups', disturbance of public order through rioting or spreading fear in direct or indirect connection with 'the small groups', armed insurrection and the concealment of weapons and ammunition, as well as giving refuge, money and other forms of help to 'the small groups'.[14]

This announcement made clear the severity with which the security services and the justice system dealt with opposition organisations, their members as well as their sympathisers. According to Amnesty International, in the first half of 1981 alone 2,444 people were executed.[15] Characteristic of the severe treatment of the opposition is the reproach of apostasy made by Khomeini against the National Front when its leaders called upon the people of Tehran to participate in a demonstration on 15/6/81 against parliament's approval of the law of retaliation (*qesas*). He threatened the leaders of the Front with the death penalty if they did not repent while the leaders of the Liberation Movement and Bani-Sadr had to make a public apology on TV and the radio because they had supported the Front's appeal.[16]

Since the prohibitions on parties after the revolution were for the most part imposed before the law on parties was passed,[17] one must again conclude that the real purpose of this law was not simply to regulate political parties. To this day, the hierocratic regime, even within the narrow framework of this law, is not prepared to tolerate opposition parties. And the fact that for a number of years there was no question of enforcing the law also leads to the same conclusion. Typically, its statutory instruments were only finally drawn up in the Ministry of the Interior and sent before the Council of Ministers in 1987.[18] It was not until the end of 1988 that the press reported that the need to take political parties seriously concerned some circles of the hierocracy and the path was cleared for setting up several political and corporate organisations.

Until this time, the authorities had always resorted to the same arguments they used when they set about annihilating the opposition organisations after the revolution. At the beginning of 1988, the minister of the interior, Hojjat al-Eslam Mohtashami, stated in an interview with *Kayhan*[19] that the law on parties had not been put into effect because parties in Iran did not have a good reputation and were unable to win the trust of the people. Even the nationalist parties had 'turned their back on the people and looked towards foreign [powers]. For this reason, parties are hated by the people and the people have driven them away.' In another interview given to *Ettela'at* on 25/2/88, Mohtashami described the parties as: 'groups which had no real contact with the people and are like foreigners with regard to the people's mentality and customs. They simply believe it is possible to win a place in the thoughts of the people by means of extravagant and mendacious propaganda.'

The prohibition of opposition parties was also in part justified by the claim that a religious community could not allow itself to be split into parties. A community that moves towards one common goal, led by a wise leader who is God's representative, could have no reason to allow itself to be divided. Differences of opinion were not so great as to justify the formation of political parties. The only possible party in such a community is Hezbollah (the Party of God) which embraces all members and consequently does not need any special organisation to represent it.

The same attitude also contributed significantly to the fact that even the Islamic parties did not survive for long. The most important of these were the Islamic Republican Party (Hezb-e Jomhuri-ye Eslami) and the Organisation of the Mojahedin of the Islamic Revolution (Sazman-e Mojahedin-e Enqelab-e Eslami). Having come into being in part as a reaction to the activities of the opposition during the first months after the revolution, these parties lost their function once the opposition parties were dissolved. But this was not the only, or even the most decisive reason for their dissolution. The Mojahedin of the Islamic Revolution disbanded itself at Khomeini's recommendation on 6/10/86[20] and the IRP on 2/6/86. In a letter to Khomeini the two spokesmen for the IRP, Rafsanjani and Khamene'i, justified its dissolution by saying that the party had achieved its goal – the establishment of the *velayat-e faqih* – and therefore no longer had any reason to exist. 'On the contrary', their letter stated, 'in the present circumstances there is a danger that forming political parties will give rise to disputes with the result that the unanimity of the nation will be impaired and energy will be wasted in fighting and eliminating one another.'[21]

Other Islamic organisations, such as the Hey'at-e Mo'talefeh-e Eslami (Islamic Coalition Association), JAMA, the Feda'iyan-e Eslam and OMMAT, ceased their activities at different times after the law on parties was passed. Three of the Islamic parties deserve special consideration: the Hojjatiyeh Association, the group around Mehdi Hashemi and the Liberation Movement (Nehzat-e Azadi) led by Mehdi Bazargan.

The Hojjatiyeh Association had existed since 1953. It was known for its conservative, quietist and unpolitical standpoint and for this reason had been attacked by several Islamicists. After the revolution it joined with the ruling legalists so that it could influence political events at government level. Its growing influence at the time had the effect of arousing resistance, especially from the radical-populist camp of the hierocracy. On 12/7/83 Khomeini finally called on the organisation 'to join the wave which is presently driving the nation forward'. The association complied with the intended sense of Khomeini's public statement and 11 days later announced it would stop all its activities. But this did not mean its complete retirement: the radical legalists repeated attacks prove that it still existed after that date and still had influence in the conservative camp of the hierocracy.[22] On 15/12/93, *Resalat* quoted a warning from 'Ali Mohammad Gharibani MP that the members of this association were occupying top offices in the ministries.[23]

The dissolution of the group around Mehdi Hashemi followed a quite different pattern. Developments reached a climax with the execution of its leaders on 29/9/87 and the subsequent annihilation of many of its members. What provoked this extreme turn of events was its radical and, for a while, rather anti-clerical stance, which before the revolution had led to the accusation that it was responsible for the murder of the conservative Ayatollah Shamsabadi. The decision to move decisively against the group was taken in 1986 when it made public the secret negotiations with the United States which eventually became known as the Iran-Contra affair. Because of the group's close connections with Ayatollah Montazeri, its fall played an important part in his dismissal from the position of designated successor to Khomeini.[24]

Although the more or less total cessation of the Liberation Movement's activities was only decided and enforced after Khomeini's death, even before that date its activities were severely restricted. By the autumn of 1988 these restrictions had reached such proportions that the party felt obliged to describe its continued existence as '[a form of] humiliation and betrayal [of its ideals]'. This statement occurs in a letter to Khomeini dated 4/10/88 in which the party describes the restrictions imposed on it through five successive phases of intensified persecution. The fifth included the arrest of 80 of its members, the occupation of its central office, the confiscation of its funds and documents and the slandering of its members as spies, apostates and hirelings of foreign powers. The letter went on to say that, in the face of such strangulation, the party had little choice but to effect 'its own honourable self-dissolution'.

There have been a number of explanations of why, by contrast to other opposition political organisations, the LMI was allowed a limited degree of activity. In its letter to Khomeini, the party itself mentions that the long-standing relationship of trust between him and its leaders, as well as political interests and propaganda considerations were responsible for its continued existence. Other reasons were the role Bazargan played in initiating and popularising the Islamic movement and later in the formation of the provisional revolutionary government, the LMI's commitment to strictly legal activities, the regime's assumption that the party was harmless and the fact that its continued existence benefited the regime's image.

Although the LMI's letter to Khomeini did nothing to stop the moves against it, the party did not dissolve itself. It continued limited activity, even after Khomeini's death, until in May 1990 it suffered its greatest set-back. This occurred after 90 well-known members and the League for the Defence of Freedom and the Sovereignty of the Iranian Nation[25] wrote a letter to President Rafsanjani about the deplorable state of affairs which had prevailed in Iran over 'the last ten years'. The letter demanded that the president rectify matters by restoring the sovereign rights to the people and by respecting the fundamental rights of the nation.

A storm of indignation and calumny broke out in the pro-government press against the signatories of this letter. A wave of arrests, albeit rather selective arrests, followed and in prison detainees were subjected to the same painful procedures which during the Islamic Republic's short history had caused so many of their predecessors to abandon their opposition and to make involuntary confessions. In secret trials which took place one year after the arrests, they were sentenced to varying terms in prison and later released or let out on parole for an unspecified period. In an interview on 9/12/91 with the special envoy of the Human Rights Commission of the United Nations, Galindo Pohl, the LMI's leaders described their organisation's situation as follows:

> Hindrances, restrictions and disturbances still exist, just as before; in many respects they are even more stringent. The office and the archive of the movement are presently in the custody of the government. Four of the active, leading members of the movement are still being held in prison. Those who have been temporarily released are constantly exposed to threats. The movement's relation to the population is confronting innumerable hindrances. In view of the present circumstances, the Liberation Movement finds itself for all practical purposes in an unavoidable state of dissolution and inactivity. It is not allowed to undertake any action, other than in an extremely narrow area. The account which the government gives of the freedom and security of opposition parties, and in particular the Liberation Movement, and the participation of these parties in elections, is blatantly false.

In the same interview the LMI's leaders mentioned that they had made an application to the Ministry of the Interior for permission to operate as a political organisation after the government had publicly declared that it would react positively to such applications. But they had received no response.[26] On 22/10/92 the party did finally receive an answer through the newspaper *Resalat*, which reported that the commission with relevant jurisdiction (known as the Commission of Article 10) within the Ministry of the Interior had rejected the application on 9/8/92. In the elections to the 5th Majles was able once more to be active in a limited fashion. Unlike other opposition groups it did not at first boycott the elections, but the credentials of all but one of its candidates were rejected and it was compelled to withdraw.

## The New Debate on Political Parties

The LMI's application, referred to in the interview with Galindo Pohl, was made against the background of a debate which began a few months after the end of the war with Iraq and continued with varying intensity for several months. On 30/11/87, Montazeri demanded that the government put into effect the law on parties.[27] Two days later the minister of the interior announced his willingness to comply with this demand.[28] In practice, however, he put off carrying out his promise until, during a parliamentary debate, he was reproached for arbitrarily postponing the implementation of the law in question.[29] As an excuse, he argued that parliament was responsible for the delay because it had not chosen its representatives for the commission set up by Art. 10 of the law.[30] Thereupon parliament proceeded to elect its representatives on 27/9/88. Two months later it was announced that the Ministry of the Interior was ready to receive applications for permission for political parties and associations to register under the law. The deadline for the initial phase of the procedure was to be 31/12/88. Meanwhile, the National Security Council held a session in order to define the tasks of the security organs and the information services in connection with possible illegalities which might be committed by the parties about to be founded. The council then announced that permission would be given to parties 'that were committed to activities in accordance with the goals of the revolution and the ruling system of the Islamic Republic, and in harmony with belief in *velayat-e faqih*.'[31]

At the same time the debate over whether parties were at all necessary continued. *Ettela'at* presented a summary of the arguments for and against concluding that they should not be allowed. The advocates of parties expressed their opinion at a 'gathering for political analysis' held in the University of Tehran. Mohammad Ebrahim Asgharzadeh, the parliamentary representative on the Commission of Article 10, described political parties as 'social engineers' and an 'achievement of humanity that must be enlisted in the process of governing society.' As a member of the commission he gave assurances that serious thought was being given to putting the law into effect. In the same gathering, the secretary of the Ministry of the Interior,

Sadr, affirmed that the implementation of the law would be accompanied by guarantees of political freedoms. His colleague in the ministry, 'Abdolvahed Musavi Lari, gave assurances that even parties that did not agree with the principle of *velayat-e faqih* would be permitted.[32]

*Kayhan* for its part formulated three questions on the issue of parties, and invited government officials to give their replies which it published over a period of three months. Most were in favour of parties. One of the most interesting was that of the former minister of heavy industry, Behzad Nabavi, who argued that there was an intellectual vacuum in the Islamic Republic. Scarcely anyone possessed a viable programme for governing the country and the vacuum must be filled by political parties. Moreover, Nabavi contested the thesis that there was no place for parties in an Islamic society maintaining that: 'Even Islamic groups can be based on differing ideologies. Their conception of Islam does not have to be identical, even though they are in agreement on the fundamentals of faith.'[33] The former minister of agriculture, Mohammad Salamati, drew attention to the contribution parties could make to the post-war reconstruction programmes. Parties could promote the population's participation in social activities and hinder capitalists from taking control of everything. They were a guarantee that freedom of speech and publication would be respected. Indeed, society needed to confront ideas in order to develop.[34]

The opponents of parties also participated in this debate. Hedayatollah Agha'i MP stated that: 'Forcing parties to exist in underdeveloped countries is a comedy that merely serves to maintain the appearance of democracy.' He went on to assert that the system of *velayat-e faqih* could not be brought into harmony with party activities in the usual sense of the word since its overriding principle was 'behaving with absolute obedience in matters of political and social relations'.[35] Mohammad Hojjati Kermani argued that in present circumstances parties would lead to anarchy.[36] Rafsanjani also took part in this debate as an opponent of parties. In a session of the Assembly for Revising the Constitution on 2/5/89, he referred to the dissolution of the Islamic Republican Party and maintained that if any party had ever had the prospect of success, it was surely this one. He went on to say that if parties were allowed to exist, leading personalities would not participate in them.[37]

The opponents of parties expressed their views chiefly in a survey which was conducted by *Resalat* and published in the issues for the month of Esfand 1367 (20 February – 20 March 1989). In a résumé of current opinion, voiced in part in this survey, the newspaper distinguished four different positions: 1) support for a single-party system, 2) approval of total freedom to form parties, 3) rejection of any kind of party system, and 4) advocacy of a restricted freedom for parties. According to *Resalat* positions 1) and 2) did not have much support whereas position 3) was supported by a considerable number of government officials and opinion leaders. Position 4) had little support. The newspaper itself supported position 4) but pointed out that the creation of parties in the usual Western sense of the word would mean giving validity to the views of the majority of the people. In a government based on ideology, however, these had no worth. 'Ideology has the power to declare any majority opinion invalid'.[38]

The debate over parties took place exclusively amongst government officials and opinion leaders. Scarcely any of these people seriously held the view that the opposition should be given the right to organise itself politically. Indeed their attitude is best illustrated by the treatment of the Liberation Movement. The debate died down after a few months, without leading to any serious results.[39] Every now and then it was simply reported that a particular religious, political or corporate group had applied for or been granted permission. The Association of Islamic Artists and Writers, the Islamic Women's Association, the Organisation of the Feda'iyan of Islam, the Party of Islamic Government Leadership, the Association of Zoroastrian Priests, and the Association of Students of the Indian Subcontinent were some of the groups mentioned in such reports.[40]

The most important groups to be legally constituted as political organisations at this time, or constituted once again, were the Union of Militant Clergy (Majma'-e Ruhaniyun-e Mobarez), the League of Militant Clergy (Jame'eh-e Ruhaniyat-e Mobarez), the Organisation of the Mojahedin of the Islamic Revolution and the Organisation of Islamic Unity.[41] The first of these had been formed as the result of a split in the second, which occurred in connection with the elections for the 3rd Majles in March 1988. The Union of Militant Clergy brought together under its aegis the radical-populist clergy of Tehran, including the president of parliament, Karrubi. However, it had ceased activity after the heavy defeat of the radical camp in the elections for the 4th Majles.[42] On the basis of an invitation issued to Karrubi by Khamene'i in the summer of 1993, the organisation had verbally agreed to resume its activities but did not do so in practice. The second organisation, whose membership consists principally of conservative clergy, exists, in the words of its ex-chairman, Ayatollah Mahdavi-Kani,[43] 'as a spiritual organisation, part of whose duty is to intervene in politics but which does not like the methods of parties as a means of furthering its [own] work.'[44] The League of Militant Clergy considers itself above political parties and on this basis demands exceptional treatment. The two other organisations rarely show much obvious sign of life. However, before the elections to the 5th Majles their activity became less secretive. In January 1996 the Organisation of Islamic Unity openly held its 3rd Congress. It also participated in the elections in a joint list with the League of Militant Clergy. It succeeded in excluding candidates favoured by Rafsanjani from this list but was not successful in getting its own core candidates elected. It has also, it appears, managed to establish its hegemony over the newspaper *Resalat* during this period. The Mojahedin of the Iranian Revolution began publication of its own fortnightly journal *'Asr-e Ma* on 19 October 1994. It participated in the elections to the 5th Majles in alliance with other state-oriented groups and, although it is difficult to calculate exactly how many, succeeded in winning a significant number of seats.

Given the tendency amongst the various power blocs participating in the hierocracy to exclude one another from governmental offices it is only natural to ask why the debate over parties should have occurred at this particular time. The following considerations are of significance in answering this question.

Firstly, with the end of the war against Iraq the argument used to counter criticism of Khomeini's one-man rule lost most of its credibility. Similarly, the fact that the war had not ended in victory undermined the belief that political forces should put aside their differences and join together against the external enemy. Since military fiasco was accompanied by government failure in all areas of domestic policy, the collapse of confidence in the leadership was further exacerbated. The result was a demand for participation in political decision-making, one manifestation of which was the debate over parties.

Secondly, it was necessary to promise participation in political, economic and social decision-making to ensure the population's participation in the reconstruction of the country and in surmounting the crisis which after the war engulfed all aspects of daily life. For a short time at least, the leaders of the Islamic state were aware of their inability to solve this problem on their own. *Resalat* quite openly connected the promises the government had made over the formation of parties with this awareness: 'If today there is talk of freedom for party activities, this has occurred precisely at a time when the burden of decision-making has outgrown the capacities of the trustees of the state.'[45] Indeed the freedom to establish parties was not the only promise made in response to the post-war crisis. An effective policy of reconstruction depended on private sector investment. Even Ayatollah Khalkhali, despite his radical, state-oriented discourse, recommended that 'business should be turned over to the private sector.'[46] The first five-year plan, drawn up at this time, relied to an unusual extent on the private sector.

Thirdly, the debate over parties owed its existence to the growing conviction within the hierocracy that there was no sense in denying their deeply rooted divergences and conflicts of interest. The dissolution of the Islamic Republican Party, which was primarily due to the conflicts between its different power blocs, had revealed this fact only too clearly. These conflicts, which were brought out in the open during the elections for the 3rd Majles and also caused the split within the League of Militant Clergy, made a mockery of any attempt to trivialise the differences between the camps. In February 1988, Farajollah Afrazideh MP described the tension caused by these disagreements as 'a hell of nerves'[47] Of course, as in the past, an attempt was made to play them down and there was still constant talk of the unity of the IRP.[48] But the conflict persisted and the split widened even further. With this situation in mind, on 16/11/87 Rafsanjani admitted that there were 'two powerful wings' within the Islamic Republic. 'Basically they represent two unorganised parties. Indeed, when they describe the positions they hold, they are two parties, not two wings.'[49] As we saw above, Rafsanjani was opposed to a party system, but other spokesmen for the hierocracy were more inclined to take account of the reality of the situation and advocated the creation of parties as a way out.

Advocates of a party system were more numerous in the radical, state-oriented camp of the hierocracy which enjoyed a great amount of power in the government and in parliament at the time the debate over enforcing the law began. During the 3rd Majles they increased the number of their MPs and benefited from Khomeini's direct protection. Yet even at this time, several factors were beginning to undermine their position and they were already in decline. Military defeat, the economic and political crisis in the economy, Khomeini's imminent death and the preponderance of the conservative clergy in the state apparatus gave them reason to fear for the future. Their only chance of countering these factors was to unite their forces. Having for so long enjoyed the advantages of the slogan of unity that oppressed the minority, they understood what awaited them if they became a minority. By advocating the creation of parties, they aimed to rally their forces and consolidate their power. The split within the League of Militant Clergy and the resumption of activity on the part of the Mojahedin of the Islamic Revolution were the practical steps which they took in this direction. Yet by adopting these measures and promoting arguments in favour of parties, the radical camp was unable to prevent its own demise. The organisations the radicals founded are now for all practical purposes defunct although every now and then they still extol the virtues of parties and stress the importance of allowing them to exist.[50]

## Suppression of the Opposition Press

Khomeini's speech of August 1979, in which he announced the pending revolutionary suppression of opposition activities, also applied to the opposition press. The opposition press had already by this date been the target of government and Hezbollah attacks.[51] The first such attack was against the newspaper *Ayandegan*, which was shut down on 8/8/79. Twelve days later, 22 other organs of the press suffered the same fate. When in July 1981 the newspapers published by the LMI, the National Front and by Bani-Sadr (*Mizan*, *Jebheh-e Melli* and *Enqelab-e Eslami*) were obliged to close, the opposition press ceased to exist. Of the 444 newspapers and magazines that had appeared during the first year after the revolution, less than a half remained a few years later. In 1981 alone, 175 newspapers were shut down. By March 1988, the total number of newspapers and periodicals published in Iran was no more than 121.[52] These were without exception loyal to the regime. This triumph over the opposition press was commented on in a book about 'the foreign controlled press' published by the Ministry of Islamic Guidance in the following terms: 'At the beginning of the revolution the Islamic state was confronted by hundreds of multifarious organs of the press, amongst which, of course, an Islamic press was not represented.' However, 'the tumultuous Islamic movement smashed the unlawful press. Since then there is truly no longer any danger emanating from that quarter, which could pose a serious threat to the Islamic ruling order.'[53]

The pressure on the press also was manifested in two laws passed at different times. The first goes back to the early months after the revolution and was approved by the Revolutionary Council on 14/8/79. The second was approved by parliament and the Guardian Council on 17/3/86. Although the first law restricted the freedom of the press, it was far less drastic than the second. Whereas the first law, for instance, made it necessary for a publication to obtain a permit from a specially created government commission, the second endowed the same commission with the additional function of exercising constant supervision over the press. This law contains three novel sections. The first stipulates that the press has a mission which includes, amongst other things, promoting the goals of the Islamic Republic, combating the artificial and divisive demarcations between the various social classes, counteracting the manifestations of imperialistic culture, furthering and propagating Islamic culture, and supporting government policies which are aimed at rejecting the West and the East (Soviet Union). In the second section, a number of measures are listed under the rubric 'Rights of the Press' which journalists must follow and which for the most part simply serve to restrict the rights of the press. These include: 'Taking account of Islamic principles' and 'the avoidance of insulting, belittling or sabotaging [the Islamic Republic].' The third section bears the title: 'Limits of the Press'. It declares that everything which can be subsumed under the concept of 'heresy' (elhad) is forbidden. Included under this rubric are the following: contradicting Islamic principles; violation of the fundamental principles of the Islamic Republic; spreading prostitution; behaviour forbidden by religion; propagating excessive consumption; extravagance, and stirring up conflicts amongst the population. Whereas the first law devoted eight articles to the powers and the formation of juries, which according to the constitution have the right to judge offences committed in this area, the law expresses its aversion for this institution by devoting only one article to the subject, in which it is simply stated that juries will be present at trials concerning the press.[54]

Even while the bill for the second law was being discussed in parliament, censorship and the prohibitions on the press were so drastic that some MPs could not refrain from characterising the law as superfluous and in fact harmful. Mohammad 'Ali Hadi MP declared that the problem with the press was not the lack of a regulatory law, but rather the fact that criticism was not tolerated and therefore the press was practising self-censorship. He compared the problem of the press to that of parliament. In parliament too everyone had to consider his words 'a thousand times' before speaking. He feared that if the bill in question were passed, the press would be hindered from publishing the little bit that it still dared to say those days. 'Ali Panahandeh MP drew attention to the population's annoyance at the way the press was obliged to toe the party line: 'The media' he stated, 'are either directly censored or they censor themselves.'[55]

After Khomeini's death, the pressure on the press was at first to some extent reduced. Under the leadership of Hojjat al-Eslam Mohammad Khatami, who represented a relatively tolerant position, the Ministry of Islamic

Guidance took a less stringent line. One result was the visible rise in the number of newspapers and journals from 102 in 1988/89 to 369 in 1992/93.[56] Several new and rather popular monthlies published authors with a known aversion to the hierocracy. These carried articles that were thoroughly critical of the regime and whose publication would have been unthinkable before Khomeini's death. Generally speaking, publications of this kind represented a more or less clearly delineated counter-culture which many government functionaries denounced as embodying the substance of what they dubbed 'a cultural invasion' or 'a cultural conspiracy'.[57]

While one part of the hierocracy tolerated this kind of press, another part attacked it with whatever means were at its disposal. Nor did these attacks spare the policies of the Ministry of Islamic Guidance. The daily newspapers *Kayhan*, *Resalat* and *Jomhuri-ye Eslami* were vehicles of this attack, along with a number of magazines such as *Sureh*, *Panzdahom-e Khordad*, *Sobh*, *Mashreq* and *al-Sarat al-Hosein*. In its issue of 27/2/91, for example, *Kayhan* indicated that there was 'a new danger of liberalism and Westernisation to be noted in the press' and hoped that 'this festering boil' would soon be excised. On 23/9/91 *Resalat* called upon the people not to take matters in their own hands in the fight against 'the cultural conspiracy' hatched by this element of the press.[58] In a joint assembly, the teaching staff and students of the Religious Academy of Qom passed a resolution in which they expressed the wish that the chief functionary responsible for cultural matters be dismissed. The Family Members of the Martyrs of the City of Mashhad demanded that the government close down 20 newspapers and journals and carry out purges in the Ministry of Islamic Guidance.[59]

If the impact of this kind of pressure cannot be described as sweeping, it has nevertheless had many consequences. In July 1992, the minister of Islamic guidance, Khatami, was forced to resign from his ministerial post. Before that some magazines had already been suppressed. The premises of the periodical *Gardun* were closed down on 10/10/91 and its editor-in-chief was arrested. The office of the magazine *Donya-ye Sokhan* was bombed by the Hezbollah. On 16/4/92, the magazine *Farad* had its premises closed down by the same group. The advocates of the new cultural policy temporarily succeeded in reversing the decision to shut down *Gardun*,[60] and *Donya-ye Sokhan* was able to appear again. But the attacks against publications of this kind did not stop and were constantly directed against new victims including 'Abbas 'Abdi, the editor-in-chief of *Salam*, a newspaper loyal to the regime. 'Abdi was denied legal representation, tried in a secret court without a jury and on the basis of charges that were never made public sentenced to a year's imprisonment.[61] This is apparently the heaviest sentence that a representative of the hierocracy has received because of his critical attitude and his affiliations with the radical camp amongst the ruling Islamic legalists. A new tactic adopted by the Ministry of Islamic Guidance and Culture consisted of refusing to allow the opposition press to buy paper subsidised by the state. Forcing a publication to purchase paper on the free market has the minimal effect that it is obliged to raise its price and thus lose a large proportion of its customers. In 1994 *Kiyan* reported another repressive measure which consists of stopping potential income for undesirable periodicals from advertisements by threatening the prospective clients with reprisals.[62] Since 1994 the pressure on journals such as these has increased. At the time of writing *Gardun, Takapu, Payam-e Daneshju, Ayneh-e Andisheh, Bahar, Bahman, Rah-e Mojahed, Jahan-e Islam* and *Tus* had all been closed down. Most of these belonged to Islamic groups and *Bahman*, which managed to publish only a few issues, was under the direction of 'Eta'ollah Mohajer, the vice-president of Iran.

The lot of the other media of mass communication, as well as that of writers, artists and scientists in the Islamic Republic over the past 15 years has been the same as that of the press. A short-lived initial freedom gave way to long-term strangulation. For the last few years, thanks to a slackening of pressure, there has again been the possibility of producing something new, albeit in an atmosphere of insecurity and constant threat.[63]

## The Violation of other Fundamental and Human Rights

A body of literature on the Islamic Republic has described in some detail the violation of fundamental rights that are more or less clearly guaranteed in the constitution. International human rights organisations have regularly investigated the matter, presented their reports and condemned what is known to have occurred. Although it has not always been possible to be precise about the extent of the abuses in question, these reports nevertheless offer a qualitatively reliable picture of the situation.[64] For this reason it is not necessary to focus on this subject in greater detail.

In many cases the violation of human rights is written into the laws of the regime and justified by reference to the *shari'a*. The clearest example of this is the Islamicised penal code which, under certain conditions, imposes maximum penalties such as stoning for adulterers, or execution for apostasy.[65]

### *Freedom of Movement and the Right to Choose a Profession*

The violation of the right to freedom of movement is above all attested by the emigration of one to two million Iranians which began immediately after the revolution. Even if the majority of exiles have not been subjected to political persecution, they are obliged to live abroad as aliens because they cannot tolerate the cultural pressure imposed on them by the compulsory Islamicisation of daily life. A significant proportion of those who remain in the country are forced to lead a double life which can be described as a kind of internal exile. To avoid harrassment and persecution by the regime's moral police agents they maintain an official life matched by a hidden life conducted within the relative safety of their homes where they take particular pleasure in the forbidden.

The freedom to choose one's profession has been especially violated by massive purges at all levels of government service designed to eliminate employees suspected of not being loyal to the regime. During the months immediately after the revolution those connected, or thought to be connected, with the old regime were ousted from their jobs in a wave of dismissals; but the purges were soon directed at participants in the revolution and even, eventually, at people loyal to the regime but in the camp that had been pushed out of power. These purges were particularly aimed at high-ranking civil servants in leading positions and teachers. In 1984 Prime Minister Musavi reported that to date 10,000 leading posts had been made vacant in this manner.[66] The same year the minister for higher education and culture announced that 3,500 university teachers had been fired or had resigned during the period after the closing of the institutions of higher education in April 1980.[67]

*The Right of Equality*

The most blatant violations of the right to equality take the form of legal discrimination against women and members of religious as well as ethnic minorities. In the case of religious minorities the violations take numerous forms. Firstly, the only religions that are recognised are the so-called religions of the Book (Zoroastrianism, Judaism and Christianity); members of other faiths are subjected to full-fledged discrimination or, as in the case of the Baha'is, active persecution. Although apostates do not form a particular closed group, they are threatened with the harshest of punishments, namely the death penalty, a threat which may be carried out suddenly at any moment that suits the interests of the hierocracy. In our discussion of political parties we saw how Khomeini threatened the opposition with the charge of apostasy and its consequences if they dared to demonstrate against the reintroduction of the law of retaliation (*qesas*). The case of Salman Rushdie is another example of the reality of this danger which is based on the *shari'a*. The fact that apostasy is currently a subject of discussion in religious circles attests to its present-day reality.[68]

The Islamicisation of the state implies, by definition, discrimination against non-Muslim citizens in the most consistent possible manner. Non-Muslims are not only excluded from leading government posts, but are also deprived of the right to take an active part in decisions which determine the form of the prevailing order. Although the Constitution of the Islamic Republic accords members of the recognised religious minorities the right to send their own representatives to parliament (Art. 64), and although those representatives enjoy the same right as their Muslim colleagues to vote in parliament, none of this has any influence whatsoever on the character of the state. As far as framing legislation in parliament is concerned, minorities participate in a process whose results at the end of the day are imprinted with the stamp of Islam. As members of the nation, they are obliged to accept and assume responsibility for decisions which were passed in the name of an exclusive religious community (*umma*). For the sake of the nation they had to make their contribution to the war with Iraq, a war, however, which was conducted in the name of Islam and with Islamic goals.[69]

Although the constitution grants religious minorities the right to behave according to their own standards in religious matters and in legal matters relating to marital status (Art. 13 and 14), in practice they have many restrictions placed upon them by governmental and quasi-governmental authorities. So far as moral practice is concerned, for example, they are frequently forced to conform to Islamic ordinances such as veiling. Discrimination against the religious minorities during the years after the revolution was the cause of their massive emigration from Iran. Between 1976 and 1986, the number of Christians in the country declined from 168,593 to 82,061 and the number of Jews fell from 62,258 to 26,354.[70]

Discrimination against the ethnic minorities has primarily taken the form of preventing them from preserving their cultural particularities. Turks, Kurds, Baluchis, Arabs, Armenians, Assyrians and other ethnic groups were not allowed to use their own languages as a means of instruction in schools. Even the constitution does not grant them this right. According to the constitution, 'local languages' may only be used 'in the press and in the mass media'. Schools are only allowed to engage in teaching the literature of these languages (Art. 15). This official attitude stems from the tendency towards authoritarianism inherent in the hierocracy and strives to establish itself wherever it can. This same tendency lies behind the policy of not allowing the ethnic minorities the right to administer the territorial areas they inhabit. The government's preference, at least in the regions inhabited by Sunnis, is to assign the higher administrative posts to functionaries from outside the area and not to local people.[71]

We have already seen in Chapter 1 how the constitution denies equal rights to women. The position of the Islamicists on the question of women had already been presented before the revolution by such leading Islamic theoreticians as Mohammad Hosein Tabataba'i (1959), Morteza Motahhari (1974 and 1980) and 'Ali Shari'ati (1971 and 1978). Despite all their efforts to project an image of Islam's high respect for women, these authors nevertheless justify in many respects discrimination against women that finds clear expression in the *shari'a*. During the period after the revolution, the ruling Islamicists put their patriarchal attitude into practice. Examples of the repressive measures they initiated include: regulations that make it more difficult for women to pursue a professional career and to participate actively in society, measures that reduce women to sexual objects, the imposition of the veil and, finally, the intensified application of ordinances of the *shari'a* that discriminate against women.

The exclusion of women from professional life after the revolution occurred primarily in government administration and especially in the judicial system. Information released on 26/5/93 by the official in charge of women's affairs in the Ministry of the Interior indicates that women's participation in professional life is decreasing every year at a rate of 2 per cent.[72] Women have also been forced out of professional life by denying them admission in several fields of study. At least this was the case up until the end of November 1993.[73] In 1988, the Ministry of Higher Education, in a letter to the periodical *Zan-e Ruz*, suggested that female university graduates would do better to use their learning in running the household and raising their children.[74] In September 1992, the Supreme Council of the Cultural Revolution recommended to women that they interest themselves in activities which concerned the life of their families. The same council listed a series of professions which it deemed suitable for women given their psychological and physical characteristics. Included were medicine, pharmacy and laboratory technology.[75] There were also certain professions from which the ruling Islamicists did not wish to exclude women and indeed were at pains to encourage women to qualify for and practice. These were professions which, according to Islamic moral law, men were not allowed to enter including teaching in girls' schools, nursing and medical activities in the women's section of hospitals, and other kinds of medical treatment for the female sex.

Compulsory wearing of the veil, the separation of the sexes in public and the other rules of chastity imposed on women reveal the sexually discriminatory attitude of the ruling Islamicists. Since taking power, they have enacted numerous laws and regulations which aim to force conformity to Islamic norms, and to ensure that the laws are observed they have created many executive organs which carry out their mission with thoroughness and zeal. Sometimes the lack of a veil or an insufficient veil is defined as prostitution, or even as an expression of conspiracy against the Islamic government, and appropriate punishments are threatened.[76] Discrimination against women in questions marital status, which had also been sanctioned by law and widely practised before the revolution, was considerably intensified afterwards. Polygamy, facilitating divorce to the advantage of men and early marriage for girls are only some of the forms this transformation has taken. The increased male dominance since the revolution has encouraged the mistreatment of women and the violation of their rights by their husbands. The growing rate of suicide amongst women is presumably connected to these developments.[77]

The discrimination against women and their exclusion from public life has met with numerous obstacles and much resistance which has reduced the impact of this policy. Firstly, the Islamicists themselves had to encourage women to take up the professions thought to be suitable for females. Secondly, the measures have provoked the persistent opposition of modern women who, at great risk to themselves, refuse to conform to the moral conceptions of the conservative Islamicists. The outward sign of this opposition is the manner in which they attempt to evade the compulsory wearing of the veil. Although they do not dare to appear in public with no veil at all, they wear their scarf in such a way that their protest is obvious. Thirdly, it is important to note the contradictory effect that has come from the hierocracy's politicisation of women who otherwise held traditional attitudes. In contrast to the conservative quietist clergy who condemn the very appearance of women in public, the ruling Islamicists quickly realised during the revolution that they could exploit for their own political ends the social importance of traditionalist women. But this presupposed that such women were snatched from their narrow social role and brought into the politically active social environment. Their inclusion in demonstrations, their active support in times of war, their mobilisation as guardians of morality, their votes in elections[78] are regularly used by the regime to achieve its goals.

The politicisation of traditionalist women was bound to influence their role in other areas of social life. It has certainly contributed to the fact that some of the women introduced into public life in this manner have become aware of the legal discrimination directed against them and have taken steps to modify the situation. The founding of women's associations and the creation of women's periodicals are two of the methods they have adopted to bring about changes. Although these associations and journals also play a part in the strategies of the ruling Islamicists directed against emancipated women or modern values concerning the position of women, they at the same time provide a forum where discrimination against women and the struggle for women's rights are discussed. One of the results of the pressure that emanates from this source has been that the regime has toned down some of the harsher aspects of the law of marriage and divorce which was put into practice in conformity with the *shari'a* immediately after the revolution.[79] Similarly, it should be mentioned that women have once more been allowed to function as lawyers, if only in lawsuits that deal with women's issues and may now be active as advisers in the civil courts.

## Ideological Justifications

The ideologues of *velayat-e faqih* have attempted to legitimate the on-going suppression of fundamental rights in the Islamic Republic. They have published numerous works whose subjects range from the nature of the Islamic form of government to critiques of humanist and liberal theories of the state to explicit justification of repressive measures and discrimination. A detailed description of the published books, treatises and articles of this kind is of course not possible but a few examples will serve to familiarise the reader with the most commonly held views and arguments. It should be noted in advance that the views sketched here are for the most part rooted in the theory of *velayat-e faqih*, that is to say in the attitude towards man and his relationship with God which that theory postulates. Consequently, we will begin our general examination of this subject by considering particular works which are specially devoted to this theory.

Paradoxically, the Islamic legitimation of repressive measures against fundamental rights begins by emphasising such principles as individuality, self-reliance, equality, the freedom of individuals in their mutual relations and the rejection of the dominance of one human being over another.

According to such principles, no one has the right to limit the freedom of another human being. An individual's freedom is only to be limited when it infringes on someone else's freedom. Ayatollah 'Amid Zanjani has declared: 'According to the world view of Islam, the individual's right to freedom and choice in all situations is indisputable and inalienable.'[80] He goes so far in emphasising the principle of individual freedom that he even denies the existence of society, which he describes as a mere agglomeration of individuals. 'A totality in the sense of a real unit in which the individual components disappear simply does not exist. Society is nothing other than harmonised objective individuals.'[81]

The more emphatically dominance of one human being over another is denied in these writings, the more clearly it is stressed that man's relationship to God is one of absolute slavery (Arabic: *ta'abbud*, Persian: *bandegi*). The dominance of one human being over another is therefore unacceptable because dominance belongs to God alone. As Creator of the world and mankind He is their owner and ruler. Consequently, as M. H. Tabataba'i had already stated before the revolution, freedom by this definition is 'freedom from slavery to the counter-God (*taghut*)'[82] By contrast, man's relationship to God can only be defined as worship, submission, obedience and the attempt to approach closer to Him in one's development.

Whereas the counter-God, according to this view, is represented by the ungodly political orders, the jurists as God's vicegerents represent the rule of God on earth. Thus, to be free from the dominance of the counter-God means acceptance of the rule of God's representatives and practising obedience to them. God's rule and the rule of the jurists mutually presuppose one another. While *velayat-e faqih* brings about the rule of God, God proclaims the necessity of *velayat-e faqih*. According to this formula, freedom reigns when all other forms of rule except *velayat-e faqih* are negated and their concepts of freedom are declared null and void.[83]

In writings such as these the rejection of political liberalism and its conception of human rights is based on this particular view of freedom. In a more philosophical mode this rejection finds expression in its debate with humanism by postulating that God is the axis of all human thought, values and endeavours. At the same time the political dimension of that axis is represented by *velayat-e faqih*. Amongst the authors who have elaborated this form of theorising the layman Shahriyar Zarshenas should be mentioned here. In *Kayhan*, one of the most zealous newspapers combating the liberal intellectual heritage, Zarshenas has almost without interruption maintained a position against the secularist, non-legalistic Islamic intelligentsia, as well as against the ideals of the Enlightenment, humanism and liberalism. 'Freedom in humanistic culture stands as the antithesis to freedom in religious culture.' The former kind of freedom 'is based on taking distance from God's glory and breaking off religious ties', whereas the latter rests on 'complete conformity to religious doctrine and closeness to God's glory'. Whereas the one view means submission to 'the lower self' (*nafs-e ammareh*) and freedom in the satanic sense, in the other view freedom takes on its true meaning 'in slavery vis-à-vis the reality of God and in liberation from material and worldly captivity.' Humanistic freedom is achieved in the government system based on democracy, but *velayat-e faqih* is the foundation on which Islamic freedom achieves its meaning and becomes a reality. Zarshenas then points out to his opponents that with regard to the dominion of the Islamic state they will search in vain for liberal freedoms. 'The Islamic revolution in Iran did not come about on the basis of democratic and humanistic ideas in order to establish the reign of freedom throughout society in the sense of Liberalism.'[84]

Elsewhere Zarshenas describes the struggle against *velayat-e faqih* as opposition to freedom and as an attempt to spread despotism and submission. For freedom can never be realised except through *velayat-e faqih* and obedience to it. A society based on the government system of *velayat-e faqih* is a truly free society. Indeed, 'true freedom is brought about by religion, the rule of God's viceregents being inherent in religion.'[85] When he was asked in an interview about what should be the limits imposed on writers, he replied: 'We believe in the freedom of the written word, but in our opinion that freedom is realised through obedience to the Islamic ordinances and regulations.'[86] Transferring the ideas of Zarshenas and other like-minded authors into practice takes the form of repeated appeals to forbid and censor the publications of intellectuals who think differently, the continual denunciation of the latter as spies, conspirators, counter-revolutionaries and apostates, as well as the violent undertakings of the Hezbollah against such persons and institutions.

Another example of a theoretical analysis of the question of freedom from the point of view of the Islamic legalists is found in a series of articles that appeared in the periodical *Howzeh* (April 1989 to February 1991) under the title 'Azadi-ye 'Aqideh' (Freedom of Belief). The unnamed authors of this series divide the various views on this subject represented by the Islamic authorities into two groups: those who approve of the use of compulsory measures in order to establish Islam and to combat unbelief, and those who are not in agreement with applying such compulsory measures. The authors underline this difference in attitude, after having stressed that Islam 'forbids with all its force the infiltration into Islamic territory of unbelief and heresy in the name of freedom of belief', and for their own part they speak up in defence of the first group and justify their view with a series of direct and indirect quotations from traditional Islamic sources. In this connection they take up in detail and with approval the concept of *jehad-e ebteda'i* (primary or offensive Holy War), to which they attribute two principle goals: the elimination of hindrances to proselytising for Islam (*da'vat*), and the elimination of oppression. Amongst the various forms of oppression is hindering people from responding to their instinctive nature (*fetrat*) and professing the Oneness of God, i.e. hindering them from becoming Muslims.

Freedom of belief in this same series of articles is measured for Muslims and non-Muslims by two different standards. Muslims enjoy such freedom in all matters concerning Islam as long as its exercise does not lead to the negation of the principles of belief. Should the latter occur consciously, rationally and for political or egotistical reasons and manifest itself in word and deed, then that amounts to apostasy which necessitates the execution of the said person. Apostasy must be punished because it leads to 'contempt for religion and the destruction of religion'.[87] The limits of freedom of belief are defined for non-Muslims by forbidding the following behaviour: spreading thoughts and beliefs which threaten the well-being of society; dishonesty in speech and hypocrisy; dishonesty when quoting others, the transmission of secrets; conspiracy; pursuing wicked political goals; harbouring subversive ideas and hatred, and disloyalty with regard to regulations and duties. Finally, there is the additional condition that non-Muslims may only exercise this lavish freedom of belief when the possibility exists for a Muslim to reply to their views. Thus, the danger will be averted that a non-Muslim's remarks might influence the true believers and cause the latter to experience doubts about their faith.[88]

The above mentioned series of articles was followed by another which bore the title 'Azadi-ye Tafakkor' (Freedom of Thought) and appeared in *Howzeh* Nos. 24 to 30 (1987–1989). Since this series, as the authors themselves acknowledge, for the most part presents the ideas which Motahhari put forward in two speeches he gave in 1969, we will quote directly from the speeches themselves.[89] Motahhari here distinguishes between thought and belief, and recognises an unlimited freedom only, as he says, in the domain of thought. Belief is only able to enjoy freedom when belief proceeds from thought. If, on the contrary, belief is the result of love, that is to say of emotion, it cannot be free because it stands in the way of thought and leads to idolatry. In this sense the prophet Abraham acted correctly when he destroyed the idols of the Israelites feeling that, as the only free-thinking person at the time, he was justified. In this connection Motahhari criticises the UN International Charter of Human Rights because it maintains that all beliefs are worthy of respect. Motahhari cannot accept this because forms of belief may well exist out of which man fashions chains for himself. In Islam the only belief that is free, is belief based on thought.

Motahhari allows freedom of thought because in his opinion thought necessarily leads to Islam. Consequently, as he sees it 'thought is not free but it is a commandment'. If a human being thinks, he will come to choose Islam. If he does not choose Islam, either he has not really thought things through or he is suffering from mental illness. Indeed, anyone who thinks and yet does not accept the path to salvation, i.e. Islam, 'must be a sick human being' who has remained attached to a belief which naturally cannot be genuinely free.[90] The idea quoted above from the periodical *Howzeh*, according to which non-Muslims should only be granted the freedom of belief if Muslims are given the possibility of responding to them, goes back to Motahhari. He formulated this point in the speeches in question after first stating that he would welcome responses to his own thoughts. But this would only be allowed if the condition he referred to above were fulfilled.

The Islamic ideologists devote a great deal of energy to recounting the disadvantages of the freedoms prevalent in the West in an effort to legitimate their own way of handling these freedoms. Typically, they reproach Western freedom as having the following unacceptable characteristics:

1. It leads to 'unbridled behaviour which works against morality and human traditions';[91] it is based on the principle of reaping the maximum enjoyment of material things and material pleasures. It hinders 'the transcendental dimension in man'; it lowers 'man to the level of animals and holds him back from the development which the nature of creation intends for him.'[92]

2. The West's idea of freedom is false because it is not a freedom for everyone but only for the capitalists, that is to say for a well-off privileged minority who dispose over all the means of enjoying freedom. This results in 'a lack of freedom for those without means – the tormented, the degenerate and the depressed majority who have little chance of enjoying freedom or putting it into practice.'[93] The West's form of freedom is the product of exploiting other people and is what creates imperialism.

3. Western freedom shows no regard for revelation. It is based exclusively on reason and this alienates man from one of the loftiest sources of blessings and benefits, i.e. divine revelation and prophecy.[94]

This conception of the nature of freedom provides the ruling Islamicists with a theoretical justification for stifling the expression of any ideas which they find undesirable. They are thus able to denounce every oppositional idea as irrational, founded on emotions, blasphemous and harmful to the Muslim community. They may then declare that the spread of such ideas is unallowable. In justifying the actual violation of fundamental rights in the Islamic Republic, frequent use is made of this form of denunciation. The most common slogan one hears in this connection is: 'Yes to freedom, but no to conspiracy!' Over the last few years the favourite reproach aimed against those who think differently is that they are agents of the so-called cultural invasion or the cultural conspiracy.

## Notes

1   *Kayhan* 28/8/79 mentions the name of 99 political organisations.

2   A reference to the National Front and The National Democratic Front.

3   *Kayhan*, 18/8/79.

4   *Kayhan*, 22/8/79.

5   Bani-Sadr (1982, p. 373) recounts that on the very eve of the revolution, i.e. 11/2/79, it was proposed within the leadership circle to attack and destroy the Feda'iyan-e Khalq and the Mojahedin-e Khalq in the heat of the moment.

6   Information on this subject can be found in Bakhash: 1986, Menashri: 1990 and Liga: 1988.

7   MM 3/3/81, p. 25.

8   Ibid., pp. 29 and 31.

9  MM 8/7/81, p. 15.

10  MM 9/7/81, p. 29.

11  Ibid., p. 27.

12  This was how Tavakkoli and Karimi expressed themselves (MM 9/7/81, p. 38).

13  MM 3/3/81, p. 26 and 4/3/81, p. 22.

14  *Payam-e Enqelab*, 5/9/81.

15  Liga: 1988, p. I/7.

16  Three other grand ayatollahs, Golpaygani, Mar'ashi and Shirazi, confirmed Khomeini's judgement by declaring the opponents of the law of blood revenge to be apostates (*Jomhuri-ye Eslami*, 15 and 16/6/81).

17  The Public Prosecutor did not even once refer to the law on parties when he dissolved the Tudeh Party in May 1983, despite the fact that the law had existed for quite some time. Instead, he based his actions on Art. 9, 24 and 26 of the constitution (*Ettela'at*, 7/5/83), which make respect for the territorial integrity of Iran into a duty and require that parties' activities be in agreement with Islamic principles.

18  *Kayhan*, 25/2/87.

19  Ibid., 2/1/88.

20  See *Kayhan* for the same day. Also the statements of Hojjat al-Eslam Khalkhali concerning this step in *Kayhan*, 12/10/86.

21  *Resalat*, 2/6/87. On this party see Ralph Kauz: 1992.

22  Between 2/1/ and 8/9/90, *Kayhan* published a series of articles against this organisation. Detailed information on this association can be found in Baghi: 1983.

23  Gharibani issued a similar warning in 1996. *Salam*, 20/5/96.

24  Concerning this group and its dissolution, much information is provided by Mohammadi Reishahri: 1990, 'Ali Reza Nurizadeh: 1986 and Ahmad Khomeini: 1989, as well as the daily press which published Mehdi Hashemi's confession on 18/3/87 and the days that immediately followed.

25  This organisation was founded at the end of the winter of 1986 as a focal point for members of the LMI and some of the members of the National Front who lived in Iran, such as 'Ali Ardalan and Asadollah Mobasheri. It carried on its work under the same tight restrictions as the LMI.

26  This information, along with the previous quotation, comes from the LMI's statement on its meeting with the envoy of the UN Human Rights Commission. A detailed report on the LMI's application can be found in the periodical *Rah-e Mojahed*, No. 72 (1993).

27  *Kayhan*.

28  Ibid., 1/12/87.

29  This reproach came from Bahonar, MM 11/9/88, p. 25.

30  MM 12/9/88, p. 20 f.

31  *Kayhan*, 20/12/88.

32  Ibid., 27/12/88.

33  *Kayhan*, 14/2/89.

34  *Kayhan*, 2/2/89.

35  *Kayhan*, 20/4/89.

36  Ibid.

37  MR I/250.

38  *Kayhan*, 1/3/89.

39  In a speech delivered in Tehran on 27/3/93 at the Friday prayers, Ayatollah Jannati expressed his joy at the fact that parties would not be allowed, because they would only lead to disputes (*Salam*, 28/3/93).

40  By 13/3/89, according to the secretary of the Ministry of the Interior, 30 groups

had applied for permission (*Kayhan*, on the same day). In February 1994, the ministry announced that 76 organisations had been given permission to operate under the law (*Salam*, 15/2/94). Three months later it stated that the number of 'active political organisations' was 31 (*Salam*, 10/5/94). But the public was told nothing about these 'activities', apart from a few sentences occasionally released for special reasons, mostly in connection with the condemnation of opponents of the regime or foreign powers.

41  The last two organisations announced their resumption of 'activities' at the beginning of January 1992 and in April 1989, respectively.

42  Hojjat al-Eslam Mohtashami announced their cessation of activity in an interview with *Salam* (16/5/93).

43  The new chairman of this party is Ayatollah Emami Kashani.

44  *Resalat*, 3/7/93.

45  *Resalat*, 1/3/89

46  *Resalat*, 5/11/88.

47  *Resalat*, 24/2/88.

48  The Central Council of the Union of Militant Clergy wrote to Khomeini stating 'this split' should not give the people the impression 'of opposition and factionalism' and offer certain unaware individuals the pretext 'for churning out propaganda against unity'. In his reply, Khomeini wrote: 'Organisational splits which have taken place for the purpose of independent expression of opinions and the founding of organisations do not constitute opposition. Opposition is when an individual fights with other people in order to impose his opinion – God preserve us from such behaviour!' (*Resalat*, 16/4/88). The intensification of the conflict during the months that followed forced Khomeini to draw up his so-called 'Charter of Brotherhood'. Afterwards, the opposing parties fraternised in a common session (*Resalat*, 5/1/89), but this state of affairs did not last for long.

49  *Kayhan*, 16/11/87.

50  *Salam* repeatedly published articles on this subject. See for instance the issues for 26/12/91, 19/3/92, 14/1/93 and 10/6/93. The process of conformity which has been observable in the newspaper has gone so far that in the issue of 9/2/94, in response to a reader's protest against the lack of permission for parties, one reads: 'Freedom to found parties has been granted, but the people themselves are not interested in founding a party.'

51  Yet on 5/3/79 (*Ettela'at*), Khomeini had forbidden his supporters in the city of Qom to insult the press or to storm the offices of the newspapers and to damage their publications.

52  *Iran Yearbook* 1989/90, Part 21, p. 4 f.

53  Vezarat-e Farhang va Ershad-e Eslami: 1983, vol. I, p. 11 f.

54  LB: 1979/80, pp. 58 and 96 ff.; LB: 1986/87, p. 665 ff.

55  MM 17/1/86, pp. 30–2.

56  These figures come from the officials dealing with the press in the above mentioned ministry. *Ettela'at*, 26/2/91 and *Salam*, 24/11/92.

57  See Asghar Schirazi, 'Gegenkultur als Ausdruck der Zivilgesellschaft in der Islamischen Republik Iran,' in F. Ibrahim and H. Wedel (eds) *Probleme der Zivillgesellschaft im Vorderen Orient*, Oplanden 1995, pp. 135–64.

58  The next day *Salam* criticised this appeal to the population as disregard for the law (24/9/91).

59  *Kayhan*, 21/4/92.

60  The court and jury, consisting at this time primarily of advocates of the new policy, found the editor-in-chief not guilty.

61  *Salam*, 25/12/93, as well as 3, 6, 8 and 12/1/94.

62  *Kiyan*, No. 18 (1994), on the cover page.

63  A report published by *Middle East Watch* in 1993 gives a detailed account of 'the

limit on freedom of expression in Iran'.

64  See for example Liga: 1988 and 1991.

65  A German translation of the 1982 Islamic penal code was published by Dara Ilzad in 1984.

66  *Kayhan*, 23/5/84.

67  *Kayhan*, 10/7/84. In 1986, Rafsanjani cited the number as 5,000 (ibid., 4/10/86). This figure may be compared with the 9,474 employed university teachers in 1990 (op. cit., 2.3.90).

68  See the treatment of this subject in *Howzeh*, No. 41 (1990) and No. 42 (1991). Despite the authors noticeable effort to adopt a lenient attitude, he concludes with the remark that: 'Only those apostates deserve the standard punishment who have consciously and out of political or sensual motives behaved or expressed themselves in some way that amounts to a denial of religion' (No. 42, p. 59). On this subject see also Shakuri: 1982, vol. I, p. 209 ff.

69  According to the figures released by Hojjat al-Eslam Mostafa Mohaqqeq Damad, 15 Jews, 330 Christian Assyrians, 200 Christian Armenians and 13 Zoroastrians died in this war. (Based on an unpublished paper entitled 'Religious Minorities in the Islamic Republic of Iran'.)

70  Markaz-e Amar-e Iran: 1990, p. 41.

71  See the objections raised by an MP from Kurdistan concerning this form of discrimination in *Resalat*, 13/1/92.

72  *Salam* 26/5/93.

73  According to *Salam*, at this time the restriction was lifted on the occasion of Women's Week.

74  *Zan-e Ruz*, 30/4/88 (quoted from Liga: 1988, p. III/24)

75  *Resalat*, 19/9/92.

76  *Ettela'at*, 8 and 28/3/83 (quoted from Liga: 1988, p. III/10 f.).

77  *Salam*, which reported on this situation on 29/9/92, at the same time pointed out that the rate of suicide in Iran is three times as high as in the United States.

78  Khomeini at the beginning of the 1960s, along with the quietist clergy, condemned votes for women as anti-Islamic.

79  See Chapter 11.

80  'Amid Zanjani: 1988–89, vol. I, p. 537.

81  Ibid.

82  Tabataba'i: 1969, p. 104.

83  'Amid Zanjani: 1988–89, vol. I, p. 553 ff.

84  Zarshenas: 1992, p. 43 ff.

85  Zarshenas: 1992a (*Kayhan*, 15/4/92).

86  Zarshenas in an interview with *Sureh*, No. 3 (1992); quoted here from *Safheh-e Avval*, No. 11 (1992), p. 18.

87  *Howzeh*, Nos. 40 and 41.

88  *Howzeh*, No. 40, p. 68 f.

89  We are quoting here from Motahhari: 1985, which includes these speeches (pp. 113–36).

90  This reasoning is also found in the writings of 'Amid Zanjani: 1988–89, vol. I, p. 555.

91  Khomeini, here quoted from T. Dezhkam: 1991.

92  M. H. Tabataba'i: 1969, p. 100 ff. See also Ayatollah Beheshti's speech on the subject of liberalism and Islamic freedom in *Resalat*, 26/6/91.

93  Beheshti, ibid.

94  Ibid.

# SEVEN

# The Power of the Clergy

## The Clergy as Government Officials

The process of adapting the application of the constitution to the concept of absolute *velayat-e faqih* was accompanied by the progressive allocation of almost all leading government posts to the clergy and many other less important posts to their lay supporters or those related to them by family ties. This process began with the Revolutionary Council, the majority of whose members belonged to this 'caste', and then extended to the three branches of the government, the Assembly of Leadership Experts, the Guardian Council, the Assessment Council, the National Security Council and the Assembly for Revising the Constitution. The administration of justice was transformed into a monopoly of the clergy. The clergy also occupied the most important seats and positions in parliament and its commissions, even though the proportion of MPs drawn from this group has decreased over successive legislative periods..

In recent years this process has been carried even further as the clergy have occupied positions in the lower levels of the administration in both the capital and the provinces. For example, in 1986, the minister for Jehad-e Sazandegi (Holy War for Reconstruction) thanked God that the clergy was represented in all the subdivisions of his organisation in the provincial capitals, the district capitals and throughout the districts.[1] Indeed the clergy's drive for government posts has been so intense that it is clear it is hindered only by its lack of professional training for certain specialised jobs and the need to exercise patronage among its lay supporters and their families. Basically, however, the clergy reserves the right to occupy state posts whenever it believes it is better qualified to fill a position or when there are no lay functionaries it feels it can trust with the job.[2]

This right is justified by a claim to possess certain unique virtues – most commonly knowledge of the *shari'a* and the role the clergy played in the revolution. According to Ayatollah Khamene'i, without the religious academies there would have been no revolution.[3] According to Khomeini himself, 'it was the clergy that carried out the uprising.'[4] This assertion forms the basis of the clergy's claim to exclusive ownership of the revolution and its subsequent fruits and is reinforced with a claim to popular consent. 'The nation', as Khomeini would have it, 'has bestowed its trust on the clergy and does what the clergy says.'[5]

## The Institutions of Clergy Power

The clergy's monopoly on power could not have been assured solely by means of the state and security apparatus that existed before the revolution. New institutions had to be created which would serve this purpose exclusively. These may be grouped according to their chief functions (though in practise many belong to more than one functional category since they carry out several different tasks simultaneously):

1. *Security organisations*: the Revolutionary Guard, the Revolutionary Committees, the Ministry of Security and Intelligence, the Basij, the Hezbollah and the Harasat.
2. *Special Courts*: the Revolutionary Courts and the Special Courts for the Clergy.
3. *Organisations for Propaganda and Supervision*: the Islamic Associations, the Representatives of the Leader, Political-Ideological Bureaux, the Organisation of Islamic Propaganda, the Council for Co-ordinating Islamic Propaganda, Jehad in the University, the Ministry of Islamic Guidance and Culture, and the Supreme Council of the Cultural Revolution.
4. *Economic Institutions*: the Foundation for the Disinherited and War-Invalids, the Foundation of Martyrs, the Foundation of the 15th of Khordad, the Committee of the Imam, as well as a series of private foundations.

From the beginning of the revolution the regime tried to involve its supporters in intelligence gathering and security. People were called upon to act as informants and to pass information about opposition activities in their neighbourhoods or work place to the official security organisations. This appeal was extremely successful. None the less, the regime also took care to build up government intelligence agencies which in 1983 were merged into the Ministry of Information (Vezarat-e Ettela'at). By law this ministry is presided over by a *mojtahed*. It co-ordinates the activities of all other information services and all state administrative organisations and institutions are obliged to send in whatever information it demands.[6]

Although the security service of the Revolutionary Guard (Sepah-e Pasdaran) has been made responsible to the Ministry of Intelligence, it can be assumed that this organisation still disposes over its own separate intelligence apparatus. The Revolutionary Guard was set up under the government of Bazargan and has since developed into an full-scale army with air force and navy branches. Its task is to combat both external and internal enemies; it is also involved in the fight against narcotics trafficking. In 1991, in the wake of the unexpected outbursts of rioting by a discontented population in several cities, the Guard formed 'a special unit for the security of the cities'.[7]

This last function is also carried out by an organisation known as the Basij (militia) which is under the direction of the Revolutionary Guard. The Basij is made up of adolescents and volunteers from amongst the lumpenproletariat. Its membership in Tehran alone has been reported as approximately 100,000[8] and in 1995 it was said to have 1.7 million members among high-school students throughout the country.[9] Since the unrest in Mashhad, Arak, Shiraz and other cities, the government has made an effort to build up the Basij by giving its members additional incentives to carry out their tasks, and by allowing it to maintain a constant presence among the urban population. Towards the end of November 1993, 120,000 Basijis carried out manoeuvres in Tehran which were openly described as a preparatory exercise for 'waging war in the city'.[10] Such manoeuvres have been repeatedly held since then.

The Revolutionary Committees (Komiteh-e Enqelab) emerged during the revolution. They originally included the members and sympathisers of an array of groups but after several purges evolved into security forces chiefly employed against the opposition. Over the years they increasingly took on more routine policing tasks and in 1991 were fused with the conventional police in a new organisation known as the Niruha-ye Entezami (Forces of Order).

The Islamic Associations (Anjomanha-ye Eslami) are located within industries, educational facilities and state administrative organisations. They belong to the group of organisations that emerged spontaneously during the revolution but after drastic purges were transformed into organs of control and propaganda. In 1986, Prime Minister Musavi praised these associations in the following terms: 'Before our intelligence services and forces of order become aware of some particular deviation, the pure heart and the political sensitivity of the Islamic Associations sound the alarm and draw attention to the signs of danger.' And he added: 'This alarm and this sensitivity are of crucial importance for the survival of the Islamic government system.'[11] On an earlier occasion he had described them as 'the ears and eyes of the Islamic government system' and had praised them in particular for their services in the struggle against the 'liberals' and Bani-Sadr.[12] Because of their interference in the management of industry the Islamic Associations for a long time lost favour with the regime. But as growing resentment amongst the population has manifested itself ever more frequently in industrial establishments the political leadership has taken a renewed interest in them. At the end of August 1992, a meeting took place between Ayatollah Khamene'i and representatives of the associations, in which Khamene'i gave them instructions 'for the consolidation of Islamic and revolutionary values' in their organisations.[13]

The Organisation for Holy War in the Universities (Jehad-e Daneshgahi) is a student organisation loyal to the ideology of the regime. It emerged in connection with the cultural revolution and is entrusted with the task of Islamicisation in the universities and combating the forces which work against this goal. It is under the supervision of the Supreme Council for the Cultural Revolution.[14] This organisation has recently been extremely active under the name of 'Ansar-e Hezbollah' and during the elections to the 5th Majles took strong action against candidates who did not belong to the conservative faction. On 2/4/1996 it held its first congress and took on the character of a political party.[15] As for the Hezbollah (Party of God) this title does not designate a separate independent organisation but loosely bound groups of thugs who are regularly sent out, usually from headquarters located in a mosque, to suppress by violent means undesirable activities of a cultural or moral nature. The Harasat (Watchmen) is a security bureau which has representatives in every state organisation and bears chief responsibility for matters of security in the administration. There is also a series of groups who constantly turn up with new names or new forms of organisation whose task is to uphold chastity and morality in the streets and to suppress sources of unrest. The Sisters of Zeinab (Khaharan-e Zeinab), the Admonishers (Nasehin) organised in groups of ten, and the Revenge of God (Sar Allah) are examples of this kind of group.

A survey of security and control organisations should include the institutions entrusted with purging government offices of employees who are not loyal to the regime or are suspicious. The most important of these are the Purging Commissions (Hey'atha-ye Paksazi), which have been active in individual government organisations since the revolution.[16] On 11/10/81 they were given the euphemistic name of Rehabilitation Commissions (Hey'atha-ye Bazsazi) which does not, of course, imply that they are now less involved with carrying out purges. Art. 14 of the law governing their function specifies no less than 17 political and military actions which could be grounds for dismissal from a government post.[17]

In connection with the subject of purges, the procedure followed when new government employees are taken on – selection or *gozinesh* – should also be mentioned. The purpose of this procedure is to ensure that politically unwanted persons do not obtain leading positions in government offices or the universities. The information the Selection Committee requires for this screening process is provided by the mosque that is closest to the applicant's place of residence and by the Ministry of Information. The applicant is also required to take an entrance exam so that his knowledge of what are called the Islamic sciences (*ma'aref-e eslami*) and his interest in Islam can be established. In the universities loyalty to the regime among students and future graduates is guaranteed by reserving up to 40 per cent or more of the places for the dependants of those killed in war, as well as for war-invalids and their children and spouses. The Guardian Council, as we saw earlier, also contributes to the process of selection by weeding out unwanted candidates in elections for parliament, for the presidency, etc.

Legal prosecution of opponents of the regime is either carried out by the Revolutionary Courts (Dadgah-e Enqelab) or the Special Courts for the Clergy (Dadgah-e Vizheh-e Ruhaniyat). The Revolutionary Courts were originally *ad hoc* institutions presided over by *shari'a* judges (*hokkam-e shar*). In 1983, these courts were obliged to attach themselves to the Ministry of Justice.[18] The execution of thousands of the regime's opponents after the revolution was ordered by them. The general fear inspired by the Revolutionary Courts is so great that whenever the government wishes to put an abrupt stop to a particular practice, such as driving up prices, it simply threatens those responsible with prosecution in the revolutionary courts. The Special Courts for the Clergy pass sentence on political or moral offences committed by the clergy. The initial step in the direction of forming these courts was taken during the first months after the revolution.[19] They were officially set up at the orders of Khomeini in July 1987.[20] By this time they had already passed sentence on 700 cases of punishable offences by so-called 'pseudo-clerics' (*ruhani-namayan*)[21] – a phrase used for clerics who fall into disfavour. By 23/1/90, according to figures released by the court's president, Hojjat al-Eslam Mohammadi Reishahri, 286 clerics had been sentenced, 14 of them to death.[22] These Special Courts are directly subordinate to the leader, follow their own rules and act independently of the ministries that would normally have jurisdiction in such cases. According to Ayatollah Khamene'i, their function is to 'protect and honour the sanctity of the clergy's outstanding dignity'.[23]

The Representatives of the Imam (Namayandegan-e Emam) are one of the most important institutions of supervision and propaganda. They act as a kind of extended arm of the leader in all the chief educational, administrative and security agencies and other state institutions, and use their considerable power to intervene in the running of those organisations.[24]

The Imams of the Friday Prayers (Emam-e Jom'eh), who lead the faithful in the performance of the Friday prayer, are appointed directly by the leader or through the Secretariat of Friday Imams in all the cities. They are in practice a powerful authority that stands over the local governors and mayors, although their official function is to supervise religious activity, propagate the doctrine of *velayat-e faqih* and agitation. In 1986, complaints about their intervention in the affairs of local government agencies reached such proportions that Ayatollah Montazeri felt obliged to warn them against such excesses. 'You gentlemen,' he declared before the General Assembly of the Imams of the Friday Prayers, 'must not aspire to draw all matters into your area of jurisdiction.'[25] In 1989, the MP Afrazideh put forward a proposal that the powers of the Imams of the Friday Prayers be clearly defined in a set of regulations.[26] The Imams of the Friday Prayers also gather information on the inhabitants of the cities, a task they carry out through the mosques. This information is then passed on to the Ministry of Intelligence. Exercising influence on the elections for parliament is also one of their tasks.

The Political-Ideological Bureaux (Daftarha-ye 'Aqidati-Siyasi) are another of the regime's organisations of control and agitation. In July 1983, Ayatollah Khamene'i described them as 'an essential and vital foundation of the regime of the Islamic Republic'.[27] They are installed in all areas of the state apparatus and are meant to provide ideological instruction to state employees and watch over them in their work place. The reports they prepare on the behaviour of employees determine whether individuals keep their job and their future career. These bureaux have also played a major role in carrying out purges in the conventional army.

The Organisation of Islamic Propaganda (Sazman-e Tablighat-e Eslami) produces and distributes publications inside and outside Iran. Having come into existence in 1981 through a transformation of the Supreme Council of

Islamic Propaganda, this organisation also promotes cultural activities of an Islamic nature.

Two kinds of economic institutions serve the hierocracy and the individuals who participate in it: public institutions that are under the control of the leader, and private institutions. The first category puts its wealth at the disposal of the informal policies pursued by the leadership and its immediate followers while the second serves the private interests of functionaries who have proved themselves useful to the hierocracy, as well as the interests of clients of those functionaries. Afrazideh once described those running the private institutions in the following terms: 'People dressed in the holy robes of the clergy who after the victory of the revolution came to hold posts and honours and then set up foundations, manufacturing enterprises and trading companies on behalf of which they availed themselves of public funds.'[28] What is special about these public foundations is the fact that, although they dispose over public funds, they only maintain a loose connection with the government and do not allow the government to determine their business policies.

The Foundation for the Disinherited and War-Invalids (Bonyad-e Mostaz'afan va Janbazan), which was set up as an institution of the revolution on 26/5/79 at the orders of Khomeini, is the largest of the public economic institutions. Its wealth, amassed through the confiscation and sequestration of properties owned by representatives of the Shah's regime and members of the Shah's family, included, by 1986, 140 factories, 230 trading companies, 282 agricultural associations and 90 movie houses, which all together employed a personnel of 150,000.[29] Since that date, it has extended its activities. War-invalids and the families of war victims are meant share in its profits and assets but in recent years the latter have complained of being neglected by the foundation.[30] Indeed towards the end of the 4th Majles a report was presented to MPs indicating extensive corruption in the organisation. The foundation has given over some of its assets to other institutions of the revolution or propaganda organisations.

The Foundation of Martyrs (Bonyad-e Shahid) was set up on 12/3/80, also at the orders of Khomeini, with the purpose of giving financial and other forms of help to the families of those who had died or gone missing in armed conflict. Through this help the foundation binds the people in question to itself and influences them in favour of the regime, in particular through setting up schools for the children of such families. The help given by this foundation is in part financed by the state. Additionally, it receives financial support by managing the sources of income granted to it or turned over to it by the Foundation for the Disinherited. By 1984, its resources already included 141 manufacturing businesses in various economic sectors.[31]

As in the case of the Foundation of Martyrs, the activities of the The Emam's Welfare Committee (Komiteh-e Emdadi-ye Emam) are financed through state disbursements and the confiscated assets which have been assigned to the committee. Financial help from religious foundations and *khoms* (the one-fifth tax) supplement these resources. The task of the committee is to impress the poor and to ensure their loyalty to the regime and the leader. To this end its dispenses help through its many branches – 1,100 in 1988 in which year, it is claimed, 1.5 million people received help from the organisation.[32]

Similarly, the Foundation of the 15th of Khordad (Bonyad-e Panzdahom-e Khordad)[33] is meant to serve the poor and the families of martyrs. But it also undertakes agitation and propaganda on behalf of the Islamic regime. It has become famous outside Iran by promising to pay $2 million for the execution of Salman Rushdie – a sum that was increased in October 1992. The foundation is financed by means of state grants and through religious donations which are encouraged by the mediation of several 'sources of imitation'. It is claimed that in 1991/92 471,886 families of martyrs, war-invalids, prisoners of war and those missing in action, as well as the poor, enjoyed benefits provided by this foundation.[34]

The Housing Foundation of the Islamic Revolution (Bonyad-e Maskan-e Enqelab-e Eslami) promotes the construction and renovation of homes for the poor and for people whose homes or businesses were damaged in the war with Iraq. In 1991/92, for example, 1,582 housing units are said to have been completed a result of the activities of this foundation and 12,453 units were under construction.[35] The foundation also encourages the construction of new homes by offering loans on favourable terms. The Housing Foundation is financed through state and private donations which at the request of Khomeini are paid into a special account.

By far the most important private institution is the Organisation of Islamic Economy created in 1979 through the fusion of the Interest-Free Credit Funds (Sanduqha-ye Qarz al-Hasaneh). Its primary task is to co-ordinate the work of the 880 funds that have been united under its management. It also undertakes trade, particularly in the areas where it is given lucrative concessions by the state. The advantages this organisation enjoys and its great financial power have repeatedly made it the target of criticism, especially by the radical camp of the hierocracy. In 1988, this institution's financial power was estimated to be 2 per cent of the total amount of money in circulation in Iran.[36]

This record will apparently be contested in the future by a newly created institution, which until its reorganisation, announced on 4 August 1994, bore the title of Institute of the Pioneers of Reconstruction (Mo'asseseh-e Pishgaman-e Sazandegi). At that time it possessed more than 80 business enterprises[37] in different sectors of the economy. It has acquired this wealth through the so-called privatisation of state industry programme by purchasing factories or the majority of their stock at favourable prices and is today engaged in buying more. It offers its stock to the different groups of people known collectively as 'the forces of Hezbollah' which include Basijis, war-invalids and the families of those killed or missing in action. The institution promises them prospects of high earnings, pointing out that the government has agreed in advance to give preferential treatment to its sister companies when handing out contracts.[38] In accordance with a law passed on 25/7/94, which is meant to regulate the handing over of the government stock to these 'forces', a central board is to be created which will shortly be taking over the tasks of this institution.

The actual number, as well as the activities, of the private economic institutions currently operating as 'a foundation' or 'an interest-free fund' are not even known to the government agencies responsible for their regulation or finance.[39] As for the public, it only learns of them and their wheeling and dealing if, as a result of the power struggle within the hierocracy, one side or the other leaks some scrap of information on the subject. For example, *Resalat*, in the course of its fight against the radical-populists within the regime, reported how the president of this foundation, Hojjat al-Eslam Hadi Ghaffari, a man famous for his acts of violence, came to possess, amongst other things, a textile factory by a transference of public assets.[40] The newspaper also reported on the Reja' Foundation, with which the former vice-president of parliament, Hojjat al-Eslam Bayat, had had lucrative ties.[41] The illegal activities of these institutions on occasion reach such proportions that the government cannot avoid taking their leaders to court. To give an idea of the degree of support that the foundations receive from the government, it is sufficient to note that the head of the Nobovvat Foundation is still alive, although as of 5/10/88 he has twice been condemned to death by the courts because of the criminal financial activities of his foundation. On 5/8/88, *Kayhan* reported that top officials in the government, members of parliament and Imams of the Friday Prayers had a share in this foundation. On 6/5/88, Ayatollah Musavi Ardebili spoke out, albeit in rather vague terms. He also condemned the additional damage that such foundations inflicted on the country's economy when they sold off state assets on the open market (*Resalat*). The deputy of the prime minister announced one month later that the foundations exploited their ties with government bureaucrats and sold state-owned property at the market price. And he actually cited the names of some of them.[42] The MP Razavi stated publicly that partisans of both wings of the hierocracy had a personal share in welfare funds, foundations and co-operatives.[43]

## Notes

1 *Kayhan*, 27/11/86. According to Arjomand (1988, p. 163) 'over ten thousand clerics ... have joined revolutionary bodies.' Hundreds more took up positions in the justice system.

2 Khomeini expressed this view in a speech he gave on 24/12/80. See Khomeini: 1987, p. 394.

3 *Resalat*, 2/12/88.

4 Khomeini: 1987, p. 379.

5 Khomeini: 1987, p. 387.

6 LB: 1983/84, pp. 306 ff. and 355.

7 *Kayhan*, 11/9/91.

8 According to the commander-in-chief of the Revolutionary Guard, Mohsen

Reza'i.(*Salam*, 28/10/92).

9  *Salam* 24/10/95. According to figures released by the Ministry of Education, 25% of the Basijis are high-school students. (*Salam*, 7/10/92).

10  A remark made by the militiaman Rahimzadeh Safavi and reported in *Salam*, 25/11/93.

11  *Kayhan*, 6/9/86.

12  *Jomhuri-ye Eslami*, 30/1/83.

13  *Resalat*, 27/8/92.

14  On 2/2/89, *Ettela'at* reported on the activities of this organisation over the last 10 years.

15  *Resalat*, 8/5/96.

16  The decision to form these commissions was taken on 4/9/79 by the Revolutionary Council. See LB: 1979/80, p. 131.

17  LB: 1981/82, p. 77 ff.

18  See the law on the jurisdictional limits of the Revolutionary Courts for pre-trial investigations and for trials in LB: 1983/84, p. 9.

19  In a speech he gave on 13/10/79 during an audience for public prosecutors and judges, Khomeini justified the formation of these courts. See the issue of *Kayhan* published the same day.

20  *Kayhan*, 7/7/87.

21  *Resalat*, 10/3/88.

22  *Kayhan* ??

23  *Resalat*, 26/10/93.

24  For further information see Chapter 4.

25  *Kayhan*, 16/6/86.

26  MM, 21/11/88, p. 19. On the same occasion, he alluded to the decreased number of participants in the Friday prayers.

27  Quoted here from Arjomand: 1988, p. 167.

28  MM 21/11/89, p. 19.

29  *Kayhan*, 5/3/86. On 8/12/92 *Resalat* reported on the assets this institution had acquired through confiscation and sequestration.

30  As an example, see report in *Salam* 18/2/92 about the sit-in staged by the war-invalids against this foundation.

31  Vezarat-e Farhang va Ershad-e Eslami: 1985, p. 517 f.

32  For these figures and further information see *Resalat*, 9/6/88, 31/8/88, 4 and 5/3/89 and 4/3/90.

33  The title is a reference to the events of 5/6/63 when an uprising began against the Shah's regime and in protest against Khomeini's arrest that same night.

34  Markaz-e Amar-e Iran: 1992, p. 218.

35  Ibid., p. 378.

36  MM 7/3/88, p. 33. For more on this subject see *Kayhan*, 15 and 16/9/87; *Resalat*, 11/5/87 and 28/9/87.

37  *Resalat*, 4/8/94.

38  On this point see *Resalat*, 28/6/94 and *Salam*, 8/4/94.

39  On 6/8/88, Ayatollah Musavi Ardebili complained (in *Resalat*) that the government registration office did not apply existing laws to these institutions so that they remain unknown to the authorities.

40  *Resalat*, 2/10/90 and 24/5/90.

41  *Resalat*, 23 and 24/4/90, as well as 10/5/90.

42  *Kayhan*, 15/9/88. See also *Resalat*, 2/11/88.

43  *Resalat*, 12/12/88.

PART THREE

# The Fate of the Constitution's
# Islamic Legalist Elements

EIGHT

# The Unavoidable Acceptance of Laws
# Alien to the *Shari'a*

One of the arguments used to legitimate the suppression of the democratic elements of the constitution was that they stood in the way of establishing an Islamic state, or in other words the full application of the *shari'a*. The Islamic rulers claimed that they could not accept a situation in which the enforcement of the classical form of the *shari'a*, which they held to be perfect, was hindered by foreign legal elements. Since they based the principle of *velayat-e faqih* on their conception of the perfection of the classical *shari'a*, they created the expectation that they would apply the *shari'a* throughout the institutions of state and social life.

## The Attempt to Enforce the Islamic Ordinances

The Constitution of the Islamic Republic does not specify whether the so-called Islamic principles (*mavazin*) or ordinances (*ahkam*) are to provide the criterion for compatibility with the *shari'a* of the laws passed by the state. However, the verbal statements of prominent legalists have placed emphasis on applying the ordinances whenever there has been a question of underlining the Islamic character of the state or justifying its legitimacy in the face of opposition. Well before the revolution, in his blueprint of the Islamic state, Khomeini insisted on the application of the *ahkam* or 'Islamic laws'. One section of his book, *The Islamic State* (1982), bears the title 'The Necessity of the Permanence of the *ahkam*' and speaks of 'putting the *ahkam* into practice' for all eternity. 'Islamic laws', writes Khomeini, 'cannot be annulled or limited by time and space.' Any objection to this proposition is 'a contradiction to the requirements of belief'.[1]

In the same work, Khomeini goes on to define the Islamic state as 'the rule of God's laws'.[2] The task of the ruler is to apply the divine *hodud* – the fixed punishments[3] the *shari'a* has established in the Islamic system of criminal law. The application of the *ahkam* is legitimated by their perfection:

> God, He is beneficent and exalted, has sent down laws and customs for all things by means of His Prophet, God grant him and his descendants blessings and salvation. God has decreed laws for man before his embryo is formed until after his burial, just as He has laws for religion and for social and governmental matters.[4]

During the first years of the Islamic Republic, the need to enforce the Islamic *ahkam* was a constant refrain in Khomeini's speeches. For example, in his message to the Assembly of Experts he stressed that the document would be invalid if even one of its articles contradicted the *ahkam*.[5] In his message to MPs on the inauguration of the 1st Majles, he warned against legislation which contradicted 'the sacred Islamic *ahkam*'.[6] On 3/6/79, in a speech to a group of women from Ahvaz, he said: 'The Islamic Republic does not mean a republic without Islamic laws ... We want a state with Islamic *ahkam*.' (*Kayhan*)

In Chapter 1 we saw that the constitution stipulates the application of both Islamic ordinances (*ahkam*) and principles (*mavazin*), and specifies that legislation must not contradict either. In practice, however, this stricture has encountered obstacles, with the result that for the most part it has proved unrealistic and has had to be abandoned. Prominent among such obstacles is the fact that the *shari'a*, because of its antiquity, does not provide *ahkam* for regulating most problems which arise in governing a modern state. The newly passed laws, or those retained from the pre-revolutionary era, are so numerous that the number of *ahkam*, by contrast, stands out as absurdly small. The ruling legalists have had no choice but to acknowledge this fact in practice, but have consistently neglected to explain how their acceptance of new facts relates to the *shari'a*.

## The Preservation of *Ancien Régime* Laws

Even before they took political power, the legalists began to apply the *ahkam* partially. In the period immediately preceding the revolution, violence was used to close down bars, shops selling spirits, or pork and sausages containing pork. Immediately after the transfer of power, the so-called *hokkam-e shar'* (*shari'a* judges), sentenced actual or alleged representatives of the old regime to death or flogging and ordered their wealth to be confiscated on the basis of Islamic criminal law.[7] In March 1979, Khomeini demanded the observance of Islamic rules of dress for women working in or frequenting the government offices.[8] Music, dance and chess were also forbidden.[9]

The first attempts at systematic Islamicisation were made in those areas of law where the contrast between the legal practice that evolved under the Pahlavis and the *shari'a* was very visible, and where it was thought that the character of the new regime could be best demonstrated. Laws that were in effect prior to the revolution and were contrary to the *shari'a* posed a major problem for the newly-appointed Islamic judges. If they did not wish to dispense justice on the basis of their individual opinion or according to the laws of the *ancien régime*, they lacked a frame of reference for their decisions. This unresolved state of affairs caused particular problems in connection with the penal code where the contradiction to Islamic criminal law was very striking.

One of the first steps towards ending this confusion was taken by the

Supreme Court when, on 14/4/81, it wrote to the Guardian Council urging it to decide whether all non-Islamic laws, resolutions and statutory instruments should be annulled and the courts instructed to dispense justice in accordance with Islamic principles which, the Supreme Court declared, it could derive from Khomeini's *fatvas*. This would prevent 'laws contradictory to Islam from being applied during the period that the Islamic Parliament had not yet approved the proposals [for eventual Islamic laws].'[10] The Guardian Council responded negatively to this offer insisting that the question of whether existing laws were compatible with the *shari'a* was within its jurisdiction. Those laws and regulations currently in force, but which in the opinion of the Supreme Court were not compatible with Islamic principles, 'should be sent to the *foqaha* in the Guardian Council for the purpose of establishing their divergence or conformity.'[11]

Although in giving this reply the Guardian Council was primarily concerned with defending its own power, its attitude sounded realistic given the legal vacuum that would be created if existing laws were annulled. In the face of the difficulties that were already emerging in connection with Islamicising the old laws, there was no prospect of finding an effective remedy if the current non-Islamic laws were annulled. The opposition of the Guardian Council to the Supreme Court's initiative, along with numerous other protests which occurred even within the Ministry of Justice, in particular against Islamicising the criminal law, led to a delay in the process of Islamicisation or in other words to a temporary de facto legalisation of the existing criminal code.

Khomeini was extremely displeased with these delays. In August 1982, his patience exhausted, in a speech to pilgrims bound for Mecca he demanded that judges hand down verdicts based, not on current laws, but on the laws of the *shari'a*. He declared his readiness to take responsibility for this decision: 'All laws from the time of *taghut* are against the *shari'a*. They must be thrown away.' He was not prepared to accept further delays – those who maintained that the existing laws must be retained should, he said, 'have their face bashed in'. In the same speech, he instructed the Guardian Council and the Supreme Court to announce that it would be a criminal offence to act according to the old laws that violated the *shari'a*. By way of justifying this order, he added: 'We maintain that our republic is Islamic. The Islamic *ahkam* must [therefore] be applied in this republic.'[12]

The pro-government press promptly announced that Khomeini's order set in motion 'the revolution in the justice system'. In compliance, the Supreme Court issued a circular ordering that 'all current laws which violate the *shari'a* are as of now cancelled and invalid.' Judges were instructed, on pain of punishment, to base their findings on valid juridical sources or on valid *fatvas* when judging an existing law to be in violation of the *shari'a*, and to continue in this manner until parliament had time to pass the necessary Islamic laws. If they were uncertain of their Islamic duty, they were instructed to consult the Supreme Court or the Bureau of the Imam which dealt with religious questions.[13] Four days after Khomeini's speech, parliament and the

Guardian Council resolved that 'the law on *hodud* and *qesas* and its ordinances' form part of the Islamic penal code.[14]

This was followed by a resolution of parliament on 5/9/82 which obliged all ministries and government institutions 'to forward within ten days all the laws they use to the Guardian Council, so that within a six-month deadline the council can judge whether their content contradicts the Islamic *ahkam.*' The Guardian Council saw this resolution as an infringement of its own powers and rejected it as contradictory to the constitution, but at the same time emphasised its readiness to co-operate with the appropriate government authorities in identifying those laws which violated Islamic principles.[15] Along with the resolution of parliament, the Guardian Council also rejected the Supreme Court's circular. In a letter addressed to the Supreme Court on 9/10/82 it insisted that the application of old laws, as long as they had not been declared contradictory to Islamic principles, was 'provisionally' allowed.[16]

Another step parliament undertook to Islamicise the laws in the spring of 1981 should be mentioned here. It consisted of setting up 'a special commission for examining laws passed by the Revolutionary Council and laws dating from before the revolution'. Four years later, however, the commission in question was dissolved. It had succeeded in examining only two laws relating to the Guilds (Nezam-e Senfi) and the protection and expansion of industry, the result of which was a bill that it put before parliament.[17] In 1987, the MP Ha'erizadeh reproached the conservative wing in parliament for being responsible for the dissolution of this commission.[18]

Although the Guardian Council reserved for itself the right to judge the relationship of existing laws to Islam, it could only act in this capacity if parliament gave it the opportunity by passing resolutions,[19] or if other state organisations approached it with corresponding proposals. On 28/7/85, however, it took the initiative and asked parliament to allow it to examine not only the acceptability of individual articles of a law but also whether the law as a whole was acceptable when it came to amending laws from the time of the counter-God (*taghut*). Otherwise, it would be necessary, the council maintained, to create a new law for every legally regulated situation. The immediate cause of this remark was the fact that parliament, in passing a bill concerning the civil courts (*dadgah-e hoquqi*), had sanctioned the Rent Law promulgated in 1977, although in the opinion of the Guardian Council that law was fundamentally in disagreement with the *shari'a.*[20]

These attempts at Islamicisation met with scant success. In a collection of 'judgements handed down by the Guardian Council' published in 1992, there are only 24 cases of this kind to be found after 12 years of activity by the council. These consist of laws and parts of laws approved either by the Revolutionary Council or promulgated in pre-revolutionary times which the Guardian Council, on the occasion of parliament passing resolutions or at the request of the Supreme Court and other government authorities, found to be in partial or complete disagreement with Islamic principles. They are overwhelmingly concerned with Islamic jurisdiction in general and the Islamic code of criminal law and criminal proceedings in particular. In a few limited cases, they involve questions of ownership or the prohibition against earning interest. It is noteworthy that the decisions formulated on these occasions by the Guardian Council were in part annulled, either by the Assessment Council or by laws that were passed later on and which the Guardian Council itself also approved.[21] The most interesting case amongst the judgements handed down by the council on the laws of the *ancien régime* is found in a letter to the Ministry of Agriculture dated 12/7/84. The letter instructs the ministry to drop 'as quickly as possible' an order it issued implying that the land reform law promulgated during the 'era of *taghut*' would remain in force. According to the council this law contradicts the *shari'a*.[22] However contrary to expectations, the law was not annulled but instead made more stringent.[23]

The fact that the Islamicisation of law only proceeded in a halting fashion does not mean that there were no significant changes in Iran's legal system. Where new structures and organisations were created on the economic, cultural, social and political level, corresponding changes in the legal system were necessary and were in part carried out. The question is not whether the Islamic Republic has or has not altered the laws of the *ancien régime*. Laws are continually amended, annulled or supplemented in every country. It is whether the numerous changes that have taken place have fulfilled the requirements of Islamicisation. By way of providing an overview of the legislative process that has brought about changes to the old laws, we may distinguish the following categories:

1. Laws which were in any case based on the *shari'a* and therefore underwent very little change.
2. Laws that contradicted the *shari'a* and were therefore partially or completely changed.
3. Laws that were considered anti-Islamic before the revolution but were later tolerated or approved.
4. Laws that have merely appeared to be Islamicised, or whose Islamicisation came up against difficulties and was abandoned.
5. Laws that have no relationship to the *shari'a* but have had to be accepted out of sheer necessity.

To the first category belong those civil laws whose codification began in 1910 and continued up to 1935. Curiously, this process took place during a period when modernisation was the principle concern of the government. Modern elements were incorporated only in those areas pertaining to commercial law and the code of civil procedure where the Islamic *ahkam* were not sufficient to deal with modern legal issues.[24] In the second category are included those laws which, under the old regime, prohibited the clergy from having access to the landed property of religious foundations.[25] The laws which most clearly belong to category four are those which allow women to vote and to stand as candidates in elections – although in the early 1960s the clergy, including Khomeini, opposed votes for women. This category also includes laws which forbid commercial transactions for interest but contain loop-holes that in practice allow such transactions. The law regulating employment, the law on wholesale supply and retailing, and the law on co-operatives are amongst those laws that were meant to be Islamicised but, after much ado, have in fact retained their secular character. We shall deal in more detail with some aspects of these laws later. At this point we should take a closer look at the laws that fall into category five.

## The Promulgation of Laws Alien to the *Shari'a*

In order to give some idea of the quantity of laws that fall within category five, it is sufficient to compare the traditional collections of Islamic *ahkam* with the law-books of the Islamic Republic published annually by the Ministry of Justice. The comparison makes clear not only the quantitative difference but also the far more important differences of substance which characterise the two forms of legal collections. We will consider here as an example of the *ahkam*-collections Khomeini's *Tahrir al-Vasila* (The Means [of Solving Problems]) and *Towzih al-Masa'el* (Clarification of Problems). The two works form a kind of handbook, both for the more simple believers who follow Khomeini as 'a source of imitation' and for judges and legislators in the Islamic Republic. The latter regularly consult *Tahrir al-Vasila* – which is more detailed than *Towzih al-Masa'el* – when they do not know what answer the *shari'a* gives to a particular problem or when they wish to verify the Islamic character of their own position.[26]

*Tahrir al-Vasila*, which Khomeini composed after 1964 while he was in exile, lists solutions to 4,397 questions, which in the traditional manner are arranged in different parts and sections. The solutions are either presented in the form of answers to concrete questions relating to the ritual or material life of believers, or as methodical exercises whose purpose is to formulate possible answers to speculative questions. In this collection, 18.2 per cent of the questions deal with regulations pertaining to ritual purity and prayer. If, under the heading of 'worship' ('*ebadat*), we add to these solutions that deal with questions about Islamic taxes (*khoms*, *zakat* and taxes relating to *waqf* foundations) the total comes to 34 per cent. Fasting is not discussed in this collection, but in the *Towzih al-Masa'el* 200 solutions are devoted to this subject. Another 14.1 per cent of the *Tahrir al-Vasila* is concerned with the Islamic legal punishments (*hodud*). Fifty-one questions deal with defence (*defa'*), 129 with 'enjoining the good and forbidding the evil' (*amr-e bel-ma'ruf va nahi al-monkar*), 44 with the adherents of 'religions of the Book' (*ahl-e zemmeh*), and 105 with 'new occurrences' (*mostahdasat*). The rest have to do with problems of civil law, as these have been expressed since the 1930s in Iranian civil law. Out of the 105 solutions devoted to 'new occurrences', 18 have to do with prayer and fasting. Solutions pertaining to marriage and divorce account for 10.2 per cent, while 20.9 per cent pertain to different business activities and relationships.

Questions that are directly or indirectly connected with public law make up 1,116 of the solutions (25.3 per cent) in the *Tahrir al-Vasila*. This category includes questions concerning Islamic dispensation of justice, Islamic punishments and the *khoms* tax, as well as 'enjoining the good and forbidding the evil', defence and relations with adherents of religions of the Book. It should, however, be pointed out that the assertion that these questions, even from the point of view of the *shari'a*, belong to the area of public law is made only in connection with the modern theory of *velayat-e faqih*.[27] Traditionally, such questions either came under the heading of worship (*'ebadat*) or were considered to be in the domain of private law. Thus the *khoms* tax and 'enjoining the good and forbidding the evil' were traditionally an aspect of *'ebadat*, and retaliation and compensation came under the heading of private law. The *ahkam* that have to do with giving testimony (*shahadat*), confession (*eqrar*) and handing down a judicial judgement (*qaza'*) were also thought of as belonging to the domain of private law, in so far as they were applied in courts convened outside the state apparatus by clerics at the request of the contending parties.

But even if we attributed all such questions dealt with in the *Tahrir al-Vasila* to the domain of public law, the solutions offered would be too primitive and meagre to meet the needs of a twentieth-century society. Iranian society has already developed to the point that its requirements, even in the area of private law, by far exceed the capacity of a work like the *Tahrir al-Vasila*. In the arena of public law, such collections are even less able to offer solutions to twentieth-century problems. We have seen how, when framing its constitution, the Islamic Republic was obliged to borrow fundamental elements from non-Islamic sources, both conceptually and in terms of content. In the area of administrative, financial and employment law, the situation is no different. And the same holds true for international law and the penal code.

The inadequacies of the *shari'a* to the needs of government in the Islamic Republic are more and more openly admitted and discussed by the ruling legalists as they are confronted with the practical problems of government. Whereas in 1979 Ayatollah Beheshti spoke casually in the Assembly of Experts of 'the many questions, laws and operational regulations ... that receive no mention in the *shari'a*' and cited the rather unproblematic example of traffic regulations,[28] in 1991 Ayatollah Khatami, the minister for Islamic guidance, felt obliged to admit that: 'We find ourselves in a vacuum with regard to questions concerning the social order and inter-personal relations.'[29] In 1988, the editors of the magazine *Howzeh* published an article in which they outlined their expectations vis-à-vis the 3rd Majles and their concern at the extent of legal problems 'which have risen to the sky like a mountain'. They considered that the reason for these problems lay in the private character of Islamic law. This had come about because the study of *feqh* during the period before the revolution had gone on in isolation from society.[30] In another article they emphasised that even the rationalists amongst the Shi'i jurists 'had not developed their ability to practice legal judgements and deductions that went beyond the limits of individual acts and decisions, and the area of commands and prohibitions affecting individuals.'[31] Even Ayatollah Azari Qomi, otherwise a defender of the perfection of the *shari'a*, was obliged to admit in a series of articles published by *Resalat* in 1989 that the *shari'a* displayed many gaps which would have to be filled by adaptations to time and place.[32]

As soon as the ruling Islamicists took up the task of legally regulating the workings of government, they were unable, given the inadequacies of the *shari'a*, to do without the laws of the *ancien régime*. That is to say, they were obliged to accept laws which were to a certain extent the result of Western-influenced change in Iranian society over a period of several decades. The Islamicists availed themselves of these laws in the hope that they could be replaced at a later date, a hope which, as we have seen, has not been fulfilled.

On the other hand, it is not the first time in the history of Islamic jurisprudence that practices and norms current in pre-Islamic society have been sanctioned either tacitly or in explicit written or oral form and then accepted into the Islamic code of morals or law. Even most of the practices contained in the 500 or so *ahkam*-verses of the Koran (*ayat-e ahkam*) were current amongst pagan Arabs before Mohammad. The ordinances that are designated as 'sanctioned ordinances'(*ahkam-e emta'i*) are consciously distinguished in Islamic law from 'the established ordinances' (*ahkam-e ta'sisiyeh*) instituted by Mohammad.[33]

If Mohammad himself subscribed in this way to the morals, customs and norms of the pagan Arabs, the same practice must have been followed to an even greater extent when, after the Prophet's death, the Muslims had close contact with the morals and customs of newly subdued peoples and empires. Indeed, according to Naser Katuzian, this is how Islamic law came about. We know that this process of assimilation from subject peoples was not only limited to the *ahkam* themselves but, to remain within the domain of jurisprudence, also included technical methods of formulating legal opinions that were borrowed from Jewish and Roman sources.[34]

Even if it is considered acceptable to designate as Islamic a legal system built in this way, its is still necessary to ask whether a state that bases its legitimacy on the *shari'a* can integrate so vast an amount of modern laws, ordinances, resolutions, regulations and statutes that are alien to the *shari'a* without damaging or forfeiting completely its identity and authenticity. In relationship to this question it is also worth remembering that the acceptance of customary practices (*'orf*) into traditional Islamic law took place over a period of several centuries and was therefore a less disturbing process. In the Islamic Republic it has been necessary to assimilate a far greater body of law within a period of a few years – a process that is well-nigh impossible for an archaic legal system, however dynamic it is meant to be. That Islamic jurisprudence and the Islamic Republic have not had the power to do this is attested by the fact that they have had to adopt a defensive position vis-à-vis most of the laws stemming from the pre-revolutionary period and have had to accept those laws with very little change.

Another procedure for assessing the ability of Shi'i law to assimilate new elements and renew itself consists in examining to what extent in the decades before the revolution jurists succeeded in responding to the needs of modern life by working out relevant regulations and incorporating them in their law-books. In the *Tahrir al-Vasila*, solutions presented under the rubric 'new occurrences' (*mostahdasat*) represent only 2.3 per cent (or 195) of all solutions. These are divided as follows: 10 on insurance, 6 on exchange bureaux, 8 on paying indemnity, 12 on banks, 7 on lotteries, 10 on artificial insemination, 7 on autopsy and organ transplantation, 10 on sex change, 11 on radio, television, etc., 18 on prayer and fasting in an aeroplane or at the earth's poles, and 6 on outer space. One also finds references to modern life here and there under other headings, but such subjects are only treated as marginal phenomena within the traditional framework.

What is striking about the *mostahdasat* is not only the limited range of subjects pertaining to modern life that they attempt to regulate legally[35] but also the brevity of their exploration of particular questions – scarcely an appropriate way of offering a solution.[36] In addition, the solutions are of a noticeably negative character. Listening to the radio or watching television is frequently forbidden or only allowed provided it does not contradict the *shari'a*. The use of exchange bureaux or banks is only permitted if interest is renounced. Lotteries are forbidden, artificial insemination is only allowed if the sperm donor is the husband of the female recipient. It is forbidden to carry out an autopsy on the corpse of a Muslim, and so on. Interestingly, many of these reservations and prohibitions have been dropped in the Islamic Republic.

Another feature of the *mostahdasat* is that, as products of a form of speculative thought, many solutions are phrased with extravagant scrupulousness. At times it seems as if the questions have been phrased in order to cause embarrassment to the grand ayatollah (though of course he himself formulated them). There is, for example, the question of how to determine when a creature or a human being on another planet attains its majority. What does Islamic law have to offer as a solution to the question that would arise if children on another planet 'develop into men within one year [of their birth]'? The answer is: 'There is no problem with establishing that they have attained their majority if their majority is manifest through ejaculation of sperm and the appearance of pubic hair.' To the question of what the Islamic ordinances say about marriage on another planet, one answer is: 'Marrying creatures on other planets is permitted, if they are possessed of reason and understanding. And this applies even if they have a different physical appearance.' Finally, it is noteworthy that most of the solutions pertaining to 'new matters' lack the kind of proof which religious law requires. Their acceptance is obviously based on the fact that it is impossible to reject them. Such is the case, for instance, when it is declared permissible to take out an insurance policy, although Islamic law is unfamiliar with insurance and has no formula for it amongst its usual contractual formulas, nor regulations to cover it. To legitimate the decision, it is explained that the conclusion of such agreements is not dependent on their being mentioned in the *shari'a*. They are allowed as long as they are not contrary to the general principles regulating agreements in the *shari'a*, e.g. the parties involved enjoy mental health, are of age, etc.[37] However, the problem here is that this type of procedure, which is rational, has rarely been followed when new questions are dealt with. Indeed, a lack of rationality is the only way to explain the superficiality of the solutions to the *mostahdasat*.

The paucity of content and the limited number of new matters accepted into the law-books can only be explained by the fact that the sources of the *shari'a* and the juridical principles (*osul-e feqh*) based on them do not allow much scope for the massive process of integration and adaptation necessary if a traditional system of law is to fulfil the juridical needs of a modern society. In Shi'i Islamic law an ordinance only has validity if it is supported by the Koran or the *sunna*. The consensus of the jurists (*ejma'*), as a third legal source, only comes into effect if it reflects the judgement of the infallible authorities (the Prophet and the Imams). Reason or intellect (*'aql*) exists as a fourth possibility, the function of which is once again chiefly to disclose the hidden ordinances of the Koran and the *sunna* concerning particular questions by applying the procedural rules laid down by the *osul-e feqh*.

In the latter connection there are, to begin with, four technical rules which are known as: the necessity of the premise (*vojub-e moqaddameh*), contradiction (*tazadd*), priority (*tarattob*) and coincidence of the command and the prohibition (*ejtema'-e amr va nahi*).[38] Moreover, intellect has another function, which operates when the jurists are unable to decide what the stipulations of the *shari'a* are concerning a particular question or action, or when they are in doubt. Assuming that the action in question is unavoidable, the jurist is allowed to support his judgement by reasoning. But even in this case, there are limits, which are defined by the so-called operative principles (*osul-e 'amaliyeh*). These are: the principle of being free (*bara'at*); the principle of caution (*ehtiyat*); the principle of choice (*takhyir*) and the precedence principle (*estehsab*). In such a case, the believer, depending on the situation he is in and depending on the action to be undertaken, may be released from a command, may base his decision on criteria of caution, may choose between two or more actions, or may base his behaviour on how people behaved in the same situation previously.[39]

These fetters on reasoning, laid down as guiding principles, restrict the capacity of Shi'i jurisprudence to adapt itself to new situations. And indeed little noteworthy progress has been made in this direction, either before or after the revolution. The paucity of legal solutions pertaining to 'new occurrences' makes this fact clear for the pre-revolutionary period. The innovative steps that have been taken since then are based less on the application of reasoning as defined by Shi'i *osul-e feqh*, than on *raison d'état*, i.e. on the rules of *maslahat* (interest), the validity of which in earlier times was always questioned by the Shi'i jurists, though not by several Sunni schools of jurisprudence.[40] Shi'i jurists were only prepared to apply such rules once they had become the rulers and were obliged to deal with the problems of state security and running the government. We will return to question of *maslahat* in Chapter 12.

## Legislation without an Islamic Content

Since the revolution, officials in the different branches of government have passed what amounts to a mountain of laws, statutory instruments, resolutions and statutes that have no demonstrable relationship to the *shari'a*. Indeed, the very subjects of this legislation are not mentioned in the traditional Shi'i law-books. For the new legislation regulates social, that is to say socially relevant, relationships which are foreign to the mercantile, agricultural or nomadic societies in which the *shari'a* came to exist. The Revolutionary Council alone, during its year and a half of legislative activity, approved 1,022 bills, only a small proportion of which had anything to do with matters dealt with in the *shari'a*. The same may be said of the 931 laws which were passed by parliament and confirmed by the Guardian Council during the first three parliaments and the 452 laws passed by the fourth up to April 1995. If, contrary to expectations, the Guardian Council, with a few exceptions, did not clarify its position at a later date with regard to the bills passed by the Revolutionary Council and if, despite its careful scrutiny, it did not establish any relation between most of parliament's resolutions and the *shari'a*, this was primarily because those resolutions for the most part by-passed the *shari'a* and did not touch upon its content. Even when the Guardian Council returned certain bills to parliament, in only about half the cases was this because they contradicted the *shari'a*.[41] The rest contradicted the constitution[42] which, as we have seen, was itself not very firmly anchored in the *shari'a*. It is interesting to note here that, in the case of legislation passed by the 4th Majles the council rejected only 31 bills as contradictory to the *shari'a* and as many as 100 as contradictory to the constitution. Indeed, the differentiation which, in accordance with the constitution the Guardian Council made between disagreement with the constitution on the one hand, and disagreement with the *shari'a*, on the other, illustrates clearly that not all the resolutions passed by parliament could be judged with the criteria of the *shari'a*.

A few theoreticians of *velayat-e faqih* occasionally found it convenient to have recourse to a means of covering up this awkward situation. They declared that every resolution which found approval with the legislative institutions of the Islamic state automatically acquired religious sanction and could be incorporated into the corpus of the *shari'a*. These resolutions corresponded to the so-called 'state ordinances' (*ahkam-e hokumati*). They belonged to the *shari'a* for the simple reason that they had been enacted by an Islamic state. By way of explaining this point, Ayatollah Montazeri made the following statement to the Assembly of Experts for Framing the Constitution: 'We have two kinds of *ahkam*, one which appears in the Koran and in *feqh* … and one which is governmental in the sense that the ruler of a particular place issues it with regard to specific cases on the basis of general [Islamic legal principles].' Such a general principle is the proposition: 'Regulate your affairs!' On this basis the state can establish traffic regulations which do not appear in the Koran or in the *sunna*. And he added that many of the laws that will pass through parliament are of this kind. 'If they are confirmed by the Guardian Council, they acquire the value of law in conformity with the *shari'a*.'[43] Madani cites these explanations extensively in the second volume of his book and adds that parliament, the Guardian Council, and the fact that the members of the latter council are appointed by the leader, guarantee that the laws have a character in conformity with the *shari'a*, and furthermore they achieve this by creating a link between the laws and the ruling jurist, i.e. the Imam.[44]

If this explanation is to have any degree of legitimating effect, then one would at least expect to hear from parliament or the Guardian Council on the basis of what principles they establish laws that are not found in the sources of the *shari'a*. But generally speaking, they do not confront this problem. One is left to assume that in all cases they base themselves on the proposition: 'Regulate your affairs!' Indeed, this proposition can in fact be applied automatically in all acts of legislation. However, such a general rule appears not only in the *shari'a*, but in every form of social doctrine.

Characteristically, bills that have no precursor in the *shari'a* or that make no attempt to establish a link with the *shari'a*, as a rule pass through the legislative institutions with relatively little friction and are enacted rather quickly. By contrast, bills relevant to the *shari'a* regularly become the object of debates that go on for years between the various legislative bodies and the representatives of different interpretations, political positions and interest groups within those bodies. For the most part, the debates hold up the process of legislation or even block it completely. In this sense the *shari'a* has proved to be the undoing of legislation, placing obstacles in its way that can only be overcome with great difficulty. When a law of this kind does finally emerge from the legislature, as a rule it no longer corresponds to any of the positions that had originally demanded its conformity with the *shari'a*.

Such a law is, in other words, in disagreement with the *shari'a*. But the people are not meant to know of the disagreement. Consequently, many tricks of religious jurisprudence are employed to cover up the discrepancy. Over the past 15 years, the history of legislation in the Islamic Republic has in a certain sense been a history of the paths taken in order to circumvent obstacles that have arisen from the disunity with regard to the *shari'a's* positions of the forces participating in legislation. In what follows we will describe some of these paths in greater detail.

# Notes

1   *The Islamic State*, p. 25.

2   Ibid., p. 47.

3   These are different from the discretionary punishments or *ta'zirat* which, as the name implies, are left to the discretion of the judge.

4   *The Islamic State*, p. 10.

5   M 1/5.

6   Majles-e Showra-ye Eslami: 1981, p. 26.

7   See the newspapers from 16/2/79 onwards.

8   'Women may frequent the ministries, but not naked [i.e. unveiled]; they must wear the veil.'(*Kayhan*, 7/3/79)

9   *Jomhuri-ye Eslami*, 17/12/80.

10   Madani: 1986–90, vol. IV, pp. 46 and 409.

11   Ibid.

12   *Kayhan*, 23/8/82.

13   *Kayhan*, 24/8/82.

14   LB: 1982/83, p. 42 ff.

15   Madani: 1986–90, vol. IV, p. 271.

16   Mehrpur: 1992, vol. III, p. 208. The doubts of the Guardian Council meant that the Islamic Penal Code was enforced on an 'experimental' basis until as late as 9/7/96 when it was announced that it had finally been made permanent. See LB: 1991/92, p. 593 ff and *Salam*, 9/7/96. See also Chapter 11.

17   Majles-e Showra-ye Eslami: 1984, p. 180; 1985a, p. 104.

18   MM 27/9/87, p. 20.

19   That is to say, by passing amendments or new formulations of previously existing laws, which resolutions then required the approval of the Guardian Council.

20   Madani: 1986–90, vol. IV, p. 389 f.

21   Mehrpur: 1992, vol. III, p. 167 ff. We will return to some of these cases later on.

22   Madani: 1988, vol. IV, p. 444 f.

23   Schirazi: 1993, *passim*.

24   The law on commerce, which contains 600 articles and was codified between 1910 and 1937, surpasses in size many times over the relevant passages found in the civil law. The law on partnerships, which is an extension of Art. 21–93 of the law on commerce, contains 300 articles and 28 notes. See Sabi: 1972, and Graf von Rotkirch: 1977.

25   On this point see Schirazi: 1988 and 1993.

26   The Guardian Council has characterised laws which contradict the two collections mentioned here as laws that contradict the *shari'a*. See Madani: 1986–90, vol. IV, p. 390.

27   This assertion is treated most extensively by Ayatollah Montazeri in his four-volume work (1988–92), where he attempts to underpin his viewpoint by citing Islamic sources. B. Johansen (1984) has pointed out (in connection with Hanafite law, which is none the less relevant here as well) that even Islamic criminal law deals with rights that pertain to the relations between private individuals. In these cases, 'the state and the justice system can only intervene if they are called upon by a private party to help him attain what is his right, or if private individuals violate the general conditions imposed upon their conduct by the law.'(p. 133).

28   M II/911.

29   *Kayhan*, 30/4/91.

30   *Howzeh*, 1988e, No. 25, p. 30; see also *Howzeh*, 1986/87, No. 14.

31   *Howzeh*: 1987/88, Nr. 23, p. 22. Rationalist jurists (*osulis*) are distinguished from the traditionalists (*akhbaris*) in that, amongst other things, they recognise not only the *sunna* as

a source of law but also formulate independent legal opinions (*ejtehad*) on the basis of reason (*'aql*).

32 These articles nevertheless bore the title: 'The Self-Sufficiency of Islamic Jurisprudence' (*Resalat*, 21/1/89 and immediately subsequent issues). Apparently, despite the awareness of gaps in the *shari'a*, it is possible to conclude that Islamic law is perfect, either by not facing the serious consequences this has, in particular with regard to the legitimacy of *velayat-e faqih*, or by ignoring the enormous extent of the actual gaps.

33 Coulson: 1964; Motahhari: (n. d.), p. 12; M. Watt: 1980, vol. I, p. 234; and see also Welhausen: 1961.

34 Katuzian: 1990; Mahmasani: 1967; M. Watt: 1980; Coulson: 1964.

35 The Grand Ayatollah Sadeq Ruhani presents in his book (1971) solutions for many questions such as 'issuing a license to broadcast news', divorce on the basis of an acquittal agreement, birth-control, road regulations and industrial alcohol. According to Azari Qomi, the reason for the paucity of new questions dealt with in Khomeini's books is that the existing *ahkam* are sufficient for all actual questions and needs of present-day society. New *ejtehad* is not required for this purpose. (*Resalat*, 1/11/87).

36 Except, of course, in the case of solutions pertaining to religion.

37 Motahhari: 1982.

38 The first rule declares an action to be required if it forms the premise of a command. The second determines whether or not carrying out one particular action removes the necessity for carrying out another action contrary to it. The third is used to decide whether fulfilling one command makes it permissible to omit a less important command that coincides with it. And the fourth is provided for cases where a choice must be made, although the action, when considered from different viewpoints, may be simultaneously required and forbidden.

39 On the subject of *osul-e feqh* see Löschner: 1971; Motahhari: n. d.; Shahabi: 1958; and Feiz: 1984.

40 Mahmasani: 1967, p. 156 ff.

41 Up until 4/9/88, 228 resolutions of parliament were declared contradictory to the constitution, while 245 contradicted the *shari'a*. These figures relate mainly to individual articles or notes, and only in a few cases to the complete text of a bill.

42 See Chapter 4.

43 M II/1083. The statement that forms the foundation of this rule is attributed to 'Ali, the first Imam of the Shi'a.

44 Madani: 1986–90, vol. II, p. 178. We will see later that the religious academies and traditional jurisprudence, which as previously is still taught in those academies, do not support this theory.

NINE

# Circumventing the *Shari'a*
# through the Rule of Emergency

The so-called rule of emergency (*qa'edeh-e zarurat*), which comes under what are known as the secondary legal categories (*'anavin-e sanaviyeh*), is often used to circumvent the *shari'a*. According to this rule, in an emergency[1] a commandment or a prohibition – in other words an ordinance – can be overlooked. In this case, the rule stipulates: 'Emergencies make it permissible to do what is forbidden.'[2] The rule of emergency is based on, amongst other things, the Koranic verses 2/173 and 6/145 where, after mentioning forbidden meat, the sentence follows: 'But if a person finds himself in a dilemma, without desiring (something of his own accord)', he will not be guilty if he eats the forbidden meat.

The Koran thus makes it perfectly clear that what is forbidden becomes permissible in an emergency on the condition that there is no desire to do it. A second and third condition for ignoring a prohibition are that there must be a continuance of the emergency and that the forbidden act must only be committed in an appropriate degree, that is in accordance with the degree of the emergency. The rule concerning this restriction says: 'Account must be taken of the extent of the emergency in question.'[3] The ordinance which, according to this rule, makes what is forbidden permissible and makes a commandment invalid is known as a secondary ordinance. It is called 'secondary' because in every case it suspends a primary ordinance of the *shari'a*.

The use of this rule in order to pass laws which, in the opinion of the Guardian Council, contradicted the *shari'a* began from the time the Revolutionary Council first undertook legislation. In particular, those laws which were intended to limit the private ownership of property, and were therefore contradictory to the sacred rule of *taslit* according to which 'people are masters over their wealth', had to be conceived of as secondary ordinances and could only be legitimised in such terms. In order to give the reader an idea of the kind of laws that this rule was applied to and the kind of arguments used to justify its application, this chapter will present a few cases in which legislators attempted to underpin their initiatives with the rule of emergency. These case studies also provide an opportunity to observe how those who upheld the classical *shari'a* opposed such attempts and the concrete results of the struggle between the opponents and the advocates of the rule of emergency.

## The Law on Urban Land

The first law passed to annul or restrict the private ownership of urban land in the Islamic Republic goes back to 1/7/79. In that law, the Revolutionary Council decided to allow persons who had come to possess large tracts of wasteland in the cities 'according to the criteria of the previous regime' a period of time to build on the land. Otherwise, it would revert to the state and be put at the disposal of the needy for the purpose of building a home. According to this law, owners of smaller plots of wasteland who had no home of their own would be given 'at least' three years to build themselves a house on their land.[4]

Since this law appeared to be too mild, even to those who had framed it, it was amended two months later. The amendment stated that all plots of land that were larger than the personal needs of their owners could 'as of now' be transferred to the state.[5] In its preamble, this law was justified primarily by reference to the fact that in Islam wasteland could not be privately owned. At so early a date after the revolution, there were few who could question the assertion that documents issued under the Shah's regime with regard to the ownership of wasteland were contradictory to the *shari'a*. None the less, opposition to the law was strong and the Revolutionary Council, realising that its initial justification was insufficient, turned to the rule of emergency. In other words it justified its action by referring to 'the interest of the nation' and the need to build homes for people.

Although the guardians of the *shari'a* did not openly fight this law, they vigorously opposed its statutory instruments[6] issued by the Council of Ministers on 29/8/79. In these, the definition of wasteland (*zamin-e mavat*) clearly violated the *shari'a*. Wasteland was a plot left vacant or fallow. But if at least three-quarters of a plot's surface had at one time been used for agricultural purposes, or a house had once stood upon not less than a quarter of a plot and had one storey roofed, it was not wasteland. These criteria, however, contradicted the *shari'a* according to which wasteland was defined as land that had never been cultivated or built on in any way.[7] Another provision of the law that drew objections concerned urban land belonging to a religious foundation (*waqf*) the use of which could not be changed without permission from the Council of Ministers. It was contrary to the *shari'a* to give the decision on the use of land belonging to a foundation to an authority other than the donor or trustees appointed by the donor.

The opposition to this law, or in this case to its statutory instruments, eventually led to its revision two years later. In legislation passed by parliament on 9/8/81 a distinction was made between urban wasteland and uncultivated land and different regulations were formulated accordingly. Wasteland whose deed of ownership had been declared null and void would, with the exception provided for by the law of 1979, be placed at the disposal of the Islamic state (Art. 4). And uncultivated land, in accordance with the *shari'a*, would be differentiated on the basis of whether its owner was known or not (Art. 6).

In cases where the owner was known, he would be allowed to cultivate up to 1,000 sq. meters for himself or to sell that amount to the state. The rest of the land was to be offered for sale to the state at a price to be fixed by the government (Art. 7 and 8). Land belonging to a foundation was to remain in the situation specified by the donor unless it was to be sold, for which transaction permission had to be sought from the Housing Ministry (Art. 9, note 2).[8]

None the less, the Guardian Council rejected this law as contrary to the *shari'a*. Its opponents in parliament had already affirmed its incompatibility with the *shari'a*. The MP Sobhani had, for example, stated: 'These multiple restrictions imposed on property owners contradict the principle of peoples' freedom to own property which is ensured in Islam by the rule of *taslit* and which says: "A person is master over his property and his life."' Sobhani approved of the idea that property whose ownership had been established illegally should be declared invalid, but he rejected the application of this procedure to land which had been acquired legally. He went on to say: 'Fundamentally, annulling the ownership of property is against the law of all religions, in particular Islam.'[9] Hojjat al-Eslam Va'ezi protested that vacant plots of urban land were being treated as wasteland. While rejecting regulations aimed at expropriation, he cited a *hadith* which declared that the property of Muslims was as sacred as their blood.[10] The provision in this bill for *waqf* land was also rejected as un-Islamic by some MPs. During its first reading, 'Askarowladi regretted that it contained no rule excepting *waqf* land.[11] Although the bill's opponents could not achieve a majority in parliament, they were untroubled since they were confident that the Guardian Council would reject it.[12]

The bill' advocates, on the other hand, naturally believed that it was in complete agreement with the *shari'a*. Mostafa Tabrizi, for example, said that ownership of land by reclamation (*ehya'*) is only permissible under an Islamic system of government. Since until now people had lived under the rule of the *taghut* all property ownership had come about in a non-Islamic way and could be considered illegal.[13] Since the existing ownership of property contradicted the *shari'a*, in the opinion of 'Ali Aghamohammadi the bill in question, in so far as it left some land to its former owners, was also contrary to the *shari'a*. He hoped that the land would not only be confiscated but also that former landowners would be forced to work for as brick-makers so that they would come to know the bitter taste of having no property.[14]

The position of the majority was located between these two extremes. It considered the restriction of property as provided for in several of the bill's articles to be contrary to the *shari'a* in the sense of the primary ordinances, but declared that this was permissible on the basis of the rule of emergency. Hojjat al-Eslam Musavi Tabrizi bowed to this justification of the bill, while pointing to the disadvantages for the public at large if ownership of urban land was not restricted. According to his colleague, Ahmad Kashani, such disadvantages included the concentration of capital and the work force in the construction sector and its inflationary effects. This would limit the construction of houses for the less well-off.[15] Tavakkoli confirmed Va'ezi's statements on the sanctity of property ownership in Islam, but remarked that the ruler (*vali-ye amr*) in the Islamic community has the authority to restrict property rights in a situation that cannot be resolved any other way. Land speculation had given rise to the current situation and the only way to deal with it was to restrict the right to own urban land.[16] The shortfall of three million homes, the lack of government funds for the purchase of land on which to build new homes, the adverse effects of increased ownership of property and the harm caused by homelessness to young couples were, according to the housing minister, other valid reasons for an appeal to the rule of emergency.[17]

Although some opponents of the bill rejected the rule of emergency as a general principle, they were willing to make an exception in this case. But they felt that parliament had no right to legislate in an area that was a matter for the ruling jurist. Thus Hojjat al-Eslam Mohammad Reza 'Abbasi-Fard declared: 'This parliament is no ruler over Muslims. It cannot take over the duty of *velayat-e faqih*. It has not been authorised by the ruling jurist to assume this task, either verbally or in writing.'[18] Hojjat al-Eslam 'Abbas Abu Torabi-Fard expressed the same view, while drawing a distinction between legislation and issuing *ahkam*. Legislation was a matter for parliament, whereas *ahkam* could only be issued by the ruling jurist, because they might be contrary to the primary ordinances of Islam. Since he did not wish to annul the primary ordinances in an absolute sense, he would have to issue *ahkam* in a limited form and for a limited duration. If this procedure were observed, then the Guardian Council could not reject the resolution because to do so would be to act against the sovereignty of *velayat-e faqih*.[19]

Despite everything, parliament passed the bill, drawing attention to the existence of an emergency, to Art. 45, 47 and 49 of the constitution and, in the preamble to the bill, to the need to obey the command of the ruling jurist. This was apparently a reference to a decision already taken but not yet put in writing: namely an authorisation Khomeini had given to parliament for laws passed on the basis of the rule of emergency. For reasons that remain unknown, it took several more months before a written authorisation was issued.

Nevertheless, reference to this point did not stop the Guardian Council from rejecting parliament's resolution, declaring Art. 7, 8 and 9 (note 2) to be contrary to the *shari'a*. The council based its judgement on the Koran, tradition and the *sunna*, as well as the rule of *taslit*. It also rejected Art. 11 which gave authority to decide whether a plot of land was wasteland to a commission made up of members of the executive branch of government pointing out that, according to the *shari'a*, it was for the competent courts to decide this matter.[20]

We have already described the content of Art. 7. Art. 8 obliged owners of cultivated and uncultivated land acquired in accordance with the *shari'a* to sell as much of their land to the state or the municipality as the latter required, at prices which the government would set or in exchange for state land located elsewhere. Furthermore, the note to Art. 9 was objected to because it made the state the owner of land acquired according to this resolution, whereas the correct view was that the state merely had the right of disposal. Art. 13 stipulated certain punishments (fines, imprisonment and expropriation)[21] – which the Guardian Council deemed to be contrary to the *shari'a* – for persons who had illegally taken possession of state-owned property.

For the government, the rejection of this bill meant interrupting a programme which, on the basis of a bill passed by the Revolutionary Council, had involved putting at the disposal of schools and public services 500,000 sq. meters of land, and which envisaged the transference of large quantities of land in the future.[22] A government that called itself revolutionary and had declared that its goal was to provide every family with a house could not sit back and accept this. Nor could the majority in parliament. In order to solve the problem and deal with similar difficulties that had arisen in the countryside in connection with land reform, there appeared to be no alternative but to use the rule of emergency. For the purpose of removing the obstacles to applying this particular law, on 27/9/81 the president of parliament, Rafsanjani, wrote to Khomeini asking him for help over those laws which had to be passed for a fixed time through the formulation of secondary ordinances to protect the interest of the state or to 'prevent evil'. Khomeini should accomplish this by enforcing his *velayat* and making use of the rights of his office as leader, as those rights are defined in the constitution. Khomeini's answer, dated 11/10/81, included the words:

> Parliament has the right to enact and carry out measures which aim at protecting the system of the Islamic Republic when the neglect of such measures would cause disturbance to the public order. And it is justified in taking all necessary steps to prevent wickedness and to avoid difficulties if the majority in parliament confirm that such a danger exists and when it is clear that the resolution is temporary and will be automatically annulled once the danger has disappeared.[23]

On the basis of this authorisation, on 8/12/81 parliament once again passed the bill rejected by the Guardian Council. However, to meet the council halfway a few small alterations were made. The preamble was made into an article emphasising that the validity of the law was for a limited period of time; property owners were given ten days to register a protest with a competent court against the commission's ruling that their plot was wasteland, and instead of the fine and imprisonment mentioned in Art. 13, provision was made for 'payment of compensation for damages caused and prohibition from any form of dealing in real estate for the next five years'.[24]

Neither these alterations nor recourse to the powers conferred by Khomeini prevented the Guardian Council from rejecting the bill once again. This time, the council argued (in a letter to parliament dated 24/12/81) that the housing emergency was not so great in every city as to warrant a general 'cancelling of the primary ordinances'. Even if it were, the crisis would not be of equal intensity in every locality and consequently applying identical criteria for 'restricting the right of ownership of property and cancelling the primary ordinances' could not be permitted. Since parliament 'with regard to this generally applied law had not taken proper account of the varying dimensions of the emergency in its assessment', its resolution was judged illogical and contrary to the *shari'a* and the bill had to be revised. Nevertheless, the council made a point of stressing that it had no intention of questioning the existence of an emergency in the area of housing nor parliament's right to declare such a state of emergency. The council had nothing against parliament being authorised to perform this function by the Imam.

The ball was once again in parliament's court. However, on this occasion the changes it made to the bill were far less significant than the Guardian Council had requested, which suggests that parliament was now sure of its ground and counted on the Guardian Council giving way. The council was obviously under intense pressure and gave its approval to a slightly altered bill passed on 18/3/82. On the other hand, this was not the only pressure which apparently motivated the council to give way. Concessions by the parliamentary majority on other parts of the bill presumably also played a role in its decision. These changes did not so much concern the question of an emergency but had to do with other matters relevant to the *shari'a*. In Art. 1 an additional reason was cited for the existence of an emergency – the need to attract capital for investment in the productive and infrastructural sector. In the bill's first draft the estimated value of public services was deducted from the market price. But now the parliamentary majority renounced such a deduction, which for the opponents of the bill was contrary to the stipulation of the *shari'a* with regard to the so-called locational price (*qeimat-e suqiyeh*) (Art. 8, note 5). In the bill's new formulation, the right to register a protest against the commission's decisions to categorise property as wasteland was extended to give competent courts priority to such cases (Art. 12). As in the older formulation, the entire bill was passed with recourse to the rule of secondary ordinances.[25]

Thus, three years after the revolution, the law on urban plots of land was finally passed. For five years the government, with reference to the existence of an emergency, was allowed to suspend primary Islamic ordinances which hold the property ownership to be a sacred right. The limited time period of five years was of no significance since it did not mean that the expropriations would be cancelled when the five years had elapsed or that the primary ordinances of Islam would be restored. If within the deadline the state was able to take possession of all the land in question, within the terms of this law there would be no property left which could form the objective basis for reintroducing the primary ordinances. With this law the Islamic state thus violated the Islamic rule on secondary ordinances pertaining to emergencies by excluding, most particularly, the possibility of reinstating the primary ordinances for the property owners concerned.

The law was put into effect and by 1987 had brought about the transference of large areas of urban land. Towards the end of February 1987 the parliamentary secretary in the Ministry of Housing announced that the total area of land transferred under the law was 529 million square meters (of which 227 wasteland, 174 million cultivated land and 129 million uncultivated land), and to 20 March 1986, 86.2 million square meters of land had been transferred to the needy of which 51 million square meters belonged to the category of cultivated and uncultivated land. Numerous complaints were lodged against the classification of property as wasteland by the relevant commission and in 54 per cent of all such cases the courts handed down rulings against the commission.[26]

In 1983, a conflict between parliament and the Guardian Council over the law once again broke out At the instigation of the Housing Ministry, parliament had recourse to powers conferred on it by Art. 73 of the constitution[27] and attempted to grant further powers to the executive on the basis of interpreting this law. Accordingly, amongst other things the transfer of property belonging to a *waqf* by its trustees could only be done with permission of the Housing Ministry and in conformity with guidelines set by urban development and housing policy (Art. 10, note 2). Owners of cultivated and uncultivated land could be obliged to hand over their property, not only to meet the needs of the government and the municipality, but also to satisfy the requirement for private housing. 'Cultivated land' was to mean any land used for agricultural or other purposes, with the sole exception of orchards. (Art. 9)

Parliament was convinced that these changes did not require the approval of the Guardian Council and that they could be passed by recourse to the rule of emergency. On 4/8/83 it voted by a two-thirds majority to pass them. However, the Guardian Council did not accept this position and letters on the subject were exchanged between it and parliament. In the end, the council declared that it was prepared to let the amendments go through in so far as they were passed with recourse to the rule of emergency. But it held the interpretation of Art. 9 to be contrary to the *shari'a* and refused to confirm it because it had not attained a two-thirds majority in parliament.[28]

This two-thirds majority was a new requirement that had to be met if parliament were to have recourse to the rule of emergency when framing legislation. It was brought in at the instigation of numerous influential members of the clergy who had spoken out against the fact that an absolute majority in parliament had been accorded the right to suspend the primary ordinances of the *shari'a*.[29] Khomeini reacted to this pressure with an ambiguous ruling. On the one hand on 24/1/82 he qualified the authority he had issued to parliament by requiring that the rule of emergency only be used on the basis of a two-thirds parliamentary majority. On the other hand he ordered that the Guardian Council could not raise any objections to resolutions passed by a two-thirds majority in parliament. Through this ruling Khomeini restricted the powers of the Guardian Council to a certain extent and made it easier for parliament to ignore the primary ordinances of Islam although he recommended that MPs formulate resolutions of this kind in a way that the Guardian Council would not have difficulty in approving.[30]

When the period of validity of the law on urban plots of land ran out at the beginning of 1987 there was still a great need for land for building homes. In the government's opinion, this could only be met by further intervention in the domain of private property. Accordingly, the period of the law's validity had to be extended or it had to be replaced with a new law. The government decided on a bill that would neither have a time limit nor be as restricted in its effect as the previous law. It justified this decision by stating that 'the housing policy and the implementation of Art. 31 of the constitution[31] both required a set of permanent regulations.' However, the bill it presented to parliament contradicted the *shari'a* to such an extent that it was unable to obtain a parliamentary majority. The president of parliament, Rafsanjani, stated on behalf of his colleagues that several parts of the bill could only be passed in parliament with recourse to the rule of emergency and hence a two-thirds majority.[32] Only in this way was it possible to save the bill which was passed after a second reading.

The bill put cultivated and uncultivated land under private ownership at the disposal of the state for the purpose of building homes and constructing municipal facilities. Once again, conservative MPs, particularly those concerned with the *shari'a,* protested, claiming that further violations of the *shari'a* were being committed. Hojjat al-Eslam Morteza Fahim Kermani asked why the problem could not be solved by appealing to the Islamic conscience of the property owners to put their land at the disposal of the state. In this way respect for the primary ordinances would remain intact. Hojjat al-Eslam Abu Taleb Mahmudi referred to the *Mizan* of the religious scholar Tabataba'i,[33] according to whom neither need (*niyaz*) nor necessity (*lozum*) constituted an emergency, i.e. was considered enough of a constraint (*ezterar*) to constitute an emergency. Hunger was not an adequate justification for violating another person's property rights. Only if someone were undeservedly threatened with death was he allowed to commit a forbidden act. Hojjat al-Eslam Khalkhali answered that if not committing a forbidden act would lead to blindness, gastritis or crippling, the situation could be defined as an emergency. The president of parliament added that 'the explosion of social problems' could also constitute an emergency.[34] A minority continued to maintain, as they had maintained five years earlier, that all private property had been acquired illegally and should be turned over to the state.

One of the arguments advanced by opponents of the bill was that the concept of emergency was being applied on too general a scale. For this reason the bill was altered to specify that the law would only apply where a crisis really did exist. The problem here was to establish in which cities a crisis could be identified. A list of 50 cities eventually had to be reduced to 36 before a two-thirds majority could be obtained for the full list. The bill was finally passed by parliament on 28/4/87. But, as expected, it met with opposition in the Guardian Council, which maintained that many of its provisions were contrary to the *shari'a*. The most interesting objection from our perspective related to Art. 9.[35] The Guardian Council maintained that the dire need referred to in the bill did not actually exist. For precisely this reason the bill itself had stipulated that the transference of vacant or built-on land (dealt with in Art. 9) could only go ahead if the Organisation of Urban Land established that there was insufficient wasteland, etc. to meet the indicated needs. Thereupon, parliament altered the regulation. It was now stipulated that, in cases where parliament itself established there was an emergency, vacant and built-on land could be used along with wasteland and state land for the indicated purpose.[36]

Another contradiction to the *shari'a* taken up by the Guardian Council concerned the fact that urban land without an owner was described as belonging to the state (*dowlat*). The *shari'a* would designate the land as belonging to the Islamic state (*hokumat*), which was itself subordinate to the ruling jurist. Therefore, it was the Imam, his representatives and the religious judges (*hokkam-e shar'*) who had the right to distribute land to the needy and those deprived of their rights. Parliament solved the problem by replacing the word 'state' with the expression 'the state of the Islamic Republic'.[37] It is noteworthy that the Guardian Council did not object to this point in the law of 1981, although there too reference was made to the state and not to the ruling jurist.

Another regulation which the Guardian Council did not object to in 1981 but now maintained was contrary to the *shari'a* concerned land belonging to a foundation (*waqf*) which according to the earlier law could only be transferred under the supervision of the Ministry of Housing. Parliament changed this regulation and placed the transference of this category of land under the supervision of the ruling jurist (Art. 10, note 2).[38] A third case in which the Guardian Council reversed its 1981 judgement concerned placing land held by the revolutionary institutions under the authority of the government. Here too the council maintained there was a contradiction to the *shari'a* which it judged would be resolved by placing such land at the disposal of the ruling jurist. Parliament yielded on these points and followed the instructions of the council (Art. 10, note 1).[39]

Two further contradictions to the *shari'a* had to do with changing an owner's use of land on the one hand, and, on the other, the validity of court rulings regarding the protests lodged against the decisions of the commission to classify property as wasteland. In the first case, parliament had made permission to undertake such a change dependent on transference of a part of the land in question to the state, and, in the second case, it had excluded any possibility of appealing against the court's ruling. On these points as well, parliament changed the text of the law to conform to the wishes of the Guardian Council.[40]

Despite such concessions parliament did not succeed in satisfying the Guardian Council which returned the changes with seven further requests.

Only with regard to Art. 9, which had been passed with recourse to the rule of emergency, did the council yield, though rather reluctantly. The council wrote: 'In the corrections undertaken to Art. 9, the emergencies there referred to have not been proven. The responsibility for this rests with parliament.' The spokesman for the competent parliamentary committee interpreted these words as follows: 'The honourable Guardian Council has passed over Art. 9 without handing down a judgement because this article was approved with a two-thirds majority. Therefore, the article may be considered to be passed.' The bill as a whole was passed after parliament, on 23/9/87, dealt with the other objections raised by the Guardian Council.

Thus it was resolved that for another five years the government could act contrary to the *shari'a* with regard to private urban land not classified as 'wasteland', and land without an owner. If parliament gave in on other issues and moved closer to the position of the *shari'a*, this was because the need to act otherwise had not yet arisen to the same degree. According to this law, there was an emergency in 32 cities including all the country's major cities except Mashhad.[41] On 16/5/89, following an accelerated procedure, parliament passed a bill with a two-thirds majority adding 28 further cities to the list. These were all located in the war zone; the return of refugees to their original homes and encouraging reconstruction in cities destroyed by the war were given as reasons to justify an emergency.[42]

The time limit set by the law of 1987 ran out in 1992. We are so far unaware of any resolution to prolong the law. However, on 26/4/92 *Kayhan* reported that the Assessment Council had decided to allow a further period of three months for registering protests against decisions of the commission for classifying property as wasteland.[43]

## Land Reform and the Rule of Emergency

Another legislative initiative undertaken after the revolution with recourse to the rule of emergency and partially approved after many years of debate between the advocates of the classical *shari'a* and the radical-populist Islamicists, restricts the private ownership of agricultural land.[44] The reason for such legislation was the extreme inequality of landownership which, despite the reforms of the 1960s and 1970s, still existed by the time of the revolution[45], as well as the fact that during the revolution 850,000 hectares of land had been occupied chiefly by farmers who owned little or no land. In this case, it was a question of productive agricultural land that had, for the most part, belonged to large or medium-scale landowners. A spirit of revolutionary egalitarianism, i.e. the desire of the new regime to present itself as a champion of those deprived of their rights, made it awkward to take away the illegally acquired land from its occupants. It was therefore deemed necessary to at least legalise the situation. On the other hand, there were *shari'a* rules which sanctioned private ownership of property and condemned illegal land seizures.

The first attempts, on the basis of the rule of emergency, to introduce laws restricting private ownership of agricultural land resulted in a bill which, although passed by the Revolutionary Council on 27/2/80, was revised four times in the space of two months (to 15/4/80) owing to the pressure of opponents. These included influential grand ayatollahs, as well as landowners. According to the April 1980 version, all wasteland and pasturage were to be transferred to the state for distribution amongst farmers. Owners of cultivated land, if they were farmers themselves, were allowed to retain land amounting to three times what an ordinary local farmer owned, i.e. three times what was necessary to provide a livelihood for a rural household. If the owner was not a farmer, he could retain twice the amount of land worked by a local farmer, provided he had no other means of earning his living. The rest of the land was to be turned over to any farmers in the immediate area who had no other way of securing their livelihood. In exchange for the improvements in productivity that had resulted from reclaiming their land, the original owners were to be paid an equivalent compensation by the government. Owners of uncultivated land put under cultivation would be able to retain the same amount allowed for cultivated land. If the land remained un-cultivated, they would lose it all to the state. The lands of mechanised farming and cattle-raising enterprises were excluded from these regulations.

The need to proceed in this manner was justified in all four versions of the bill by verbal formulations which, if not always explicitly, made clear reference to the rule of emergency. These included expressions such as: 'social needs', 'the requirements of rule', the need 'for national self-sufficiency' in agricultural production and 'ensuring a livelihood for rural households'. Moreover, cultivated and vacant land was only to be transferred if it turned out that the need for land could not be satisfied, or satisfied adequately, by transference of wasteland and confiscated land. Likewise, farmers were only to receive land if they could not earn their livelihood any other way.

The opposition to these regulations, which were considered to be contrary to the *shari'a*, was so great that Khomeini was obliged to forbid their implementation, at least as far as cultivated and vacant land was concerned. But this was not the last attempt to undertake legislation of this kind. The next took the form of a bill passed by parliament in December 1982 and explicitly based on the rule of emergency and the authorisation Khomeini had given to parliament to use the rule. For this reason the bill's validity was restricted to a period of five years. Recourse to the rule of emergency was justified, in addition to the points indicated in the law of 1980, by the need to prevent emigration from the countryside.

In the case of some regulations, the 1982 bill made the law of 1980 less stringent, which could not have pleased the radicals in parliament. The radicals went on the assumption that Islam did not allow private ownership of land. What they accepted as Islamic was simply the right of exploitation, which was acquired through personal work and consequently limited to the amount of land an individual exploited. The radicals had recourse to history to prove the illegality of the existing ownership of land. In their view landownership also violated other rules of the *shari'a*, for instance the rule of *zarar*, which amongst other things declares every right to be cancelled if that right causes harm to other people, and the rule of *'otlat*, which declares it is not permissible to let land lie fallow.

One of the arguments used by opponents of the bill was that dividing up land holdings for redistribution would diminish the yield of the land per hectare and consequently work against increasing agricultural productivity and self-sufficiency. In their view, the migration of farmers from the countryside was not caused by their lack of land, but by the difference in the standard of living in the country and the city. What was necessary, therefore, was not the division of land holdings but an increase in production through reclamation of wasteland and other technical measures.

In the opinion of the Guardian Council, parliament's recourse to the rule of emergency contradicted the *shari'a* on several grounds. Firstly, wasteland, as well as state and confiscated land, could also be made available for transference to farmers by applying the primary ordinances of Islam. Secondly, the need for the transference of cultivated and vacant land could only be established once the distribution of the first mentioned category of land proved to be inadequate to meet the existing needs. Thirdly, the ruling system of the Islamic Republic could not be set up on the basis of secondary ordinances and temporary emergencies.[46] But this is exactly what the government and parliament, at least when dealing with certain problems, were trying to do by repeatedly using this rule to legitimate their legislative undertakings.

On these grounds parliament's resolution was rejected and a solution of the land question was further postponed. The issue was not taken up again until May 1985 but the new bill again encountered the opposition of the Guardian Council. In this bill attention was primarily directed to settling the issue of the land that had been occupied by farmers. Ownership of the land was to be transferred to the occupants if they fulfilled certain conditions. They must be landless or own very little land, live in the locality and have no other means of earning their livelihood. Otherwise, the land in question was to be returned to its original owner. However, if the former owner was obliged to give away his land, he would receive 'a fair price' for it after his 'legal and religious debts' had been deducted. If the owner were himself a farmer residing in the locality without other means of ensuring his livelihood, a portion of his land would be returned to him. An owner of uncultivated land would be given a year's grace to put his land under cultivation, either through his own labour or through a tenant or a sharecropper, and in that case he could retain the land. Otherwise, the government would sell his land at a fair price and provide him with the proceeds. The essential point was the exploitation of the land.

This bill was justified by reference to an existing crisis and passed by parliament with the necessary two-thirds majority. Nevertheless, the Guardian Council rejected it on 2/6/85. This time the council based its decision on a flaw in procedure. The two-thirds majority made it impossible for the Guardian Council to throw out the resolution because it contradicted the primary Islamic ordinances, but the procedural mistake was sufficient grounds for once again deferring suspension of the primary ordinances. The council objected that parliament had not treated the bill in question as a new bill in which case the usual procedure would have to be followed, but as an amendment to the bill of 1982 which had already been rejected.

In the end, the struggle of the Guardian Council on behalf of the classical *shari'a* was just as unsuccessful as the effort of the radical-populists to put through their version of Islamic law. Towards the end of October 1986, the opposing parties found a form of regulation which, though it did not correspond to the *shari'a*, offered a solution to problems which could no longer be deferred. Parliament passed a bill by a two-thirds majority with a validity of three years which was limited to regulating the transference of the occupied land to the present occupants. The advocates of this solution argued that a crisis existed because if the lands in question were returned to their former owners the consequence would be an uprising of the farmers and the disruption of governmental order.[47] In Kurdistan, where the rebels had taken steps to redistribute land, such a decision would appear to be additional proof that the Islamic regime was a friend of the feudal lords. Moreover, if the farmers, who had taken part in the war against Iraq in such great numbers and whose participation was essential to the war effort, were snubbed they might then turn their back on the war. Another point was the fact that the Imam, the president, the prime minister and the president of parliament had for many years assured the farmers that the land would be given to them. What would happen if these promises were broken and the farmers were forced to swallow this 'pill of despair'? 'What consequences would such an act have for the war?'[48]

The Guardian Council did not oppose this resolution. However, it was able to add the qualification that cultivated and vacant land that had not been occupied would be excluded. To that extent, for the time being at least, the *shari'a* remained unviolated as far as unoccupied land was concerned. However, on 16/8/88 the Assessment Council decided to take a further step against the primary ordinances pertaining to these matters. This consisted of including uncultivated land amongst the land to be transferred, under the same conditions that were specified in the law of 1985. Another step undertaken by the Assessment Council concerned the formation of small-scale agricultural co-operatives (*mosha*). Most of the previous bills had stipulated that the farmers who received land would have to join such co-operatives. The Guardian Council saw a contradiction to the *shari'a* in this measure as well, but this did not seem important to the Assessment Council.

Although the law of October 1986 was valid for only three years, expropriations based on it were still being carried out in mid-1994. Figures released by the Ministry of Agriculture show that up to 26 January of the same year 677,304 hectares of occupied land had been transferred to the occupants.[49] This is the scale on which the *shari'a* has been openly violated. In addition, 81,959 hectares of cultivated and vacant land, which did not come under the category of occupied land, has also been transferred. The figure of over 14,000 *mosha'* co-operatives said to exist by January 1994 [50] throws light on another area in which the *shari'a* has been sacrificed for practical purposes.

## The Rule of Emergency and the Rent Law

The rule of emergency has also been applied to the Rent Law. To begin with a legislative initiative was presented that, it was claimed, corresponded fully to the primary Islamic ordinances. This was debated in parliament on 11 and 13/4/82 in a first reading and in a second reading between 2 and 10/1/83, after which it was passed. This 'fully Islamicised' Rent Law, was supposed to replace the corresponding law of 1977. Its text was formulated by the Parliamentary Committee for Judiciary Affairs, in which the clergy usually form the majority. Hojjat al-Eslam Musavi Tabrizi, extolling its virtues, claimed that the committee which formulated the bill had made an effort to apply 'the highest degree of consideration for the *shari'a*'. Most of its articles, he said, would reproduce ordinances that had always been 'known and un-disputed' in the books of Islamic law. He expressed his delight that there was 'happily no great disagreement exists among us over these matters'.[51]

According to Musavi Tabrizi, by contrast to the Rent Law of 1977, the bill was Islamic because it did not contain clauses dealing with mortgages (*rahn*) and terminable business contracts (*bey'-e shart*). The same was true of the right to adjust rent, which according to the old law could be claimed before a court every three years. According to the new bill, the question was to be solved solely between the contracting parties – a provision that accords with Islamic law in which business contracts concern the two parties involved and not a third party, in this case the state. By way of justifying this Islamic revision of the old law, which was clearly to the tenant's disadvantage, the MP Hojjat al-Eslam Mohammad Khamene'i stated:

> Those of us who are in parliament must know where our duty lies. Is our duty to uphold Islam and the undisputed formulations of *feqh*, or to protect the weak and do what is best for them? Included amongst the undisputed ordinances relating to the question of renting, is the recognition of an owner's right to own and dispose of his property as he wishes. If it is necessary to protect the weak, a different way must be found. This religion is perfect. Go and find the correct way. The amount of rent and the rental period are to be specified in a rental contract. Tenancy comes to an end as soon as the rental period has elapsed … Muslims adhere to agreed upon conditions and Muslims are true to their promises. These are the rules of *feqh*.'

His colleague Hojjat al-Eslam Movahhedi Savoji drew the attention of MPs to the warnings of opponents of the bill, who believed that this kind of legislation would create great tensions in society. Landlords would put intense pressure on their tenants now that the latter had lost state protection. But he then reported a conversation he had had with members of the Guardian Council who were not at all convinced that the Islamic Rent Law would produce such tensions. They had told him: 'For once try putting the Islamic laws into practice to see if they really would lead to difficulties.' Convinced of the need for this experiment, Savoji presented arguments to support it. Amongst other things, he cited the example of students of the religious academies in Qom who followed Islamic law in questions to do with renting. 'As soon as the contract's time limit runs out, they are prepared to vacate [their room] or to enter into a new rental contract. This ought to provide people with an example to follow. We should apply the primary ordinances to the Rent Law without bringing in secondary regulations, in order to see what the result will be.'[52]

This legislative initiative unambiguously contravened a bill which the Revolutionary Council had passed two and a half years earlier. On 29/10/79, disregarding the Islamic ordinances, the council had intervened on a far-reaching scale in the regulations affecting rent by confirming the Rent Law of 1977 but lowering the rent for almost all housing by 20 per cent. A few weeks later, it resolved that the courts should not adjust rents on the basis of the Central Bank's price index, but on the basis of assessments such as 'the fair market value of the day'.[53]

By contrast, the Islamic law removed state protection from tenants to such an extent, and contradicted the populist slogans of the revolutionary government so blatantly, that many felt it would be better to withdraw the bill immediately. Indeed the MP Morteza Alviri argued that the bill could not compare with the law of 1977.[54] He and other opponents of the bill pointed out that it would encourage landlords to force tenants to vacate their lodgings since landlords could hope to draw up rental contracts that were more favourable to themselves. The parliamentary secretary of the Ministry of Justice noted an additional danger – namely that courts would be swamped with the number of complaints which would arise if this bill were passed. He enumerated seven points in the bill which he objected to. The MP 'Azam Taleqani stated: 'We are always saying the revolution belongs to the weaker members of society.' She went on to ask: 'What is there in this bill which favours the weak?' Turning to the members of the Judiciary Committee, she demanded to know: 'Islam's actual answer to the tenant who is required by a landlord to leave his lodgings and who then turns to a court of arbitration only to be immediately presented with an order of eviction?'[55]

In the end the opponents of this bill managed to ensure that it only passed its second reading with considerable changes which, however, caused the Guardian Council to oppose it. The council maintained that ten points in the bill were incompatible with the *shari'a*. For instance, in Art. 9 it was left to the discretion of the courts to accord tenants a period of time to vacate their lodgings if immediate eviction would cause them distress. A note to this article obliged the Supreme Court to create a special court for the purpose of examining all orders of eviction. If an eviction order was issued against a tenant who had fallen into arrears with his rent, he could be granted time to make up what he owed. In view of the urban housing crisis and because of the need to freeze rents for a period of five years, Art. 14 granted the Ministry of Housing the right to determine the rent of lodgings on the basis of the size and quality of a habitable unit. The Supreme Court was charged with the task of establishing in which cities there was a crisis (note 1). A tenant would have the right to complain before a court about a rise in rent and to demand to be reimbursed if he had paid too much (note 2). If a landlord refused to rent a habitable unit without good reason, a commission specially appointed for the purpose would have the right to act as his deputy, rent it on his behalf and transfer the rent to his account (note 3).[56]

The Guardian Council considered that Art. 9 was contrary to the *shari'a* because it did not take account of the possible dilemma of the owner or the fact that, in cases where other lodgings were available, no urgent need would arise for the tenant if he had to vacate his lodgings. The council objected to Art. 14 because parliament, despite the authorisation it had been given by Khomeini, had transferred to the Supreme Court the right to establish whether an emergency existed. The same objection was levelled against note 3 of Art. 14. Moreover, the Guardian Council judged that it was not correct that a commission should intervene when payment of rent was refused since the decision in such cases rightfully lay with the ruling jurist and the religious judges (*hokkam-e shar'*) who were his deputies.

Similar criticism was voiced in parliament by the opponents of the disputed article. One MP considered that the generalisation of an emergency was not justifiable. The minister of justice invited those MPs who denied the existence of an emergency to follow for half an hour the work of a court of arbitration in order to see what problems this question had created for society.[57] The MP Hojjat al-Eslam Va'ezi put his finger on the main point when, quoting numerous *hadiths*, he declared the state's intervention in private commerce to be contrary to the *shari'a*. This policy amounted to curtailing people's freedom, and furthermore appeared to deny the intelligence of individuals who engaged in business with one another. 'A person who concludes a business deal is of necessity logical. He does not buy when prices are high.' His colleague Khalkhali based his answer on the character of the state. If one accepted that the state was Islamic, then one had to go along with the practice that 'exchange rates and prices could be fixed on the basis of *fatvas* issued by well-known jurists'. Ayatollah Yazdi had doubts about the claim that rejecting this bill would cause damage to the Islamic community or ruling system. On the other hand, his colleague Zavvare'i drew attention to the high level of rents in Tehran and other large cities. Even people with middle-range incomes could not afford them. 'Therefore, it is necessary to freeze rents for a limited period.' Aghamohammadi warned that if this law were passed people would be forced to break it because they would simply be unable to act in accordance with its stipulations. Hojjat al-Eslam Ansari replied that if you looked at matters in such a way, you would have to blame the Koran for encouraging people to commit sins. Indeed, the Koran contained regulations whose violation constituted a sin. If you judged things that way, you would end up saying that 'the prophets, God forbid, had made committing sins a prerequisite for the development of mankind'.[58]

The Guardian Council's opposition to this bill forced parliament to resume its debate on 5/2/83. Parliament resolved to take account of the urgent situation of the landlord as well. With regard to the tenant, an emergency would only come into effect if there was in fact a lack of available lodgings. This time parliament itself would designate which cities had a housing crisis. The validity of those parts of the bill which had recourse to the rule of emergency would be subject to a five-year time limit. These and other changes were undertaken in order to satisfy the Guardian Council. Nevertheless, the council still raised an objection to note 3 of Art. 14. On 2/5/83, parliament also changed the note in question and thereby transferred to religious judges competence to decide about renting an empty house.[59]

In later years as well, whenever the government and parliament wished to supplement or amend the Rent Law in ways that violated the primary ordinances of the shari'a, they met with opposition from the Guardian Council and were obliged to push their programme through by applying the rule of emergency. Such was the case on 17/9/85 when they nullified the vast number of accumulating orders of eviction that property owners had demanded against schools. But although this resolution obtained a two-thirds majority in parliament, it could only be put through once its validity was limited to five years.[60]

On another occasion, towards the end of September 1986, the issue concerned the accommodation the government had rented for war refugees and war invalids, whose eviction, once again, could only be prevented by recourse to the rule of emergency and with the proviso that the law in question would only be valid for five years.[61]

In 1990, Art. 9 of the law was supplemented by two notes which, as in the previously mentioned case, went into effect because the Guardian Council did not rule on them within the deadline set by the constitution. Thereafter, the time limit for the supplement of September 1986 was extended by two years.[62] The fact that the Guardian Council twice refused to render its verdict on a resolution passed by parliament prompts the conclusion that at the end of the day the council has failed in its struggle against attempts to suspend the primary ordinances of the shari'a the council.

As in the case of urban land, by means of this law and numerous other measures, the Islamic regime has given partial relief to many of the needy; but generally speaking this procedure has not alleviated the housing crisis. Indeed, it has got worse. The enormous rise in rents since the early 1980s has not been matched by a rise in income, particularly amongst people in the lower and middle-income brackets, testifying to the dire proportions of the crisis. But despite the deterioration in the situation since the law of 1983 was passed, its time limit was not extended in 1988, or to put it more correctly, no visible steps were taken in that direction.

In 1984, the government and parliament attempted to apply the regulations of Art. 9 of the 1983 Rent Law to commercial premises, again citing the rule of emergency. The Guardian Council rejected the move and since then parliament has not made any further effort to put through the amendment. Consequently, the regulations of the 1977 law are still valid in this case. According to this law, eviction from commercial premises after the contracted rental period has ended depends on a series of conditions, which 'naturally were not in agreement with the principles of the *shari'a*'.[63]

## The Emergency in Domestic Trade

Although the Guardian Council rejected the attempt to apply the rule of emergency to the case of commercial premises, despite the fact that they could not guarantee the application of the primary Islamic ordinances, matters took a turn in the opposite direction when it came to bills regulating the buying and selling of goods. In this case, the Guardian Council itself recommended that government and parliament justify their legislation with reference to the rule of emergency. However, the government and parliament refused to take up this suggestion, the relevant bill was opposed by the Guardian Council, and further efforts to pass the law were abandoned, without however renouncing the actual policy.

On 20/4/83, parliament obliged the government to present it with a draft bill within three months which would serve to regulate the buying and selling of goods within the country. The bill was submitted to parliament on 15/1/84 and passed after a second reading on 11/4/85. According to the bill, responsibility for the buying and selling of goods was transferred to the Ministry of Commerce. The bill established three categories of goods: essential, necessary and ordinary. The responsibility of the Ministry of Commerce for the buying and selling of goods increased in the reverse order of this sequence. In an emergency, the ministry was even allowed to intervene in the retail trade. Moreover, in the case of those goods that it purchased itself, the ministry was authorised to work out its own policy with regard to stockpiling, price-fixing and selling whenever this was in the interest of the nation. Determining when this was in the nation's interest lay with the same ministry. Likewise, it was to decide what shares the private, state and co-operative sectors were to have in the buying and selling of necessary goods. Its duties also included determining the amounts of essential and necessary goods that would be stockpiled and the amounts that would be made available for consumption, applying pressure to change the population's pattern of consumption in order to stop extravagance and the pursuit of luxury, and designating the organisations that were to be responsible for selling goods on the basis of consultation with the guilds concerned and after consideration of the particular goods involved.[64]

The primary reason for this far-reaching nationalisation of domestic trade was the scarcity of goods brought about by the war with Iraq and the decrease in revenues from oil exports which had been followed by rocketing prices. But the government was also encouraged to monopolise trade for its own advantage by the self-interest of officials and their clients in the private commercial sector.

On 5/5/85, the Guardian Council, as might be expected, rejected this bill completely as contrary to the *shari'a* and the constitution. It argued that the bill had: a) turned over trade to the Ministry of Commerce forever, not just for a temporary period of emergency; b) created a state monopoly over many goods; c) given the state the right to set up its own trading enterprises; d) entrusted the Ministry of Commerce with deciding what was in the interest of the ruling system so far as the sale of imported and domestically produced goods was concerned; e) moved in the direction of depriving people of their right to manage their own affairs and restricting an individual's choice of profession, and f) transformed the state into a wholesale entrepreneur by conferring on it authority over the whole system of merchandising. 'Therefore, the bill in its present form and with its present content is in violation of Articles 33 and 43 of the constitution, and in the opinion of the majority of the *foqaha* is incompatible with the principles of the *shari'a*.[65]

On 20/10/85, the government withdrew its bill although the Guardian Council had indicated its readiness to accept it if it were passed as an emergency regulation.[66] The fact of the matter was that in practice the government had already brought a great part of domestic trade under its control and was in a position to extend that control further without having to base its action on the rule of emergency. How far the government went in that direction was described by the spokesman of the merchants of Tehran in November 1986 when he said that state control of domestic trade had already extended to retailing and had thus attained the level of 100 per cent.[67]

The far-reaching intervention of the state in domestic trade corresponded to a state-oriented populist tendency which continued until the beginning of the presidency of Hashemi Rafsanjani, and which had been reinforced by the scarcity of goods and self-interest of many government officials. By referring to the scarcity of goods and the inflation which resulted from it, the state could justify this policy even in the eyes of those members of the clergy such as Ayatollah Montazeri who, on the basis of the classical *shari'a*, warned against state intervention in the affairs of the bazaar.[68] This policy was finally abandoned, at first with hesitation and for a long time only partially, when Rafsanjani formed his government and switched to a commercial policy adapted to the market economy. The change was influenced by the conservative camp, which by then had strengthened its position in the regime, by the collapse of the Eastern Bloc, pressure from the World Bank and factors with a similar effect in the world market. On 28/6/90 the minister of commerce declared that the government would turn commerce over to the private corporations. On the 27 August 1990, his deputy promised that controls over trade in 900 kinds of merchandise would be lifted. On 20/2/91, the Supreme Council of the Economy resolved to close down the state centres for the buying and selling of goods. The Central Bank issued the same resolution on 13/10/91. The repetition of similar resolutions and declarations of intent was an indication that there was massive resistance to this change in policy on the part of interested circles. But however successful this new policy may prove to be, it has no firmer basis in the ordinances of the *shari'a* than the state's intervention in domestic trade during the period before 1988. If the new policy appears to come closer to the primary ordinances, this is simply due to the influence of social, economic and political factors, as was the case with the state's intervention in trade.

## The Emergency in Foreign Trade

The bill for nationalising foreign trade was on the whole handled the same way as the bill for the buying and selling of goods. Here too the government under Prime Minister Musavi insisted on taking complete control of trade, a policy which was only relaxed when Rafsanjani became president. Similarly, although the Guardian Council recommended that the bill be passed as an emergency regulation, parliament and the government did not go along with their suggestion. And again the government abandoned its efforts to create a legal basis for a policy which it had already put into practice on the widest possible scale, disregarding in practice the primary ordinances.[69]

The nationalisation of foreign trade had already been stipulated in the constitution (Art. 44). From this point of view, the constitution itself was contrary to the primary Islamic ordinances – a consequence of the pressure exerted by revolutionary forces which believed in a state monopoly of foreign trade.[70] In accordance with the constitution, on 17/3/81 parliament obliged the government to present within two months a bill to deal with this subject. The bill was sent to parliament on 20/5/81 and passed after a second reading in April 1983.

Art. 1 of this bill stipulated that, for the purpose of putting into practice Art. 44 of the constitution, the government was to create the organisations necessary to nationalise foreign trade. Art. 2 justified nationalisation on the basis of a Koranic verse that says God will not allow unbelievers to rule over Muslims and the policy of 'neither the West nor the Eastern Bloc'. Foreign trade had to be regulated in such a way that 'the economic, political and cultural dominance of unbelievers and foreigners over Muslims' would be hindered, that the country's well-being would not be 'founded on a single economic and political axis in the world' and that priority would be given to trading with Muslims and the peoples of the world who had been deprived of their rights. In addition to a series of other economic goals that were to be met through the nationalisation of foreign trade, the bill was meant to help the government discourage forms of commercial transaction forbidden in Islam, the passion for luxury goods and entertainment, and to introduce an Islamic pattern of consumption. The bill named a number of organisations which were to be entrusted with the management of foreign trade.[71] Some of these had already been formed in relationship to the bill on domestic trade which had been passed by the Revolutionary Council on 9/4/80.

As the other cases discussed in this chapter, advocates of the nationalisation of foreign trade not only saw no contradiction between the bill and the *shari'a* but, on the contrary, were firmly convinced that there was a perfect congruence between the two. They repeatedly quoted the Koranic verse cited above and emphasised, as did the spokesman for the Parliamentary Committee for Commercial Affairs, 'Ali Akbar Ma'sumi, that in the past 'the channel for trade was the channel through which the unbelievers had established their dominance over the Muslims.' This channel had to be closed because 'God rejects every form of dominance by unbelievers over the Muslims.' Ma'sumi also referred to Khomeini's book *Tahrir al-Vasila*, which rules that all forms of foreign trade which entail a danger that foreigners may establish political dominance over the territory of Islam and the Muslims must be avoided. 'Therefore', Ma'sumi concluded, 'the nationalisation of foreign trade springs from the depths of our ideology. We want to put it into practice as a commandment from God.' Foreign trade, in this view, only gives rise to the dangers inherent in dealing with foreigners if it is left in private hands, because private merchants are exclusively concerned with making profits and are not interested in the welfare of the Islamic country.

The opponents of the bill answered: 'In Islam trade has always been free for Muslims. It is a precious blessing from God. Other conceptions of trade are therefore contrary to Islamic principles.' The MP Va'ezi, who made this statement, by way of supporting his position cited several passages from the sacred sources. He then reproached Ma'sumi for distorting the sense of the quotation from the *Tahrir al-Vasila* to defend his view. In Va'ezi's opinion, Khomeini was not referring to nationalisation of trade but 'avoiding' foreigners. The MP Taheri expressed the view that the bill in question could only be advocated on the basis of the rule of emergency and for a limited period. Otherwise, it would contradict the *shari'a*. Many opponents of the bill remarked that its goals could be achieved if the state would merely exercise supervision over foreign trade. Nationalisation was not necessary for that purpose.[72]

The position of the opponents of the bill contradicted Art. 44 of the constitution which, in dividing the branches of the economy into a state, private and co-operative sector, designated foreign trade as part of the state sector. But they solved their problem by referring to a passage in the same article of the constitution which declared that the rights of ownership in all three sectors were protected as long as 'they did not violate the framework of Islamic laws'. Although they did not say so explicitly, they took this to mean that the constitution itself would not be respecting this condition if it turned foreign trade over to the state.

The Guardian Council was clear on this question. On 11/6/82, it stated in its ruling on the bill that there could well be laws that were in agreement with the constitution but which were contrary to the *shari'a*. It rejected the bill because, 'by placing all exports and imports under the direct and monopolistic control of the state' it contradicted the principles of the *shari'a*.[73] A few months later but still in connection with this bill, a member of the Guardian Council, Ayatollah Mahdavi-Kani, in a letter he sent to the press regarding the relationship between the *shari'a* and the constitution, expressed the view that the Guardian Council had the authority to declare invalid any article of the constitution which in its particular or general meaning contradicted the *shari'a*. He based his view on Art. 4 of the constitution itself, which likewise made the validity of the constitution dependent on being congruent with the *shari'a*.[74]

In this letter Mahdavi-Kani also rejected one of the favourite arguments used by the advocates of the bill, namely that the state is the owner of the foreign currency obtained through oil and as such has the exclusive right to decide whether for the purpose of foreign trade it will be put at the disposal of the private sector or not. Those who argued this position based themselves on a *fatva* issued by Khomeini which says that the foreign currency obtained from oil exports 'belongs to the state and is the property of the Islamic state.' It 'must be spent on administering the country and in the interest of the nation.'[75] But Mahdavi-Kani was of the opinion that owning foreign currency was in no way a justification for the state's monopoly over foreign trade. 'What justifies the monopoly are the demands of the public interest and the existence of social emergencies.' The Islamic state could only exclude the private sector from foreign trade under these special circumstances. And he went one step further and stated that even the state monopoly on the export of oil and the imports which depended on the currency earned from it were contrary to Islamic principles unless it was justifiable in terms of the public interest.

Parliament's reaction to the ruling of the Guardian Council was as long in coming as was its anger at this ruling. The unavoidable corrections to the bill were not made until 22/4/84 but they were not sufficient to satisfy the Guardian Council. A second round of corrections was made on 21/6/84 and the bill was renamed a 'Draft Bill on the Form of Activity in Foreign Trade', a step apparently meant to prevent antagonism arising from the concept of 'nationalisation'. But the Guardian Council still would not yield. When a third attempt failed, the government and parliament gave up trying to transform their bill into a law, without of course abandoning the state monopoly on foreign trade. Later, when the Assessment Council had been formed, it also examined this issue,[76] without however passing a resolution that we know of. The dismantling of the state monopoly on foreign trade only began, as in the case of domestic trade, once the radical-populists in the regime had lost their dominance in the government, i.e. after Khomeini's death which was followed by the election of Rafsanjani as president.

The Guardian Council's ruling on the bill for nationalising foreign trade, as in the case of domestic trade, included a recommendation that parliament should pass the bill with recourse to the rule of emergency and with a two-thirds majority. Although it would not have been difficult to obtain a two-thirds majority in parliament the bill was abandoned because its advocates were confident that the state monopoly could be maintained without it. Their ideological and economic commitment to the monopoly was so strong that they did not want to restrict their scope of action with the reservations associated with secondary ordinances. Crucially the amendments they had made to the bill in their attempt to satisfy the Guardian Council were insufficient in the council's eyes because they never went so far as to restrict the monopoly. Thus, the Guardian Council's last ruling stated: 'The bill which regulates the distribution of foreign currency amongst the state, co-operative and private sectors allows the portion allotted to the state to exceed the usual limits. This share reaches proportions amounting to a monopoly or semi-monopoly.'[77]

## The Punishment of Speculators

The Bill to Increase Punishments for Speculators and Those Responsible for High Prices, which passed its first reading on 31/7/86, acquired the status of a law 21 months later on 24/4/88[78] after it was justified by declaring an emergency and had received a two-thirds majority. By this time the bill had been sent back and forth four times between parliament and the Guardian Council.

Before the bill was debated in parliament, the government had launched several large-scale propaganda campaigns against speculators and those attempting to drive up prices, publicly attacking them and condemning them to harsh penalties. In other words, the content of the bill had already been implemented. The immediate cause for applying these measures was a rate of inflation that was running in double figures. Like the *ancien régime*, which had introduced criminal legislation against speculation in 1974, the Islamic government found it convenient to shift the blame for inflation onto retailers in particular, despite the fact that it had itself imposed far-reaching controls on domestic trade. As might be expected, given that the causes of speculation and inflation cannot be eliminated by means of legal penalties, this bill, and subsequent more stringent bills were no more successful than parallel measures taken under the Pahlavis.

Formulating a bill especially directed against speculation (*ehtekar*) was very difficult because the *shari'a* only conceived of speculation as illegal when it involved wheat, barley, raisins, dates, fat and olives, i.e. products which in earlier times were in general use and the hoarding of which was forbidden.[79] Although there were some jurists such as Ayatollah Montazeri (1988) who had no legal objections to extending the range of goods which came under the relevant ordinances of the *shari'a* other authorities, including Khomeini himself, were against any such extension.[80] Consequently, other ways had to be found to undertake the necessary extension without acting against the *shari'a* in too obvious a manner. This sleight-of-hand was achieved by distinguishing between the concept of 'speculation' in the sense of the *shari'a* and speculation in the sense of an activity involving other commodities. Thus, to begin with Art. 1 and 2 of the bill made speculation involving the six above mentioned commodities punishable under the law, whereas Art. 3 stipulated that speculation involving all goods designated as essential was also forbidden and would be punishable under the law. The procedure was justified by pointing out that speculation involving other essential goods led to the same consequences which the *shari'a* had declared were forbidden. The text of this article stipulated: 'Anyone who keeps hidden more than a one-year supply of goods that are considered essential for the public, or refuses to sell them, with the intention of pushing up their price, comes under the definition of 'speculator' (*dar hokm-e mohtaker ast*) and will be punished with the penalties provided for speculation.'[81] This meant that he could not be designated a speculator in the sense of the *shari'a* but that he was acting like a speculator and therefore must be punished accordingly. To work out this formulation, a three-man commission was set up which sought advice in old law-books and from living jurists.[82]

Given the artificial character of this formulation, even many MPs were not satisfied with the article and foresaw that the Guardian Council would reject it. Consequently, it was proposed that Art. 3 of the bill be passed with recourse to an emergency and with the necessary two-thirds majority. The president of parliament announced that the Guardian Council had already made a recommendation to that effect. In the end, this solution was adopted and the article was approved with a limited time period of five years. The Guardian Council confirmed the bill on the condition that 'the amount of commodities involved exceeded a one-year supply for consumption.'[83]

## The Limitations of the Rule of Emergency

The rule of emergency was also used in more minor cases. For example, the employment of foreign doctors had to be justified on this basis while on another occasion it was used to oblige Iranian doctors to work at the front during the war. Each time the Guardian Council criticised the measure and one set of changes or another to the original formulations of the bills had to be undertaken before the council was satisfied.[84]

We have seen how the legislators in the Islamic Republic could not avoid departing from the primary ordinances of the *shari'a* when they set about regulating many essential questions of government. In two of the cases we have examined, the issue was landownership which is a central theme both in Islamic law and in the books that have been written on Islamic economics over the past decades. Issues like this are naturally of great concern in a country where industry does not have a dominant significance and land-ownership is still a major source of employment and income for large sections of the population.[85]

Although the spokesmen for the radical-populist position in the debate over landownership based their views on Islam, i.e. on the *shari'a*, and although they cited relevant religious sources, or their own interpretation of these sources, to support their approach, they could not convince the Guardian Council and the religious authorities that stand behind the council. The latter based their views on the form of classical source interpretation which had been carried out for centuries in the religious seminaries and, in the name of the primary ordinances of the *shari'a*, they fought against any arbitrary restriction of the right of private ownership. For them, the right of ownership could only be restricted on the basis of the other primary ordinances of the *shari'a*, that for example forbid the acquisition of property by illegal seizure (*ghasb*) or by means of the so-called prohibited forms of employment (*makaseb-e moharrameh*) such as selling wine, etc.

None the less, a large, temporarily dominant, majority in parliament and in the government, moved by the revolutionary mood, its own understanding of Islam or simply by self-interest, was passionately concerned to restrict this sacred right or to suspend it altogether. At the time before the Guardian Council existed and laws were passed by the Revolutionary Council alone or decreed by the leader, there was at least no constitutional barrier to putting such an undertaking into practice. But once the Guardian Council had been created, the advocates of radical-populist laws could only realise their intentions by circumventing the legislature or by relying on the rule of emergency, in which case they might succeed in achieving at least part of what they had originally wanted. In the first case, they disregarded the primary ordinances directly, whereas in the latter case they ignored them indirectly while formally acknowledging their validity. The existing social and political pressure hindered the Guardian Council from successfully opposing this use of the rule of emergency.

We label this form of recourse to the rule of emergency as formal because the original conditions for its application were disregarded. Even though the validity of the resolutions passed in this manner were restricted by a time limit, whenever necessary the date of expiration was so often extended that the object of the right in question, although suspended temporarily, finally ceased to exist. Moreover, the condition which stipulated that the normally forbidden act should not be something one desired was ignored completely: the radical-populists fought with all their strength to put through bills which aimed at committing a prohibited act.

Since the purely formal character of this recourse to the rule of emergency disturbed many of the ruling clergy, they thought up an explanation according to which the secondary ordinances which were formulated on the basis of an emergency were just as Islamic as the primary ordinances. As Ayatollah Azari Qomi put it, both sets of ordinances together formed 'the most important element of the divine ruling system'.[86] Ayatollah Montazeri indicated that he was in agreement when he said that the Islamic ordinances would consist of the primary as well as the secondary ordinances. But he added, in all honesty, that the foundation of Islamic law would be provided by the primary Islamic ordinances.[87] This view was endorsed by the Guardian Council when, in its ruling on the bill restricting the ownership of agriculturally productive land passed by parliament in December 1982, it emphasised that the ruling system of the Islamic Republic could not be constructed on secondary ordinances. Like every other legal system, the Islamic could not get around the fact that secondary ordinances were reserved for emergencies which were by definition of a temporary nature.

Although they held the primary Islamic ordinances to be sacred, strong political and social pressures meant that the protectors of those ordinances could not, in practice, prevent violations of them in the name of the rule of emergency. In such cases the Guardian Council limited its efforts to preventing excesses in the application of the rule of emergency. But it was hardly content with this situation. On 25/6/85, in a letter to Khomeini, the secretary of the Guardian Council pointed to particular excesses and demanded that they cease. He also expressed his fear that parliament, as in the first legislative period, would pass laws that were contrary to the *shari'a* and declare 'in the name of necessity that every commandment was a prohibition and every prohibition was a commandment.' He warned of the danger that, through the rousing of public sentiment and pressure exerted by influential persons in parliament, similar actions would be repeated.[88] Montazeri described it as 'an insult to Islamic *feqh* and the ordinances of God ... if we do everything we wish in the name of an emergency'.[89] Grand Ayatollah Golpaygani complained about the anti-Islamic regulations that were being passed in the Islamic Republic and expressed the hope that in the future loyalty would be maintained to the primary Islamic ordinances and not to 'ordinances that God's bondsmen attempt to pass off as divine decrees in the name of an emergency'.[90]

As for the reason parliament has over-applied the rule of emergency, Mehrpur (1992a), who was himself a lay member of the Guardian Council for several years, gives the following explanation:

> Parliament has formulated resolutions and passed them, for example in the domain of the economy, in view of what is in the general interest of society and out of consideration for the position of the weak and the needy, as well as the egalitarian and upright position of Islam and its fight against the accumulation of treasures and riches ... [But] the Guardian Council has examined these resolutions by applying the known rules and principles of *feqh*, and rejected them because in many cases they have been contrary to the principles of *feqh* and sometimes to the articles of the constitution.'

If Mehrpur had left out the connection with Islam in his remarks on parliament's motives, he could simply have said: 'parliament has passed resolutions on the basis of a set of views about society which are not in agreement with the social views embodied in *feqh*. And therefore the Guardian Council rejected those resolutions.'

When Khomeini gave parliament the authority to declare emergencies, the Guardian Council rightly saw this as a restriction of its own powers and protested. Although Khomeini rejected their reproach, it was clear that he had revoked the Guardian Council's power to enforce the *shari'a* with regard to a series of fundamental resolutions passed by parliament. For a long time the council would not accept this loss of power and gave vent to its anger by contesting the resolutions of parliament based on the rule of emergency. But restricting the powers of the Guardian Council vis-à-vis parliament meant restricting the link between legislation and the *shari'a*.

We saw earlier how, for example, Azari Qomi, in an attempt to gloss over the disregard for the *shari'a* that had clearly manifested itself in the incorrect application of the rule of emergency, maintained that secondary ordinances were identical with the primary ordinances. Similar attempts were made by other ayatollahs and hojjat al-eslams. Khomeini's personal representative in matters concerning *fatvas*, Hojjat al-Eslam Qadiri, for example, actually denied the existence of secondary ordinances. 'In our view all the ordinances of the *shari'a* apply to their own particular objects and are primary ordinances ... It never happens that two ordinances apply to the same object so that one of them can be a primary and the other a secondary ordinance.'[91] In connection with the debate over ownership of agricultural land, Hojjat al-Eslam Musavi Tabrizi explained that in an emergency the rule of *taslit* (individuals are masters over their wealth) loses its validity in the sense that it is no longer a primary ordinance. If in such a situation a person has his land confiscated, it does not mean that the primary ordinance has been annulled. In cases like this the primary ordinance is the ordinance that forms the basis for the confiscation.[92]

The radical-populist camp within parliament and the government, which had proposed the bills to restrict private ownership of land, at first showed no inclination to use the rule of emergency. Either they paid no attention to the stipulations of the *shari'a* on the questions they were engaged with or they relied on their own interpretations of the *shari'a* and its sources. Recourse to the rule of emergency only became necessary when they encountered the opposition of the Guardian Council. For its part, the council was convinced that the problems that had to be dealt with could best be solved with the help of the primary ordinances. Of course the spokesmen for the radical-populist camp said the same thing; the problem was that both sides interpreted the primary ordinances differently, or to resolve one and the same issue, wanted to apply two different primary ordinances. In any case, sorting out the legal difficulties in this area proved to be irrelevant since the result of these discussions either over the form a law was to take, or on the level of day-to-day practice, had little or nothing to do with the primary ordinances as understood by the Guardian Council or the radical camp.

The basic aversion of the radical-populists to using the rule of emergency also expressed itself, as mentioned earlier, in their disregard for the proper conditions for the rule's application. This disregard manifested itself, for instance, in the unauthorised but unavoidable extension of the object of the intended legal measure, this object being allegedly or actually in a state of emergency. On the basis partly of their egalitarian principles, and partly their state-oriented ideological views, they showed no willingness to delimit the area affected by an emergency, nor were they concerned to document the existence or the extent of an emergency by statistics or any other method. Only under pressure from the Guardian Council did they eventually devote themselves to tasks of this kind. This was, however, frequently no more than an exercise on paper. The executive often took action beyond the geographical boundaries of the emergency as defined by a law. The time limit imposed on the validity of a law, which had been a condition for passing it under the rule of emergency, served no practical purpose if the object or the right protected by the primary ordinances was in fact annihilated once and for all by applying the law in question.

The reasons given for declaring states of emergency revealed strong ideological characteristics or indications of self-interest. Among these, one in particular was especially effective in convincing the Guardian Council: namely 'the requirements of holding power' or 'the interests of the Islamic ruling system'. The power of justification which this explanation possessed went far beyond the application of the rule of emergency and far more radical steps for resolving problems raised by the *shari'a* could be legitimated by reference to it. This question is dealt with at greater length in Chapters 11 to 13.

The restriction of the power of the Guardian Council by authorising parliament to pass laws without consulting the council also amounted to an infringement of the functions assigned to that institution in the constitution. Since the constitutional task of the Guardian Council is first and foremost the protection of the *shari'a*, such restriction of its powers led directly to a loosening of the connection of legislation with the *shari'a*.

## Notes

1 There are those like Hojjat al-Eslam Musavi Tabrizi, for instance, who stretch the idea of 'emergency' or necessity (*zarurat*) so far that it comes to include compulsion (*ezterar*), distress (*'osr*), unwillingness (*ekrah*), secrecy (*taqiyyeh*), disadvantage (*zarar*), etc. All these would provide one with a valid excuse for committing what is forbidden (MM 5/4/87, p. 28 f.). Ayatollah Azari Qomi reckons that the rules defined previously: premise of the forbidden, priority and contradiction, also belong to the secondary legal categories (*Resalat*, 12/1/88). Ayatollah Yazdi expresses the same view in *Resalat*, 22/12/87.

2 Ja'fari Langarudi: 1984, p. 775.

3 Ibid., p. 776.

4 LB: 1979/80, p. 60 f.

5 Ibid., p. 95.

6 Ibid., p. 31 ff.

7 In *feqh*, another kind of wasteland is land that was once cultivated but has then become barren through neglect (*mavat-e bel-'araz*). This defintion comes close to the concept

of uncultivated land (*bayer*) – land that was once cultivated but gradually reverted to being wasteland.

8  Mehrpur: 1992, p. 69 ff.

9  MM 21/12/80, p. 25; 3/8/81, p. 23.

10  MM 28/7/81, p. 10; 3/8/81, p. 14 f.

11  MM 21/12/80. p. 26.

12  Va'ezi said: 'Even if parliament approves this bill, the Guardian Council will reject it.' (MM 21/12/80, p. 27.)

13  Ibid.

14  Ibid., p. 28.

15  MM 27/6/81, p. 17 ff.

16  MM 28/7/81, p. 32 f.

17  Ibid., p. 35 f.

18  MM 28/7/81, p. 46.

19  MM 5/8/81, p. 10.

20  Mehrpur: 1992, vol. I, p. 68 f.

21  On this subject see Chapter 11.

22  This information is based on a statement by the minister of housing (MM 21/12/ 80, p. 29).

23  Majles-e Showra-ye Eslami: 1982, p. 66.

24  Mehrpur: 1992, vol. I, p. 74 ff.

25  LB: 1981/82, p. 195 ff.

26  MM 24/2/87, p. 36 f.

27  This article confers upon parliament the right to interpret laws.

28  Madani: 1986–90, vol. IV, p. 306 ff.

29  As spokesman for his colleagues, Ayatollah Jannati, a member of the Guardian Council, expressed this protest openly. He was especially annoyed that this right had been conferred on a parliament whose members for the most part did not dispose over the knowledge of Islamic jurisprudence which in this case was considered to be absolutely necessary (*Ettela'at*, 2/6/84).

30  Majles-e Showra-ye Eslami: 1982a, p. 20 ff.

31  'Every Iranian family and every individual has the right to his own living space in accordance with his personal needs. The state is obliged to assure the necessary conditions for putting this principle into practice, with priority being given to the needy, in particular villagers and workers.'

32  MM 24/2/87, p. 20 ff.

33  Tabataba'i's multi-volume work that deals with Koranic interpretation.

34  MM 5/4/87, p. 28 ff.

35  This article states: 'The Ministry of Housing and Urban Development is obliged to obtain the land it needs for building homes and for public services from the supply of state wasteland and land without an owner. If this supply proves to be inadequate, it is to take possession of uncultivated land, or should the need arise, of land that has been built on in cities. A list of the particular cities is appended. Establishing what it needs in the way of land and whether that land is lacking is carried out at the suggestion of the chairman of the Organization of Urban Land and with the permission of the general assembly of that organization.' Furthermore, the owners are obliged to sell their land to the state at a price fixed by the government.

36  MM 7/7/87, p. 23 ff.

37  Ibid., p. 21 ff. The Guardian Council was not satisfied with this. It wanted the term '*vali-ye faqih*' to be used. Consequently, this is the expression found in LB: 1987/88, where the relevant law is published. The decision to adopt this term was taken by parliament in

a session on 13/9/87 under pressure from the Guardian Council. Rafsanjani commented on this change with the remark: 'In our opinion this distinction between the Islamic state and the *vali-ye faqih* is not correct. The two are identical.' (Ibid., p. 21)

38  MM 12/7/87, p. 21.

39  Ibid.

40  Ibid.

41  LB: 1987/88, p. 531 ff.

42  MM 18/7/89, p. 25 ff.; 19/7/89, p. 20 ff.

43  This resolution is not contained in LB: 1992/93. In connection with the 'statutory instruments for constructing new cities' which were passed by the Council of Ministers on 6/8/92, it is stated that the expropriation of land in the border area of the cities will be carried out in accordance with the 1987 law (Art. 7). Ibid., p. 32 ff.

44  No legislative initiative, virtually up to October 1986, aroused so much political and social concern. See Schirazi: 1987 and 1993.

45  At this time there were more than two and a half million farmers who either owned very little land or none at all.

46  Madani: 1986–90, vol. IV, p. 274.

47  MM 23/10/86, pp. 25 and 28.

48  MM 19/5/85, p. 21 ff.; 21/10/86, p. 29 f.

49  *Resalat*, 26/1/94.

50  Ibid.

51  MM 11/4/82, p. 26 f.

52  MM 13/4/82. p.18.

53  LB: 1979/80, p. 244 f.

54  MM 10/4/82, p. 26.

55  MM 13/4/82, p. 18 ff.

56  Mehrpur: 1992, vol. I, p. 309 ff.

57  MM 4/1/83, pp. 21 and 34.

58  MM 9/1/83, p. 20 ff.

59  MM 9/1/83, p. 25; Mehrpur: 1992, vol. I, p. 313; LB: 1982/83, p. 12 ff.

60  MM 15/9/85, p. 32; 17/9/85, p. 20 f.;19/9/85, p. 20 ff.

61  This law was automatically passed because the Guardian Council did not react within the ten-day deadline (LB: 1986/87, p. 379)

62  LB: 1990/91, p. 417.

63  Mehrpur: 1992, vol. II, p. 161.

64  MM 9/4/85, p. 22 ff.; 11/4/85, p. 19 ff.

65  Madani: 1986–90, vol. IV, p. 367 f.

66  See the secretary of the Guardian Council, Ayatollah Emami Kashani, in *Kayhan*, 9/6/87, and member of the council, M. Alef, in part 5 and 6 of his series of articles in *Resalat*, 7 and 8/6/87.

67  *Resalat*, 19/11/86.

68  Alef (1987) quotes these statements by way of confirming the position of the Guardian Council.

69  One could maintain that the government's conduct, as in the case of domestic trade, had been secured through a bill passed by the Revolutionary Council on 10/5/80 (LB: 1980/81, p. 75 ff.). However, the government and parliament must have considered this insufficient since they formulated new laws.

70  The MP Rajab 'Ali Taheri indicated this when the relevant bill was debated in parliament (MM 26/11/81, p. 22).

71  Mehrpur: 1992, vol. I, p. 161 f.; MM 4 to 10/4/82.

72  MM 26/11/81, p. 20 ff.

73  Mehrpur: 1992, vol. I, p. 160 f.

74  This is a further indication that the founders of the Islamic Republic were not sure of the agreement between the constitution of this state and the *shari'a*, or that they wished to leave the way open for questioning the constitution at any time in the name of the *shari'a*. For Mahdavi-Kani's letter see Madani: 1986–1990, vol. IV, p. 234 ff.

75  *Kayhan*, 30/11/82.

76  *Kayhan-e Hava'i*, 8/6/88.

77  Mehrpur: 1992, vol. I, p. 178.

78  LB: 1988/89, p. 152 f.

79  And yet not all of these products were widely consumed or consumed in large amounts.

80  On this subject see the series of articles by Ayatollah Azari Qomi in *Resalat*, 12/7/87 ff. and 22/8/87 ff., as well as ibid. 28/8/86, 2/10/86 and 14/6/87.

81  MM 31/7/86, p. 20.

82  MM 29/7/86, p. 32 ff.

83  Madani: 1986–90, vol. VI, p. 379 ff.; on this point see also Emami Kashani: 1992. Besides Art. 3, the penalties stipulated in the bill were problematic and contrary to the ordinances of the *shari'a*. These are discussed in Chapter 11.

84  On the two cases mentioned see Madani: 1986–1990, vol. IV, pp. 210 and 366. The difficulty which arose over the observance of Islamic burial rituals after the earthquake of 1990 in Northern Iran obliged the grand ayatollahs to suspend them by reference to the rule of emergency. This was an example of the application of the rule in accordance with its real purpose.

85  Around 30 per cent of the Iranian labour force is active in the agricultural sector.

86  *Resalat*, 27/7/92.

87  Quoted from Ayatollah Emami Kashani in *Kayhan*, 9/6/87.

88  Mehrpur: 1992a.

89  Quoted from Ayatollah Emami Kashani in *Kayhan*, 9/6/87.

90  *Kayhan*, 17/8/85.

91  *Pasdar-e Eslam*, No. 1 (1981), p. 30 f.

92  MM 2/3/82, p. 30.

# TEN

# Circumventing the *Shariʿa* through Secondary Contractual Conditions

Another way of circumventing obstacles to legislation arising from the *shariʿa* or the primary ordinances was to use the possibilities offered by the so-called binding secondary contractual conditions (*shart-e zemn-e ʿaqd*). In cases where a legal undertaking based on contracts between private individuals could not be reconciled with the form of contracts recognised by the *shariʿa* it could be justified, as far as its content was concerned, as a secondary condition of the contract. The *shariʿa* recognises such secondary conditions and allows them, though only under clearly defined circumstances. Iranian civil law, which is firmly based on the *shariʿa*, recognises two categories of secondary contractual conditions: those which do not in any way contradict the contract itself, and those that are contrary to the contract. To the latter category belong those conditions that 'contradict the requirements of the contract' and those whose object is formulated in a vague and unspecified manner (Art. 233 f.). ʿAli Feiz defines three kinds of invalid secondary conditions: first those which contradict the Holy Book, second those which make a commandment into a prohibition and a prohibition into a commandment, and third those which are not in accord with the content of the contract.[1] Khomeini writes in the *Tahrir al-Vasila*, where he enumerates the secondary conditions of the marriage contract, that those which contradict the *shariʿa* are null and void.[2]

However, whenever parliament enlisted the secondary contractual conditions in order to put through a piece of legislation, it violated these requirements for applying the rule. Consequently, bills of this kind met with the opposition of the Guardian Council. Without renouncing the advantages of secondary contractual conditions, parliament and the executive were forced to use other strategies in order to confer a legal character on their undertakings. Although the application of the rule of secondary contractual conditions did not always secure the goal they had in mind, the history of attempts to use it is instructive. Two major examples of such attempts are documented in this chapter.

## The Labour Law as a Secondary Contractual Condition

The Labour Law has been the most important example of an attempt to introduce legislation contrary to the *shariʿa* by means of the secondary contractual conditions. It occupied the legislators of the Islamic Republic for 10 years and, like the discussions surrounding the legal regulation of landownership, attracted a great deal of attention. The professed intention behind the law was to take a decisive step towards Islamicising labour legislation and annulling the old pre-revolutionary laws.

The Labour Law in effect before the revolution dated from March 1958 and, together with a few subsequent amendments, was among the mass of old laws which retained their validity in the Islamic Republic for many years. The first attempt to work out an Islamic Labour Law took place when Ahmad Tavakkoli, the spokesman for the conservative camp in the regime, was head of the Ministry of Labour. On 21/12/82 Tavakkoli presented a new draft bill at a press conference where he detailed some of the measures used to ensure that it was in complete agreement with the *shari'a*. Amongst other things, there had been numerous discussions with 'the lordly *'ulama'*, he had himself consulted the Imam who had emphasised that the Labour Law must be drawn up in co-operation with the *'ulama*, and the final version of the draft bill had been checked by the Supreme Council of the Economy in which the Imam's representatives had been present. The next step had been to consult the Guardian Council who had endorsed the methods adopted to work out the bill, made a few general observations and given their opinion on several points. In addition, the bill had been presented to Ayatollah Montazeri, Hojjat al-Eslam Khamene'i, Hojjat al-Eslam Rafsanjani and others. In short, it was based 'on the views of the Imam and the *fatvas* of famous Islamic jurists'. It therefore had the value of an Islamic ordinance. Even more important, it was based not on methods which had to do with the new ordinances (*ahkam-e mostahdaseh*), but on traditional *feqh* and specifically the Islamic ordinances of 'leasing' (*ejareh*) which had not not been changed through the centuries.[3]

A glance at the text of this bill[4] is enough to confirm the great effort that went into making it conform to these ordinances. Although the object of the bill – the contract of employment – is a product of modern times, in particular of industrial production, in spirit it was entirely consonant with the tradition in which the *shari'a* had developed. This spirit finds expression in the many concepts employed in the bill such as *ojrat* (remuneration, rent), *hiyazat* (measures which precede an act of seizure), *khiyar* (the right to give notice), *saman* (counter-value), etc.,[5] as well as in the content of many of its articles which do not reflect the conditions current in a world of industry and labour but rather an environment in which, for example, it is decided whether the objects gathered together on common land[6] belong to 'the owner of the labour' (*saheb-e kar*) or to 'the recipient of the labour' (*kar-pazir*).

According to this bill, the most important questions to be dealt with in a law regulating relations between employers and employees – such as the number of work hours, the duration of the contract, dismissal, vacations, pay and the employment of women and children etc – were to be settled in contracts which were to be concluded between the individual employer and employee. In short the new labour law belonged exclusively to the domain of private law. In this sense it was in conformity with the *shari'a* which, as we saw in Chapter 8, almost never operates beyond the confines of private law. The bill could not, however, totally ignore the state, because this would all too blatantly have run counter to real employment requirements. But it only allowed the state to intervene when circumstances made it unavoidable. Accordingly, a limit on the hours of work on dangerous and harmful activities was to be ensured by statutory instruments approved by the Council of Ministers (Art. 45). In situations where there was an emergency, a minimum wage was to be proposed for a specified time period by the Ministry of Labour and approved by the leader (Art. 46). Moreover, the government was to supervise the hygienic and technical conditions in factories and to intervene as a mediator whenever disagreements arose between the partners to the contract (Art. 100 ff.).

The bill was based on Islamic ordinances of leasing in the sense that it considered an employment contract to be a lease in which the employee's labour represented the object of the contract. Labour was to be placed at the disposal of the employer for a specified period and for a defined task. Consequently, its remuneration was not described as a wage (*mozd*) but as rent (*ojrat*). '*Ojrat* is cash or any other thing that has value which is given to an employee in exchange for his labour' (Art. 3). The description of the relationship between the employer and the employee in the contract was firmly based on the ordinances of Islamic jurisprudence. In Khomeini's *Tahrir al-Vasila* two kinds of lease are distinguished. One has to do with property (*'ayani*) e.g. 'an animal or a house', and the other with people, e.g. 'when a free man hires himself out for the purpose [of undertaking] a particular job.'[7]

In Khomeini's book the rules for 'taking possession of labour' are formulated in a manner which reflects the world in which *feqh* originally developed. For example, the book establishes the conditions under which a child hired out by its guardian can cancel the lease, or how women can be hired to breast-feed infants, or what the legal position is if a lessee engages two other persons to carry out two different jobs. Nevertheless in its section on leasing, the *Tahrir al-Vasila* is more concerned with the leasing of things and animals and only marginally with the conditions of a lease that regulates the labour of people. Seen in this light, the bill drafted by Tavakkoli is a novelty since for the first time it formulates an entire labour law on the basis of leasing.

In the bill several questions are regulated by making use of secondary contractual conditions, but this is done in conformity with the relevant stipulations of the *shari'a*. For instance, secondary conditions were only to be concluded between the partners of the contract and the government had no role in this matter. Art. 32 states for example, that: 'The employer can, in addition to the contract with the employee, agree to the condition that he will provide a retirement plan, accident insurance, insurance against disability, a pension scheme, etc.' The use of the word 'can' rather than 'must' is significant here. The employer was not obliged to respond to the demands of employees for such conditions. In a subsequent article (33), the word 'can' is used again, but since this particular qualification favoured the employer, the phrasing is unambiguous: 'The employer can enforce the disciplinary regulations for his work places as secondary conditions of the contract of employment concluded with the employee, once those regulations have been confirmed by the Ministry of Labour and Social Affairs.'

In both these cases, the regulations in question do not appear in the traditional contract of leasing. Thus, they were brought into the contract of employment as secondary conditions which were in agreement with the *shari'a* primarily because they did not compromise the private character of the contract. If the article just mentioned tolerated the intervention of an outsider, it did not contradict the *shari'a*, at least in its content, to the extent that it was the the well-to-do party, the employer, who would decide whether government regulations would be brought in or not.

From the very beginning this bill met with such violent opposition from the workers and their official and non-official representatives and sympathisers that it could not even be passed in the Council of Ministers[8] and was consigned to the waste-paper basket without ever reaching parliament. The protests were chiefly directed at the fact that the bill, by declaring that a contract of employment was solely a matter for the parties involved, left employees totally unprotected. From this point of view, it ignored the interests of the employees to a far greater extent than the old Labour Law.

The failure of this project meant it became urgent to draft a new bill which would on the one hand include the state protection and the employment rights that the people demanded of a revolutionary government and which were provided for in internationally recognised labour laws, and on the other hand be, at least formally speaking, 'Islamic'. In those areas where the Islamic ordinances on leasing could not provide a solution, other ways would have to be found to fulfil these requirements. However, this task proved increasingly impossible to carry out in practice. Between December 1982 and the beginning of November 1986, three bills were worked out, none of which was able to meet the government's criteria. The difficulties the government encountered in its efforts to take account of the *shari'a* can be gleaned from information made public in 1986 by the deputy minister of labour, Mohammad Salamati, which allows us to follow the process that finally led to the passage of a labour law in the same year.

To start with, an attempt was made to solve the problem with the help of the rule of emergency. It was thought that considerable parts of the labour law could be approved as secondary ordinances. It was considered acceptable to resort to these measures because employers were not obliged by the primary Islamic ordinances to observe the regulations for the protection of employees. But the use of the rule of emergency entailed two serious problems which in the end compelled the government to abandon this approach to a solution. Firstly, the rights of employees provided for in a labour law could not be passed as concessions granted for a limited period and, secondly, a draft bill consisting of 198 articles had no chance of obtaining for all its parts that were based on the rule of emergency the two-thirds majority necessary to neutralise the expected opposition of the Guardian Council. The fear was that the result would be a mutilated torso rather than a fully adequate labour law with all its parts intact.

Another solution considered for a while was to base the law on the Islamic ordinances governing partnership (*sherakat*). A relation of partnership might be postulated between three parties: the employer, the employee and the state. The state would be involved as a partner because, as a supplier of public services, it made an indispensable contribution to the functioning of business concerns. The state would then exercise the rights it acquired in this way by demanding that measures for the protection of employees be enforced and that employees' rights be recognised. The advantage of this solution was that it could be supported on the basis of primary Islamic ordinances. It appears, however, that the proposal was not taken seriously and was subsequently dropped.[9] There remained the possibility of resorting to the secondary contractual conditions. However, Salamati saw seven difficulties with this particular solution, most of them to do with the implementation of the law. For example, the only way the protective measures and the rights provided for employees by a law of this kind could be enforced would be by threatening to withdraw state services (electricity, water, etc.) from the employers. But such a threat would be difficult to carry out in practice if an employer refused to submit. Indeed, a law like this would turn out to be unenforceable. According to Salamati, these were the obstacles that caused the relevant parliamentary committee to give up the idea of legitimating the bill that was before the plenary session of parliament through the secondary contractual conditions.[10] Consequently, the new draft bill, which was passed by parliament on 19/10/86 after its first reading, contained no reference to these conditions.

Not only did this draft bill contain no reference to secondary contractual conditions, it also had no other legitimating positive relation to the *shari'a*. It was therefore certain it would be rejected by the Guardian Council. In the 12 months that elapsed between the first and second reading – the second reading began on 1/10/87 – this consideration eventually convinced MPs that the bill could only be put through if an attempt was made to give it legitimacy by using secondary contractual conditions. However, since the MPs knew that they were unlikely to convince the Guardian Council with an argument which they themselves hardly found plausible, they turned to Khomeini for help.

Khomeini had already expressed his support for the bill in 1985. At that time he had stated:

> The government can, in exchange for their observation of the legal regulations
> and the conditions it has set, place at the disposal of the owners of industries
> raw materials and other government facilities. Conversely, the government can

refuse to make available to them those raw materials and other facilities, in the event that they oppose the adoption of legal regulations.[11]

But this order did not fully break the resistance of the Guardian Council which evaded the issue on the pretext that Khomeini's statement had validity only in connection with newly founded companies. It could not be used to force already existing companies to observe the conditions in question.[12]

The opposition of the Guardian Council led the government to appeal to Khomeini again. The letter which the minister of labour and social affairs composed for this purpose, contained the question:

> Is it allowed to impose binding conditions on companies in exchange for public and state services and facilities such as water, electricity, telephone lines, fuel, foreign currency, raw materials, harbour and docking facilities, roads, the banking system, administrative equipment, etc., independently of whether they have made use of these facilities in the past and continue to do so, or whether this is a recent situation?[13]

Khomeini's reply was succinct: 'whatever the past or temporary case, binding conditions can be imposed.'

The pertinent *fatva* was issued three weeks after the bill had actually been passed in parliament. The entire bill was legitimised by reference to secondary contractual conditions. Art. 1 formulated the legitimation by means of this rule as follows: 'All employers, employees and companies operating in the industrial, agricultural and service sectors that in one form or another make use of state facilities such as foreign currency, energy, raw materials and bank credit, are obliged to conform to this law.' Acting in violation of the law would entail penalties which were set out in a separate section of the bill.[14]

The government pinned high hopes on Khomeini's *fatva* upon which it counted to disarm the Guardian Council. In a press interview, the minister of labour said that although the *fatva* was issued in connection with the Labour Law, 'in the future it would be a complete and comprehensive guide for the Islamic government in all matters'. Then he added: 'Whenever the government wishes to intervene in social issues, it can legitimate its action with the help of this great *fatva* of the Imam ... From now on, every law such as the Labour Law and any regulations issued by the government can simply be formulated and passed as secondary contractual conditions,' without having to confront the question of legitimacy. He went a step further declaring that: 'This *fatva* will from now on release the government from dependence on secondary ordinances, or limit their use to very rare cases.'[15]

The *fatva*, and this kind of hopeful and grand interpretation which followed in its wake, caused the Guardian Council to write Khomeini a letter that testified to their irritation and confusion, asking him for further clarification. In the letter it was stated:

> There are people who hold the view that the government, on the basis of this *fatva*, is authorised to replace the noble and certain Islamic regulations with 'any

form of regulations pertaining to social, economic, commercial, municipal and agricultural matters or to matters affecting employment and the family,' and to use the services and facilities which are exclusively at its disposal, and which people are forced or virtually forced to rely on, as a means of putting through its general political measures, even if that entails prohibiting activities which the shari'a allows or imposing prohibited activities.

In the same letter the Guardian Council went on to express its approval of the principle that people should come to agree on legitimate conditions in their relations with one another or with the government, where the latter does not dispose over monopolistic privileges. But the application of the rule in question, in view of the existence of a state monopoly in the area of public services, gives rise to the apprehension that 'the Islamic regulations in matters of leasing, sharecropping, trade, the family, etc., would little by little be undermined, suppressed and finally changed ... The people referred to ... wish to use this fatva in order to establish the social and economic system' they desire.[16]

Far from deterring Khomeini the warning implied in this letter led him to come out even more openly in support of the government's position. In his reply he wrote that the government 'without any condition ... in all matters under its jurisdiction' could demand a price for its services and facilities when the population made use of them. Moreover, the areas where it could demand such a price were not restricted to those mentioned in the letter of the minister of labour.[17]

Nevertheless, Khomeini's fatva did not move the Guardian Council to give its approval to the legislation. In its letter to parliament, the council wrote that in more than 100 of its articles, notes and individual sentences, the bill contained contradictions to the shari'a and the constitution. The letter begins with what was apparently intended to be a vaguely formulated sentence which even the government would not be able to interpret correctly:

> To begin with, it is necessary to state that the complaints expressed concerning this law from the viewpoint of the shari'a are based on the understanding of the contents of Art. 1 which oblige certain people to obey this law under legal compulsion. Therefore, the examination and judging of the other cases[18] is carried out directly and not in connection with the said article. Naturally, the Guardian Council, once the Islamic Majles has taken account of the fatva of his Excellency the Imam Khomeini ... and made the corrections [to the law], will examine these and judge them with regard to the [said] fatva.[19]

With the help of an exchange of letters that subsequently took place between the council and parliament, as well as the relevant parliamentary debates, these sentences can be deciphered as follows: a) The Guardian Council finds that there is a series of contradictions between this bill and the shari'a; b) the council is prepared to pass it with recourse to Khomeini's fatva, and c) it will only do so if parliament undertakes a few corrections to the bill, which will presumably have the function of helping the Guardian Council to save face.

The contradictions to the *shari'a*, which the Guardian Council established in its first ruling on the bill sprang from the situation, with which we are already familiar, that the *shari'a* does not allow the intervention of a third party, in this case the government, in bilateral contracts, contracts of employment being included in this category. In connection with Art. 36 of the bill, which regulates arrangements for paying salaries, the Guardian Council wrote: 'Obliging workers and employers to conform to conditions and cases which they have not agreed to along with the contract or which do not appear amongst the specifications of the contract, is in contradiction to the *shari'a*.' Concerning the duration of the validity of an employment contract, the Guardian Council was of the view that 'this must be specified by the partners of the contract in each case to hand. A compulsory fixing of the duration by means of statutory instruments or by law is contrary to the *shari'a*.'[20]

Although Khomeini's *fatva* of 7/12/87 confirmed the practice of resorting to secondary contractual conditions, and although the minister of labour took this *fatva* to be the solution to all problems of legislation, it was issued at a time when Khomeini signed several other *fatvas* of far more fundamental significance which, amongst other things, made it unnecessary to apply the rule of secondary contractual conditions. The high point of this phase was reached in a letter Khomeini wrote to President Khamene'i on 7/1/88 in which he declared that the state is 'a branch of the absolute trusteeship of the Prophet ... and constitutes one of the primary ordinances of Islam [which] has precedence over all the other derived ordinances such as prayer, fasting and the pilgrimage.' Consequently, the ruler could suspend all the derived ordinances (*ahkam-e far'iyeh*) when it was in the interest of the country and of Islam to do so. The state thus acquired the absolute power of the Prophet and could, on this basis, enforce any condition in the contract of employment or in all other areas.[21]

We will return to this issue later. So far as the Labour Law was concerned Khomeini's letter meant that it was no longer necessary to support it by recourse to the rule of secondary contractual conditions. Those of its stipulations that were contrary to the *shari'a* had now acquired a far stronger source of legitimation. It was therefore decided to remove references to this rule from the first article of the bill. The Guardian Council still found numerous other contradictions to the *shari'a* in the bill. Parliament was not, however, prepared to correct these and preferred to forward the bill unchanged to the Assessment Council [22] which, it was hoped, would dismiss the objections expressed by the Guardian Council. The strategy failed; the Assessment Council sent the bill back without approval on procedural grounds and thus forced parliament to come to terms with the wishes of the Guardian Council.[23]

This time parliament conformed to the wishes of the Guardian Council and changed the objectionable passages. It also changed the text of Art. 1, eliminating the reference to the secondary contractual conditions. The result was therefore legitimated solely by the *fatva* contained in Khomeini's letter to

Khamene'i. From this perspective, the spokesman of the Parliamentary Committee for Labour was able to quote a member of the Guardian Council, Ayatollah Yazdi, and declare that the law would rightfully belong to the category of Islamically sanctioned ordinances (*ahkam-e emzá'iyeh*),[24] discussed in Chapter 8. These had 'already existed before the Islamic legislators and were taken over by them into Islamic law.'

The last point, taken directly from Yazdi, represents an attempt to find a place within the tradition of the *shari'a* for a law which is *per se* contrary to it. But it provided no answer to the question of why the legislators in the Islamic Republic had to take this long detour, only to announce after so many years that the solution lay in sanctioning as 'Islamic' already existing laws which had originated from foreign sources.

Although the Labour Law was corrected as far as possible in accordance with the wishes of the Guardian Council, its opposition to the document was not completely dispelled. The council still found in the revised text 32 contradictions to the *shari'a* and 33 contradictions to the constitution.[25] The bill was therefore sent once more to the Assessment Council for a final judgement on this tiresome question.[26] The Assessment Council worked on it for more than ten months before giving its approval on 20/11/90.

The Labour Law of the Islamic Republic which finally emerged from this lengthy process has many points in common with the old, non-Islamic law of 1958 as well as with the labour laws of other countries.[27] The most important difference is that the new law gives more advantages to the workers than the 1958 law.[28] Employees no longer work at the orders of their employer but at their request. Means of transport, according to the new law, come under the concept of 'the company' so that an accident which happens on the way to work is classified as an industrial accident. Dismissal is linked to many more conditions which favour the employee than had been the case in the old law. The working week has been reduced from 48 to 44 hours, and statutory holidays have been increased from 12 days to one month.

These and several other minor differences have enabled the regime's propagandists to characterise the 1958 law as a product of the era of *taghut* (the counter-God) and to celebrate the new law as Islamic. Yet to claim that a series of quantitative differences give an Islamic character to the new law is hardly convincing. Any regime that claims to pass exemplary laws to protect the weaker elements of the population attaches importance to quantitative improvements of this kind. Furthermore, in the case of Iran, which is not in a position to fulfil the necessary economic, infrastructural, organisational, cultural and medical requirements on the basis of which the new advantages promised to the workers can be realised, the improvements are a matter of the letter rather than the practice of the law. Indeed, the government is already thinking seriously of revising the Labour Law, and cancelling some of the concessions that have been made to the employees.[29]

The rule of secondary contractual conditions was also applied in connection with two other legislative undertakings that were meant to define the rights of employees vis-à-vis their employers. The first was the 'Legislative Initiative to Exempt Employers with Under Five Workers from Paying Insurance Contributions'. The bill, which consisted of a single article, was passed by parliament on 31/1/83 and, as is clear from its title, exempted owners of workshops involved with industrial or handicraft production who make use of state services (such as electricity, water, telephones and roads) from paying insurance contributions if they employed no more than five employees. Note 1 of the bill declared: 'In cases where a business does not make use of state services, it is not obliged to pay insurance contributions for its workers.'[30] Even if it was not stated explicitly, it was perfectly clear that, by referring to the use of state services and the possibility of denying them to certain businesses, this legislation aimed at putting pressure on employers to pay insurance contributions on behalf of their workers. On several occasions during the debate over the bill attention was drawn to its contradiction to the *shari'a* and ways were sought to solve this problem.[31] Finally, at the suggestion of the Guardian Council, note 1 was removed on the grounds that it would indirectly establish the intervention of the state in the relation between the partners of a contract, which was contrary to the *shari'a*. The legislative initiative was then passed, the *shari'a* remained un-violated, and the government for the time being was satisfied that it had discussed state services as a means of putting through its own desired secondary contractual conditions.

The second time secondary contractual conditions proposed by the government came under discussion was in connection with the bill regarding insurance for the unemployed, which once again stipulated that the employers were obliged to pay a contribution on behalf of their employees. The bill was passed after a second reading on 26/2/87 and 3/3/87 but then, as had been expected, was rejected by the Guardian Council. In the council's view, if the bill became law employers would be forced by the government to assume a particular task, and this was contrary to the *shari'a*. In its ruling the council made it clear that it had no objection to the obligation itself if it were concluded between employers and employees as a secondary contractual condition.[32] But parliament would not comply with this wish. Instead, it changed its resolution to stipulate that employees as well as employers were obliged to conform to this law. The secondary contractual conditions were included in the bill, not, however, as an agreement between the partners to the contract but as an agreement between the government and the employers. Surprisingly, despite all expectations and warnings to the contrary[33] the Guardian Council this time yielded and allowed parliament's resolution to pass, even though it contradicted the *shari'a*.[34]

## The Marriage and Divorce Law

In accordance with its patriarchal character, Islamic law discriminates against women in numerous respects. Polygamy and women's lack of rights in matters of divorce provide some of the more striking examples of this discrimination. Iranian civil law before the revolution conformed almost completely in these questions to the position of the *shari'a*. Only in 1967 did the government attempt to introduce changes that would make the law less stringent. The result of this attempt was the Family Protection Law in accordance with which: a) husbands could only divorce their wives with approval of a law court; b) wives were given the right to petition a court for divorce; c) the court was to grant a divorce if both spouses agreed, or if it was established by the court that the marriage was ruined; d) in addition to the grounds recognised by the *shari'a*,[35] the wife could petition for divorce if her husband had been sentenced to five years or more imprisonment for a criminal act, if he suffered from a disease which impaired family life, or if without her permission he took a second wife, abandoned family life or was prosecuted for a crime which damaged the dignity of the family and the wife; e) the court could only allow a man to take a second wife if it had established the fact that he was financially capable of doing so and could fulfil the rule of impartiality in his treatment of both wives. So that these innovations would not be in violation of the *shari'a*, the law declared that they were to be written into the marriage document in the form of secondary contractual conditions, and that the wife's right in matters of divorce was to be indicated as having been conferred on her through irrevocable authorisation by her husband. Accordingly, the husband had to accept as a secondary contractual condition of the marriage that his wife, as his authorised representative, acquired the right to divorce him through the courts.[36]

Before the revolution the Family Protection Law met with intense opposition from conservative members of the clergy, who saw in it an unacceptable violation of the *shari'a*. Khomeini wrote in his book *Towzih al-Masa'el* under solution number 2836:

> The law which was passed in recent years by illegitimate parliaments that violated the *shari'a* as a family protection law by order of agents of the foreign powers for the purpose of annihilating Islam and destroying the family hearth of the Muslims is contradictory to the Islamic ordinances ... Whoever has approved it is, from the point of view of the *shari'a* and the law, a criminal. Women who are divorced at the order of the courts have not obtained a valid divorce and shall be considered as married women. If they marry [once again], they are adulteresses. Whoever knowingly marries them is an adulterer and deserves the *hadd*-punishments of the *shari'a*. Their children are illegitimate from the point of view of the *shari'a*. They cannot inherit as wives, and the other relevant regulations of the *shari'a* pertaining to adultery shall be applied to them. And all this is the case, whether the courts declare their divorce directly or oblige their husband to undertake the divorce.

Naturally, the annulment of this law was one of the first undertakings carried out within the framework of Islamicisation of the laws after the revolution. Already on 26/2/79, the minister of the interior, Ahmad Sadr Hajj Seyyed Javadi, informed the press that the application of the Family

Protection Law had been stopped by order of the leader and the competent special courts had been dissolved by fiat of the Bureau of the Leader.[37] On 9/8/79, the minister repeated this announcement when he informed the press about his talk with Khomeini. On that occasion, he made it clear that the courts dealing with matters of divorce and family conflicts were already judging cases in accordance with the *shari'a*.[38] Two months later, the Revolutionary Council passed the Bill on Special Civil Courts according to which the pre-revolutionary ordinances of the civil law with regard to matters of divorce were to be enforced once more.[39]

Although the ordinances of the law of 1967 contradicted the *shari'a*, they were still closer to the conceptions which a portion of traditionalist Muslim women themselves had of their rights. Indeed they joined the fight against enforcing the pertinent civil law and demanded that the leadership of the revolution renounce any such plans. The pressure from women was so great that Khomeini had to promise a group of women who visited him in Qom on 29/10/79 and presented him with complaints of this kind that they could make use of the law of divorce with the help of secondary contractual conditions. Moreover, he formulated this answer in written form, stating:

> If women when concluding marriage set it as a condition that in matters of divorce they are the authorised representative [of their husband] in absolute terms, i.e. that they may divorce him whenever they wish, or in relative terms, i.e. if he mistreats them or, for instance, takes another wife, then there are no other obstacles for them; they may obtain a divorce.[40]

But since this *fatva* did not solve the problem of women who were already married and the latter wished for a fuller statement from Khomeini, a few days later he declared that women in that situation could turn to jurists. The jurists had the right to issue a divorce if a husband mistreated his wife and she lodged a complaint with them against him.[41]

These declarations did not fully satisfy the demands of women who were obliged to intensify their campaign. In 1982 they finally succeeded in getting the government to take steps to enforce the 1967 law, if not as an official law, none the less in terms of its actual content. The Ministry of Justice ordered that 12 secondary contractual conditions were to be written into marriage documents and that the registry offices were to invite persons getting married to sign them.[42] This order contained a new element that had been lacking in the law of 1967. Indeed, the new conditions required that the husband turn over to his wife half the wealth or the equivalent thereof that he had acquired during the period of their marriage if the divorce, in the ruling of the court, was not due to the wife's refusal to fulfil her marital duties or because of sexual misbehaviour on her part. In this respect, the order even went a step further than the law of 1967. However, it was up to the couples themselves to decide whether they would comply with the invitation completely, not at all or only in part.[43]

The chief obstacle to implementing this 'solution' in practice was that husbands, law courts and the registry offices did not feel bound to follow the order and often preferred the more comfortable choice of deciding in favour of conformity to the *shari'a*. Amongst others, the press was highly critical of this practice and demanded that further solutions be found.[44] The numerous complaints arising from the disregard in practice of the secondary contractual conditions have in recent years led many officials to take steps to give them a legal foundation. Moreover, officials feel pressure from the fact that the divorce rate has been increasing, as some would have it because of the ease with which husbands, according to the *shari'a*, can declare divorce.[45]

During the debate on the Legislative Initiative for Correcting the Divorce Law in November 1989 and September 1991, these facts, supported by reports and statistics, were discussed in great detail. However, the discussion also gave spokesmen for the *shari'a* an opportunity to complain about the violation of Islamic law by the regulations which had been in force up to this time. They requested that parliament restore the legal provisions of the *shari'a*. The advocates of the 'legislative initiative' for their part justified their position by pointing out that they had recourse to the rule of secondary contractual conditions. Moreover, they drew attention to the fact that in Islam divorce was considered one of the most abominable acts and had to be discouraged. As a proof of the conformity of their bill, they emphasised that it had been confirmed by a parliamentary commission which included such respectable *'ulama* as 'Amid Zanjani, Bayat, Salimi, etc.[46] The fact that almost four years went by between the introduction of this initiative and its passage after a second reading testifies to the strength of the conservative legalists' opposition. But passing the bill in parliament did not solve the problem because the Guardian Council promptly rejected it. What is especially interesting from our point of view is that this time the rejection was not because of the secondary contractual conditions but primarily because of the following stipulation: a husband who wants a divorce on grounds that are not upright and honest will be ordered by the courts to pay compensation to his wife for all such work as she undertook during their life together but which the *shari'a* does not define as obligatory. The Guardian Council found that this rule was contrary to the *shari'a* and requested that parliament correct it. But since parliament was unwilling to comply, the bill was forwarded to the Assessment Council.

This referral made it clear that the problem could not be resolved by the *shari'a*. In this case other criteria were being applied which, as we will see in Chapter 12, were summed up under the heading of interests of state. On 19/11/92, the Assessment Council approved of the parliamentary legislative initiative, but only after making a few changes which were to the disadvantage of women. The law, which consists of a single article along with six notes, gives the decision regarding divorces, as did the law of 1967, to the competent courts. If the courts come to the conclusion that the marriage partners cannot get along together, divorce is then permissible. When coming to a decision concerning a petition for divorce and the consequences it will entail with regard to financial matters and the custody of children, the courts are to take account of all the secondary contractual conditions entered into at the time of marriage. Note 6 stipulates that 'after the divorce' the wife can apply for payment of compensation for work which she undertook during her married life but which the *shari'a* does not define as obligatory. To begin with the court attempts to facilitate a mutually agreed upon settlement. But in cases where such a settlement cannot be reached it acts in accordance with whatever binding conditions were entered into at the time of marriage inside or outside the marriage contract. Otherwise, the court establishes a fixed sum for the wife which depends on whether the work in question was carried out as a voluntary donation (*tabarro*) or not. In any case, such a sum only goes to the wife if she is not the partner petitioning for divorce and is not herself responsible for the divorce because of her refusal to carry out her marital duties, difficult behaviour or sexual misconduct. The law contains two other rules which are contrary to the *shari'a*: the presence of a woman in the courts as an adviser is allowed; and the divorce only comes into force once the husband has returned the wife's dowry (*mahr*), the furnishings and belongings (*jahizeh*) the wife brought to the marriage, and paid any maintenance (*nafaqeh*) required of him.[47]

When the Assessment Council passed this law the result was, if not explicitly, none the less in terms of the actual meaning, that the law of 1967 (which was contrary to the *shari'a*) was partially rehabilitated, and all those men and women who had divorced after 1967 and therefore stood accused of adultery by Khomeini, were now pronounced innocent. Although the new law, in terms of the stipulations of civil law governing marriage and divorce, made a small contribution towards decreasing discrimination against women, it was still far from satisfying the expectations even of those women, jurists and journalists who were loyal to the regime. In fact, it even created new problems which are still discussed in those circles. *Resalat*, through interviews with judges, has brought the discussion into the open and drawn attention to the problems, weaknesses and forms of discrimination which even so conservative a newspaper as this finds are associated with this law and its implementation.[48]

## The Problem of Secondary Contractual Conditions

The use of the rule of secondary contractual conditions in the form parliament and the government had in mind was contrary to the *shari'a* mainly because these conditions were not only to be negotiated between the partners of the contract but also the state was to intervene as a third partner. As private law, the *shari'a* does not allow such a third partner. Even under the changed circumstances, i.e. where the *shari'a* is meant to provide the foundation for the state, it is conceived of as private law and opposes the recognition of the state as a third partner. The *shari'a* cannot assimilate the idea that it is to serve as the legal foundation for a state that, amongst other things, claims to be the representative of the people i.e. that is also their representative when they enter into contracts. The *shari'a* does not accept that the state is authorised by the people, i.e. by the partners to the contract, to intervene in bilateral relations between the contracting partners. The state is either a usurper, in which case the *shari'a* accords it no rights, or the state is the Imam, who represents God not the people. If a third party has the right to intervene in contractual relations between private persons it could only be the Imam, whom the Guardian Council obeys, if not always with enthusiasm.[49] The Guardian Council insists on such a conception of the *shari'a* and therefore rejects, whenever it acts consistently, any intervention by the state in relations based on private law. When the council is put under pressure by the government, parliament, the public and even by the leader, or when it has doubts itself about the correctness of its position, it permits the use of secondary contractual conditions, though this is contrary to the *shari'a*. But when the council stands firm, the opposite side finds another way, with or without recourse to secondary contractual conditions, to put through legislation that contradicts the *shari'a*. In such cases an appeal is made to the Assessment Council and thus to the interests of the ruling system. Sometimes if it merely acts in conformity to the outward form of the *shari'a*, that is sufficient. Otherwise, as the state it is prepared to do what it cannot avoid in the given circumstances. Furthermore, the contradiction between what the majority in parliament understood as secondary contractual conditions and what the *shari'a* understood them to be was based on the fact that, as far as their content was concerned, the conditions parliament drew up were irreconcilable with the main conditions of the individual contractual categories as set forth in the classical law-books. For example, the secondary contractual conditions provided for the marriage contract, and partially approved, contradict the husband's rights in divorce as laid down in the *shari'a*. However, as in the case of the rule of emergency, in the end this question has not been resolved either by primary or secondary ordinances, but by an appeal to the interest of the ruling system and by having recourse to so-called state ordinances.

## Notes

1 'As in the case where a person buys something under the condition that the buyer is not the owner of the thing' (1984, p. 167).

2 Vol. III, p. 539.

3 *Kayhan*, 22/12/82.

4 See *Kayhan*, 21/12/82.

5 It is true that these concepts are also found in the Iranian civil code which itself is based on the *shari'a*. But in the case of a law of employment such concepts particularly stand out as anachronisms.

6 Common land, i.e. land which everyone is free to make use of.

7 Vol. II, p. 485 ff.

8 Three years later the spokesman of the Parliamentary Committee for Labour and Social Affairs explained that the protests against this bill were so violent it had to be removed from the agenda of the Council of Ministers (MM 19/10/86, p. 30). But Tavakkoli thought these protests had been stirred up by Marxists. In defence of his position he stated: 'In order to regulate relations between human beings, we base ourselves on Islam, as it is defined in *feqh*.' (*Kayhan*, 21/12/82).

9 Apparently, because the *shari'a* does not allow partnership in connection with labour, i.e. the so-called *sherkat-e abdan*.

10 *Kayhan*, 8/11/86.

11 From an interview with Salamati in *Kayhan*, 8/12/87.

12 Ibid.

13 Ibid.

14 MM 1/10/ and 11//11/87.

15 *Kayhan*, 8/12/87.

16 This letter is dated 17/12/87. See Mehrpur: 1992a, or *Howzeh*, No. 23 (1987), p. 30 f.

17 Ibid.

18 By 'other cases' is meant the other articles and their notes, etc.

19 Mehrpur: 1992a; Salamati in his interview with *Kayhan*, 6/1/88.

20 From an interview Salamati gave in *Kayhan*, 6/1/88.

21 *Kayhan*, 31/8/88.

22 *Kayhan*, 31/8/88.

23 See the letter of the Assessment Council to parliament in: MM 19/9/89, p. 22.

24 Ibid.

25 Based on the statement of Hosein Qazizadeh MP in *Kayhan*, 8/11/89.

26 This was done at the suggestion of the Guardian Council according to Ayatollah Jannati, a member of the council (*Kayhan*, 25/11/89).

27 These were referred to in the drafting of the Islamic law, according to the spokesman of the Parliamentary Committee for Labour and Social Affairs (*Kayhan*, 13/2/90).

28 On this point see 'Arabi: 1991. On the 1958 law see Hojjati Ashrafi: 1984.

29 Every now and then the daily press reports on such proposals and the protests directed against them. For example, on 27/11/93 *Salam* reported on a scheme put forward by the Plan and Budget Organisation, according to which within the framework of the national budget the salary of workers would be fixed on the basis of their productivity, not the number of hours they worked.

30 MM 31/1/83, p. 16.

31 MM 30 and 31/1/83, and 13/3/83.

32 MM 14/6/87, p. 25 f.

33 Ibid.

34 LB: 1987/88, p. 221 ff.

35 Such grounds included: the husband's refusal to provide support for his wife, neglect of other marital duties, mistreatment of the wife beyond the limits within which it is possible to maintain a common life together, incurable and contagious disease on the part of the husband, and payment of compensation to the husband by the wife.

36 Hamidi: n. d.

37 *Ettela'at*.

38 *Kayhan*, 9/8/79.

39 LB: 1979/80, p. 180.

40 *Kayhan*, 30/10/79.

41 *Kayhan*, 3/11/79.

42 This is according to Ayatollah Mohammad Musavi Bojnurdi, member of the Supreme Court. Bojnurdi admitted that civil law discriminates against women and for that reason

must be revised (*Kayhan*, 8/8/91).

43  This information is based on the author's correspondence with a Tehran judge. See also the comments of Hojjat al-Eslam Mahdavi Kermani, the president of the Special Civil Courts (*Kayhan*, 26/10/88).

44  See, for example, *Resalat* 7/8/92 and 19/12/92.

45  According to the MP Hosein Harati, the divorce rate in 1985/86 was twice as high as before the revolution. He announced that 85% of the divorces were carried out in registry offices. This means that only 15% were decided by the courts (MM 20/10/91, p. 24). The MP Jowhar al-Shari'eh Dastgheib complained before a plenary session of parliament that the courts would not even allow women to speak (MM 24/9/91, pp. 26 and 31).

46  MM 19/11/89, p. 22 ff. and 24/9/91, p. 24 ff., as well as 16/10/91, p. 23 ff.

47  LB: 1992/93, p. 490 ff.

48  See, for example, the issues of 7 and 18/12/92, as well as 6 and 21/8/93.

49  In the classical law-books too, the divine legislator intervenes in contracts concluded according to private law by giving them certain forms and imposing certain conditions.

# ELEVEN

# State Ordinances

Islamic penal law consists of four parts: *lex talionis* or retaliation (*qesas*), compensation (*diyat*), fixed punishments (*hodud*) and discretionary punishments (*ta'zirat*). The Islamic regime insisted that these laws should be put into practice but in the case of each category encountered obstacles which forced it, to a greater or a lesser degree, to deviate from the ordinances of the *shari'a*, both in the text of its laws and in practice. Since it is not possible to deal here with all the problems associated with the Islamic penal code, we will in this chapter focus on the discretionary punishments, which provide a good illustration of the complications and consequences which a present-day legal system must face if it tries to base itself on the use of Islamic penal regulations.

## The Discretionary Punishments in Shi'i Law

The special problem involved in the application of the discretionary punishments stems from the fact that they have to do with crimes which only became relevant for the *shari'a* once the Islamic state had been set up, namely with political crimes and crimes in the area of public law. In classical *feqh* such punishments form part of the law of moral behaviour and receive only marginal treatment. In the *Shara'i' al-Islam*, written by the great thirteenth-century jurist 'Alammeh Mohaqqeq Helli, discretionary punishments are dealt with in a mere three pages and relate to sodomy and necrophilia,[1] whereas the other penal categories are treated in 94 pages. In Khomeini's *Tahrir al-Vasila* they are entirely missing, although several pages of this book are devoted to the other three penal categories.

The main problem raised by the use of the *ta'zirat* in the judicial process of the Islamic Republic is that, according to the *shari'a*, the penalties they impose cannot be fixed. The *shari'a* dictates that it must be left to the discretion of the judges to determine the extent of a punishment. Parliament and the government nevertheless attempted to establish fixed penalties for the *ta'zirat*, visible in all their efforts to cast them in the form of a law. They had to do this because in practice judges often imposed very different penalties for the same crimes. A second problem arose because the severity of discretionary punishments cannot exceed the limits set by the *shari'a* for the fixed penalties.[2] Moreover, they are to be graded in terms of severity so that a judge has the possibility of adjusting them to what he estimates will be their effect. A fourth problem was that according to the *shari'a* the offences in question were to be punished by whipping. Parliament, however, considered punishments involving imprisonment and fines. Whereas it was relatively easy to resolve the second, third and fourth problems the first proved more intractable.

## The Introduction of State Discretionary Punishments

Discussions on the issue of legislation and the Islamic punishments began on 9 August 1983 when the Parliamentary Committee for Judicial and Legal Affairs passed the Islamic Penal Code, which included stipulations on the *ta'zirat*, as an experimental measure that was to last for five years. The Guardian Council was unable to block this law or delay its implementation because it failed to present its ruling within the deadline set for the purpose.[3] However, its view was published at a later date. It consisted of 42 points, each containing several complaints of a contradiction to the *shari'a* in one or more of the 159 articles and notes that made up the law. There was not a single article of the law which, according to the Guardian Council, did not in several places contradict the *shari'a*. But the council's chief criticism was the following:

> Because according to the *shari'a* when the discretionary punishments are applied it is the judge's decision that is valid with regard to determining the penalty, the kind of penalty or acquittal, and because fixing [the punishments] in many cases results in not carrying out the appropriate penalty or leads to discrimination against an offender, these fixed punishments are contrary to the *shari'a*. Therefore, the bill must be corrected in this respect.[4]

Despite this ruling, the Islamic Penal Code remained in force. In the interim, with the help of Khomeini, another solution was found for the *ta'zirat*, which consisted in renaming them as 'state discretionary punishments' (*ta'zirat-e hokumati*). This tactic offered the advantage of regulating the discretionary punishments, in the name of the Islamic state, in a way that would take account of the requirements of running the government while disregarding the relevant ordinances of the *shari'a*.

Meanwhile, without waiting for the results of this experiment, a lengthy process of re-writing began.[5] This came to a conclusion, after much coming and going between parliament and the Guardian Council, towards the end of the 4th Majles when it was announced in the press on 9/6/96 that the Islamic Penal Code (of the *ta'zirat*) had at last been approved by both bodies.

But before matters reached this point and the designated five-year period had run out, the Guardian Council voiced its objections whenever discretionary punishments for any particular offence were formulated in a law that was to be passed. An example worth mentioning here is the Bill to Increase Penalties for Bribe Taking, Embezzlement and Fraud which was rejected by the Guardian Council in the version that had been passed by parliament.

The council commented on the prescribed penalty provided in this bill as follows: 'Since it is the judge's right to determine the form and the severity of punishments when applying the *ta'zirat* and since the punishments must be less than those of the fixed penalties, the bill is contrary to the principles of the *shari'a*.'[6]

The solution, which was found with the help of Khomeini, emerged when parliament was debating the Bill to Increase Penalties for Speculation and Persons Driving Up Prices discussed in Chapter 9. Parliament and government both had an interest in fixing the highest possible penalties for this category of offence. This involved violating the *ta'zirat*-ordinances with respect to both the form and the severity of punishments. What emerged from the debate on this legislative initiative was that the competent parliamentary committee, knowing in advance what the attitude of the Guardian Council would be, turned to Khomeini for guidance asking him whether:

> ... it is permissible to fix as *ta'zirat* such penalties as arrest, exile, closing down a business, suspension from service, fines and in general any punishment which is calculated to stop certain offences, or whether when applying these punishments one must be content with the *ta'zirat* that exist in written form.

Given its content the solution to this problem could not be based on the *shari'a*, Khomeini's reply thus attempted a ruling which at least formally speaking would not conflict with the *shari'a*:

> When applying *ta'zirat* in conformity with the *shari'a*, it is advisable to be content with the penalties that have been fixed in written form, unless [the offence] has a public character such as speculation and driving up prices, which along with the state regulations concerns the second question.

A second question, posed in the same letter to Khomeini, was more detailed and, in an attempt to clarify a whole series of problems in one go, had far greater scope:

> In parliament laws are passed for the purposes of governing which deal with [matters concerning] smuggling, customs formalities, violation of traffic regulations, municipal administration and generally with state ordinances (*ahkam-e soltaniyeh*). In order to oblige the population to obey these laws, any particular law stipulates penalties to be imposed on offenders. Do these penalties come under the heading of *ta'zirat* as defined by the *shari'a*? Are the *ta'zirat* which conform to the *shari'a* related to these or are these of another kind and substance, being independent from the *ta'zirat*? Must they be obeyed if they do not cause one to commit any form of wrong-doing?

In his reply Khomeini wrote that the state ordinances were to be distinct from the *ta'zirat* provided in the *shari'a*. 'Offenders can be punished with preventive penalties, to be determined by the ruler or his representatives.'[7]

Thus in order to achieve his dual goal Khomeini divided the discretionary punishments into two separate groups. The first, which did not present a problem, were to be calmly applied in accordance with the ordinances of the *shari'a*. But the second group of discretionary punishments were set apart from those normally dealt with by the *ta'zirat*, and this meant that they could be freely applied as an aspect of state ordinances. In this way parliament and executive were given a free hand to fix the form and severity of punishments as they saw fit. By way of justifying his *fatva*, Khomeini endowed his state ordinances with the status of primary Islamic ordinances, which as such could naturally not be contradictory to the *shari'a*, even if they suspended some part of the *shari'a*'s stipulations.

Although the Parliamentary Committee for Judicial and Legal Affairs expected that these *fatvas* would break the opposition of the Guardian Council, the council did not give up easily. Amongst other things, it objected to the fact that the punishments did not comply with the rule requiring that penalties be graduated.[8] In the event, their objections proved to be effective in so far as the bill that was finally passed was so toned down that it inspired little fear among speculators or persons attempting to drive up prices. Consequently, the government preferred to put its legislation before the Assessment Council which complied with its wishes and on 14/3/89 passed a series of stringent but graduated penalties which did not exclude the whip for those who disrupted trade by driving up prices, for speculation or for other undesirable activities. The law in question bore the title 'The State Discretionary Punishments Law'.[9] This was supplemented by yet another *fatva* from Khomeini, in answer to a question put to him by Prime Minister Musavi, which gave the government a free hand to fix prices and to exercise the supervision required to ensure that they were observed.[10]

Khomeini's two *fatvas* and the law approved by the Assessment Council, introduced the concept of 'state discretionary punishments'– a novelty which represented a special form of deviation from the *shari'a* – to the Islamic Republic. The attribution of the term 'state' to this form of discretionary punishment virtually signified 'contrary to the *shari'a*'. The *ta'zirat* which conformed to the *shari'a* were accordingly relegated to the traditional sections of the books of *feqh*. The partial fixing of the penalties imposed by the *ta'zirat* deprived these of much of their distinctive meaning, that is, the right of the judge to exercise his discretion in determining the penalties.

In the period that followed, the concept *ta'zirat-e hokumati* regularly came up whenever it was necessary to fix discretionary punishments for particular offences. The following laws could be mentioned as examples of this: the Regulations for Implementing the Discretionary Punishments for Citizens and Civil Servants in Municipal Authorities passed on 15/6/88; the Law on State Discretionary Punishments in Hygienic and Therapeutic Matters[11] passed on 14/12/89, and the statutory instruments issued to regulate the Investigatory Methods of the Commission for Discretionary Punishments in the Government Sector[12] passed on 5/5/90. On 18/12/90, the Assessment Council resolved to give the judiciary jurisdiction over all matters that concern the dispensation of justice in connection with discretionary punishments in the government sector.[13]

## The Guardian Council and the State

Putting aside cases of profane self-interest, the opposition of the Guardian Council to government intervention in the economy, in the courts and in social affairs, stems from the fact that the council, basing itself on the *shari'a*, has a conception of a social order in which the state plays little or no significant role. Under such a system, social relationships in these spheres are mostly based on bilateral contracts between individuals whose form and content are regulated within the framework of the *shari'a*. If a third party intervenes in this relationship, it is at the wish of the partners to the contract and usually in the form of an arbitrating judge known as a *hakem-e shar'*.[14] This attitude has clearly manifested itself in the rulings handed down by the Guardian Council with respect to all the laws discussed in this section of the book. For the Guardian Council, a relationship involving lease should be regulated only by the lessor and the lessee, as should the relationship between the employer and the employee. The state should not be involved in shaping laws governing the ownership of land and should have no part in regulating the affairs between buyers and sellers of goods. Marriage and divorce are likewise an affair for married couples to be regulated on a mutual basis or by the husband alone. And decisions about both the imposition and execution of Islamic penalties are the concern, not of the state, but of the *hakem-e shar'*. This approach is equally clear in many other rulings handed down by the Guardian Council on parliamentary resolutions which regulate relations between individuals or between an individual and the state. This trend merits a study in its own right – here we can only present a brief account of a few representative examples.

On 19/10/81, the Guardian Council rejected parliament's interpretation of a bill passed on 15/3/7 justifying its ruling with reference to 'the rights of individuals or corporate bodies' which cannot be abolished without their agreement. The bill dealt with the question of whether a suspended construction project for a new university complex, which had originally been entrusted to a private firm, should be resumed. The council ruled that the decision should be made by the Ministry of Housing and Urban Planning or by the Mortgage Bank.[15]

On 23/2/82, parliament resolved that university graduates who, in return for a grant, had committed themselves to service in the university system but had not been given a post, would as an alternative be required to fulfil their obligation by serving in other government institutions. The Guardian Council, however, ruled that the transference of a compulsory service was contrary to the *shari'a*, because it would be a violation of the personal rights of the graduates if they were not in agreement with the alternative form of work.[16] In yet another case, parliament introduced a mineral resources bill which aimed at nationalisation. The Guardian Council ruled that the bill was contrary to the *shari'a* because it included mineral resources on private property or *waqf* land, or resources used to meet private needs. The problem was only resolved after long negotiations, and when Khomeini issued a *fatva* which drastically restricted, in the government's favour, the use landowners could make of the mineral resources on their property and imposed on such use a maximum limit as defined by the concept of 'normal practice'.[17]

The Guardian Council also declared proposed legislation on the just distribution of water to be contrary to the *shari'a* because, amongst other things, it obliged the owners of water sources to sell whatever water they did not need themselves. In the council's view, such a resolution could only be passed in emergencies and then only for a limited period of time. The Guardian Council also found another provision of this bill to be in contradiction to the *shari'a* – namely that disagreements between the government and the owners of water resources were to be decided by the executive and not by the courts.[18] Finally, on 11/1/83, parliament resolved that the wealth of Iranians who had fled abroad would be confiscated, justifying its decision by stating that such people subscribed to counter-revolutionary attitudes. However, the Guardian Council ruled that, from the standpoint of the *shari'a*, flight from Iran did not justify the infringement of property rights.[19]

There are clear historical reasons why the *shari'a* has the character of private law. In the past rulers usually kept jurists from intervening in the affairs of government, or jurists themselves judged it desirable to remain aloof from the state. The rulers ran the state on the basis of customary law or more often despotically. Rulers only involved the *'ulama* in governmental issues when they sought religious confirmation for their decisions. When the *'ulama* complied with the wishes of those in power, it was rarely on the basis of the *shari'a* and their attitude was at best justified by the rule of *taqiyyeh* (dissimulation for the sake of caution) or by means of secondary ordinances.[20]

Given the private character of *shari'a* law the Guardian Council, as protectors of the *shari'a*, could not but reject or restrict those resolutions of parliament which gave the state the right to intervene in the affairs of citizens in the sphere of private or public law. It was in this sense impossible for the council to play an effective role as an organ of state, especially while the state was represented by a parliament and government which was in favour of state intervention and state welfare. Although both the *shari'a* and its guardians had emerged from their traditional marginal position, and although the Guardian Council was supposed to support a government that needed a free hand to promote its political programme on a world-wide scale, it was unable to react positively to these requirements. The difficulties were, moreover, exacerbated by the fact that the was modern and differed in numerous respects from that in which the *shari'a* had developed. Many jurists did not understand how, given this new society, they should incorporate the state into the system of the *shari'a* or how they were to define the relationship between the established *shari'a* and the new laws that continually had to be passed. This dilemma is repeatedly manifested in MPs' statements. For example, in a debate over divorce Hojjat al-Eslam 'Abbas 'Abbasi asked what would happen if the court did not approve a petition for divorce but the husband had proclaimed the divorce in accordance with his rights as stipulated in the *shari'a*. And he went on to ask: 'Is such a divorce legal or not? Is the wife divorced or isn't she?' His own answer was: 'Yes, of course she is divorced.'[21] Other MPs, such as Va'ezi, expressed the view that laws were unnecessary and irrelevant because the Islamic law books were adequate for this purpose. People could finally regulate their relations by following the prescriptions of the *Tahrir al-Vasila*.[22]

The attitude of the Guardian Council, on the one hand, and parliament's attempts to pass resolutions that would open the path to state intervention on the other hand entangled legislation in a multitude of complications, the numerous rejections of parliamentary resolutions by the Guardian Council being only one dimension of this problem. Others which had an effect on the government's legislative programme included prolonging the process of legislation, watering down the effect of resolutions, renouncing the framing of laws and resorting to actions that were not legally sanctioned. The comparison that was drawn in Chapter 5 between the number of parliamentary resolutions that were rejected by the Guardian Council and the total number of laws passed in each legislative period indicates the dimensions of this problem. The passage of laws was prolonged because of the repeated rejections, in some cases, as for instance in that of the Labour Law and the Law on Co-operatives, from the 1st through the 4th Majles. Quite often parliament was obliged to delete many passages from the text of a law in order to satisfy the Guardian Council.[23] Deletions and corrections often went so far that the final text no longer bore any resemblance to the intentions which had originally moved the government to formulate the bill and it had to be withdrawn. The government would then either give up its undertaking or would attempt to achieve its goals without legislation.[24]

As we already saw in Chapter 5, the rulings on the resolutions of parliament handed down by the Guardian Council aroused violent protests on the part of the radical-populists. On the other hand, the Guardian Council received support and encouragement from the powerful conservative camp, especially from members of the clergy. Khomeini defended the council against what he considered to be exaggerated criticism but at the same time demanded that it should take account of present-day requirements in its rulings and not always follow the letter of the *shari'a*. He himself set an example and, ignoring the ordinances of the *shari'a*, resolved many legislative problems through *fatvas*. He was also prepared to restrict the powers of the Guardian Council in order to make sure his own decisions would be effective.

## The Supremacy of State Ordinances over *shari'a* Ordinances

Khomeini, as both a religious authority and a political leader, was uniquely able to both neutralise any opposition to his *fatvas* and simultaneously confer on them an appearance of congruence with the *shari'a*. The high point of this kind of activity by Khomeini was reached when, in his letter of January

1988 to President Khamene'i discussed above, he characterised the 'trustee-ship' (*velayat*), that is to say the state, as the most important of all God's ordinances and raised the decisions of the state above all other Islamic ordinances, which were thus demoted to derivative status. Just a few days before this, on 1/1/88 in a Friday sermon, Khamene'i had stated with reference to Khomeini's *fatvas* on the secondary contractual conditions that the leader only meant those conditions which 'fall within the framework of the ordinances accepted by Islam and not any others.'[25] Khomeini abruptly rejected this conservative interpretation and wrote:

> From your comments during the Friday prayers it would appear that you do not believe it is correct [to characterise] the state as an absolute trusteeship which God conferred upon the noble Prophet, God bless him and his family and grant them salvation, and that the state is the most important of God's ordinances and has precedence over all other derived ordinances of God. Interpreting what I have said to mean that the state [only] has its powers within the framework of the ordinances of God contradicts my statements. If the powers of the state were [only] operational within the framework of the ordinances of God, the extent of God's sovereignty and the absolute trusteeship given to the Prophet would be a meaningless phenomenon devoid of content.

If the content of this letter is interpreted in the light of the *fatvas* which preceded it and the decisions which were subsequently based on it (see Chapter 12), the following conclusions can be drawn:

1. The state understood as an ordinance of God stands above all God's other ordinances, which are therefore declared to be derivative. The latter, amongst which are included the commandments to prayer and going on the pilgrimage, can be suspended by the state.
2. The state possesses absolute power which extends to every level of state authority.
3. The basis for the state's absolute power lies in the absoluteness of God's sovereignty, which God conferred on the Prophet and after him on the Imams and the jurists.
4. Although the suspension of the derived ordinances of God by the state only has a temporary validity, this condition loses its meaning when concrete cases are involved where decisions have permanent effect.
5. Likewise, the interests of state which justify the suspension of divine ordinances are, by virtue of their character, not usually ephemeral phenom-ena so there is no reason to suppose that after a time the *status quo ante* might be restored and the suspended divine ordinances have validity once more.

By means of his *fatvas*, Khomeini gave the state a free hand to suspend 'the derived ordinances' of the *shari'a* wherever the state deemed this necessary. This decision was legitimated by reference to the existence of an *Islamic* state whose decisions are therefore Islamic. Such a state does not have to feel bound to the Islamic ordinances which in this case are declared to be derivative.[26] The question which remains unanswered, however, is how a state which declares it is necessary to suspend the Islamic ordinances whenever this furthers its interests can still be described as Islamic.

Due to Khomeini's *fatvas*, the concept 'state ordinances' came into use. By analogy the decrees and *fatvas* which Khomeini issued in his capacity as ruling jurist with absolute power could also be considered as a form of state ordinance. But the concept *hokm-e hokumati* only acquired actuality after the decrees and *fatvas* Khomeini issued at the end of 1987 and the beginning of 1988. It was also at this time that instruction was given to the believers to the effect that state ordinances were the most important of the primary ordinances. An indication of the surprise which this ruling caused is the amazed reaction of the Guardian Council and the fact that President Khamene'i just a few days earlier believed he was meant to interpret state ordinances in terms of the conceptions which had been normal up to this time.

As usual, shortly after the concept of *hokm-e hokumati* was introduced, the theoreticians of the regime began to justify it and explaining its connection with other fundamental concepts such as divine, primary and secondary ordinances. Once again the most detailed and extensive comments, which at the same time were full of obscurities and contradictions, originated with Ayatollah Azari Qomi, who published them in *Resalat*, beginning on 6/1/88. Undoubtedly, the most important statement can be paraphrased as follows: Since state ordinances stand above the constitution, parliament and the Guardian Council, they are capable of annulling or suspending the decisions of these bodies. But we see that the Imam has not ordered this. On the contrary, he has turned over to the state his right to issue state ordinances.[27]

## Notes

1 See the edition of M. T. Daneshpazhuh: 1983–85, vol. IV, p. 1900.

2 The fixed penalty for certain criminal acts is 75 strokes of the whip. An offence which is punishable by whipping should not, if it is to be judged according to the ordinances of the *ta'zirat*, be punished with more than 74 strokes of the whip. See Ayatollah Emami Kashani's statement in *Resalat*, 2/10/86.

3 LB: 1983/84, p. 369 ff.

4 Madani: 1986–90, vol. IV, p. 312; Mehrpur: 1992, vol. I, p. 405 ff. Mehrpur here emphasises that the law could not even fix a maximum and a minimum penalty for the discretionary punishments (p. 430).

5 On 30/5/94, *Resalat* reported that the Parliamentary Committee for Judicial Affairs had passed 64 of the 224 articles of the new version of the law.

6 Madani: 1986–90, vol. IV, p. 394 ff. For other examples see ibid., pp. 194 f., 355 ff. and ibid., vol. VI, p. 358 f.

7 MM 30/7/86, p. 30 f. See also the information given by Ayatollah Yazdi in *Ettela'at*, 30/5/90.

8 Madani: 1986–90, vol. VI, p. 379 ff.

9 LB: 1988/89, p. 810 ff.

10 The question was formulated on 19/5/87, and the answer to it bears the date 21/

5/87. See *Howzeh*, no. 23 (1987), p. 27, as well as *Kayhan*, 23 and 27/7/87, where information released by the minister of trade and the prime minister was published.

11  LB: 1988/89, pp. 466 ff. and 824 ff.

12  LB: 1990/91, p. 366 ff.

13  Ibid., p. 677.

14  Characteristic of this point of view, which does not yet accept the concept of a state, is the meaning attributed to the term *hakem-e shar'*. Literally it is one who rules according to the *shari'a*. However, in current usage in the Islamic Republic it is often a title to designate judges. At the same time, when the leader or his representatives are intended, it means ruler. This ambivalence is based on the conception of the Imam as the ruler who is the head of all branches of government, including the judiciary. This conception of the state may be consistent with *velayat-e faqih*, but it is contradictory to the form of state outlined in the constitution.

15  LB: 1979/80, p. 611; Madani: 1988, vol. IV, p. 206 f.

16  Madani: 1986–90, vol. IV, p. 224 f.

17  Ibid., p. 239 ff.; *Howzeh*, no. 23 (1987), p. 31. The 'normal practice' referred to here is ancient and excludes the modes of exploitation offered by modern technology.

18  Madani: 1986–90, vol. IV, p. 245 ff.

19  Ibid., p. 291 f.

20  *Howzeh*, No. 23 (1987), p. 22.

21  MM 19/11/89, p. 22.

22  MM 15/4/82, p. 17.

23  Madani: 1986–90, vol. IV, p. 183.

24  The number of such withdrawals during the Ist Majles was 110, in the 2nd Majles 45 and in the 3rd Majles, as far as we know, 10. (Majles-e Showra-ye Eslami: 1986, 1990; and the president of parliament, Karrubi, in *Salam*, 4/5/92.)

25  *Kayhan*, 2/1/88.

26  Ayatollah Hosein Rasti Kashani undertook to explain why this should be so in a lead article in *Resalat* (29/7/86) where he quotes the following statement of Khomeini: 'Safeguarding Islam is a higher duty than safeguarding the Islamic ordinances.' Ayatollah Rasti Kashani added that by safeguarding Islam was meant the safeguarding of the Islamic state. Therefore, it makes no sense 'if many people go on asking why here and there, and in this or that case, the Islamic ordinances cannot be put into practice.'

27  'state ordinances are the responsibility of the Imam. He confers them on whichever government authority he wishes' (Rafsanjani, 9/12/87).

## TWELVE

# The Interests of the Ruling System as a Standard for Legislation

### 'Interest' (*maslahat*) in Shi'i Law

State ordinances base their legitimacy on the interests (sing. *maslahat*) of the Islamic state or government. Whenever its interests are at stake the state can suspend the primary Islamic ordinances, temporarily or permanently, by issuing state ordinances. The resort to *maslahat* to justify various government, or private actions has played an important role throughout the history of Islam. The practice was accepted by most of the Sunni schools of jurisprudence as the rule of *esteslah* (taking account of interests) and *masaleh-e morsaleh* (consideration of interests without deriving them from the *shari'a*). However, the Twelver Shi'a have always rejected it as *bed'at* (forbidden innovation).[1] According to Ayatollah Ebrahim Jannati, Shi'i law rejects the rule of *masaleh-e morsaleh* because it may cause too much harm: it could be interpreted as an admission that Islamic legislation suffers from deficiencies, and it establishes the possibility that different opinions may be represented at the same time and that conflicts may break out between them. In addition *masaleh-e morsaleh* are inferences based on conjecture (*zanniyat*), and are therefore prohibited in Islamic law.[2] Shi'i jurists rejected the rule of *esteslah*, writes Jannati: 'Because they are of the view that all principles [underlying ordinances] and all general laws, in the various religious, political, ethical, legal and other areas, have already been given to us. Consequently, we have no need to resort to this source in order to establish ordinances for new events and new subjects.'[3]

Despite these long-standing objections, in 1987/88 the ruling jurists came to accept, inevitably perhaps, that they had to make use of these two rules in the interests of their system of government. Indeed they were obliged to extend the scope of *maslahat* even further since they were now confronted with what they described as a mass of new events (*havades-e vaqe'eh*) and new questions which would require more than simply creating ordinances for which there were no analogues in the sources. In the name of *maslahat*, interest, they would have to do nothing less than suspend the ordinances of the *shari'a*. At this time apologetic writings by ayatollahs such as Azari Qomi served to justify this revision. The periodical *Howzeh* published a survey of the previous use of the rule of *maslahat* in Islamic history and the various attitudes of Islamic jurists to it. An attempt was made to show that the Shi'i

233

Imams had based their statements and actions on this rule. In its very first article on the subject, *Howzeh* came to the conclusion that 'the Prophet ... and Imam 'Ali ... had not forbidden the use of *maslahat* when making regulations concerning behaviour. They had not claimed that this method was permitted for themselves alone, nor had they warned people against it.'[4] At the very centre of these justifications stands Khomeini's pronouncement: 'The interest of the ruling system belongs to the issues that transcend everything else, and we must pursue it.'[5]

## The Council for Assessing the Interests of the Ruling System

The first state ordinance Khomeini issued after his letter to Khamene'i, ordered the creation of an Assessment Council. A scenario was devised for the purpose of issuing this order involving an appeal to Khomeini, in a letter dated 3/2/88, by the presidents of the three branches of the government, Ahmad Khomeini and Prime Minister Musavi. Complaining about the difficulties caused by the lengthy legislative procedure, they asked him to comment on a rumour that he intended to create an authority which would 'promulgate state ordinances after taking account of the interests of the ruling system and of society, in those cases where disagreement between parliament and the Guardian Council could not be resolved on the basis of the *shari'a* or the constitution.' They then expressed their wish that he employ haste in carrying out this intention.[6] In his written reply dated 6/2/88, Khomeini ordered the formation of the Assessment Council and specified who would sit on it. Taking into consideration the contradiction between this order and the constitution, he at the same time gave assurances that there was really no need for this 'phase' and that it was being introduced only 'for the sake of extreme caution'. Moreover, he indicated that the Assessment Council could pass its resolutions with a majority of the members who were present.[7]

One of the first steps taken by the Assessment Council – which began its work in the second half of February 1988 – was to draft its own statutes. The only power it conferred on itself was to decide what was in the interest of the ruling system. This power would only be exercised if it proved impossible to resolve a conflict between parliament and the Guardian Council. But in giving his view on the council's statutes, Khomeini extended its powers allowing it to decide on any subject that the majority of those present during a session with the necessary quorum deemed worthy of discussion.[8] In effect this turned the Assessment Council into a legislative authority capable of framing legislation independently of parliament and the Guardian Council. However, as we saw in Chapter 5, protests from many MPs and the Guardian Council led to a formal revocation of these extended powers, although in practice the Assessment Council continued to promulgate laws independently.[9]

Later in the summer of 1989 there was also talk in the Assembly for Revising the Constitution about the reasons behind the formation of the

Assessment Council and its role in the legislative system and the concept of *maslahat* which gives legitimacy to its decisions. Rafsanjani said the need for the council stemmed from the failure of attempts to resolve the problems of legislation with the help of the rule of emergency. The limited period of validity of laws passed on this basis, the difficulty of attaining the necessary two-thirds majority, and the continued opposition of the Guardian Council to parliament's resolutions even when all these requirements had been fulfilled, greatly restricted the effectiveness of the rule of emergency as a legislative strategy. On the other hand, the Guardian Council itself had not infrequently reached its decisions on the basis of *maslahat*.[10] Hojjat al-Eslam Kho'iniha thought that, in principle, legislation was nothing but taking account of interests. Fundamentally, parliament also worked on this basis.[11] Without wishing to deny that *maslahat* and the *shari'a* would contradict one another, Ayatollah Yazdi emphasised that:

> Taking account of interests means that, independently of laws and independently of the *shari'a*, interests demand that a particular decision be taken. In other words, *maslahat* means, if we want to grasp it more precisely, the overstepping of limits in an emergency for the sake of interests. We wish to overlook a law of the *shari'a* or of the constitution, i.e. to undertake an action contrary to the *shari'a* and contrary to the law, because of interest.[12]

These statements were made in response to Ayatollah Emami Kashani, a member of the Guardian Council, who proposed that the Assessment Council should be abolished and its function assigned to the Guardian Council. Emami Kashani's proposal was based on the argument that the protectors of the *shari'a* could at the same time be the authority that was concerned with considering interests. He remarked that the Guardian Council had not judged the resolutions of parliament on the basis of secondary and state ordinances, nor on the basis of ordinances of the *velayat-e faqih*, because the council saw it as its task to formulate its opinion on the basis of the primary ordinances. But now that Khomeini in his testament had urged the council to give its rulings with attention to the needs of the country, and on the basis of the secondary ordinances and the ordinances pertaining to *velayat-e faqih*, the Assessment Council would no longer have a function because the Guardian Council could take over its tasks.[13]

Emami Kashani's proposal expressed the disquiet of the Guardian Council over the Assessment Council. But it was rejected by the Assembly for Revising the Constitution because most members of the assembly were not prepared to accept that the *shari'a* would no longer have a protector and that legislation would be completely turned over to *maslahat*. If the *shari'a* were put aside there would be no purpose in allowing the Guardian Council to exist. As Ayatollah Amini pointed out, parliament itself would be able to carry out the task of determining interest.[14] Parliamentary spokesmen in the Assembly for Revising the Constitution also protested against the independent legislative activities of the Assessment Council.[15] Although the Assembly for Revising the Constitution in response restricted the Assessment Council's decision-making powers to cases involving conflict between parliament and the Guardian Council,[16] the Assessment Council continued to legislate. Furthermore, the Assembly for Revising the Constitution resolved that the appointment of members to the Assessment Council would be a prerogative of the leader, taking it to be tacitly agreed that in this connection Khamene'i would follow the same path as Khomeini.[17]

The leaders of the regime expected that the Assessment Council would resolve all the problems they had been confronted in the area of legislation. On 7/1/88, the day Khomeini's letter to Khamene'i was published, Rafsanjani declared triumphantly, and with the Guardian Council in mind: 'I ask those gentlemen who have been appointed by the Imam to take seriously the views of the Imam and not to allow their own views or the views of others to be an obstacle to implementing the Imam's decree.' Indeed, by means of this decree 'the way has been barred to wrong guidance and false piety and they will not be allowed in the name of Islam to block the capacity of the state to act'.[18] Ayatollah Musavi Ardebili remarked that the decree issued in this letter along with those issued during the pervious months 'constituted the most important of all the achievements of the revolution'.[19] Prime Minister Musavi went a step further and declared that this 'message' of the Imam 'can make it possible for the government to deal effectively in every situation with the complications and problems that burden the international community.'[20] The minister of the interior rejoiced at the fact that Khomeini's most recent *fatvas* 'had led the community of Muslims out of a dead end'.[21] Everyone rejoiced that with the help of *maslahat* they were freed from the fetters of the *shari'a* and could now look ahead to the future with hope. The Guardian Council, for its part, promised to take account of the *fatvas* and declared that it was prepared to revise its procedure of rejecting parliament's resolutions on this new basis.[22]

The most important legislative decisions of the Assessment Council to date have already been discussed in connection with secondary contractual conditions and discretionary punishments. But many other significant legislative undertakings were placed before the council because of the disagreement between parliament and the Guardian Council. By the summer of 1992, the Assessment Council had passed some 50 or so bills as laws, perhaps less than half of the bills that had come before it to be judged.[23] Given the relatively large number of bills it has to decide on, the optimism over the potential of this body to solve its legislative problems was clearly exaggerated. The Assessment Council has too few members and too large a workload, to deal with the numerous contested – and therefore complicated bills, which are placed before it by parliament and the government. But however many laws are passed or rejected by the Assessment Council each year, the significant point for this study is that the decision to set it up was based on the practical experience of long-standing that in a modern-day society like Iran it was not possible, by following either the ordinances or the so-called principles of the classical *shari'a*, to frame laws that would solve problems without raising new ones.

## Precedents for the Rule of *maslahat*

Because the *fatvas* issued towards the end of 1987 and at the beginning of 1988 eventually established *maslahat* as a formal principle of legislation, it should not be assumed that this was the first time it was used in the affairs of the Islamic Republic. On the contrary, what occurred was simply the official sanctioning of a practice which had been recognised for some time and which was now supplemented by the creation of a formal institution. A cursory glance at the history of the Islamic Republic makes it clear that the basis for the most fundamental decisions through all phases of the state's development and on all levels of government was the interest of the ruling system – or more correctly, the interest of those persons, groups and camps who participated in power. Even decisions regarding the form of the state, i.e. how it was to be transformed into a hierocracy based on the concept of *velayat-e faqih*, were taken in conformity with this principle. This includes those strategies which, before the proclamation of the rule of *maslahat* in Khomeini's *fatvas* had brought about the suppression of the *shari'a* as the basis of legislation – the rule of emergency and the secondary contractual conditions. If account had to be taken of the *shari'a* in these decisions this too was to a great extent for the sake of the interests that were involved. When consideration of the *shari'a* was no longer so necessary because of the widespread familiarity with the difficulties of running a government based on it, a further step was taken and *maslahat* was declared to be the finally decisive principle of legislation. The particular ordinances of the *shari'a*, such as the rules on clothing, which were still enforced, occasionally by violent methods, do not contradict this assertion because their observance, at least partially, is also due to the principle of *maslahat*.[24]

The recourse to *maslahat* is evident from the earliest days of the revolution. The edicts of the Revolutionary Council in the spring of 1980 to limit private ownership of agricultural land present several examples of this. According to the bill of 1/3/80, when turning over large estates to the farmers 'the interest of society' is to be constantly borne in mind. In the bills of 19/3/80 and 15/4/80, 'the requirements of trusteeship' and 'the ordinances of the ruler' are referred to. 'The interest of the Islamic community', as Ayatollah Beheshti stated, had played a decisive role in the latter bill.[25] Ayatollah Meshkini confirmed that if 'the interests of society' require it, the ruling jurist can take away legitimately acquired property from a person.[26]

Another example of recourse to the notion of interest is the Law on Direct Taxation, promulgated on March 1988 after lengthy delays. This law formally sanctioned the de facto situation that had prevailed ever since the founding of the Islamic Republic, and in so doing reversed an opinion that had held sway amongst Shi'i jurists for several centuries. Tax in the form of alms (*zakat*), the one-fifth tax (*khoms*) and the poll tax (*jeziyeh*) were the only kinds of tax which the classical Shi'i law unanimously sanctioned before this time. *Zakat* was to be paid to the poor by Muslims who owned camels, cattle, sheep, silver and gold coins, as well as by producers of raisins, wheat and barley. On the other hand, *khoms* was to be paid to imams, or to grand ayatollahs as representatives of the latter, by Muslims who owned mineral resources, valuables, wealth lawfully and unlawfully acquired, the profits of trade or a handicraft, wartime booty and plots of land which adherents of the other religions of the Book bought from Muslims. The poll-tax was to be levied on adherents of the other religions of the book by the Imam or the Islamic state.[27] Shi'i jurists rejected all other forms of tax (apart from a few exceptions)[28] which in their view were levied by fundamentally illegitimate rulers. In the *Tahrir al-Vasila*, such taxes are condemned as 'tithes, tolls and every other form of injustice'.[29] In *The Islamic State* Khomeini writes: 'When the Islamic state is realised, it will have to be run with just these taxes that we have, i.e. *khoms* and *zakat*, the latter of these being naturally quite small, as well as *jeziyeh* and *kharaj* (to be levied on national productive agricultural land)' (p. 29).

Once the Islamic state came into existence, however, it was immediately clear that its financial needs could not be secured through the religious taxes. In any case the ayatollahs and the religious academies were not prepared to give up their revenues from *khoms* on which their independence was tradition-ally based.[30] There was no alternative but to abandon the *shari'a* and demand that Muslims pay several forms of taxes, direct and indirect, in the tradition of the illegitimate rulers. To justify this about-face, both rational and religious-sounding arguments were used and references were made to state ordinances based on considerations of interest as well as to the rule of emergency and the secondary contractual conditions.

The debate on this subject began in the Assembly of Experts that dealt with framing the constitution.[31] It was taken up again in public here and there,[32] until the first direct taxation law was discussed in parliament. The intention of this bill was to replace pre-revolutionary laws which remained in force. In the debate surrounding its first reading, three positions became distinguishable. First, taxes based on customary law were contrary to the *shari'a*. The one-fifth tax and the alms-tax were sufficient to run the state. Second, to run the state taxes based on customary law are unavoidable, but could only be allowed on the basis of the rule of emergency and secondary ordinances. Third, the levying of taxes belongs to the powers of the ruling jurist who can impose any form of taxation on Muslims if it is required by the interests of the Islamic ruling system. Hojjat al-Eslam Fakhreddin Rahimi, who took the first position, based his arguments on the classical *shari'a* and in particular criticised the fact that the opening paragraph of the bill stated that it was inspired by Islamic ordinances. He emphasised that it was forbidden in Islam to take people's property away from them. One could not demand that Muslims pay both the one-fifth tax as well as other forms of tax.[33] Hojjat al-Eslam Mohammad Baqer Akhundi described the bill, because of its contradictions to the *shari'a*, as being more dangerous for the revolution than the United States and the Soviet Union.[34] Referring to the *Tahrir al-Vasila*, Ayatollah Azari Qomi rejected it because it was not based on the rule of emergency.[35] And the Guardian Council adopted the same position.[36] The advocates of the third position drew attention to the fact that no state could carry out its tasks without taxes. The spokesman for the Parliamentary Committee for Economy and Finances, Mohammad Khaza'i, said, 'As long as the world continues to exist, the system of taxation will remain in society … Taxation is a means in the service of achieving the goals of the Islamic state.'[37] For Hojjat al-Eslam Bayat taxes belonged to the primary ordinances of Islam.[38] But the decisive word was spoken by Khomeini. In an interview he gave to *Resalat*, Hojjat al-Eslam Hosein Shahrudi, Khaza'i's successor on the parliamentary committee, described how recourse was had to Khomeini who declared that taxes were one of 'the primary laws of the state'.[39] Thus, the resistance of many opponents of taxation that contradicts the *shari'a*, was broken. None the less, it was another three years before the bill got its second reading and was passed in parliament.[40] It only became a law because the Guardian Council preferred to abstain from handing down a ruling on it.[41]

Another example of *maslahat* in the economic sphere concerns the Islamic regulation of banking, at the centre of which is the issue of interest (*reba*). The first step in this direction was already taken in the budget law for 1358 (1979/80). This led to the passage in 1983 of the Law On Banking Without Interest.[42] However, in reality these legislative measures achieved little more than a prohibition on the use of the old terms for earning interest, and their replacement with new terms. Instead of *reba*, the terms *karmozd* (handling fee), *sud-e qat'i* (fixed earning), *sud-e mowred-e entezar* (expected earnings) and so on came into use, as well as *tahsilat* (payment facilities) and similar terms in place of *vam* (loan). This had to happen, as otherwise the banking system could not function. Five years later, Hojjat al-Eslam Movahhedi Savoji complained in parliament that in practice the banks were charging between 8 and 10 per cent interest.[43] On 4/7/90, the newspapers reported that earnings (*sud*) had risen to 13 per cent for long-term deposits of five years and to 10 per cent for one-year deposits. In later years further increases were announced every now and then.[44] At the Grand Congress of the Hezbollah on Banking, held in Tehran at the end of August 1992, Ayatollah Jannati, a member of the Guardian Council, complained that banking transactions had in part been organised in contradiction to the *shari'a* and requested that this be stopped. The congress passed a resolution requesting the banks not to engage in transactions that involved interest.[45] Somewhat later, the Islamic economist 'Ali Sadeqi wrote an article in *Ettela'at* (20/9/92) in which he admitted clearly, if not explicitly, that in the given circumstances banks cannot renounce transactions involving interest.[46]

A dramatic example of an action based on *maslahat* in the political domain was the choice of Hojjat al-Eslam Khamene'i as the successor to Khomeini in his capacity as leader. This choice was made despite the fact that, as we saw in Chapters 4 and 5, it was tantamount to establishing a separation between the *marja'iyat* and the office of leader. There was consequently a risk that one of the central legitimating pillars of *velayat-e faqih* would be undermined, a risk which could not, however, be avoided under the prevailing circumstances. So that this breach would not be too apparent, another decision was taken which was likewise based on interest: the uncustomary conferring of the title of ayatollah on Khamene'i who until then had been addressed as a hojjat al-eslam.[47]

Khamene'i's appointment as the successor to Khomeini was accompanied by a justification of this unexpected act. Recourse was had by such figures as Ayatollah Azari Qomi[48] to the advantages offered by the new legalised rule of *maslahat*. Qomi came to the conclusion that 'all problems of the system, its government offices and even the office of the leader, were to be decided after taking account of what was in the state's interest.' Since the state represented the highest principle, everything had to be done to protect it. He went so far as to declare that the existence of the state had such overriding importance that even if out of some necessity a depraved infidel came to preside over it, it was the duty of believers to obey him.[49]

Other examples in the political sphere concern foreign policy, which slowly and reluctantly abandoned its pan-Islamic anti-national stance and submitted to the requirements imposed on it by Iran's geo-strategic, national and economic circumstances. The unwilling halt to the war with Iraq, and the approval in practice of the West's policy towards Iraq in the second Gulf War followed upon this shift in foreign policy.[50]

Also in the area of the arts, entertainment and the domain of morality, the leaders of the Islamic state have had to abandon, completely or in part, the maintenance of several of the *shari'a's* prohibitions on the grounds of the interests of the state. The best example of this is music. Despite his condemnation of music in the *Tahrir al-Vasila*, Khomeini not only came to declare that it would be tolerated in practice but that it was, at least partially, useful. In his book Khomeini says of music:

> Performing and listening to singing (*ghena'*), as well as making money from it, are forbidden. *Ghena'* means not only making one's voice attractive, but also includes the drawing out and varying of the voice in a way that induces merriment and which is suited to gatherings for the purpose of amusement and having fun. And it also includes musical instruments. It makes no difference whether it is used to accompany the holy word such as the Koran or prayer or as a dirge or to accompany prose or poetry. Indeed, the penance is doubled when it is used in connection with worshipping the sublime God.'

The only exception to this general prohibition is the performance of female singers at weddings, under the condition that caution is exercised and the singing takes place in gatherings held immediately before or after the wedding night, i.e. 'not in just any gathering whatsoever'. In any case it is more advisable 'if singing is avoided altogether' (vol. II, p. 351). In another passage in the same book listening to singing and suchlike on the radio or a tape recorder is declared to be forbidden (vol. IV, p. 485). In his *Towzih al-Masa'el*, Khomeini also forbids making money by means of playing musical instruments or games of chance (p. 23).

Despite these and other more stringent prohibitions, music in all its courtly, mystical and folkloristic varieties had been cultivated for centuries in Iran. And for much of the twentieth century the mass media, supported by the government, had aimed at its widespread diffusion. Furthermore, during the 1979 revolution music and song were used as a highly effective means of mobilisation. All the same, in the wake of the revolution, after an initial period of tolerance, the ruling clergy began to fight against it. Music was prohibited on radio and television, music schools were closed down, and musicians, in particular female singers, were maltreated.[51] This was followed by the prohibition of imported cassette players and video cassettes and the regular deployment of the forces of order to confiscate such equipment which had been imported earlier or recently smuggled in.

However, given the impossibility of eliminating music completely from the life of the people, the more sensible of the Islamic republic's leaders gradually became aware that concessions had to be made. Some went a step further and realised the advantages that certain forms of music offered for achieving the propaganda and cultural-political goals of the Islamic state. The ground was prepared for an about-turn in policy enshrined in the indispensable *fatva* from Khomeini. The question put to Khomeini was: 'Is there any problem with the buying and selling of instruments for fun and amusement, if they facilitate licit enjoyment such as playing songs?' The expected and perhaps pre-arranged answer was that there is no problem in buying and selling of 'ambivalent instruments' for the purpose of permitted enjoyments.[52] This *fatva* was followed by another which legitimised music on radio and television with the words that such broadcasts were 'on the whole unproblematic'.[53] Thus music, in particular classical Iranian music, which was not considered frivolous could once more be performed in public, though under certain restrictions.

The new policy towards music was legitimated by pointing to the interests of the ruling system. Ayatollah Azari Qomi wrote that committing a forbidden act in the form of listening to music is permissible

> when the ruler of the Muslims established that it is in the interest of society to permit music and when it is clear to him that if he does not allow it, people will turn to foreign and counter-revolutionary radio broadcasts and be alienated from the radio of the Islamic Republic, with the result that they could be influenced by the poisonous propaganda of the enemy.

Music is permissible 'when [it is established that] if music is permitted by the ruler, the people will be influenced by the correct Islamic propaganda and their inclination for the Islamic laws and regulations will increase'. Azari Qomi believed that in this case it was even better 'if the order of the leader was absolute, i.e. not qualified in terms of time'.[54] A year and a half earlier, Qomi had declared before the advocates of music broadcasts on radio and television that the Imam had forbidden music in his book and laid down the relevant guidelines on this issue.[55] The kind of trick this consideration of interests could contrive is illustrated by a passage in a speech of Khomeini's son Ahmad in which he describes a meeting between his father and the presidents of the three branches of government. On that occasion Rafsanjani put the following question to Khomeini: 'Previously you declared that music was forbidden. Why do you no longer object to it?' The answer given by the Imam was: 'Let us assume that the music in question was broadcast by the radio of Saudi Arabia. Then I would forbid it, because wherever Taghut is in power, opposition to what he undertakes is allowed and such opposition conforms to *maslahat*. But here where the Islamic state is in power, a different form of regulation is valid.'[56]

In the same two *fatvas* Khomeini declared several other violations of morality permissible. One of these was playing chess. The question which led to the rehabilitation of this game was: How would matters stand with regard to chess 'if it completely lost its character as a game of chance, and if as [is customary] nowadays it were only enjoyed as an intellectual game'? Khomeini replied that chess was allowed on the condition that it was not practised as a game of chance.[57] The fact that no one had previously come up with the idea of allowing chess under this condition can only be explained the same way as the music broadcast by the Saudi Arabian radio. Moreover, inappropriate forms of dress from an Islamic point of view were permitted in the case of actresses and athletes such as wrestlers and football players when their performances were transmitted on television. 'Watching these kinds of films and theatrical performances is in no way contrary to the *shari'a*. Indeed, many of them are instructive. Broadcasting them is not a problem from the standpoint of the *shari'a*. The same is true of sports broadcasts.'[58]

In 1993, a further practice previously considered immoral was transferred to the category of permissible actions because the interest of the ruling system. The guardians of public morals had fought a fierce but hopeless battle against the trade in radio and video cassettes. The unstoppable flood of smuggled video films finally forced the rulers to rethink their policy in this area. Instead of forbidding videos, they have now switched to building up their own distribution network which is meant to lend out censored versions of films. The deputy of the minister for Islamic guidance and culture announced on 15/8/93 that 4,000 such centres would soon be opened.[59] In this case *maslahat* led to the decision that if 'an immoral practice' cannot be stopped completely, the Islamic state itself will undertake a controlled propagation of the immoral practice. The rapidly proliferating dish-antennae which are used to receive foreign TV stations were also dealt with in a similar way. On 15/4/94, the minister of the interior, 'Ali Mohammad Besharati, announced that the government had forbidden them. But here also he came up against the rule of *maslahat* which recommended a decision similar to that taken in the case of videos. It remains a technical problem how to censor foreign TV transmissions from within Iran.

In setting up a form of state that was unknown to the *shari'a*, the ruling jurists also took over a system of justice for which they found no guidelines in the books used for centuries to deal with the subject of *qaza'* (judgement). But it was in the interest of their newly-won power that they take over an organisation for dispensing justice which had emerged in Iran as a consequence of the twentieth-century modernisation of the old justice system and which presented numerous similarities to its Western model. The takeover of this system along with its corresponding judicial authority has been called 'a legal revolution' by Said Amir Arjomand. In order to make clear what this 'revolution' involved, I will here cite Amir Arjomand's comments on the issue and add a few remarks of my own.

A judicial judgement in Shi'i law, by contrast with 'judge law', has to do with 'jurists' law' which is more at home dealing with juridical questions in treatises and in books. Whereas 'jurists' law' scarcely concerns itself with the administration of justice, the latter function forms part of the state in the case of 'judge law'. Whereas 'judge law' includes public law and criminal law, 'jurists' law' concentrates on private law. Even the ordinances of the penal code in the latter are an element of private law which regulates people's relations with one another and with God. If 'judge law' is distinguished by its formal and impersonal character, the personal aspect of 'jurists' law' is even further reinforced by the fact that it does not dispose over any kind of hierarchical organisation and does not deliver a ruling on the basis of circumstantial evidence but rather on the basis of a confession, an oath and testimony. Arjomand also mentions the traditional reluctance of Shi'i jurists to take up a judicial function which must now be overcome.

With the setting up of the Islamic state, Shi'i law had to undertake to dissociate itself from these traits:

> From being a jurists' law it was to be transformed into the law of state. Law finding as the typical activity of the Islamic jurists was to be replaced by legislation and codification. Shi'i law was to be extended to cover public law fully. It was also to cover criminal justice. Its public provisions, unenforced for a millennium, were to become fully operative. From the point of view of procedure, Shi'i law was to be enforced through the modified mechanism of an inherited judiciary modelled on the West European civil law system. All this meant that the moral idealism of Shi'i law had to give way, at least partially, to practical realism, its procedural informality to a formally rationalised bureaucratic court system, and often impractical personalism to more impersonal and efficient procedures involving much greater reliance on written documents and impersonal forms of evidence.[60]

The transformation of Shi'i law in the Islamic Republic becomes more apparent if one looks at what has happened to Islamic legal regulations since the revolution. We have already given some representative examples. Especially noteworthy is the transformation in the area of criminal law, the Islamicisation of which has been pursued by the ruling jurists with special vigour. They have nevertheless been forced to adopt many reforms which could only be justified as requirements of government. We have discussed changes relating to the discretionary punishments in Chapter 11. With regard to the legal stipulations laid down by the Islamic *hodud*, *qesas* and *diyat*, the legislators are so unsure of themselves that, at the time of writing, these are still put into practice on an experimental basis only. The punishments which the *shari'a* actually prescribes for crimes such as adultery (stoning) or theft (chopping off a limb), are only exceptionally imposed, even if one assumes that information on this subject is not always published.[61] Installing students from the religious academies as judges because of the lack of learned or willing jurists, allowing lawyers or female legal advisers to be present in the courts, all of which is contrary to the *shari'a*, are decisions that are only justifiable as requirements of government. Other examples are the numerous breaches of the law and the judicial abuses which occur on a daily basis in the justice system for political reasons as well as for personal gain – abuses that occasionally reach such proportions that members of parliament have been moved to speak out in protest.[62]

## Notes

1  On this subject see Mahmasani: 1967; Coulson: 1964; Jannati: 1990a. After criticising other definitions of *masaleh-e morsaleh*, Jannati offered his own: 'Promulgating ordinances for new occurrences and phenomena on the basis of rational reflection and consideration of interests, in cases where no pertinent established text (*nass*) is available, either in a general or in a specified form.' But he added that throughout history recourse had not always been had to a *nass* in practice. Thus, the above definition is a qualified and a special definition. In an unqualified and general definition the requirement of referring to a *nass* must be dropped. Accordingly, *masaleh-e morsaleh* would 'mean promulgating ordinances for new derivations and questions on the basis of rational reflection and consideration of interests, even when these contradict the Book, established texts and Tradition.' On the other hand, according to Jannati the definition of the concept *esteslah* was as follows: '*Esteslah* is an ordinance which is based on interest, and this occurs when it is impossible to draw analogies because no pertinent stipulation exists in the *shari'a*, and when no relevant *nass* is available. The difference between *masaleh-e morsaleh* and *esteslah* is that 'the latter applies to an event concerning which interests and their contrary are taken into account', whereas in the case of the former 'considerations are only concerned with interests'.

2  Ibid., p. 61.

3  Ibid., p. 71.

4  *Howzeh*, No. 28 (1988), p. 158. This series of articles, published in nos. 28 to 42, was not continued in the later issues, although it has not yet been completed. In the 5th to 7th part of the series, examples of the use of *maslahat* in the life of Imam 'Ali are cited.

5  Quoted from Ayatollah Azari Qomi's series of articles in *Resalat* (3/4/89 ff.). The

last part of the series bore the heading: 'Sacrificing Everything in the Interest of the Ruling System' (*Resalat*, 9/4/89).

6 Mehrpur: 1992a.

7 MR II/846.

8 MR II/856.

9 On this subject see Mehrpur: 1992a, Parts 3 and 4.

10 MR III/1536.

11 Ibid.

12 MR II/838.

13 In this connection Khomeini's testament contains a contradiction. On the one hand, he wanted from the Guardian Council 'laws which were in contradiction to the pure *shari'a* and the constitution to be hindered without any compromise', while on the other hand he wanted the Guardian Council to take account of the needs of the country. That could happen one time with the help of the secondary ordinances and another time according to the ordinances of *velayat-e faqih*. By the latter he meant the state ordinances. See the Supplement of *Resalat*, 6/3/89.

14 MR II/853.

15 Views to this effect were expressed by Bayat, Najaf-Qoli Habibi and Musavi Ardebili (MR II/842 f. and 846).

16 The new Art. 112, which was pertinent to this issue, states: 'The council for determining the interests of the ruling system is to be formed in order to determine what is in the interest of the ruling order in those cases where the Guardian Council declares a resolution of parliament to be contrary to the *shari'a* or the constitution, and yet parliament does not comply with the demands of the Guardian Council out of consideration of the interests of the ruling system ...'

17 On 14/11/92, Khamene'i once again confirmed the members of the council. These are the presidents of the three branches of government, the clerics who are members of the Guardian Council, an alternating minister and an alternating spokesman of one of the permanent parliamentary committees, the first deputy of the president (at the time Hasan Habibi), Mir Hosein Musavi, as well as the *ayatollah*s and *hojjat al-eslam*s Mahdavi-Kani, Hasan Sane'i, Ahmad Khomeini, Musavi Kho'iniha, Mohammad 'Ali Movahhedi Kermani, Mohammad Reza Tavassoli, 'Abdollah Nuri and Ruhani. (See *Ettela'at* for the same day).

18 *Kayhan*, 7/1/88.

19 *Kayhan*, 18/1/88.

20 *Kayhan*, 10/1/88.

21 *Kayhan*, 13/1/88.

22 Ibid.

23 Mehrpur (1992a, 23/2/91) states that the number of bills forwarded by parliament to the Assessment Council represents 10 to 12 % of the bills parliament passed. Reckoning that parliament passed about 1,000 resolutions, this means 100–120 individual bills.

24 For example, the patriarchal attitude of those other than the rulers is also partially responsible for this.

25 *Ettela'at*, 4/9/81.

26 *Ettela'at*, 3/2/81.

27 Khomeini: *Tahrir al-Wasila*, vol. II, pp. 5 ff. and 79 ff.

28 Several *'alem* close to the government pronounced that the state had the right to collect *kharaj*, a tax levied on cultivated land which has been peacefully acquired by Muslims. See Modarresi Tabataba'i: 1983, vol. II, p. 72 ff.

29 Vol. II, p. 359.

30 MM 20/12/84, p. 28. Only after Khamene'i had become the Leader and he had experienced difficulty in establishing himself as the religious leader in face of the religious

authorities in Qom and Najaf, did several of his protectors demand that these revenues be passed on to the leader, but even so, not for the sake of the state but for the running of the religious academies. See Ayatollah Azari Qomi in *Resalat*, 10/6, 12/6 and 18/7/88.

31  M III/1410 ff.

32  See for example the statements of Ayatollah Meshkini in *Kayhan*, 3/2/82.

33  MM 20/12/84, p. 24.

34  Ibid., p. 21. See also pp. 23 and 25, as well as MM 18/12/84, p. 31.

35  In an interview in the periodical *Pasdar-e Eslam*, no. 35 (1984), p. 28 f. His position was later undermined when Khomeini, with recourse to *velayat-e faqih*, declared it legal to levy tax and gave the power to decide to do so to parliament, the Guardian Council and the government. Azari Qomi himself made statements to this effect in *Resalat*, 17/9/89 and 13/8/91.

36  Emami Kashani in an interview in *Kayhan*, 23/12/84.

37  MM 18/12/84, p. 21.

38  Ibid., p. 28. See also his book, p. 269 ff.

39  Already on 17/12/83, Khomeini had supposedly declared the opponents of levying taxes to be ignorant. He had asked them if they thought the costs of the war and running the government could be met by the 1/5th tax alone. See *Howzeh*: 1990, p. 12.

40  MM 21/1 up to 22/2/88.

41  Majles-e Showra-ye Eslami: 1990, p. 18. Regarding the system of taxation in the Islamic Republic of Iran see also Rosskopf: 1990.

42  LB: 1983/84, p. 335 ff.

43  MM 27/10/89.

44  For example, see *Salam*, 17/3/93.

45  *Resalat*, 26/8/92.

46  See also Hojjat al-Eslam Mosahabi, *Resalat*, 7/9/92, as well as the discussion of the same problem in *Resalat*, 1/9/93 and issues that immediately followed.

47  On this subject see Schirazi: 1991.

48  See his series of articles entitled '*Maslahat-e Nezam*' (The Interests of the Ruling System) that appeared in *Resalat* between 3 and 9/4/89.

49  *Resalat*, 30/4/89.

50  For a discussion of Iran's policy in the second Gulf War see Schirazi: 1991a and 1992.

51  See Liga: 1988, p. V/1 ff.

52  *Howzeh*, No. 28 (1988a), p. 20. By 'ambivalent instruments' (*alat-e moshtarakeh*) were understood instruments which can be used for licit as well as illicit purposes.

53  The pertinent question came from Esma'il Ferdowsipur, a member of the supervisory council for radio and television (*Resalat*, 22/12/87). The *fatva* itself is dated 19/4/87. In connection with the publication of this *fatva*, the public was informed that the Imam himself would listen to the radio and television music broadcasts and that he had no objection to them.

54  *Resalat*, 13/1/88.

55  *Resalat*, 26/6/86.

56  *Kayhan*, 27/6/90.

57  *Howzeh*, No. 28 (1988a), p. 20.

58  However, he did specify two conditions with regard to actresses. Firstly, the make-up artists of the actresses must be close members of their family (*mahram*). Secondly, viewers must not watch the film in question with erotic intentions. (*Resalat*, 22/12/87).

59  *Salam*, 15/8/93.

60  Arjomand, 1988: 184 f.

61  A female legal adviser, in a lecture she gave outside Iran, recounted how many

judges look for grounds to avoid applying the penalties prescribed for adultery. (Based on ms. of the lecture).

62  190 signed a letter addressed to the president of parliament in which they complained about conditions in the Ministry of Justice (*Kayhan*, 19/1/89). See also the reports of *Kayhan* on the Ministry of Justice which were published in several issues between 16/1 and 22/2/89. With regard to the structure of the justice system in the Islamic Republic see Madani: 1986–90, vol. VI, 1990.

# THIRTEEN

# A Problematic Criterion of Legitimacy

So far we have seen how the ordinances of the *shari'a* were, in the Islamic republic, overlaid by a mass of laws with a secular foundation, and how essential laws could only be passed by legitimating them through recourse to secondary ordinances, secondary contractual conditions and in the name of the 'interests of the ruling system'. We must now deal with a question which throws additional light on the relationship between legislation and the *shari'a* in the Islamic Republic – namely the criteria the Guardian Council applies when it examines the resolutions of parliament or other institutions.

In Chapter 5 we pointed out that only in exceptional cases does the Guardian Council give its reasons for rejecting parliamentary resolutions as contrary to the *shari'a*. Occasionally, to use Madani's words, it points in 'the direction of the contradiction', or the desired corrections, but often in so vague and brief a form that it is difficult even for experts to understand. Although MPs have insisted on being informed of the council's reasoning, and Montazeri and other authorities have made similar recommendations, the council has not changed its behaviour. There are indications that from time to time it has presented its reasons for rejecting parliamentary resolutions by word of mouth to the president of parliament, members of the competent parliamentary committees, or to Khomeini; but such cases are in all likelihood exceptions. The Guardian Council has insisted that it will formulate its views on the basis of its own *ejtehad* and that it is not obliged to give reasons for them. Nor is there any access to these reasons through the minutes of the council because no such minutes exist.[1]

Nevertheless, 'The Views of the Guardian Council',[2] which record its rulings on parliamentary resolutions, make it clear that the criteria on which these views are based are not the Islamic ordinances (*ahkam*) but the so-called Islamic principles (*mavazin*), the meaning and identity of which are only rarely the object of agreed upon interpretation. Although there are collections of the Shi'i ordinances, for example in the *Tahrir al-Vasila*, we find almost no case in the rulings of the Guardian Council where its judgement is based on a contradiction between a parliamentary bill and the *ahkam*.[3] Assuming that the concept *mavazin* is occasionally used synonymously with *ahkam*, and that it is theoretically possible to use the *ahkam* in this context,[4] it is important to ask why the Guardian Council has avoided recourse to the *ahkam*. There could be two answers to this question: either there are, in most cases, no pertinent *ahkam* on which the council can base its ruling, or the council thinks it is advisable to resort to criteria that have deliberately been left undefined in order to allow more room for desirable interpretations.

The Guardian Council's formal rejections of individual articles, notes and so on of bills passed by parliament are usually worded in one of the following ways: 'It contradicts the principles of the *shari'a*'; 'a contradiction exists from the standpoint of the *shari'a*'; 'it does not agree with the principles of the *shari'a*'; 'it is against the principles of the *shari'a*'; 'it cannot be confirmed from the standpoint of the principles of the *shari'a*.' There is a great difference between the formulations which refer to a contradiction between a resolution and the *shari'a*, and those that establish a lack of agreement between them. Whereas in the first case the lack of contradiction would be sufficient for the validity of the resolution, in the second agreement with the *shari'a* is required. In the first case there is the possibility that the *shari'a* makes no provisions for the problem at hand, while, on the other hand, the second formulation excludes any such possibility. Since the Guardian Council in most cases makes use of the first formulation, one can assume that it is aware that Shi'i law does not offer sufficient fundamental criteria even in the form of principles for a bill to claim to be in agreement with them. The more sensible jurists expect nothing further than this from the Guardian Council. This was what Ayatollah Yazdi meant when he said in the Assembly for Revising the Constitution that the task of the Guardian Council would be to hinder any parliamentary resolutions that were in contradiction to the *shari'a*. He added: 'Agreement is not necessary.'[5] Madani confirms our view that even when the Guardian Council speaks of a lack of agreement between a resolution and the *shari'a*, in most cases it is not actually seeking to establish agreement but rather to remove a contradiction.[6]

With respect to this issue the preliminary draft of the constitution had emphasised the desirability of striving for a lack of contradiction between the laws passed by parliament and 'those particular principles of Islam which were indisputable' (Art. 66). What was intended by the notion 'indisputable' (*mosallam*) was that there should be a consensus over their validity. As for giving a definition of compatibility, the competent commission of the Assembly of Experts stated that all laws and regulations that were passed must be 'in full consideration of Islamic principles'. To justify this formulation Ayatollah Beheshti pointed out that not all regulations could be taken directly from the Koran and the *sunna*. With regard to traffic regulations, for instance, it was necessary to take account of the experience of experts on the subject. In such cases it was sufficient that legislation be carried out 'taking into consideration the restrictions imposed by the Book and Tradition'. Ayatollah Montazeri objected that the expression 'taking into consideration' might give rise to the misunderstanding that in addition to Islamic principles other principles were to be considered, such as those of international law or the UN International Charter of Human Rights. Therefore, he proposed that the term 'compatibility' should be used even 'in cases where parliament passed laws which did not appear in explicit form in the Islamic legal sources.'

Akbar Parvaresh demanded that the expression 'taking into consideration' only be applied to regulations, which as such were of less importance and by their nature mutable. But 'the laws of the noble Prophet ... are immutable values.' Therefore laws must, without exception, be taken from the Koran and Tradition. In contrast to Parvaresh, Taheri Khorramabadi was of the opinion that compatibility with Islamic principles must also be a binding condition for regulations, 'but that under other circumstances it was sufficient if no contradiction to Islamic principles existed.' He did not make clear what he meant by 'other circumstances'.

As we saw in Chapter 3, their awareness that requiring parliamentary and government resolutions to agree with the *shari'a* was an untenable position led the members of the Assembly of Experts for Framing the Constitution to formulate the relevant articles of the constitution in vague terms. In various articles they employed the concepts '*mavazin*', '*ahkam*', '*moghayarat*' (contradiction) and '*entebaq*' (agreement) without any more precise definition. Art. 4 requires that all laws and regulations be passed 'on the basis of Islamic principles'. Art. 72 demands that parliament avoid passing laws 'which are in contradiction to the principles and ordinances of the religion of the country, or to the constitution.' Art. 91 states that the Guardian Council will be formed 'in order to hinder contradictions between the resolutions of parliament [on the one hand] and the Islamic ordinances and the constitution [on the other].' Art. 94 makes it the duty of the Guardian Council to examine the resolutions of parliament 'as to their agreement with the principles of Islam and the constitution', while Art. 96 stipulates that the task of 'establishing that there is no contradiction between the resolutions of parliament and the Islamic ordinances' is reserved for the six clerics who are members of the Guardian Council.

Ayatollah 'Amid Zanjani represented the position that where the constitution speaks of principles, it requires that parliamentary resolutions agree with them, whereas where it speaks of the relationship between parliamentary resolutions and the Islamic ordinances, it requires a lack of contradiction between them. He confirms our assumption that it is not a question of agreement in the latter case, because Islam does not have pertinent ordinances for many new laws and regulations. However, these can 'agree with the general rules of *feqh* and its principles of action'. In this connection, along with the general rules (*qava'ed-e kolli*) Zanjani also counts the principles of reason (*osul-e 'aqliyeh*) and the principles of action (*osul-e 'amaliyeh*) as belonging to the Islamic *mavazin*.[7]

The extent to which the Islamic principles themselves are disputed is well illustrated by the fact that even amongst the members of the clergy in the Guardian Council there is seldom agreement concerning them.[8] Since this was predictable, it was already stipulated in the constitution that for resolutions to be valid they would have to be approved by an absolute majority (Art. 91). However, establishing on the basis of majority views that a resolution does not contradict the *shari'a*, which is meant to represent the very ordinances of

God, is held by many Shi'i authorities to be a highly controversial matter.[9] Since God's ordinances cannot be disputed, the views of a majority or a minority should not have any relevance.[10] But because this principle cannot be maintained in practice, yet again the domain of the *shari'a* must be abandoned in order to make it at all possible to reach decisions. Even the fact that in the *osul-e feqh* (the principles of jurisprudence) the possibility is recognised that ordinances may be lacking or disputed, especially when dealing with new occurrences, and that in such cases with the help of *ejtehad* new ordinances may be derived from the existing 'general ordinances' (*kolliyat*), principles and sources, this does not change anything with regard to the above conclusion. For although *ejtehad* implies disagreement and error in drawing judicial inferences, it is not normally conceived as so unreliable a method of reaching a ruling that it will lead to disagreement in most cases, with the result that almost all the decisions of the Guardian Council are not unanimous but are reached by a majority.[11] This last fact is also an indication that, even for the Guardian Council, not many principles are so clearly established as to provide the council with a reliable source on which to base its rulings.

The creation of the Assessment Council and its adoption into the constitution did not prevent the Guardian Council from evaluating parliamentary resolutions by the *shari'a* and rejecting them when it judged this was possible and necessary.[12] The difference since the formation of the Assessment Council is that parliament is no longer obliged to comply with the recommendations of the Guardian Council. Parliament can reject them and turn the decision over to the Assessment Council in the hope of an acceptable outcome. Yet despite this, there are many cases where parliament takes account of the recommendations of the Guardian Council and corrects its resolutions as the council requests. However, this happens only in the case of resolutions on subjects which do not involve conflicts of interest or serious differences in points of view. It should nevertheless be noted that the relationship between parliament and the Guardian Council during the 4th Majles, in contrast to previous periods, was characterised by a degree of harmony, even though the council continued to reject many parliamentary resolutions.

The fact that parliament, both before and after the creation of the Assessment Council, has carried out many of the Guardian Council's wishes and recommendations on the *shari'a*, would appear to contradict the thesis presented in Part III of this book, namely that legislation in the Islamic Republic has increasingly freed itself of any link with the *shari'a* and thereby freed the constitution from its legalistic components. But this possible objection can be refuted in four ways:

1. Firstly, in cases where parliament has complied with the Guardian Council it has mostly been a question of resolutions which are of no real significance for influencing the character of the state.
2. In many instances there is agreement between the ordinances of the *shari'a* and those of a secular legal system. If, for example, through the

perseverance of the Guardian Council, the nationalisation of foreign trade is not sanctioned, at least not as far as the law is concerned, taking such a decision, or vetoing it, could just as well occur in any other legal system which defends the right to private property. If one bears in mind that the theoreticians and the advocates of the Islamic state declare it to be the most legitimate and the best, not because of what it has in common with other forms of government but on the basis of its special features, then there is nothing wrong in taking precisely those special features as a measure of whether the claims it has put forward are tenable.

3. Similarly, in many cases the enforcement of ordinances of the *shari'a*, such as the dress regulations, can be explained not so much in terms of a desire to observe the will of God, as a way of serving the interests of the rulers. For how can a state call itself Islamic if it does not even apply those ordinances which help it to save face? The enforcement of ordinances dealing with morality is something everyone can observe in daily life and which not only convinces loyal followers that a genuinely Islamic state exists, but also enables the rulers to free themselves of the ordinances of the *shari'a* in spheres where it is unavoidable and desirable.

4. Finally, one should bear in mind that when parliament complies with the wishes of the Guardian Council, it renounces resolutions which, for its part, it holds to be Islamic and believes are congruent with the *shari'a*. For parliament also calls itself Islamic and justifies its resolutions on the basis of its own understanding of Islam.

## Notes

1 This information is based on a personal conversation with Mehrpur, a former member of the Guardian Council.

2 These are contained in the law books published each year and can also be found in Mehrpur: 1992, Madani: 1986–90, and in a two-volume collection published by the Edareh-e Koll-e Qavanin va Moqarrarat-e Keshvar: 1993, although not in complete form.

3 One of the few exceptions is note 2 of the Law on the Classification of Property as Wasteland and Cancellation of the Relevant Land Registers, passed on 12/6/86. See Madani: 1986–90, vol. IV, p. 373.

4 In Chapter 1 it was noted that some *ahkam* were taken into the constitution.

5 MM II/838.

6 Madani, 1986–90, vol. IV, p. 174.

7 'Amid Zanjani: 1988–89, vol. I, p. 395 f.

8 As we have seen, there is no agreement among the jurists even on such principles as the rule of emergency, the rule of *maslahat* and the secondary contractual conditions.

9 'Allameh M. H. Tabataba'i (1969) makes his so-called unalterable Islamic regulations, as well as 'the alterable regulations' issued by means of *velayat* on the basis of reason, independent of the majority view (p. 45 ff.). In *The Islamic State*, Khomeini counts amongst the characteristics which distinguish an Islamic state from the other forms of constitutional government the fact that in the Islamic state 'the framing of laws is independent of the views of the people and the majority' (p. 47). This corresponds to his conceptions of the legislative power in the Islamic state, a power reserved for God alone. In his book, which

first appeared in 1909, the Grand Ayatollah Na'ini defended constitutionalism against such figures as Sheikh F. Nuri, who has been highly praised by Khomeini, and refuted Nuri's position that a state based on the views of the majority was invalid. But even Na'ini restricted the decision-making power of the majority to such laws and regulations which dealt with areas that were not provided for in the *shari'a* (edition of 1955, p. 80 ff.).

10 It is a question here of resolutions which, in the view of the Guardian Council, can be examined with reference to the *shari'a*, i.e. that the *shari'a* does provide indications for examining them.

11 In most cases the decisions of the Guardian Council are not unanimous but based on a majority (Madani: 1986–90, vol. IV, p. 173). With regard to decisions taken on the basis of the *shari'a*, this means, according to the council's statutes, at least 4 out of the 6 votes (ibid., p. 175). Although the text of the official findings issued by the Guardian Council does indicate whether the decision was unanimous or based on a majority, there is no way of knowing how often a decision was hindered by the absence of a necessary majority.

12 Between 31/7/91 and 7/8/93, the Guardian Council established that there were contradictions to the *shari'a* in at least 18 parliamentary resolutions. This figure is based on the author's own calculations.

PART FOUR

The Crisis of the *shari'a*

# FOURTEEN

# An Awareness of Crisis

The complications of a system of legislation and government based on the *shari'a* eventually gave rise to a widespread discussion of the deficiencies of the *shari'a* itself, and of Islamic jurisprudence and the religious seminaries, both amongst those who participated in government power and those Islamicists who had been excluded from it. The participants in this discussion can be distinguished by their social position, as well as their views. Besides the so-called *foqaha*, theologians, philosophers, law students, journalists and scientists have all made their contributions. These appeared in professional journals such as *Howzeh*, *Nur-e 'Elm*, *Rahnamun*, *Farhang*, *Kayhan-e Andisheh*, *Kayhan-e Farhangi*, and in newspapers and magazines such as *Salam*, *Resalat*, *Kiyan* and *Iran-e Farda*. A number of tendencies became visible in this discussion. To begin with one can contrast a conservative with a reform-minded position. The former camp consists primarily of jurists whose attitude towards the Islamic state is one of quietist reserve. Their position finds expression not so much in the explicit contribution they make to the discussion as in the reproaches which the reform-minded group level against them. The second tendency is prevalent among many of the *foqaha* who participate in power, and most especially amongst the intellectuals outside the religious seminaries. Within the ranks of the reform-minded Islamicists three distinct positions can be observed.

There is, firstly, a cautious position which approves of reform only in so far as it justifies *velayat-e faqih* and the practical consequences of that concept in government policy and legislation. Otherwise, it insists on maintaining views based on so-called traditional *feqh*. The clerics in the Guardian Council adopt this position together with many of the teaching staff at the religious academies, members of the Assembly of Leadership Experts and the Imams of the Friday Prayers. Together they form a powerful grouping supported by lay Islamicists of the kind who publish their views in the newspaper *Resalat*.

A second group within the reform-minded camp is distinguished by its willingness to apply far-reaching measures in adapting the *shari'a* to present-day requirements, in particular to the needs of government, and to approve whatever reform of *feqh* and the organisation of the religious seminaries is necessary to achieve this end. Representatives of this group are prepared to overstep many of the limits imposed by traditional *feqh*, to interpret old sources in new ways and to abandon many of the *shari'a's* ordinances in the name of *zarurat* and *maslahat*. In the discussions surrounding legislation, they have always spoken out against the views of the Guardian Council. The magazine *Howzeh* and the newspaper *Salam* support these reformers who are chiefly to be found amongst the students at the religious seminaries and their younger teachers. The differences between this group and the first are most clearly expressed in the positions they take in discussions about practical government policies.

The third group, whose adherents and sympathisers are more to be found amongst Islamic or Islamicist intellectuals, advocate a radical reform of the conception of Islam which begins with Islam's view of man and the world, and aims for an eventual reform of the totality of the so-called Islamic sciences (*ma'aref-e eslami*). Politically, this group more or less openly criticises the concept of *velayat-e faqih* and demands that it be replaced by what many of them refer to as 'scientific management'. By this they mean that the government should be run by modern experts. Under the editorial staff that was in charge till 1990, *Kiyan* and *Kayhan-e Farhangi* have provided the best-known platforms for this group. Because of their attitude towards *velayat-e faqih* and the fact that the group is chiefly made up of intellectuals, we designate its position as external and for this reason will discuss it at greater length.[1]

The debate on the deficiencies of *feqh* and the need for reform is far too extensive to be treated in detail. What follows is no more than a sketch of the positions which have emerged in the contributions of some of the best known spokesmen of the various camps and is limited to the issues surrounding *feqh* and the religious academies. Theological or philosophical positions will be left aside, except where they expressly provide a point of departure for criticising legalistic positions. Despite its brevity our presentation should be sufficient to familiarise the reader with the crisis affecting the conception of Islam and the *shari'a* in the Islamic Republic and the solutions proffered to overcome this crisis.

## The Shortcomings of Traditional Jurisprudence

The most important defect of *feqh* is its one-sided preoccupation with private law, discussed at some length earlier in the book. The preoccupation has also been noted by the editors of the periodical *Howzeh*. For example, in an article written in 1987 *Howzeh* regretted that 'the capacity of *ejtehad* and *estenbat*' did not go beyond the limits of individual actions and regulations concerning private persons, and that those who were engaged 'in research in the oasis of state ordinances and the guidance of society' could be counted on one's fingers. Even they were only concerned with questions which had to do with the necessity of rule and avoided the task of deriving state ordinances from the sources.[2] In another article, the fact that *feqh* even dealt with financial questions of a social nature as if they were private was taken to be the clearest proof of its predominantly private character. 'A single glance into the books of Shi'i *feqh* that deal with questions of finance reveals that it was not drawn up as a system for guiding a real society. That is precisely why the indications of governing and the state are so vague.'[3]

Ayatollah Ebrahim Jannati cites as another deficiency of *feqh* that it is disproportionately concerned with questions of worship. In his view the 'supposed deficiencies' of *feqh* would disappear if one third of the effort that went into the subject of rules of ritual purity and prayer were devoted to questions dealt with under other headings. He referred to the deficiencies as 'supposed' because in his view it was not *feqh* itself which was deficient, but the jurists.[4] Hojjat al-Eslam Hojjati Kermani objected to those ordinances of *feqh* whose content was based on superstition or which gave the false impression they had come about through consensus. To this category he relegated ordinances on conversing with women, the appearance of women before government authorities, their participation in elections, the questions of music and wearing a beard.[5]

In this discussion not only was attention drawn to the lack of state ordinances in traditional *feqh* but also to the fact that, although jurists had now become rulers, *feqh* still suffered from the same deficiency. Ayatollah Khatami, the former minister for Islamic guidance and culture, described the situation as a vacuum he greatly regretted.[6] The editors of *Howzeh* characterised what they called 'the fundamental problem of present-day *feqh*' as 'flight from the [new] facts' and as 'avoiding problems which [modern] civilisation has created. A *feqh* of this kind is forced to seek its identity in outmoded forms and issue its *fatvas* for a fictive society ... Every passage of present-day *feqh* confirms this statement.'[7] Ayatollah Azari Qomi declared that, despite the reforms of *feqh* introduced by Khomeini, 'politics has not found its way into [jurisprudence]. It has managed only to change the look of the curriculum in the seminaries to a very limited extent.'[8]

For some participants in the discussion, the absence of state ordinances was only part of a greater deficiency described as a lack of attention to issues relating to the new world. 'Ignorance of New Subjects' is the title of one part of a series of articles on '*Feqh* and the Creation of a Healthy Economy' published in *Howzeh*. In these articles it is argued that in general *feqh* has not paid attention to contemporary issues and in particular has neglected the economy.[9] As an example of new questions *feqh* has neglected to address, Hojjat al-Eslam Bayat mentions the radio and television organisations, as well as the arts, which in his view should be discussed and examined by Islam in all their dimensions. He also mentions the system property-ownership, concerning which *feqh* must dispose over clear definitions. Another such question in his view is birth-control which has similarly been neglected.[10] With these deficiencies in mind, Ayatollah Jannati comes to the conclusion that 'our *feqh* ... belongs to schools and old-fashioned personal questions that have long since ceased to be current.' It deals with issues whose content has no present-day relevance. Many jurists are satisfied simply to reiterate frequently-repeated ordinances without paying attention to their content or concerning themselves with new subjects.[11]

But even in those areas where *feqh* has dealt with new questions, these have not been solved according to the rules of *feqh*. Ayatollah Makarem Shirazi points out that the ordinances formulated for these questions in the books of *feqh* lack the proofs required from the point of view of the principles of *feqh* (*osul-e feqh*).[12] Ahmad Khomeini expressed himself along the same lines in connection with the new *fatvas* his father had issued in order to solve the questions of legislation, etc. He remarked that the required juridical proofs from the verses of the Koran and the *sunna* must be provided for them by 'the honourable professors of the city of Qom'. Before making this request he had announced that Khomeini himself had not produced the proofs for his *fatvas*.[13]

## The Defects of the Religious Academies

Most articles on the deficiencies of *feqh* also criticise the religious academies where *feqh* is preserved, developed and taught. The criticism encompasses the organisation, administration and financing of the academies, as well as their educational methods and curriculum. Many critics consider the decentralised structure of the academies to be their most important organisational and administrative problem and hold this chiefly responsible for the fact that a policy of reform cannot be implemented in the individual academies and therefore in the system as a whole. Traditionally, the organisation of the academies revolves around the households of individual grand ayatollahs. Whereas previously their homes had been the locality where the respective *marja's* did their teaching, 'in recent times' they had developed into 'centres for the receipt, administration and distribution of money, as well as negative rivalries and, not infrequently, the formation of spiritual cliques.' Which is why 'their scholarly soundness and their wholesome normative principles' show signs of fading.[14] Criticism of the decentralised organisation and administration of the academies comes chiefly from the ranks of the ruling clergy who advocate government control over these institutions as a means of stopping their enemies from gaining greater power. In opposition to this centralising tendency are those members of the academies whose motto in this regard appears to be 'order in disorder'.

Likewise, the decentralised collection of religious taxes, specifically the *khoms*, is often criticised from this standpoint. Since the tax provides the financial basis for the independence of the grand ayatollahs, the state would prefer these sums to go into a central fund which would possibly be under the control of those who hold power in the academies.[15] Criticism of this kind is based on more credible reformist motives when it emphasises that the direct payment of taxes to grand ayatollahs results in their dependence on the mass (*'avam*) of contributors and an obligation, in the exercise of *ejtehad*, to take account of the usually conservative stance of the masses and therefore to issue rulings against reforms.[16]

Many articles in the press criticise the system of education in the academies in great detail. Indeed, the criticism extends over the whole range of problems, from the process of selecting applicants for study to the very goals of the study program. The abilities of applicants to the academies are not tested, there is no fixed study program, textbooks date from previous centuries and to a great extent treat subjects that no longer have present-day relevance, and generally speaking 'the system of education is not directed towards a defined goal'. This lack of an ultimate goal leads many students to make of the academies a self-contained, enclosed world for themselves. For students with a sense of responsibility, 'study for the sake of study is their most sacred motto.'[17] Furthermore, the academies do not attempt new research. Instead they produce *resalehs* which always contain the same contents, commentaries on old books and commentaries on commentaries. As Ayatollah Jannati points out, since the death of Grand Ayatollah Abolhasan Esfahani in 1945, 360 *resalehs* of this kind have been composed.[18]

Another problem with the academies is their concentration on *feqh*, as if 'the Islamic sciences could be reduced to *feqh* and its *osul*.' Koranic interpretation, theology, philosophy and ethics are relegated to an obscure marginal life which depends on the personal interests of the professors and the students. The way the academies deal with the other Islamic sciences makes it clear how they stand in relation to the modern sciences and the human sciences,[19] which are still roundly ignored. Moreover, after the foundation of the Islamic state the academies developed a new problem – namely that the teaching staff became totally involved in politics and ceased to concern itself any longer with teaching. Hojjat al-Eslam Bayat has remarked: 'I know some Imams of the Friday Prayers who no longer read any books and don't do any teaching.'[20]

The following remarks by Mohammad Reza Hakimi read like a résumé of all these criticisms:

> The general situation in the academies today, the particular features they display and the way they are administered, are neither in agreement with the methods and tasks of our great and vigilant forefathers, nor with conditions in the present-day world. The academies have still not found an answer to any of today's problems. Although Islam has attained dominion in this country, the academies are still unable to say what the political philosophy of Islam is, how the government is to be run in accordance with Islam and what practical ethical principles should guide statesmen and government authorities. And many other such questions remain unanswered.[21]

## The Causes of the Crisis

The conservative and moderate critics of *feqh* and the academies do not seek the reasons for the deficiencies they have described in the *shari'a* itself. Rather, the jurists themselves are blamed. According to Jannati: 'We are the ones [who are responsible], for we have not applied ourselves adequately.' Had we done so, 'Islamic *feqh* would not have left a single question unanswered.'[22]

Like all the advocates of *velayat-e faqih*, Hojjat al-Eslam Hojjati Kermani is in no doubt that *feqh* possesses a potential universality which must be actualised by means of *ejtehad* and the sciences.[23] For Ayatollah Makarem Shirazi the proof of this universality lies in the fact that, in the conception of the Muslims, Islam is not limited by ordinances which are bound to time and place: 'Therefore, it must have solutions for all the needs of every people throughout all the regions of the world and at all times, not simply for religious questions but also for questions regarding economics, politics, law and all other matters that pertain to individuals and societies.'[24]

According to Ayatollah Mohammad Taqi Jaʿfari and many others, the reason the *ʿulama* have not dealt with such questions is that rulers have always been treated them as enemies. Consequently, they have exercised caution and, since the people could not turn to them for solutions on these questions, they have felt no compulsion to think about them or to issue pertinent *fatvas*. This situation, which continued up to the time of the Islamic revolution, led to the isolation of *feqh* and the *foqaha*.[25]

A complex of attitudes, which present-day jurists cultivate in conformity with old traditions, has also been held responsible for the deficiencies. For example, 'reverence for the views held by *foqaha* who have passed away.' Thus views expressed by living jurists retain a strong flavour of the past. Their formulations are far removed from the reality of contemporary life and with the passage of time have developed into a kind of cancerous growth at the margin of society.[26] This reverence occasionally goes so far that the views of the ancients are declared to be sacred. The editorial staff of *Howzeh* called this 'the sickness of sacralisation' (*taqaddos-zadegi*). In their view, 'what, more than any other cause, has injured the development of *ejtehad* throughout the history of *feqh* is the reverence for and sacralisation of *fatvas* and declarations which, according to the very nature of *ejtehad*, did not deserve to be treated in this way.' This attitude has brought about the stagnation and crippling of *feqh* and *ejtehad*.[27]

The sickness of sacralisation is reinforced by 'the cult of personality' (*shakhsiyat-zadegi*). This operates where extreme veneration for a personality or a theory and self-effacement before the greatness of a particular human being leads to paralysis of the creative will of a legal researcher and forces him to accept the views of that authority without any opposition.[28] Both illnesses include a third – 'the sickness of imitation' (*taqlid-zadegi*). This reproach is especially levelled against the academies from outside. But it has even been attested within the academies as a explanation for why *feqh* lags so far behind contemporary reality.[29]

One consequence of these sicknesses is described as ignorance of the fact that the jurists are clinging to ordinances which no longer have any relevance to their objects, which have been completely transformed under changing conditions of time, place and technology. ʿAbbas ʿAbdi has examined this lack of relevance in a series of articles entitled 'The Sociology of Iranian Law', in which he shows through numerous examples taken from the legal system of the Islamic Republic how jurists and legislators, by disregarding 'the principle which postulates the mutability of laws' and 'the principle which prescribes harmonising laws with their external requirements', pass laws or issue regulations which do not correspond to any object or whose object is no longer the same. The three-month period (*'eddeh*) a divorced wife must wait before remarrying in order to establish whether she is pregnant, is still adhered to although pregnancy can be established much sooner by means of modern medical techniques. Despite modern methods of criminology, the oath, confession and testimony are still employed as Islamic means of proof in the courts. The regulations concerning interest are still declared to be inviolable although everyone now knows that in the current galloping inflation they favour debtors. On the basis of these and many other examples, 'Abdi comes to the conclusion that Islamic law has fallen prey to formalism.[30] Khomeini cites other examples in his letter to Hojjat al-Eslam Qadiri where, amongst other things, he asks him whether he thinks the regulations that forbid betting – with the exception of wagers on horse racing and archery – should still be applied today with the same exceptions. He points out that these days Islamic territory can no longer be defended by horsemen or bows and arrows and Muslims must be encouraged to acquire the necessary skills in using modern weapons, and that includes encouragement through allowing wagers.[31]

The editors of the periodical *Nur-e 'Elm* give another reason why the academies have become ivory towers – namely that, in formulating their views, they always assume the existence of an Islamic ideal state of affairs: 'In practice one is dealing with a day-to-day reality which operates on a far lower level. This gap constitutes a practical obstacle to the academies and the government system ever drawing close together.' In the view of *Nur-e 'Elm*, the insistence on primary ordinances and the lack of attention to the rule of emergency are amongst the manifestations of this idealistic tendency.[32]

According to *Howzeh*, jurists are also prevented from addressing new questions by 'the sickness of hyper-caution' (*ehtiyat-zadegi*). This 'scourge on *ejtehad*', will, they argue destroy it and bring an end to the ability to practice *estenbat* (drawing inferences). Jurists who suffer from 'the sickness of hyper-caution' completely lose their capacity to form views on new occurrences and real events.[33] Coupled with this is an abstract and unsystematic way of looking at things which dominates whenever jurists – 'without concerning themselves with such high ideals and goals as justice' – express themselves about a real case at hand like the employment law.[34] In 1988, *Howzeh* also mentioned the fear of eclecticism as one of the obstacles which stood in the way of the regeneration of *feqh* and the academies.[35]

Before leaving this subject it should be mentioned that 'international unbelief' (*kofr-e jahani*) has also been held to be responsible – by Ayatollah Jannati – for the stagnation of *feqh*. Through its hirelings and untrustworthy elements inside the country *kofr-e jahani* is not only out to hinder Islam, which now rules over Iran, from influencing Islamic societies but endeavours to drive from the arena of actual practice a dynamic and progressive *feqh* which is based on *ejtehad*.[36] According to Rafsanjani, imperialistic powers send their informers into the academies in order to create by this means their own circles of influence.[37]

## Who is to Blame?

The sources we have so far cited hold a particular group responsible for the diverse sicknesses they diagnose.[38] They are, according to the advocates of *velayat-e faqih*, a conservative, quietist clergy who refuse to recognise the regime or to support it actively. The harsh view of this group is reflected in the negative phrases used to describe them: 'shameless jurists', 'fools affecting pious behaviour', 'informers', 'petrified', 'simpletons', 'narrow-minded', 'mentally retarded', 'incompetent and with bad taste', men 'who not only refuse to march with the times and are incompetent to think about new issues, but reject every new thought and every correct conception of Islam branding it as unbelief'.[39]

In a lead article *Howzeh* described them as clerics caught 'in a frozen mental state and inward ineptitude' who are set on separating the clergy from the state, and religion from politics. The authors of this particular article ask 'how anyone concerned with the organisational reform of the academies can calmly stand by and out of fear be silent in the face of this luxuriant growth of weeds, these persons of bad taste and petrified ideas, who think along the lines of mullahs with fixed appointments from 500 years ago.'[40] Khomeini described such clerics as 'unaware and pro-foreign', and reproached them for working against the revolution and 'the true Muhammadan Islam'. In his view, while making a display of false piety they were attacking the foundations of Islam in a manner that led one to believe that they saw this as their real task. He warned against underestimating 'the danger posed by those who were committed to petrified ideas, and the fools who made a display of sanctity in the academies.' He urged his 'dear students not to let out of their sight for one moment these multicoloured snakes,' for they were 'agitators on behalf of the American Islam, and enemies of the Prophet.'[41]

According the radical wing of the legalistic Islamicists, these characteristics were more or less shared by 'conservative fellow-travellers', meaning, as many of the radicals' descriptions make clear, members of the Assembly of Leadership Experts and the Guardian Council. To the authors of *Howzeh*, the positions adopted by the Guardian Council on questions such as the Labour Law, landownership and taxes provided clear proof of the council's abstract attitude in legal questions, an attitude which neglected the ideals of Islam and was influenced by formal externals in matters to do with *fatvas*.[42] To the radical legalists anyone like this could not be characterised as a reformer but merely as a person pretending to be a reformer. 'They find themselves confronted by a *fait accompli*, feel they are incapable of opposing the onslaught of ideas, and so they join the movement.' But they do everything in their power to slow down the course of reform or to lead it in the wrong direction.[43]

## Notes

1 The author is aware that a more detailed treatment of the subject would require further differentiation of this division of positions.

2 *Howzeh*, No. 23 (1987), p. 22.

3 *Howzeh*, No. 28 (1988a), p. 11.

4 *Howzeh*: 1986, p. 87. See also his article in *Kayhan-e Andisheh*: 1990.

5 *Ettela'at*, 23/12/92.

6 *Salam*, 1/5/91.

7 *Howzeh*, No. 29 (1988), p. 6 f.

8 *Kayhan*, 29/2/91.

9 *Howzeh*, No. 25 (1987a), p. 136.

10 See his interview in *Howzeh*, No. 37/38 (1990), p. 129.

11 1990, p. 29.

12 *Ettela'at*, 17/3/92.

13 See his speech at the closing session of the Ninth Conference of Islamic Thought (*Kayhan*, 5/2/92).

14 The view expressed by Hojjat al-Eslam 'Abbas Mokhlesi in his article 'Obstacles to Reforming the Organisation of the Religious Academies', *Ettela'at*, 30/1/93.

15 *Resalat*, 20/19/92.

16 The view of Mokhlesi See *Ettela'at*, 3/1/93 and *Howzeh*, No. 27 (1988b), p. 65.

17 *Howzeh*, No. 28 (1988a), p. 14.

18 Jannati: 1990, p. 34. *Resaleh* is another name for the books which appear in standard form with the title *Towzih al-Masa'el* and contain solutions to questions about the *shari'a*. Ayatollahs who aspire to the position of *marja'* attempt to publish a *resaleh* of this kind.

19 In these sources, by human sciences are meant the social sciences and sometimes psychology.

20 *Howzeh*, No. 37/38 (1990), p. 136.

21 From a series of articles published in *Howzeh*, Nos. 1 and 2 (1983). See also the articles criticising *feqh* and the academies in Nos. 4–14 (1986/87) of the same periodical, and Bonyad-e Farhangi-ye Baqer al-'Olum in *Ettela'at*, 2, 10 and 17/10/92.

22 Jannati: 1987, p. 13.

23 *Ettela'at*, 24/2/92. On this point see also Khomeini's testament in the supplement to *Resalat*, 6/6/89, p. 4.

24 *Ettela'at*, 18/3/92.

25 See his interview in *Howzeh*, Nr. 20 (1987), p. 35 f. Cf. also Jannati: 1990, p. 23, and the series of articles which began to appear in *Resalat* on 24/10/87.

26 *Howzeh*, No. 31 (1989), p. 32.

27 *Howzeh*, No. 28 (1988a), p. 8 f.

28 *Howzeh*, No. 27 (1988c), p. 166.

29 See the statement of Jannati: 1990, p. 24 f.

30 *Salam*, 9/9 until 15/10/91. The editors of *Howzeh* (1987a, p. 132 f.) describe this formalism as a sickness characterised by a jurist being satisfied with externals (*zaher-zadegi*) when practising *efta'* (issuing a new *fatva*) or when conducting legal research.

31 *Howzeh*, No. 28 (1989), p. 21. Ayatollah Makarem Shirazi (1992, Part III) gives as an example the prohibition against selling human blood and organs which makes no sense

because, in contrast to earlier times, these may today be used for medical purposes.

32  Cited here from *Resalat*, 23/2/92.

33  No. 28 (1988a), p. 14.

34  *Howzeh*, No. 20 (1987a), p. 133 ff.

35  1988c: p. 156 ff.

36  Jannati: 1990, p. 37 f.

37  See his interview in *Howzeh*, No. 11 (1985).

38  Although they are rarely mentioned as individuals, they well known to observers as targets of reproach. Those known to be opponents of the regime, become victims of various forms of mistreatment.

39  *Howzeh*, No. 5 (1984), p. 3 ff.

40  *Howzeh*, No. 14 (1986/87), pp. 34 and 38.

41  Cited from Khomeini's message 'Showing the Way', which was intended for the clergy and published in *Resalat*, 25/2/89.

42  *Howzeh*, No. 25 (1987a), p. 132 ff.

43  *Howzeh*, No. 35 (1989a), p. 72.

FIFTEEN

# The Search for Solutions

## The Demand for Reform of the Academies

The urgency to the reformers of the issues posed by the deficiencies of the *shari'a* is evident in the their constant warnings of the dangers of neglect. In 1986 *Howzeh* thought that if reforms were not carried out a collapse of the academies would follow.[1] A few months later, the journal warned that the future of the clergy was in jeopardy. The danger was all the more serious because the failure of the religious academies to implement reforms would entail the defeat of the Islamic revolution which, in its turn, would mean abandoning the dominion of Islam for years or even for centuries.[2] In another issue, *Howzeh* maintains that hesitation over reform would call into question the very existence of religion.[3]

Most of the time criticism of *feqh* and the religious academies occurs in conjunction with proposals for the rectification of their shortcomings. These are either presented individually or appear as part of a blueprint for reform which the authors consider to be all-embracing. The most important proposals so far as the academies are concerned may be summarised as follows:

1. A centralised organisation should be set up on a scientific basis for running the academies without giving encouragement to bureaucratic and dictatorial tendencies.
2. The finances of the academies should be centrally organised, preferably under the direction of the ruling jurists.
3. There must be a thoroughgoing reform of the system of education in the academies encompassing the method of selecting students, the organisation of the study program, the content of textbooks, areas of specialised study and teaching the human sciences.
4. Specialised personnel should be trained to take over management positions at every level of the government apparatus. There should be a legally sanctioned monopoly over such positions for suitably qualified graduates of the academies in the areas of culture, the legal system, the intelligence service and Islamic guidance.
5. Propaganda methods must be brought up to date because throughout industrial societies people have become highly sophisticated and can no longer be influenced by the old methods.[4]

Similarly ideas for the reform of *feqh* and its deficiencies are frequently put forward. On the basis of a critique *feqh*'s abstract approach to dealing with the ordinances of the *shari'a*, the demand has been raised for comprehensive systematisation. Concerning the use of caution (*ehtiyat*) as a method of reaching a judgement, nowadays, as Hojjat al-Eslam Hojjati Kermani puts it, it is taken for granted that one is prepared to put caution aside, i.e. to have the courage to question the usual *fatvas*. All dogmatic adherence to the *ahkam* and *fatvas* of the famous jurists would today be in violation of the rule of caution. Doubt as to their validity is permissible because they cannot be taken as identical with the ordinances of God.[5] Permission to doubt is at the same time a rejection of imitation, which critics have associated with the sickness of the cult of personality or sacralisation. 'The true *mojtaheds* must tear down the barriers of imitation in their discourse of *ejtehad*' and in its place apply the principles of *ejtehad* in all questions. They must do this even when the result runs counter to the usual *fatvas*. As examples of questions where this approach must be taken, Ayatollah Jannati mentions the banking system, foreign currency, the commission business (*mozarebeh*), music, women becoming judges, taxes, birth-control, chess, landownership and 'many other matters'.[6]

The criticism of imitation as the dominant method in *feqh* is reinforced in the appeal to take account of the role of time when issuing a *fatva*. Time not only creates new facts which require new ordinances that are lacking in current *feqh*, but also possesses the characteristic of making old ordinances devoid of an object. Taking account of the role of time would, according to Ahmad Khomeini, free legislators of the need to constantly resort to secondary ordinances and to violate primary ordinances. For the disappearance of an object from the area of jurisdiction of a primary ordinance does no harm to the latter. The ordinance itself will remain unchanged but will not have to be applied to the particular matter in question, which by now has become the object of another ordinance.[7]

In order to work out new ordinances for new facts by means of *ejtehad*, it is necessary to acquire knowledge of those facts. However, opinions differ as to whether the jurists themselves should be experts (*karshenas*) on new matters or whether they should seek such knowledge from specialists. Whereas Ayatollah M. T. Ja'fari is satisfied if *mojtaheds* receive aid from 'aware and upright experts',[8] M. R. Hakimi (1983) wants 'the academies to possess everything, and ... to be informed on all dimensions of present-day thought.' It is the advocates of the latter position who are in favour of the curriculum of the religious academies also including the human sciences and even some of the natural sciences.

Amongst the new facts the academies should deal with, knowledge of the state is the top priority. Awareness of the lack of state ordinances in the *shari'a* and the newly won responsibilities of political power have increased pressure on the academies to acquire and transmit 'expert knowledge'. According to *Howzeh*, what could liberate *feqh* from 'the sickness of concentrating on private law' would be new treatises on questions concerning the state and the social dimension of human beings. 'Should the academies not reflect on the demands of the time ... and the relation of *feqh* to the state and not apply *ejtehad* to this issue with success, they will no doubt soon fall into the claws of "time's annihilation".' *Feqh* would then necessarily disappear from the arena of life forever.[9] In a letter to the members of the Society of Teachers of the Academy of Qom, Khamene'i declared that turning attention to 'state *feqh*', discovering the divine ordinances pertaining to all questions about the state, and considering all the ordinances of *feqh* from the viewpoint of the state constituted one of the most fundamental duties of Islamic jurisprudence today. These matters were indispensable for 'establishing an exemplary society and a refreshing Islamic life'.[10]

New facts could not be dealt with without specialised training. This would be necessary even if one wished to revive the Islamic sciences that had fallen into neglect. According to Ayatollah Ja'fari, the expansion of subjects dealt with in the separate areas of *feqh*, theology, logic, literature, exegesis, *hadith* and other Islamic sciences had attained such dimensions that a person could spend a whole lifetime studying and carrying out research in just one of these disciplines.[11] Ayatollah Ja'fari went on to add that if one were to move in the direction of specialisation, it would be necessary to separate 'research' from religious propaganda. Under present conditions it was impossible for someone involved in propaganda activities to find sufficient time to engage in research.[12]

At this point it would be appropriate to ask how prepared individual reformers are to accept the consequences of their attitude towards traditional *feqh* and their insistence on adapting the *shari'a* to the needs of the time. One way of assessing such willingness would be to look at how far they are willing to go in revising the conventional Islamic ordinances, or in other words the extent to which these reformers are prepared to drop or replace the ordinances. It is also important to consider the motive for each case for which the revision of a particular ordinance is accepted. Leaving aside the quiet abandonment of the rather embarrassing ordinances on slaves in the new *feqh*-books and considering Khomeini's rulings on music, chess, the rules of emergency and the interest of state as a direct outcome of the pressures of government, there is scarcely an example of significance in which there have been signs of revision.

Even Ayatollah Motahhari (murdered on 1/5/79), who the legalists recognised as the greatest reformer, was not prepared to renounce such ordinances as the Islamic fixed punishments (*hodud*), although he devoted entire lectures to the subject of 'Islam and the Needs of the Times'.[13] Although he spoke in these lectures of the possibility of distinguishing between 'the constant' and 'the changeable' Islamic ordinances, he devoted all his attention to enumerating those ordinances which were constant. At the same time, he engaged in polemic against, for example, Habib Bourgiba, the former President of Tunisia, who wanted to forbid fasting for economic reasons, and held to the prohibition against eating pork although he admitted there were apparently no hygienic grounds for maintaining the ban.[14] Moreover, when it came to specifying which ordinances were changeable, he would either cloak himself in a cloud of caution and vagueness or shift the discussion to the area of new facts where it was easy to revise the relevant ordinances because they had not existed in the traditional *shari'a*.

Although the practical demands of government and legislation made the negation and revision of many Islamic ordinances inevitable, the official form of *feqh* has hardly moved in this direction. In such an atmosphere, the status of declarations of a cleric such as Hojjati Kermani who states that joy, hand clapping, cheerful music and dance at weddings and at national and religious celebrations are permissible, that sports halls should be built for the students in the academies, or that joyful celebrations should be held in mosques, and then engages in polemic with the opponents of this interpretation of Islam is hazardous. Hojjati Kermani is himself aware of the danger but has said that he is prepared 'to sacrifice' himself because 'otherwise the revolution will be sacrificed'. However, in order to legitimate his proposals in terms of *feqh* he draws attention to the fact that many of its prohibitions are the result of misinterpretations of Islam. Since in his view many of the ordinances are based on conjecture (*zanniyat*), he urges jurists not to insist on them so adamantly. They should not believe that in such cases it is a question of divine ordinances and must, like Imam Khomeini, show courage and distinguish undisputed ordinances from those based on conjecture.[15]

Declaring that many ordinances are based on conjecture is one approach to expanding the possibilities of revision. Another is to point out that *fatvas* have been influenced by the conditions of life affecting the jurists. According to Mehdi Nasiri, the editor-in-chief of *Kayhan*, 'the *fatvas* of an Arab display the characteristics of an Arab and the *fatvas* of a non-Arab those of a non-Arab.'[16] The Imam of the Shafe'i school of jurisprudence, Mohammad Shafe'i, changed 90 of his *fatvas* and legal views when he travelled from Baghdad to Egypt, which Jannati takes as proof of how local conditions have an effect on *fatvas*.[17]

The latest proposal for reforming *feqh* and the religious academies involves the use of computers to collect and arrange the ordinances and traditions. This proposal seems to have encountered fewer objections based on Islamic law.[18]

## Dynamic Versus Traditional Jurisprudence

For some time now in discussions of the reform of *feqh* the concept of 'dynamic *feqh*' (*feqh-e puya*) has been used as a counterpoint to the concept of 'traditional *feqh*' (*feqh-e sonnati*). Although they have rarely presented themselves as a uniform movement in the debate, the advocates and supporters of *feqh-e puya* have been the targets of violent attacks by the dominant authorities in the academies. It is also clear from the violent polemic against them that they are primarily from amongst the ranks of the lay Islamicists. Not wishing to abandon the ground of *feqh* altogether, they advocate a more radical reform of Shi'i jurisprudence than has hitherto been proposed, and have consequently showed little respect for the representatives of traditional *feqh* and its content, methods and principles. They have been characterised by their opponents as laymen who attribute whatever view they wish to *feqh* and Islam without knowing anything about the subject and are prepared to translate and interpret the Koran according to their own ideas thus distorting its meaning.[19] In the view of *Resalat*, this is a group of eclectic intellectuals who express opinions on questions of *feqh* and Islam without any scholarly justification whatsoever. They are influenced by Westernised intellectuals and in part by pro-East bloc thinkers, are against the clergy, and denied the latter's legitimacy. Unfortunately, their number is not small.[20] According to Azari Qomi, the advocates of *feqh-e puya* have attempted to lead *feqh* in the direction 'of ordinances that are fashionable and correspond to the progress made in the natural sciences' without the times justifying such a step. In contrast to Khomeini, who only wished to revise a few ordinances to take account of changes in time and place, this group intend to a comprehensive change.[21]

The advocates of dynamic *feqh* always represented the most radical positions within the regime with respect to all socially and politically relevant decisions on the level of legislation. This is why the attempts of the conservative legalists to expel their opponents from positions of power and leadership have been, in the first instance, directed against them. Fearing this pressure many have given in. Others have proved obstinate and brought reprisals upon themselves. When Khomeini came out in support of the advocates of traditional *feqh* (which according to *Ettela'at*[22] was as early as the year 1981), the fear of the 'dynamists' was increased. In 1989, in his testament, which was specifically addressed to the clergy, Khomeini urged them 'on the position of traditional *feqh* which is the expression of prophethood and the imamate, as well as a guarantee of the development and greatness of the community, not to yield one millimetre and not to give in to the temptation of the devil and the enemies of truth and religion.'[23]

A tactic which used in the fight against the advocates of dynamic *feqh* and which has proved to be very effective consists of maintaining that traditional *feqh* was itself so dynamic that there is no need of any additional dynamism. The supposed proof of this is the development traditional *feqh* has undergone in previous centuries. This capacity for development gives traditional *feqh* sufficient power to prove its worth in the present and in the future. If the capacity for development of traditional *feqh* is acknowledged, it is necessary to take account of the methods of *ejtehad* it employed. *Feqh* would only suffer stagnation if the inferences (*estenbat*) which had been arrived at within its framework were declared sacred and its proper methods ignored. Consequently, traditional *feqh*, understood as a method, is in itself sufficiently dynamic to cater for the needs of the time.

In this connection, Ayatollah Yusef Sane'i said in a discussion organised by the periodical *Kayhan-e Andisheh*, 'Criticism of the Methods of *Feqh* and Education in the Academies': '*Feqh* and dynamism are two truths joined with one another. The uniform and eternal truth which they have formed is called [traditional] *feqh*.' He went on to say that the dynamism of *feqh* was embodied in its movement that proceeded with adherence to its own special principles, rules and guidelines. An alternative dynamic, *feqh* would only exist if one practised *ejtehad* independently of these principles. But this would no be *feqh* at all; it would be a new artificial phenomenon which had nothing to do with Islam or *feqh*. Ayatollah 'Ali 'Abedi agreed with him arguing that to be traditional and dynamic were two characteristics of *feqh* and *ejtehad*. In reality it was traditional *feqh* that was dynamic. *Ejtehad* that was dynamic, but was not traditional and based on the rules and foundations of the *shari'a*, could not be called *ejtehad* from the standpoint of the *shari'a*. However, Ayatollah Jannati distinguished between a negative and a positive dynamism. Negative dynamism was represented by the formulation and adoption of *ahkam* on the basis of *ra'y* (personal judgement), *maslahat*, *qiyas* (drawing conclusions by analogy) and *estehsab* (personal opinion supported by preference), whereas by contrast positive dynamism prevailed in traditional *feqh*.[24]

The massive and many-sided pressure exerted on the advocates of dynamic *feqh* on the one hand, and the attempt to take the wind out of their sails by pointing to the dynamic content of traditional *feqh* on the other, has proved very successful. This obstruction of the development of *feqh-e puya* has strengthened the stagnant powers of the allegedly dynamic traditional *feqh* and has in part been responsible for the fact that so far the reform of *feqh* and the academies has not occurred.

## The Absence of Reform

Alongside the growing awareness of the deficiencies of *feqh* and the academies there have been signs, particularly in recent years, of doubts about the effectiveness of any potential reform. But before looking at representative attitudes on this issue, we should note that the current awareness of the need for reform has its roots in pre-revolutionary times. Already in the 1960s and 1970s, reformers such as Motahhari, Tabataba'i, Shari'ati and Taleqani had spoken about the deficiencies of *feqh* and the academies and called for reform. As early as 1962, a discussion of this subject took place which dealt with many of the problems and reform measures, and aroused interest in many quarters.[25] Along with others, Motahhari, who was recognised as an authority, especially by the legalistic Islamicists, continued the discussion in subsequent years, notably in his lectures entitled 'Islam and the Needs of the Times' (1983).

The extent to which Motahhari was a pioneer of the debate that began amongst the legalists after the revolution is revealed by the numerous references they make to his work to confirm their position. Furthermore, so far as content is concerned, the post-revolutionary debate in legalist circles has not gone beyond Motahhari's contribution. The difference between the pre and post-revolutionary debate lies chiefly in its breadth, for it has now come to involve the academies almost completely. Moreover, the simple fact that Motahhari's demands had to be reiterated once again after the revolution is an indication that they had not previously had any significant impact.

In words filled with emotion, *Howzeh* repeatedly regrets that reform has not been implemented. In 1987, the periodical stated that the awareness of many reformers in the academies had until now 'not had the desired effect'.[26] In 1988, in a lead article, *Howzeh* criticised the fact that Imam Khomeini's repeated appeals for the academies to practice a new *ejtehad* for new questions 'had found no positive echo'. The academies had persisted in their traditional methods without paying heed to the demands of the times.[27] Although in 1989 *Howzeh* welcomed the 'foundation stones' of reform,[28] four issues later 'the hopes that never bloomed and the blossoms that had fallen prey to the plundering of autumn' were mourned.[29] By 1991 we read that the only notable innovations were of an informal nature, were based on individual initiative and had to be described as inadequate.[30] One year later, the writers in the periodical were on the verge of rejoicing at the arrival of the season of blossoming ideals because the leader Khamene'i, in an interview with them, had stressed the need for reform, but in the next sentence it stated: 'There is serious fear because in practice efforts have not brought any real results.' *Howzeh* lamented the prevalence of factional thinking in the academies and emphasised that as long as there was no change in this respect reform would not be possible.[31] Almost two years later, i.e. towards the end of 1993, we read that although 'some efforts of a theoretical and practical nature' have been undertaken on the path to reform, none the less these represent no more than 'a first step'. 'The goal lies miles away in the distance.'[32]

The opinions expressed by the writers of *Howzeh* were shared by other insiders. In 1989, Ayatollah Jannati stated in the round of discussions organised by the periodical *Kayhan-e Andisheh* that although the means for the progress and development of *feqh* were available, as far as content was concerned 'none of the required work has been carried out'.[33] In the summer of 1992, Hojjat al-Eslam Mohsen Kadivar wrote in the same periodical[34] that the measures undertaken over the previous twelve years to reform the Academy of Qom 'counted for nothing when compared with the tasks that faced the academies'. Ayatollah Khatami has repeatedly stated the view that since the revolution no work has been done comparable to that achieved by Motahhari. On the contrary, many people have opposed his ideas for reform.[35] Even conservative legalists such as Ayatollah Azari Qomi are dissatisfied. In 1992, Azari Qomi stated that 'the academies have not fulfilled their mission …' and compared their work with the time-honoured practice of discussing whether or not the urine of bats is ritually impure.[36] In 1995, asked whether the academies deal with problems that are of importance to society he replied: 'No. Sadly change, whether political, economic or social, has had no impact on *feqh*.'[37] In 1994, Ayatollah Mohammad Sadeq Ha'eri Shirazi regretted that the academies still felt they were competent to solve the question of what the *shari'a* commanded and what it forbade. They did not occupy themselves with the human sciences regardless of the fact that the Koran was the source for all human sciences; 'religion' and 'the human sciences' were in reality one and the same, and the real mission of the academies was to derive these sciences from the Koran and to disseminate them to the universities so that the latter would not be influenced any longer by Western human sciences, i.e. by Western religions.[38]

The practical measures that have been taken so far add up to very little. From time to time the academy in Qom organises seminars in which the need for reform, especially of the academies, is discussed and in which relevant resolutions are passed. Occasionally, as in October 1991, the students take the initiative and put together a collection of signatures to present to the leader with a petition in which they express the wish that, for example, a panel be created for revising the curricula of the seminaries.[39]

The formation of an administrative council for the Academy of Qom is the most important measure adopted since the revolution. But this also appears to be a difficult undertaking, for its purpose and chances of success are doubted even by that section of the clergy loyal to the regime. The first steps to set up the council were taken in 1981, but it was abolished almost immediately because of serious rivalries and opposition within the academy. Towards the end of October 1992 it was reconstituted as a result of a compromise effected amongst the supporters of several groups within the academy loyal to the regime. The alleged task of the council, now as previously, is to implement reforms in the academy's system of education and administration. However, its first real priority is to facilitate supervision over the academy by members of the clergy loyal to the regime which, as Hojjat al-Eslam 'Abbas Mokhlesi has stated, is not only of little help in the implementation of reform but actually stands in its way.[40]

How far the work of this council has progressed since its foundation can be ascertained from an interview with Ayatollah Mo'men, its chairman, published in *Resalat* on 24 and 25/4/94. On the reform of textbooks, or more correctly, the lack of any such reform, Mo'men stated: 'The textbooks presently in use in the academy are those which have been used in teaching for years, perhaps for centuries ... In connection with literature and logic, it is perhaps necessary that the texts be changed.' On the question of specialisation, he reported that matters have remained at the level of planning although teaching in psychology, sociology, economics, philosophy, religions, Arabic literature and especially jurisprudence 'will soon begin'. To ward off the cultural invasion, he felt that a department of research should be created. On the question of government and the tasks it poses for *feqh*, he stated with an eye to the future that: 'We must see to it that in the academy *feqh* concentrates on questions which have arisen through the creation of the Islamic state.' But only now is the academy occupying itself in detail with the question of *velayat-e faqih*.[41]

# Notes

1 *Howzeh*, No. 14 (1986/87), p. 31.

2 *Howzeh*, No. 26 (1988d), p. 41.

3 *Howzeh*, No. 28 (1988a), p. 7.

4 See Bonyad-e Farhangi-ye Baqer al-'Olum: 1992; Hadavi Tehrani: 1992; Kadivar: 1992; *Howzeh*: 1986/87a; the resolution of the students and teachers of the Academy of Mashhad in *Kayhan*, 23/2 to 18/3/92.

5 *Ettela'at*, 21/2/92.

6 Jannati: 1990, p. 25.

7 He drew his colleagues' attention to the fact that all too frequent cancellation of primary ordinances by means of secondary ordinances would lead to the conclusion that 'the primary ordinances of Islam are not adequate for governing society' (*Kayhan*, 5/2/92). Ahmad Khomeini made these remarks while attempting to explain his father's reforms of *feqh*.

8 In an interview he gave in *Howzeh*, No. 20 (1987), p. 31.

9 *Howzeh*, No. 28 (1988a), p. 12.

10 *Salam*, 16/11/92. See also Makarem Shirazi in *Ettela'at*, 18/3 and 13/6/92.

11 See his interview in *Howzeh*, No. 19 (1987), p. 37. Cf. also *Howzeh*, No. 20 (1987a), p. 141 and No. 35 (1989a), p. 20.

12 *Howzeh*, No. 35 (1989a), p. 21.

13 Motahhari: 1983, p. 106 f.

14 Ibid., pp. 44 f. and 50. He stated he did not know the possible reasons the divine legislator had for forbidding pork.

15 Hojjati Kermani: 1992. However, he remarked that the Imam had not shown courage in his *'fatvas* dealing purely with *feqh'*. Hojjati displayed such courage himself perhaps partly because his colleagues did not take him entirely seriously and allowed him certain liberties.

16 *Kayhan*, 24/10/89.

17 Jannati: 1990, p. 22.

18 For Azari Qomi's views on the use of computers in religious academies see his interview in *Kayhan*, 29/2/92.

19 *Ettela'at*, 28/1/87.

20 *Resalat*, 26/10/89.

21 *Resalat*, 18/9/89.

22 27/1/87

23 Supplement to *Resalat*, 6/6/89. On another occasion, he declared that he believed in the traditional *feqh* of the Javaheri school of *ejtehad* and would not permit any deviation from it (*Resalat*, 25/2/89). Mohammad Hasan Javaheri lived in the 19th century and was the author of a multi-volume collection of legal questions entitled *Jawahir al-Kalam* which is still used for teaching in the academies today.

24 *Kayhan-e Andisheh*, No. 22 (1989), pp. 6–32. On this subject see also *Howzeh*, 1989; Azari Qomi in *Resalat*, 20/12/86, 11/1/87, 6/2/87 and 19/3/87; ibid.: a series of articles published on 19/9 to 4/11/87 and 18/5 to 30/5/89; Jannati: 1986.

25 Participants in the discussion included the *ayatollah*s M. H. Tabataba'i, M. Taleqani, 'A. Zanjani, Morteza Jazayeri, M. Motahhari, M. Beheshti and the layman Mehdi Bazargan. The minutes of the talks were published at the beginning of 1963 in Tehran and were chosen for the book of the year award. A. K. S. Lambton reported on this event in an article (1964).

26 *Howzeh*, No. 20 (1987a), p. 50.

27 *Howzeh*, No. 28 (1988a), p. 16.

28 Apparently, this was a reference to the setting up of a council for running the academy of the city of Qom, which was a compromise reached at that time by the supporters of Khomeini and the followers of Ayatollah Golpayegani after years of efforts (*Howzeh*, No. 31, 1989b, p. 59).

29  *Howzeh*, 1989a, p. 3.

30  *Howzeh*, No. 42 (1991), p. 21.

31  *Howzeh*, 1992, p. 31 f.

32  *Howzeh,* No. 58, 1993, p. 3.

33  *Kayhan-e Andisheh*, No. 22, 1989.

34  *Kayhan-e Andisheh,* No. 42, p. 6.

35  *Kayhan*, 1/5/91.

36  *Resalat*, 17/11/92.

37  *Salam*, 25/10/95 and 16/11/95.

38  Cf. his interview in *Resalat*, 4/5/94.

39  See *Kayhan*, 12/10/91.

40  *Ettela'at*, 6/2/92.

41  On the development of the administrative council see Bonyad-e Farhangi-ye Baqer al-'Olum: 1992. On 4–6 February 1996 a Conference to Examine Imam Khomeini's Principles of *feqh'* was convened in Qom. Hojjat al-Eslam Mohammad Mehdi Faqih, the organiser, announced that 'The purpose of this conference is to consider the problems of time and place and discover the ways in which *feqh* is capable of responding to the problems of humankind ... the reform we have all been waiting for.' *Resalat*, 7/2/96.

# SIXTEEN

# Criticism from Outside

There is also a category of criticism which comes from Islamic reformers who, depending on tactical or other considerations, distance themselves more or less openly from the concept of *velayat-e faqih*. When the author of the lead article in a 1992 issue of the journal *Ayeneh-e Andisheh*[1] 'having first taken a survey of the consequences of guiding the revolution on the basis of *feqh*', concludes that this guidance is sick and suffering from historically conditioned weaknesses, and when he demands that it be replaced by people who are 'responsible and motivated by patriotic-liberal (*melli*) ideals and who base their thought on science', he is, in the given circumstances, clearly expressing the views of those who were once Islamicists, or may still be Islamicists, but who no longer want to have anything to do with the concept of *velayat-e faqih*.

Advocates of this third line of Islamic reform can be found, as groups or individuals, in various positions along the spectrum of Islamic-minded intellectuals among the laity and even the clergy. In the political arena the Liberation Movement, whose critical attitude to *velayat-e faqih* was described at some length in Part I, can be counted among this group. That its members have maintained their position, despite the pressure on them to conform in recent years, is confirmed by a book published in 1988 which is critical of the conception of the Islamic state contained in the notion of the absolute *velayat-e faqih*. The book argues that 'after the end of era of the Prophet the acts of divine communication, there are no grounds for the dominion of one group of people over another on the pretext of being God's representatives,' and that absolute *velayat-e faqih* is nothing but 'autocracy and religious despotism' which will destroy 'freedom, personality and independence'.[2]

Again in response to the declaration of the absolute *velayat-e faqih* the leader of Ommat, Habibollah Peiman, published a pamphlet in which he argued that '*feqh* with its current methods and principles cannot be reconciled with the needs of today's society.' In his view, 'the superficial changes in *feqh* and the more open attitude to it over the last few years have not created the necessary dynamism and cannot produce a congruence with the demands made on it.' The source of these problems, according to Peiman, lies in the fundamental world view of *feqh*. The theory of *velayat-e faqih* may indeed contribute to eliminating the long-standing obstacles *feqh* has placed in the way of legislation, the state and the solution of social problems, but it could also very easily become the theoretical foundation of a centralised, exploitative and capitalistic state 'in which the mass of people no longer have the legal possibility of resistance, or of expressing disagreement and protest.' Peiman hoped that 'the right to legislation, to establishing the interests of society and to choosing the trustees who regulate public affairs be concentrated completely in the hands of the people.' To this end, it would be necessary to declare the whole of existing *feqh* with its foundations, ordinances and principles invalid.[3]

Radical criticism outside the circle of the ruling clergy is carried on by a large number of other Islamic intellectuals, amongst whom two draw the greatest amount of attention: Mohammad Mojtahed Shabestari, a theologian who is a member of the clergy, and the layman ʿAbdolkarim Sorush who is a professor of philosophy. The ideas of both men are available in numerous publications. Since they represent the position of the third group of reformers most clearly, a brief description of the key points of their ideas, in so far as they affect the debate we are examining, is in order.

## Mohammad Mojtahed Shabestari

Shabestari, whose articles usually appeared in the periodical *Kayhan-e Farhangi*, argues that although religion and the state have been merged in the Islamic Republic, legislation is totally devoid of any theoretical foundation. Resolutions passed on the basis of the rules of *zarurat* and *maslahat* are merely reactive. The religious academies are not in a position to conduct a serious discussion about, for example, what they understand by the concepts 'ownership', 'employment' and 'exploitation'. Not only have they paid no attention to these problems; they do not even allow discussion of them.[4] Moreover, the issues which have arisen in the Islamic Republic are not of a juristic kind and can only be resolved if they are discussed in the context of anthropology, theology and sociology. What must be aimed for is that 'in our religious culture' new views 'on the social transformation of people' be expressed and accepted.[5]

This goal cannot be achieved unless account is taken of modern philosophy and the modern sciences, and the information which they have made available. Such information serves the purpose of acquiring knowledge of the laws that govern social processes. Knowledge of this kind is necessary if we are to set ourselves the task of drawing up plans for regulating the social life of human beings.[6]

From this standpoint Shabestari criticises the particular understanding of Islam current in the religious academies which displays no connection with the modern sciences, especially not with the human sciences. Since the Koran and the message proclaimed by the Prophet can only be properly understood today with reference to the sciences, it is necessary to question the interpretations laid down by the academies. As products of a human understanding of religion that is ignorant of the modern sciences, *fatvas* issued on this basis are devoid of any claim to sacredness. No *fatva* imposes a religiously binding duty on people. As a collection of *fatvas*, *feqh* represents the product of the theoretical work carried out by jurists and therefore, like every other intellectual discipline, must be seen as a human endeavour. To describe the products of such endeavour, with all its limits of time and place and its fallibility, as ordinances of the *shari'a* and to take them to be unchanging, would be not only to attribute something to religion that is alien to its nature but also to help stagnation prevail over Islamic societies.[7]

Another critical feature in Shabestari's thought which runs counter to the official interpretation of Islam is his historically oriented view of the commands and prohibitions contained in the Koran and the *sunna*. These are contingent phenomena which correspond to the political and social conditions of the time in which they were proclaimed. They cannot therefore be understood as absolute and timeless. Only the 'fundamental values' (*osul-e arzeshi*) laid down by God and the Prophet possess that character, and they must be applied in concrete terms by Muslims in every day and age in accordance with the prevailing conditions of life. To maintain that the statements of the Prophet have a binding character for all people until the Day of Judgement, is to proceed on the basis of theological, philosophical and aesthetic considerations which are not necessarily correct.[8]

Shabestari has also contested the interpretation that the jurists give to the proposition that Islam is perfect, thus simultaneously contesting the legitimating foundations of *velayat-e faqih*. The perfection of religion does not mean that it has an answer to every question. It means simply that God has expressed what He wished to communicate to man in perfect form. The notion that statements are to be found in the Koran and the *sunna* concerning everything that occurs in politics and economics, will only lead people into error. 'Religion does not wish to replace science and technology, and lay claim to the place of reason ... God has only offered answers for some of the needs of human beings. As for other needs, He has left it to reason and human effort to supply the answer.' Furthermore, it would be false to want to measure the perfection of religion in terms of human needs. That would be an attempt to define the content of religion by means of man, more specifically by means of man's needs.[9]

Shabestari also questions the assertion that God has a legislative function. God only establishes values, not laws. 'Eternal divine mercy only requires the determination of the direction of human resolutions and measures, and not the determination of laws ... The primary reason for sending the prophets was to proclaim truths and lay down eternal values, not to make laws.' This is confirmed by the fact that most Islamic laws were borrowed from moral practices and habits, as well as the customary law, current amongst the Arabs at the time of Mohammed. 'The sacred precinct which people are forbidden to enter concerns values and not the determination of individual cases affected by those values or their specific realisation in changing social circumstances.'[10]

Following close behind the negation of God's legislative function is the negation of this function in connection with the Islamic jurists. According to Shabestari the jurists have only two functions: establishing fundamental Islamic values in politics and economics, and determining whether or not in a given society laws, regulations and political decisions correspond to these values. Moreover, since such judgements are of a human character, they do not possess any binding force. The people are free to compare them with the opinion of experts on politics and economics and make their own choice.[11]

The logical conclusion that Shabestari draws from these considerations is that Islam has not provided any particular system of government for regulating man's political and social life. 'According to the teaching of the Koran, it is not consistent with the dignity of religion to define the forms and methods of governing the state.' Religion only determines the relevant values, which include justice. What is important in determining the form of the state from the standpoint of religion is the exclusion of contradictions to the values religion has postulated. It cannot be said of any government system that it automatically corresponds to certain standards. No one can claim to make Islam a reality or create an Islamic constitution. What is correct is to work for a constitution that does not disagree with Islam. 'If the people, on the basis of their own experience and knowledge, come to the conclusion that a form of government based on elections and a system of councils will better guarantee justice, then religious duty clearly lies in the creation of a system based on these principles.'[12] Shabestari goes so far as to declare that the values anchored in the Koran and the *sunna* have no predetermined definitions. Rather, they represent universal and abstract formulations which in every new case must be checked and interpreted with regard to the concrete capabilities, needs, realities and possibilities of the people involved.[13]

Similarly, Shabestari denies the assertion made by the proponents of *velayat-e faqih* that political actions, including the founding of a state, are a religious duty or a form of worship. Instead, such actions are for every person a right or a practical measure (*tadbir*). People who cite Koranic verses and the *sunna* to assert that founding a state is a religious commandment both confuse different concepts in these sources, and interpret their meaning erroneously.

> The identity of religion and politics does not mean that a political action is [necessarily] one in conformity with the *shariʿa* undertaken for the purpose of achieving a closer relationship with God. Rather, such is the case when an action aims at creating and leading a good life which, if the action then pursues the above mentioned purpose, will lead to attaining satisfaction and God's love.[14]

Shabestari questions the validity of another of the claims of the jurists, namely to a monopoly over the process of forming opinions in matters of religion and law. Anyone who has acquired the appropriate knowledge can practice *ejtehad*. No one can make a monopoly of the right to express opinions on whether a government system, a law or a government policy is or is not congruent with the fundamental values of religion. *Ejtehad* is not susceptible to a monopoly because the knowledge acquired through it is human knowledge. No one has the right to impose his understanding of the law on others or to forbid others from discussing alternative interpretations of the law. Since all opinions possess the same worth, space in Muslim society for thought and discussion of fundamental values, government systems, laws and politics must be kept open for everyone. Such space will offer the possibility of observing and controlling how the jurists deal with the law.[15] Since the fundamental political values recognised by Islam do not represent 'truths based on the *shari'a*', the interpretation of these values and the decision about whether a particular political system is in agreement with them is a matter for all people. The matter depends on the level of political development of the people, and on the technological and political information available to them. 'Although the religious scholars can and must lead this general cultural and intellectual process, the acceptance of such a form of leadership cannot be equated with imitation.'[16]

The last of Shabestari's ideas we should take note of here concerns the distortion which, in his view, the religious institutions create in humankind's relationship with God. They are responsible, on the one hand, for the reification of God and, on the other, for restricting human freedom and self-reliance. However, since these institutions cannot be removed from the world, they must constantly be subjected to a process of purification.[17] Shabestari considers denying the jurists' claim to a monopoly over judging religious questions as a useful way of accomplishing this.[18]

## 'Abdolkarim Sorush

The ideas of Sorush come from even further outside the established frameworks of religious thought. A layman who works within the university system, Sorush has made the 'lords' in the academies the target of his free-ranging irreverent remarks. In recent years he has drawn attention to himself particularly through a critique he published in *Kayhan-e Farhangi* under the title 'Theoretical Contraction and Expansion of the *Shari'a*' or 'A Theory of the Development of Religious Knowledge', which later appeared in expanded form as a book with the first of these titles. In this book he argues that, firstly, on the basis of epistemological considerations, religious knowledge is dependent on the development of knowledge in general. Consequently, religious knowledge must be described as changeable and as endowed with a worldly and human character. Being utterly devoid of sacredness, it is obliged to adapt itself to the development of the sciences. Secondly, he poses fundamental questions about the validity and the use of *feqh*. Thirdly, from this relativisation of the knowledge cultivated in the academies, he derives certain political conclusions which lead to the demand that 'a religious-democratic state' replace the regime based on *velayat-e faqih*.

The intended audience for this epistemologically constructed criticism of the understanding of the Islam the *foqaha* have declared sacred is in part the jurists themselves, whom Sorush tries to win over to the view that their religious rulings are human, and in part the jurists' supporters, particularly amongst students and government functionaries. He appeals to the latter to give up their imitation of authority and encourages them to think independently and carry out their own research on religious questions. For whatever reasons, Sorush is concerned to emphasise that he is not out to reform religion, or to clarify how people conceive of religion, how this conception is transformed, and why the reform of religion is bound to remain incomplete as long as insight into these processes is lacking.[19]

The starting point for Sorush's critique of the conception of Islam put forward by the academies, in other words for the reform of Islam, is the assertion that such reform is chiefly a matter of establishing what is changeable and what is not changeable over time. By this method, which he has not always applied consistently, Sorush comes to the conclusion that religion itself is an unchanging entity, whereas the religious sciences are subject to constant transformation. Religion is characterised by its lack of contradiction, freedom from doubt, perfection, sacredness, unchangeablity, divinity, and so on, whereas the religious sciences are continually subject to change, contradictions, disunity and depend on the other sciences. Indeed, they have no access to revelation and are products of human effort.[20]

According to Sorush, the connection between the religious and the non-religious sciences is of the same nature as that between the non-religious sciences in general. They are all in a state of flux. When a transformation takes place in one part of the stormy sea of the human sciences, the wave it creates sets the whole sea in motion.[21] By this Sorush does not, as his critics maintain, wish to give the impression that truth is a relative matter. On the contrary, in his view this constant process of transformation moves in a forward and cumulative direction.

According to Sorush, the connection between the sciences appears in different forms. These include:

1. Connections based on common methods, so that methodological transformation in one discipline entails transformation in the others.
2. Connections between the productive disciplines like mathematics, philosophy and the fundamental medical disciplines on the one hand, and the consumer-oriented disciplines like medicine, law and Koranic exegesis on the other.
3. Connections based on dialogue between the sciences, so that they ask questions and receive answers from one another.[22]

Apart from these forms of connection between the various scientific disciplines, Sorush distinguishes four special forms of connection between the religious and the non-religious sciences which can be summarised as follows:

1. Non-religious sciences ask the religious sciences questions which have a present-day relevance, and demand answers which must correspond to the present and the state of today's non-religious sciences. Because of the increase and differentiation of such questions, the *shari'a* has the opportunity to manifest itself more effectively.

2. The transformation of the non-religious sciences necessitates the transformation of the religious sciences in harmony with the former. The correct understanding of the *shari'a* cannot deviate from a correct understanding of nature. In this case, the non-religious sciences become the judge over religious understanding and eliminate a false understanding of religion.

3. The non-religious sciences produce processes of transformation in the *shari'a*, while they provide new definitions of the concepts which have entered into the *shari'a* during its transformation. Man's conception of the sun in the eleventh century, by which God swears an oath, is quite different from that of people in our century.

4. The non-religious sciences influence the expectations which people have of religion, so that science's transformation entails the transformation of human expectations of religion.

In the development of the non-religious sciences, Sorush sees a source for the development of the religious sciences and therefore for their drawing closer to the truth. A better knowledge of the cosmos, in his view, leads to a better knowledge of God and the Prophet. The most important point, however, is that, as the religious sciences develop, precise knowledge of what is unchanging in religion increases.[23] Sorush energetically contests the notion that the development of the non-religious sciences could affect the kernel of religion or bring it into doubt.

On the basis of his epistemological approach, Sorush, as already mentioned, draws two concrete conclusions which have a direct bearing on the conception of Islam represented by the religious academies. Firstly, this conception is not consistent with the requirements imposed on religion by the modern sciences, and secondly the religious authorities are not in a position to meet these requirements because they have inadequate knowledge of the modern sciences. 'The religious knowledge of our clergy is basically restricted to *feqh* ... Their knowledge of other subjects is quantitatively and qualitatively small. Therefore, it is no wonder that they equate Islam with *feqh* or characterise *feqh* as the most important of the Islamic sciences.'[24]

For Sorush no error is as serious as reducing Islam to *feqh*. This is not simply the result of the clergy's narrow-mindedness but also comes from their wish to be 'a source of imitation' and to exercise undisputed rule over others. 'What the *foqaha*'s form of Islam today suggests is that the substance of religion can be reduced to imitation and *feqh*. There is no place for a dialogue between the imitator and the imitated, but only for *fatvas*, on the one hand, and imitation, on the other.'[25] In an essay which he wrote in honour of Abu Hamed Ghazali and Molla Mohsen Feiz Kashani (two prominent theologians from the eleventh and seventeenth centuries respect-ively),[26] Sorush articulates his opinion of the jurists by quoting their words:

> Jurists who reduce research in religion to knowledge of *feqh* ... especially that group of jurists who only concern themselves with the offences (*khelafiyat*) dealt with in *feqh* and pay no attention to anything but disputes, suppressing their opponents and boasting victory over their enemies ... and take pleasure in exposing the misdeeds and the weaknesses of their fellow-men, were fiercely derided and scolded by Ghazali and Feiz Kashani and deemed to be afflicted with arrogance and intellectual opacity. Ghazali referred to the second group in particular as 'beasts of prey amongst men' because their effort was directed to strife and their nature tended towards tormenting other persons.

In another passage, Sorush quotes Ghazali where the latter speaks of jurists as people who have ceased to struggle against their own shortcomings and instead are ever urging others to do so. It is the same with:

> ... that wretched student of *feqh* who has fallen prey to love of the world, passion, hypocrisy, envy, arrogance and other deadly character traits and who will probably leave this world before repenting and thus come face to face with the wrath of God. None the less, he has dropped everything else and turned to studying the ordinances which deal with advance sales, leases, ritual purification, criminal punishments, blood-money, lodging complaints, witnesses and the book on menstruation.[27]

In a lecture at the University of Isfahan, Sorush attacked the jurists directly and accused them of vulgarity, hypocrisy and hunger for power. He reminded his audience that in the classical critical literature of Iran the hunger for power of the jurists and their craving for pleasure have always been the object of reproach. And he entreated his listeners to reflect on the negative effects of the religious academies' access to political power: 'One of the consequences has been that they now speak the language of power and have abandoned the language of logic.'[28]

For Sorush the reduction of religion to no more than *feqh* is also an offence because under the Islamic Republic the jurists have used it as a weapon to suppress the diversity of religious thought that prevailed before the revolution. 'Before the revolution one could find no trace of emphasis on the legal aspects of Islam in the writings, in the ideas or in the lectures of our thinkers.' The concepts 'Islam based on *feqh*' or 'Islam of the *resaleh*' were unknown. Formerly the anthropological and cosmological aspects of Islam, along with certain mystical ideas, were dominant. Islam 'based on research' had the upper hand, whereas today the Islam of imitation prevails.[29]

Sorush also denies the sacredness which the jurists are pleased to attribute to their discipline and its products. This he denies from his epistemological viewpoint and often in a biting language. He demands that the academies declare that their syllabus has been created by human beings and is therefore wholly devoid of any sacredness.[30] The law they teach is not only devoid of sacredness but also lacks the capacity to guide society. Creating order and stability, solving or helping solve problems, eliminating difficulties – these are capacities *feqh* possesses in the context of simple and undifferentiated societies that have few needs. In societies in which 'the conception of another pattern of life, another strand of social interaction and new needs' was not even possible, in which 'the regular patterns affecting social life, the market, the family, professions and the state had not yet been discovered, one might assume that problems could be solved by means of the ordinances of *feqh* and the skill of the jurists.' But today can anyone deny 'that *feqh* is not in a position to clear away the dust that is raised by industry, trade and obscure international political relations?' Can anyone maintain that all the problems in the world are of a legal nature? Consequently, one cannot expect them to be resolved by *feqh*. Today's world has need of experts, scientists, managers and organisers of leisure to solve its problems, not jurists.

Nevertheless, Sorush does concede certain tasks to *feqh* and the jurists, but these he formulates in rather vague terms. The task of *feqh* today consists in ascertaining values, 'defining the boundaries in the field of human endeavour beyond which humankind must not step. Everything else is a matter for science.' For example, when traffic regulations are drawn up, *feqh* has the right to declare that they should not violate the legitimate right to ownership, but it is not its task to draft the actual regulations.[31]

Sorush does not attach any importance to the ideas produced in the academies for solving the current problems of religion. *Ejtehad* is also ineffective in this respect, the contemporary stagnation of *feqh* being a clear proof of this. Along with Shabestari, he believes that the problems lie much deeper, in the views of man and the world held by the religious authorities, and that they cannot be solved until those views are renovated through adaptation to the modern sciences.[32]

Sorush's criticism of the jurists also contains a clear appeal to his public to recognise their own potential as experts in the modern sciences, to value their own capacity and right to be leaders of the state and not to allow their relation with the jurists to be determined by imitation.

> Your task is firstly to inform the *'ulama* about the serious problems of the day, and secondly to engage in a critical dialogue with them ... Have no doubts about it! As long as you are simply imitators, you will not be able to move the *'ulama* to educate themselves about matters outside the realm of *feqh*.[33]

Sorush's criticism of *feqh* and the jurists indicates the position he holds on the political ambitions they cherish. Indeed he has recently advocated a form of government he calls 'religious democracy'. However, his inclination to political liberalism was visible earlier in his sympathy for the liberal philosopher Karl Popper. In one of his articles inspired by *sapire aude* (dare to know), according to Kant the most important motto of the Enlightenment, Sorush devotes his attention to 'studying the liberal school from its beginning to the present day' in such a way that makes clear his admiration of this school. At the same time he maintains that 'no believer can be a liberal' because there are values which a believer cannot doubt and which cannot be the object of investigation. Nevertheless, 'liberalisation of the economy and the state in the sense of renouncing the absolute concentration of power and information, and understood as abandoning totalitarian *étatisme*, is a matter which can also be talked about and discussed in a religious society.' This has nothing to do with philosophical liberalism but is based on scientific considerations which are in harmony with the fundamental principles of the *shariʿa*.[34]

In 1992, Sorush read a paper entitled 'A Religious Democratic State?' in a seminar on the theme 'Human Rights Between Universality and Cultural Determinism' organised by the German Oriental Institute of Hamburg.[35] He bases his answer to the question of whether a religious democratic state can exist on his epistemological approach to the religious sciences. Since all forms of the democratic state are based on reason (*ʿaql*):

> the religious democratic state means rendering flexible the conception of religion by emphasising the role of reason in that conception; however, [we do not mean] individual reason but social reason, which is the product of the participation of everyone and the result of the experience of humanity.

According to Sorush, the application of reason to the conception of religion is justified because the latter, in contrast to religion itself, is itself the product of reason, in particular of social reason.

> Democratic states are those which allow social reason to judge controversies, and they see the solution to problems in it. Religious states reserve this judgement for religion, and dictatorial states reserve it for individual violence. But as we know, it is never religion itself that judges but a particular conception of religion, and this conception is a matter of reason.

Building on this consideration, Sorush comes to the conclusion that the democratisation of a religious state is possible. To achieve this it is not necessary to abandon religious faith. Democratic religious states, by way of being religious, make religion their leader and their judge when resolving their conflicts and problems. So that they can be democratic, they make their conception of religion based on *ejtehad* more flexible to bring it into harmony with reason. 'In this manner, liberalism is denied but democracy, based on social reason, is connected to a rational and learned faith. Thus, one of the preconditions for a religious democratic state is created.' Sorush's religious democratic state presupposes the existence of a corresponding religious society. In such a society any form of non-religious government would be undemocratic. How such a state and the society which provides that state's foundation are to come about Sorush does not say. What is perfectly clear is that in addressing the question he originally posed, he gives two negative replies. Firstly, he denies the validity of those ideas that dispute the agreement between democracy and a state based on religion, and secondly he says no to the non-democratic religious state with which he presently finds himself confronted.

In this paper Sorush also goes into the question of the religious state's relation to human rights, in particular to freedom. He comes to the conclusion that the religious state and freedom are mutually dependent. Indeed, the legitimacy of the one stems from the respect it gives to the other. 'If humanity is a precondition for the justification of a religion, it is also a precondition for the legitimacy of the religious state. Therefore, consideration for human rights (such as justice and freedom) not only guarantees the democratic nature of a state but guarantees its religious nature as well.

Sorush expresses his deep respect for freedom in another lecture entitled 'Reason and Freedom' delivered in the spring of 1992 at Beheshti University (formerly the National University) in Tehran.[36] Here he maintains that reason and freedom are dependent on one another because reason without freedom can no longer be reason. This is the same relationship as exists between humanity and freedom. 'Just as humanity is not possible without freedom, reason cannot exist without freedom.' He enumerates the various forms of mutual interdependence of reason and freedom, and formulates them in sentences such as: 'Freedom is the precondition for the liberation of reason from ideology', 'Reason is by its nature a free zone ... if lack of freedom and constraint enter this zone, it loses its quality of reason'; 'Just as reason is nourished by reason, so freedom is nourished by freedom'; 'Discovering the errors made by reason is only possible through reason, and the elimination of the mistakes of freedom is only possible through freedom'; 'Freedom is the greatest right'.

Sorush's attempt to be an intermediary between religion and democracy also finds expression in his criticism of Shari'ati's conception of Islam. He accuses Shari'ati of ideologising Islam, which he takes to be a big mistake. Thus in a three-part lecture delivered in a mosque, he enumerated the negative epistemological, social and political characteristics and consequences peculiar to ideologies, and then, in a second step, related these to the ideologisation of Islam as Shari'ati had practised it.[37] In this case, Shari'ati obviously functions as a representative of others who have justified their claim to rule by ideologising Islam and have exercised rule while making use of all the privileges they have acquired in this manner.

### The Reaction to Shabestari and Sorush

Shabestari and Sorush are treated differently by their opponents in legalist, Islamicist circles. Whereas the former seldom evokes audible reactions, the latter has been the target of attacks which are aimed at the positions represented by both men. The reason for this lies, first of all, in the rather provocative manner in which Sorush behaves, and in the way he promotes his views and treats his opponents and secondly, in all probability, to the fact that he is not a cleric. A large number of attacks on Sorush have been published in the Iranian press – sometimes several times during one week in the different newspapers and magazines that officially or semi-officially support *velayat-e faqih*. If he happens to give a talk somewhere, it is certain that a flood of responses will inundate the reading public.[38] Amongst his opponents there are such authorities as Ayatollah Makarem Shirazi, the chairman of the Administrative Council of the Academy of Qom. The reproaches levelled against Sorush chiefly refer to the damage his speeches and writings cause to the authority and dignity of the clergy. He is accused of 'speaking the same language as the enemy', 'being in step with the widespread conspiracies hatched by the enemies of the clergy' and 'consciously or unconsciously' devoting most of his efforts 'to weakening the clergy'.[39] Ayatollah Makarem Shirazi considers his speech at the University of Isfahan as 'a conspiracy' and 'a large and powerful injection of poison against the academies', the Islamic sciences and 'in a certain sense against Islam itself'.[40] Occasionally, the polemic against Sorush displays a higher quality. Clerics like Sadeq Larijani, Hosein Qaʾem-maqami and Jaʿfar Sobhani enter into what may be called a scientific dispute with him and in this way maintain the discourse on the reform of the conception of Islam.[41]

Through their attempt to free the Islamic state from the burden of the Islamic jurists and the Islamic law they champion, Shabestari, Sorush and other like-minded Islamic intellectuals have taken the most consistent steps to eliminate the obstacles that stand in the way of running the state and passing legislation. To varying degrees, their attempt has also contributed to a reconciliation of Islam and democracy. As for the practical effect of their ideas or the influence they have on Islamicists, the academies or amongst the general public, this cannot be estimated with accuracy in circumstances which cause many to adopt an attitude of secrecy (*taqiyyeh*) about their thought. A positive reaction to these ideas on the part of the majority in the established system of power can scarcely be expected under prevailing conditions, for such a reaction would depend on first eliminating the very conditions that guarantee their interests. On the other hand, it would not be justifiable to link the question of the ultimate effect of these ideas to the future development of the Islamic state, because the efforts to reform Islam and its relation to the state must continue even if the Islamic state ceases to exist. Sorush himself, though he rejects the ideologisation of Islam, makes this mistake in clinging to the idea of an Islamic, albeit a democratic, state. As already mentioned, he explains that the democratic state must be Islamic because the underlying society is Islamic. What he does not explain is why this society, which allegedly is thoroughly Islamic, has the desire to impose on itself an Islamic state.

## Notes

1 *Ayeneh-e Andisheh* : Nos 6/7, 1992.
2 Nehzat-e Azadi: 1988, pp. 145 and 150.

3   1988, pp. 9, 13 f., 17 and 25.

4   See his interview in *Howzeh*, No. 42 (1990), p. 109.

5   Shabestari: 1987–90, No. 1 (1987), p. 11 and No. 2 (1989), p. 15.

6   Ibid., No. 2 (1989).

7   Ibid., No. 6 (1987), No. 2 (1989); 'Shahid Motahhari' in *Kayhan*, 11/5/86 and his interview in *Kayhan*, 10/9/87.

8   Shabestari: 1987–90, No. 2 (1989), p. 14 and his interview in *Howzeh*, No. 46 (1991), p. 129 f.

9   See Shabestari's interview in *Howzeh*, No. 48 (1992), p. 130 ff.; 1987–90, No. 5 (1989), p. 14. Mohammad Sa'idi (1989) also put forward this view when, amongst other things, he wrote: 'If we say that religion or the Koran are perfect, we mean they are perfect in terms of the goals they pursue.'

10  Shabestari: 1987–90, No. 2 (1989), p. 16; cf. his interview in *Howzeh*, No. 42 (1991).

11  Ibid.: 1987–90, No. 5 (1989), p. 15.

12  1987–90, No. 4 (1989), p. 11 f.

13  Ibid., p. 20 f.; ibid., No. 2 (1989), p. 16; and his interview in *Howzeh*, No. 42 (1991).

14  Shabestari: 1987–1990, No. 2 (1991), p. 19 f. and No. 5 (1989), p. 14.

15  Ibid., No. 5 (1989), p. 14 f.

16  Shabestari: 1987–90, No. 2 (1990), p. 21 f.and his interview in *Howzeh*, No. 46 (1991), p. 134.

17  Shabestari: 1992, p. 70 f.

18  Shabestari: 1987–90, No. 5 (1989), No. 2 (1990); *Howzeh*, No. 46 (1991), p. 134.

19  Sorush: 1991, p. 8 of the Foreword.

20  Sorush: 1991, Foreword, p. 6 ff.; 1991a, No. 2, p. 7 ff.; 1989, No. 4, p. 7. In this explanation Sorush avoids an attempt to define the concept 'religion'. He is obviously uncertain what ultimately remains unchangeable and where the boundaries can be drawn between religion and the religious sciences. It is this uncertainty which explains why he occasionally (1991a, 1989) equates religion with the Book, the *sunna* and the *shari'a*, although the last two are not spared in his criticism.

21  Sorush: 1989, No. 5, p. 6.

22  Sorush: 1989, No. 9, p. 11 f.

23  Sorush: 1990, No. 1, p. 13; 1989, No. 4, p. 11 and No. 9, p. 11 f. Sorush feels that it was his merit to have explained these kinds of connections. He admitted, while countering a criticism of Peiman's (1992), that before him Shari'ati had discussed the connection between religious and non-religious sciences, but he believes it was his accomplishment to have worked out the connections more precisely (1992).

24  Cited here from his speech before the gathering of the members of Jehad-e Daneshgahi published in *Kiyan*, No. 1 (1991), p. 13.

25  Ibid.

26  Sorush: 1989a, p. 12.

27  Ibid.: p. 13.

28  *Salam*, 6/1/93.

29  *Kiyan*, No. 1 (1991), p. 13.

30  Ibid.

31  Sorush: 1989a, p. 38 f.

32  In an interview with the author in Tehran (6/9/92), Sorush expressed his conviction that these proposals for reform were useless. They had arisen as a reaction

to external pressure and were devoid of any foundation. When students were sent abroad to study philosophy, it was not with the intention of integrating new perspectives into their own conceptions and drawing out the consequences of this, but merely to indulge in polemics against philosophy. Moreover, in this conversation he criticised the lack of historical judgement on the question of *ahkam* in the academies. They would divest the *ahkam* of sacredness, if they had any notion of historical change.

33   *Kiyan*, No. 1 (1991), p. 15.

34   Sorush: 1990a, p. 41.

35   The complete text of the talk was published in *Kiyan*, No. 14 (1993) and in *Spektrum Iran*, No. 4 (1992). Here we are quoting from *Kiyan*.

36   Published under the same title in *Kiyan*, No. 5 (1992).

37   See the complete text of the lecture published in *Kiyan*, No. 14 (1993a).

38   In response to his lecture at the University of Isfahan in January 1993, to 14 February eleven detailed rebuttals were published in *Kayhan* and *Resalat* alone.

39   *Resalat*, 10/2/93.

40   *Salam*, 6/1/93.

41   We cannot here go into their writings at greater length. M. Borqeʾi (1992) deals with them briefly.

# Conclusions

In Parts II and III of this book we followed the stages by which the Constitution of the Islamic Republic of Iran almost completely divested itself of its democratic and legalistic elements, thereby resolving in practice the major contradictions written into it. Since this process effected no changes in the text of the document, eventually a great gap developed between text and practice, a problem discussed in Parts II and III. This closing chapter summarises the analysis set out in the book, presents some conclusions and adds further details on the present situation and future prospects of the Islamic state. But before addressing these points, we return briefly to the subject of the historical context from which the contradictions in the constitution emerged.

## The Constitution in Historical Perspective

The 'historical environment' in which the constitution of the Islamic republic was framed was characterised by a series of crises. Iranian society had risen against the Pahlavi monarchy under a constellation of contradictory social, economic, political and cultural interests of its classes, strata and other segments which interacted to some extent with international factors. It was caught in a phase of wild transition from a loosely formed complex of different modes of production to a modern industrial nation with corresponding cultural values. A society with a political culture deeply marked by millennia of despotism, but also by a spirit of revolt, it had, over the decades preceding the revolution, absorbed elements of the democratic system of values. Yet this is also a society with a split conception of itself which, in its search for a new identity, has become entangled in further conflicts. It includes groups which identify with values typical, or held to be typical, of modern industrial societies, groups that think they can cling to values which define what they believe to be their traditional identity and groups seeking an identity which includes both modern and traditional elements. An additional difficulty Iranian society faces in this search for a new form of self-understanding is that has neither broken spontaneously with tradition, nor yet is in a position to form a new independent identity. The principle source of its new values is a foreign culture whose political and economic behaviour towards Iran has been aggressive, and the search for identity has – until very recently – been conducted within a framework of rivalry between two systems seeking international hegemony and of international capital's dominance over

markets and value systems. In this context the various sources of dissatisfaction are experienced differently by each social segment depending on its
position. This is true in a certain sense even of the issue of freedom and
independence vis-à-vis the world powers, the lack of which is perceived by
all in common. Consequently, the expectations people had of the revolution
also varied greatly.

By the time of the revolution Iranian society had already experienced
more than a century of political struggle carried on by its urban classes. An
array of political movements and organisations had each attempted to put
their stamp on the struggle, to seize a vanguard position and to direct events
towards the alternative it believed would satisfy its own demands and the
general demands of society. Among these groups there were liberal and left-
wing movements as well as Islamic and modernist state-socialist elements.

As a force that only in the 1960s again attained a position of leadership
in the political struggle, the Islamicists enjoyed several advantages over their
rivals. For one thing, there was no living memory of the alternative they had
to offer. For another, their vanguard position in the revolutionary struggle
was favoured by the fact that their demand for the rule of Islam offered
hope to various classes of the population that through Islam they might
retrieve a lost, and in their eyes, authentic identity. Thirdly, the Islamicists'
radical stance towards the modernist-despotic regime of the Shah offered
the political forces that were determined to overthrow his regime by any
means and at any cost the prospect of achieving their goal. For these and
other reasons the conviction was fostered among the forces of opposition
that they should concede the leadership of the struggle to the Islamicists, i.e.
the Islamic clergy – or at least accept the clergy as comrades in arms and
for the moment ignore their conservative attitudes. Given the apparent
certainty that the clergy would not be capable of governing the state after
the fall of the Shah's regime and would have to hand over power to others,
even the opponents of the Islamicists accepted their leadership of the
revolution.

It was against this background that the Islamicists in general and the
Islamicist clergy in particular step by step assumed the leadership of the
revolution. To safeguard their position they were obliged to commit themselves to fulfilling not only their specific interests but also the demands of
the whole spectrum of social groups participating in the struggle. Hence it
was necessary to draft a constitution that offered a framework within which
common interests and goals might be achieved, and made it possible for the
struggle over special interests to be conducted by peaceful means.

A constitution entirely based on Islamic principles would clearly have had
difficulty in accommodating diverse interest groups. The preliminary draft,
however, satisfied the whole of the modern-Islamicist camp, and the moderate
secularists, recognising that the Islamicists had already achieved a position of
dominance, were also prepared to give it their approval – at least for the
period until they themselves were in a position to take power. Although this

version made considerable concessions to the legalists, by placing parliament at the centre of legislation it nevertheless presented fewer obstacles to the development of the democratic rights of the non-Islamic opposition than the later, post-revolution version.

The constitution framed by the Assembly of Experts satisfies non of these requirements. Indeed it is not even capable of creating peace within the Islamicist camp. It is, in fact, the constitution of the hierocratically oriented Islamicists, the product of a social stratum which, in the decades of modernisation, had been forced to relinquish more and more of its positions of power and was, after the revolution, able to exploit a scarcely hoped for historical chance not only to retrieve lost ground but to realise a dream it had not even dared to speak of openly in bygone centuries. If this constitution, despite everything, contains elements that contradict its overall hierocratic spirit, the reason lies in the multiplicity of interests which motivated the various strata of the population to participate in the revolution and which in subsequent years could still not be entirely ignored.

The alien elements in the constitution reflect the uncertainty of its authors as to whether, in the given circumstances, they could dare to take further steps in the direction of their real goal. The tactic employed by the legalistic clergy under Khomeini's leadership was to assess the balance of forces at a given moment and adjust their immediate goals to what could be achieved in each situation. The replacement of the monarchy with the *velayat-e faqih* was already, at the beginning of the 1970s, Khomeini's aim. But as long as the overthrow of the prevailing order seemed an impossible task, it was not spoken of openly. Then, when the revolution gained momentum, approval was conferred on the preliminary draft of the constitution for as long as it was uncertain whether *velayat-e faqih* could be established. As soon as the formation of an Islamic Republic uncontaminated by democracy appeared to be within the realm of possibility, vehement protest was voiced first of all against the plan to call the post-revolutionary state an 'Islamic Democratic Republic', although this title had been agreed in the Revolutionary Council. Then, once he sensed that there was a reasonable chance of success, Khomeini took steps to ensure that the preliminary draft would be set aside for a constitution that enshrined the *velayat-e faqih*, by pushing for an Assembly of Experts instead of the promised Constituent Assembly.

The wisdom of this tactic, with its many uncertainties, was to a great extent borne out by the way opponents of *velayat-e faqih* reacted to it. Instead of uniting to defend themselves against the clergy's thrust for power, they split into numerous groups. Failing to recognise the common danger that threatened them, they were unaware that it could only be warded off successfully if they united their forces. There are many reasons for this fragmentation; the more obvious are as follows:

1. The drive for exclusive leadership which characterised the behaviour of the clergy was also characteristic of most other groups, especially the

more radical political organisations. They would enter into alliances only if they could be the dominant partner. Potential allies would reject compromise even when it was justified on grounds of the distribution of power, let alone necessary if democratic norms were to be observed and established.

2. The moderates, who given the socioeconomic structure of Iran should have held the leadership were, due to their intrinsically non-revolutionary inclinations, their internal divisions and their deficient organisation, utterly incapable of gaining the upper hand vis-à-vis a political movement intoxicated with revolutionary zeal and hungering for radical solutions.

3. The radical organisations were unable to seize the leadership of the revolution because they ignored the real capacities of their society and dreamed of unattainable goals. They were committed to the ideal of a government system based on councils and strove to replace capitalism with a people's democracy or a classless, divinely sanctioned society. Wanting to attain these goals as quickly as possible they aroused the loathing of the moderates with whom they had, in any case, from the outset rejected any form of alliance.

4. Democratic values were not high on the list of priorities especially amongst groups with a Leninist outlook, whether communists or radical Islamicists. What these groups took to be anti-imperialism and egalitarianism had a much more important place in their scale of values. Consequently, they allowed themselves to be influenced by Khomeini's populist slogans. If they felt loyalty to anything at all, it was to Khomeini's leadership, an attitude Khomeini was able to exploit for his own ends.

5. The behaviour of the moderate Islamicists was bound by deep-seated inhibitions which greatly reduced their ability to resist the hierocratic legalists. As Islamicists their attitude to Khomeini was credulous and submissive rather than independent and self-confident. Khomeini understood how to intimidate them with his overbearing style of leadership and they were afraid of being damned by him as infidels and of being excluded from government power.

The fact that the hierocratic legalists tolerated the inclusion of democratic elements in the constitution did not mean that they were prepared to regulate their behaviour accordingly. Nor did it mean that the Islamic state was conceived in a way that would guarantee the promotion or the enforcement of these elements. The intention was to get rid of the constitution's democratic elements as quickly as possible. Since it was not necessary or advisable to change the text, the process of elimination was carried out in the practical running of the state, in particular by concentrating power in the hands of the leader, undermining and disempowering representative institutions, suppressing fundamental democratic rights and carrying the implementation of *velayat-e faqih* to its logical conclusion.

For all practical purposes, this process began immediately after the change-over of power but only gained real momentum after the fall of Bazargan's government.

## The Real Distribution of Power

### The Distribution of Power Among Official State Institutions

Among the formal state institutions that have access to power the Islamic parliament is surely the weakest. Its legislative power consists solely of its participation in the drawing up of draft bills. Through such legislative initiatives, parliament attempts to demonstrate its independence vis-à-vis the government, but the success of even this limited activity depends on whether the official and non-official institutions of power that stand over it confirm its resolutions. The work of parliament, and its jurisdiction, are increasingly defined as professional expertise (*kar-shenasi*) brought to bear in the formulation of bills and must be distinguished from actual legislation. Indeed, this task corresponds to the function assigned to parliament in Khomeini's book *The Islamic State*, namely 'planning-work'.[1]

Although in emergencies Khomeini allowed parliament, if it had a two-thirds majority, to jump the hurdles created by the Guardian Council and thus attain a greater share in the power to legislate, in practice it rarely enjoyed this power. Once the Assessment Council was established and laws could be passed on the basis of *maslahat*, parliament lost even this limited privilege, because there was no longer any need for the rule of emergency. Even though parliament primarily drafts its resolutions on the basis of reasons of state,[2] it can only do this within the framework of its function of expertise and within its real area of jurisdiction. It has no authority to pass, on the basis of reasons of state, resolutions which do not take account of the *shari'a*.

Through its vote of confidence, parliament can decide on the composition of the Council of Ministers, yet when it exercises this prerogative it does so as the extended arm of those institutions of authority and those power blocs which, amongst other things, decide on its own composition. If parliament has a share in power, this is not because of the constitution but because its members happen to be participants in the unofficial distribution of power. However, it should be noted here that, a few exceptional cases aside, MPs are relatively low rank functionaries within the governmental class and do not dispose over a power base of any great consequence. The most influential among them is the president of parliament who is chosen for this office precisely because of the influence he has personally acquired outside parliament. During the four legislative periods to date, the Islamic parliament has chiefly served as an arena where the opposing camps and blocs that participate in power present their positions, disavow their adversaries and introduce resolutions which, if passed as laws, contribute to the expansion of their areas of power and satisfy their particular interests.

The relatively open debates that take place in parliament are of course partly rooted in the tradition of the Shi'i religious academies where a multiplicity of views within a certain framework is generally tolerated and disputes between the representatives of contrary positions are commonplace. But the more important reason lies in the splintering of power that has occurred between the different camps and blocs, and the fact that no one side is strong enough to suppress its opponents completely. If in the future, due to whatever developments, the democratic principle of representation were to achieve significant importance in the Islamic Republic, then it would have to take place by means of parliament. But as long as this institution remains under the guardianship of numerous official and unofficial councils, circles of power, etc., it will not be capable of positioning itself for this role.

If the text of the constitution (before its 1989 revision) were to be taken literally, the Guardian Council would have to be described as the real source of legislation. Although it had no part in formulating laws, it decided whether or not a draft text could become a law. But the Guardian Council lost this position as a result of two parallel processes which reached their high point in the creation of the Assessment Council: the concentration of legislative power in the hands of Khomeini, and the eventual separation of legislation from the *shari'a*, whose protector the Guardian Council was meant to be. Khomeini's death did not reverse this process because the Assessment Council had by then already been established and anchored in the constitution. This council reaches decisions on the basis of the interests of the government system, which are often irreconcilable with the *shari'a*.

The Guardian Council still examines the resolutions of parliament in relationship to the *shari'a*, although it also observes Khomeini's recommendation[3] that it should take account of the interests of the ruling system. Its insistence on the *shari'a* is partly to be explained by the fact that it has never come to accept the principle that laws are to be conceived as 'state ordinances' and passed in the interest of the ruling system, that is to say, in the interest of the particular political camps dominating that system. But also, as guardian of the *shari'a*, it has no choice but to declare its judgment if a law contradicts the *shari'a*, even if it knows that this is no longer a hindrance to the Assessment Council's approval of the law. A statement made by Ayatollah Emami Kashani, a member of the Guardian Council, in the Assembly for Revising the Constitution is interesting in this connection. He pointed out that members of the Guardian Council who are also members of the Assessment Council would decide over one and the same subject in a session of the Guardian Council according to the standards of the *shari'a* and in a session of the Assessment Council according to the criteria of *maslahat*.[4] In the Guardian Council they participate in decisions about who may be candidates for parliament, or the presidency and the Council of Leadership Experts. But in the Assessment Council they make decisions as representatives of the clerics who dominate the hierocracy.

The Assessment Council is the highest legislative institution, although while Khomeini was alive it was second to the leader. Since his death it has been able to extend its power because Khomeini's successor is not strong enough to impose his authority on it. Individual members of this council dispose over varying degrees of influence in the state, which is susceptible to periodic fluctuations. Hence Ayatollah Mahdavi-Kani, the *éminence grise* amongst his peers, disposes over a considerable power base now as before; but the former prime minister, Musavi, and the former public prosecutor, Hojjat al-Eslam Kho'iniha, apparently retain their seats on the council only for reasons of political expedience. The fact that they have learned to be obedient has also, no doubt, worked in their favour.

Again, as long as Khomeini was alive, the leader was the highest authority in government and therefore the highest legislative authority, even if all his powers were not officially recognised. His decisions, communicated in the form of *fatvas*, decrees or recommendations, could only be questioned if a relatively large group of people with their own power, for the most part jurists, thought this desirable. Even so no one ever wanted, or was able, to contest the supremacy of the leader as represented by Khomeini. He stood outside and above the state. Not only did he unite all the branches of the state in his hands, he even exercised the power to shape the constitution. Only when Khamene'i became leader did some representatives of the radical camp, which was massively excluded from positions of power especially during elections to the 4th Majles, suddenly recall that in the constitution, alongside the principle of *velayat-e faqih*, there were elements of 'republicanism'. It has thus become clear that obedience to the leader, and the central role of his office in the state of the jurists, depends greatly on the particular person who is the leader. Khamene'i became leader as an emergency solution and has ever since been trying to exploit his official position, while at the same time bolstering his office by intervening unofficially in religious and governmental processes of decision-making. But he cannot succeed at this as long as he is obliged to depend exclusively on the conservative clergy for his support. On the personal level, he lacks the necessary force of persuasion to steer a middle course between the different power blocs. Moreover, by now the conservative camp has come to exert so strong a dominance over the state that they are unwilling to let him to manoeuvre in this way.

Formally speaking, the Assembly of Leadership Experts stands above the leader because it can dismiss him and choose another in his place. By exploiting this power the majority in the council can, at any given moment, put pressure on the leader to bow to their will. Under Khomeini it could not, of course, exercise this power and even now it only uses it discretely at moments when it feels its intervention is appropriate. The members of the Assembly of Leadership Experts are for all practical purposes the leading clerics who support the concept of *velayat-e faqih*. Because of their position both in the state and the religious academies, their power is sufficient to influence significantly the direction of government policies.

The Council for National Security, the Supreme Council of the Cultural Revolution and members of the judiciary also dispose over legislative power, if unofficially. The first of these bodies is among the most powerful in the Islamic Republic. Given the fact that any question arising in the country can easily be transformed into a question of security, the Council for National Security makes decisions in many cases for which it has no jurisdiction conferred on it by the constitution.

The government in its executive capacity also disposes over much unofficial legislative power. Through resolutions and statutory instruments which manipulate the contents of laws, or through refusing to enforce laws, or through putting into practice bills rejected by the legislature, the government creates a sphere of action for itself which is not provided for in the constitution. Generally speaking, it is on the executive level of government that deviation from the law and the exercise of personal or client-oriented power takes place. Although the organisation of the executive is formally based on the principle of centralisation, the power over which it disposes is fragmented into a network of personal, client-patron relationships producing a form of anarchic decentralisation.[5] From the highest to the lowest level of the government apparatus functionaries attempt to use their position to acquire personal advantage over rivals in the system and to promote the interests of their clients, thus opening a breach in the hierarchical, centralised executive apparatus. Since this personalised utilisation of executive power has almost become the rule, the government apparatus is full of such breaches. Among the beneficiaries of this system multiple competitive and co-operative relations exist which all revolve around the axis of personal and group interests.

The clients of these functionaries consist on the one hand of influential business men, entrepreneurs and colleagues with whom they exploit government contracts and resources in exchange for financial remuneration or a share of profits. On the other hand, at a lower level, the clientele consists of ordinary people who are forced to pay out bribes whenever they come in contact with the government apparatus.[6] As a rule such payments are made to remove a barrier set up by a civil servant to prevent them from using a public service or in order to by-pass the bureaucracy. On this low level, only disadvantages exist for the clients of the state, disadvantages that become ever greater as economic and administrative power is concentrated in the hands of the government. On the higher level, as time goes by clients draw greater and greater benefits from the patronage system. This situation helps to explain the persistence of étatist tendencies in state policy and the high-level opposition in recent years to the decision to privatise government and nationalised enterprises and services.[7]

Focusing again on the government, the special role of the president must be mentioned, especially after Khomeini's death and the revision of the constitution. In addition to his position as head of the executive branch, the president is also chairman of the Assessment Council, the Council for National Security and the Supreme Council of the Cultural Revolution, as well as a member of the three-man presidium of the Leadership Council.

Despite this, the real power he exercises depends on his unofficial relations with the other powerholders around him. If he is faced with a strong leader – the situation of Khamene'i vis-à-vis Khomeini – then his influence will be minimal. But if the leader is weak, as was clearly the case to begin with when Rafsanjani was president and Khamene'i the leader, then the president's influence will increase. If the leader succeeds in forming a powerful alliance with his personal rivals and opponents, as Khamene'i was able to do at a later stage, then the president may not even be able to put together a cabinet that is unified and submissive to him. The situation is similar with regard to the president's position vis-à-vis parliament, the Assessment Council and the other institutions of power. Naturally, his influence also depends on the extent to which he is successful in deflecting from himself responsibility for the failure of government policies, an extremely difficult task which Rafsanjani has recently been less and less capable of performing.[8]

## The Unofficial Power of the Institutions of the Revolution

If the term 'institutions of the revolution' is taken to mean not only those institutions that are officially described as such but also those more or less organised groups, structures and institutions which arose as a result of the revolution and in which the holders of power came together, then the meeting places where the ruling clergy encountered one another must also be considered. The most important of these are the religious academies, the League of the Militant Clergy of Tehran[9] and the organisation in which the Imams of the Friday Prayers gather. The greatest amount of power in the Islamic state lies in their hands and it is from among their members that the most influential offices in the state are recruited. Even though the lay civil servants, technocrats and bureaucrats who are in competition with them increasingly disapprove of the influence of the clergy and every now and then rebel in various ways against them, at present they do not constitute a visible danger to the position of the ruling clergy.

The official institutions of the revolution possess other organisations that are active outside the state apparatus and through which the clergy and its lay allies can exercise influence. Although the Revolutionary Guards have now developed into an army – or perhaps precisely because of this – they form without a doubt the strongest institution of the revolution. They defend the hierocracy against its opponents and at the same time are an instrument through which the distribution of power can be influenced. However, there has so far been no sign of the Revolutionary Guards attempting to become independent of the other holders of power.

A special role is played by the daily newspapers, the most important of which are *Kayhan*, *Ettela'at*, *Jomhuri-ye Eslami*, *Resalat*, *Salam*, *Abrar* and most recently, *Hamshahri*, *Iran* and *Akhbar*. Each of these roughly represents a specific power bloc in the Islamic state. As in the case of parliament, these newspapers provide a platform on which both the fight against the regime's opponents and the internal arguments between its power blocs is carried out. Their relatively small circulation[10] justifies the conclusion that their influence does not extend to a broad public but primarily affects those segments of the population that are loyal to the regime.

## The Impotence of the People

Since the Islamic Republic came into being, institutions guaranteeing the sovereignty of the people have been suppressed to such an extent or so consistently ignored that of these only a few reluctantly tolerated traces have survived. Parliamentary and presidential elections, and elections to the Assembly of Leadership Experts cannot be regarded as an expression of the sovereignty of the people because the election regulations do not allow opposition candidates to stand. For this reason an increasing proportion of the electorate does not exercise its vote. Those who do participate do not do so with the necessary democratic attitude. Some, like the architects of the election regulations themselves, believe that only Hezbollah should have the right to vote. For a large proportion of them, however, opportunistic motives or fear of suffering eventual disadvantages play a preponderant role. The exclusion of a part of the electorate from the right to stand as candidates, or in effect to vote, has created a situation which justifies the view that the ruling Islamicists have in their own mind divided the population into two categories: those who submit to, or willingly approve of, the conditions the Islamicists have laid down, and those who do not. The first category have the right to vote; the second category do not. In the language of *feqh*, the first make up the *umma*, whereas the second represent a conglomerate of multifarious components which cannot be counted as belonging to the *umma*.

Nor has the concept of the sovereignty of the people been put into practice on the lower levels of government. The local councils provided for in the constitution still do not exist. The Islamic associations of blue and white-collar workers and civil servants have been colonised by the followers of Hezbollah and serve primarily as a means of control and propaganda. Those non-Islamicist or liberal-Islamicist technocrats and bureaucrats whose services the regime cannot do without have achieved a certain form of participation in power. Likewise, the possibility of participation in power is offered through personal relations with functionaries of the regime who as a rule are prepared to use their influence on behalf of people outside the state apparatus in exchange for money or other advantages.

Democratic freedoms, which are the only means of assuring the proper participation of citizens in political life, are suppressed in the widest sense in the Islamic Republic. Opposition organisations or even independent professional associations are not tolerated. The appearance of a few journals that represent, or are close to, the views of secularist or liberal-Islamic intellectuals does not disprove this point. This phenomenon is more properly interpreted as an indication that certain circles in the regime believe that it is to their advantage to allow limited activity in this sphere. It is also flows from two other factors. On the one hand, the decentralising, particularistic forces at work in the state have served to create, as a side effect, 'spaces' in which dissent can sometimes emerge, if only temporarily. On the other hand, the domain of the intellect is too differentiated for the government to be able to impose uniformity on it or to suppress it completely, especially in a situation in which the intelligentsia in the service of the hierocracy cannot satisfy the evident demand for products of this kind. In a complex, highly differentiated society such as that of Iran, with its exceptionally large urban population, its modern middle class, its academics, experts and students, and a bourgeois movement that has already been under way for decades, the suppression of freedoms in general and of an opposition press in particular cannot be maintained in the long run. Independent intellectuals find other ways to communicate with the public and to promote their views. They do not disappear when they face suppression but simply wait for the next opportunity to make themselves noticed. Thus, when asked in 1992 about progress towards reviving the Union of Writers, forbidden in 1981, the poet Ahmad Shamlu replied that the Union of Writers did not have to be revived since it lives on as an idea in the minds of all its members: 'it is not dead because it has never accepted its abolition.'[11]

The articles published in these periodicals for the most part deal with cultural matters and developmental policies. However, strikingly, they also include reports, interviews and articles that more or less openly advocate political participation, a democratic form of government and democratic rights. They convey clearly enough to their readers the critical attitudes of the intelligentsia and the population in general to prevailing practices in Iran, and occasionally – generally in periodicals with a religious tendency – they go so far as to question the foundations of *velayat-e faqih*. On the whole they reflect a secularist or Islamic non-legalist culture and have consequently been branded by the spokesmen of the hierocracy as products of 'the cultural invasion', 'the cultural conspiracy', 'the culture struggle', etc. Yet, despite the attention they attract, they have only an indirect influence on political life in the Islamic Republic and therefore cannot be understood as a form of direct participation in politics.[12]

Another form of participation in public life in the Islamic Republic expresses itself in acts which are contrary to Islamic morals and regulations. Among the more common are drinking alcohol, listening to forbidden music, holding parties at which the guests dance, and ignoring clothing regulations. These activities are so widespread that life in today's Iran would be unimaginable without them.

## The Separation of the State and Religion

Part III of this book described how legislation has increasingly, and across a wide front, abandoned the ground of the *shari'a* and how decisions in this area, as elsewhere, came increasingly to be based reasons of state. The result of this process has been a far-reaching separation between Islam and the practice of government.[13] But in order to fully address the question of the relationship of the state to religion in post-revolutionary Iran it is necessary to ask whether and to what extent religion as defined by the *shari'a* has contributed to facilitating and shaping modern forms of life – institutions, communications media, as well as norms, in short those modern 'products' which are demanded, consumed and valued in the life of the population as a whole and which even the legalists would not gladly renounce.

The answer to the question is negative for the simple reason that the material and intellectual products of modern civilisation consumed in the Islamic Republic are of foreign and non-Islamic origin and have found their way into the life of the country by direct importation or at best by imitation. This is true even for certain products of theological, philosophical and political, let alone scientific, thought. The only relationship the legalists have been able to create between their conception of Islam and the products of modern civilisation is reactive. Although they do not wish to reject these modern products completely, they can only accept them by employing certain legal tricks transparent to everyone. But legal tricks are scarcely a suitable method of justifying the assertion that in Iran today Islam rules the state. Under present circumstances, the unity between religion and the state has only been achieved to the extent that in a few rudimentary areas of social life Islamic ordinances have been applied, at times through different forms of violence. These are no more than a handful of ordinances relating to civil, penal and customary law which even in their classical formulation cannot satisfy the ruling legalists, a fact made clear by the desire for their reform in legalist circles.[14] Given this situation the Islamicists cannot speak of the unity of religion and the state, if by this notion they understand a situation in which all aspects of life and government are defined by religion.

The unity of religion and the state, and the contribution of the ruling Islamicists to establishing such a unity, can best be scrutinised from the perspective of the problems the Islamicists have created, by imposing prohibitions of various kinds, for the integration of modern thought and life into Iranian society on a basis of positive criticism and creative participation. The most important of the obstacles they have created has been to the development of liberties, including free thought, free action and free human beings capable of independently acquiring modern knowledge and of creatively and critically shaping their lives on the basis of their own independent experiences. By demanding the imitation of dogmatic authorities, ordering obedience, and attempting to force thought and behaviour into the mould demanded by their concept of religion which, for all the changes it has undergone, remains conservative, they have taken away people's initiative and creative resources and made them into passive consumers of the products of modern civilisation.

The legalists have attempted to legitimate their rule over Iran, and to achieve the unity of religion and the state on the basis of the alleged perfection of the classical *shari'a* and their special knowledge of it. But they were unable to find this perfection in the ordinances of the *shari'a* and therefore had recourse to undefined and disputed principles of *feqh*, such as *ejtehad*. *Ejtehad*, allegedly founded on proper principles, led them to the rules of *zarurat* and *maslahat* which are provided for emergencies and temporary phenomena, which they used to pass laws of permanent effect. In so doing, they based legislation and government on the same principles that underlie secular forms of the state. Although the Guardian Council declared that an Islamic state could not be built on the basis of the secondary ordinances of Islam and opposed the use of *maslahat* as a principle of legislation, when its members took their place on the Assessment Council where decisions were to be made in the name of reasons of state, they were themselves unable to maintain their own objections and protests.

Viewed in this way, on the level of legislation the Islamic Republic has from the beginning experienced a separation rather than a unity of religion and the state. On another level the process has been supplemented by a development which may be characterised as a separation of the clergy from their religious functions. While members of the clergy have held on to their turbans and robes ever more tenaciously, they have at the same time increasingly taken over the offices of state and thus neglected their religious duties. Indeed, they have been transformed into state functionaries. It is not they, the bearers of religious authority, who have conquered the state and subordinated it to the rule of religion. Instead the reverse has happened: the state has conquered the clergy and along with them religion. In this connection, several authors speak of a form of Caesaropapism which has managed to establish itself in Iran since the revolution.[15]

Given that the classical *shari'a* also emerged by internalising and sanctioning customary law, it should be asked at this point whether we are now witnessing a similar process, namely a transformation of the conception of Islam which has found expression by abandoning the ground occupied by the classical *shari'a* and accepting the modern contents of legislation and government? The failed search for unity and the separation in practice of religion and the state would from this point of view concern the old conception of Islam and the possibility that it has been replaced by a new conception capable of restoring a unity between religion and the state on a new basis. A conclusion on these lines[16] cannot yet be drawn because, for it to hold, the ruling Islamicists would themselves have to represent the new conception of Islam. We have seen, however, that the legalists still brandish the banner of the traditional *shari'a*. They have not yet succeeded in integrating into their understanding of Islamic law the products of legislation in their state and the principles on which these are based. On the other hand, the modern Islamicists, not least because of their experience they have had of the legalists, are on the way to developing a conception of Islam which, when it reaches maturity, will probably no longer contain the principle of religious dominance over the state. An important question here is whether an old legal system can absorb so many foreign elements in so short a period without losing its own identity. Can the original identity remain if what is new comes to dominate the old and attacks its very substance? This book has argued that it cannot.

The failure to Islamicise legislation has created an atmosphere of crisis within the religious academies where at first the cry was raised for a reform of *feqh* and the religious academies themselves. But in time, with the evident lack of serious progress toward reform, this cry faded. Ideas from outside the academies, proffered by the Islamicist intellectuals, were received by the religious authorities with great suspicion and abruptly rejected. In the end the reform efforts within the religious academies proved ineffective because reform would have had to go beyond the limits set by the authorities and therefore could not be accepted. A consistent policy of reform would mean the abandonment of Islamic law and consequently the liberation of legislation and government from the constraints of *feqh*. This the academies cannot allow, both for internal and external reasons: internally because they stand to lose their chief occupation, the exercise of their expertise in *feqh*, and externally because their claim to power, which is legitimated by their knowledge of *feqh*, would be undermined.

The separation of the state from religion on the basis of a thoroughgoing reform of Islam cannot be carried out to the full. All that can be contemplated is the assimilation of many rules of *feqh*, without contradiction, into a modern judicial system. Moreover, it is possible that these rules turn out to be the same as those which occur in other judicial systems.[17]

## The Hierocracy

One of the characteristics that enable people to refer plausibly to the post-revolutionary Iranian state as Islamic is the fact that it is ruled by the clergy. In the name of Islam the new masters have annulled the sovereignty of the people, and in the name of the Islamic state they have annulled the Islamic ordinances. What is still enforced of these ordinances is sufficient, in the view of the clergy, to call their state Islamic. But this form of Islam is no longer that integral whole which had been described as 'perfect' and able, potentially, to solve all the world's problems. Its purpose now is to legitimate the rule of the clergy in the eyes of an ever dwindling portion of the population. In this book this form of rule is termed hierocracy, albeit one that has separated itself from the traditional religious foundations of legitimation which it had originally emphasised, without finding new foundations which it can convincingly define and relate clearly to the *shari'a*, that is to say, to Islam.[18]

Before the revolution the clergy received money for their upkeep from the population in the form of fees for performing religious rituals; today they draw a salary from the state treasury. In addition many of them have acquired an income through state transactions or by offering to use their influence in the state apparatus on behalf of clients in return for money or other advantages. The access of the ruling clergy to state sources of income, and the possibility of assuring economic advantages for themselves by means of political power, has led to increasing independence from the people. The independence that flows from this change is augmented by the fact that to a large extent, the state does not acquire its revenues through taxation,[19] which would make it dependent on the people and the private sector, but through oil revenues over which it has exclusive charge. Government control of the large industrial companies and services industries also contributes to this state of affairs. The clergy's control over this relatively autonomous state economic power justifies speaking of it as the chief component of a state class which is to a large degree independent of the will of the people. As a state class, the clergy are supplemented by officials drawn from the laity who carry out their functions in a relationship of dependency on the clergy.

The clergy's access to state sources of income has made possible a life-style so luxurious that its more cautious or conscientious members began quite early on to warn their colleagues of the consequences. Already in 1982, Rafsanjani demanded that the clergy maintain the life-style common amongst the students at the religious academies before the revolution.[20] Ayatollah Montazeri repeatedly expressed the same demand.[21] In August 1991, Khamene'i voiced his displeasure with those functionaries who lived in the luxurious houses of ministers of the Shah's era and indulged in expensive wedding ceremonies.[22] On 30 October of the same year, *Resalat* warned that the people would lose their trust in the state because of the tendency of government officials to live in luxury.

By and large, the ruling class presents a unified front against its opponents outside the regime. But those within the regime attempt to exclude one another from power and compete on the basis of political, economic and other interests, including ideological orientation. The power struggles taking place within the state class have often caused observers, as well as the participants, to divide the contenders into groups which they designate with terms such as 'camps', 'blocs', 'factions', 'currents', 'wings', etc.[23] When this occurs there is a tendency to distinguish two groups, one characterised as 'radical', 'extremist', 'fundamentalist', etc. and the other as 'moderate', 'pragmatic', 'conservative', etc.[24] It would in fact be more correct to speak of three camps. The first might be described as 'radical', 'populist' *étatiste*, 'extremist' or 'social-radical'; the second as 'pragmatic' or 'moderate', and the third as 'ultra-conservative'.

An attempt to make more precise distinctions would have to take account of the fact that those who comprise the state class are rarely willing to subordinate themselves to the constraints of formal organisation such as is normal in parties and factions. Impelled by individualistic motives and attitudes, they tend to avoid defining themselves in fixed terms either with regard to organisations or political programmes. Perhaps the firmest bond amongst them occurs in the form of loose cliques, alliances and blocs which are normally grouped around influential individuals. Several cliques form a particular camp, the coherence of which, however, remains rather undeveloped. The boundaries between the camps are fluid in two senses. On the one hand, many people regularly switch sides, while on the other hand, as a result of these shifts, they do not commit themselves to fixed programmes. Moreover, connections are constantly made between camps for purely practical reasons, with the result that conflict between them partially disappears for longer or shorter periods of time. Any attempt to establish the inner structure of the government class and to investigate the relationship between its camps should focus attention on the essential interests and practical issues which divide them from one another or bring them together. These include among other questions: i) the role of the state in the economy; ii) the reform of the *shari'a*; iii) Iran's relationship with the United States; iv) how to deal with moral regulations and v) the treatment of non-Islamic intellectuals. Whereas iii) has brought the radical and the conservative camp together in an alliance against the moderates, they remain divided over points ii), iv) and v). While the moderates ally themselves with the conservatives over point i), they stand much closer to the radicals with regard to points ii), iv) and v). Thus, many adherents of the radical camp take up the same position as the conservatives on the matter of moral regulations. The same is true of their views on secular intellectuals. In order to establish the practical position held by a particular camp or its separate groups and blocs, it is necessary to observe them over a long period. For there is always a good chance that the positions adopted at any given moment are the result of tactical power play. They may be abandoned as soon as a shift in the power structure makes it necessary. The best example of this is the conservative camp's ant-*étatiste* policy that has slackened markedly over the last few years, one explanation for which is the fact that since the death of Khomeini this camp has managed to assert its dominance over the state.

## Notes

1   In this book, parliament is called 'the Planning Assembly' (Majles-e Barnameh-rizi) (p. 48).

2   Parliament promulgates laws on the basis of *estehsan* and *esteslah*, according to the MP Zavvare'i in *Resalat*, 9 and 10/6/87.

3   Khomeini made this kind of 'fatherly remark' in various places including a letter written on 31/12/88. For the text see M. Kadivar: 1992a, p. 86.

4   'That is to say, when the government wishes to take away people's plots of land ... we say in the morning in the Council of Guardians that this is contrary to the holy *shari'a* of Islam ... and in the evening when we are in the Assessment Council, we give our permission for this to be done because this is what *maslahat* demands' (MR I/208).

5   In 1986 (16 January), *Resalat* was already comparing the administrative system to a poisonous millipede and a horrific octopus whose demands were every day becoming more vociferous.

6  In a talk with the Friday Imams published in *Resalat* 8/7/92, Rafsanjani stated: 'The worst practice that we encounter in the government apparatus is bribery and extortion.' Afrazideh said in a session of parliament on 13/5/93: 'Bribery, favouritism in conferring offices and the replacement of guidelines by personal relations have reached such proportions that practices of this kind are no longer tolerable.'

7  In a lead article in *Howzeh* (No. 29, 1988, p. 3 ff.) 'unauthorised behaviour and fragmentation in guiding society' are declared to be 'a spreading sickness of the revolution … which manifests itself in the splitting apart and growing independence of institutions, organisations and branches of government.' The article also speaks of 'the politics of cliques … dominant in the ministries and in many organisations. It's a question of organised groups that arrive and depart in accordance with the change of ministers and chiefs of government institutions.'

8  On the evolution of the position of the president in the Islamic Republic, see Milani: 1993. Milani wrote this article when the weaknesses of Rafsanjani's position were still not visible and thus attributed too great an importance to the presidency as an institution.

9  And earlier on its rival the Union of Militant Clergy.

10  The total circulation of daily newspapers, according to *Salam* (11/4/94) is not quite 1.5 million. According to the figures released by the deputy of the president of the Ministry for Islamic Guidance and Culture in the province of Khorasan, there are all together 21 daily newspapers (*Salam*, 3/10/94).

11  *Ayeneh-e Andisheh*, No. 72 (1992).

12  Over the past two years the periodicals have come under increased pressure which at the time of writing shows no sign of easing.

13  What is meant here is the legalistic conception of Islam. In this context, one cannot speak of the other interpretations of Islam because they were not shared by the ruling Islamicists and because their proponents were unable to participate in the running of government.

14  Even an exponent of conservatism such as H. Mehrpur feels obliged to deal with the problems that occur in practice because of the application of the Islamic penalties. See his article in *Ettela'at*, 19/6/93.

15  Houchang Chehabi (1991) deals with the question of whether the Islamic Republic is a theocratic state from a different standpoint based on Max Weber's definition of theocracy. He concludes that 'the attempt to found a theocracy in Iran has only had a superficial success' (p. 87). See also Chehabi 1993.

16  Büttner (1991) raises this question in his article 'Possibilities and Limits of an Islamic Integration of Society'. He sees a possible middle path between 'the ethicising of religion' and its 'dogmatisation' which consists of adapting and Islamicising 'practices and solutions to problems' which Muslims find 'useful and appropriate and which do not unambiguously contradict the basic rules of their religion'. But on the decision to follow this path, he concludes by asking whether the slogan 'Islam is the solution!' can still be justified (p. 16).

17  N. Katuzian pleads for retaining many ordinances which are already established by the Koran and therefore difficult to annul such as the inheritance law, which should, however, be accompanied by provisions that compensate women for the disadvantages it imposes on them. See the interview he gave in *Iran-e Farda*, No. 11 (1994), p. 6–8.

18  The Persian term that can be used to designate this form of a state is '*akhund-salari*', literally 'the rule of priests' but 'hierocracy' gives greater emphasis to the estrangement of the rulers from religion. Abrahamian (1993) characterises this form of state as populist and compares the position held in it by Khomeini with that of 'El Lider, El Conductor, Jefe Maximo (Chief Boss), and O Pais do Povo (Father of the Poor)' (p. 38) encountered in several Latin-American states.

19  Despite the increasing share of taxes in the state's revenues since the revolution (chiefly due to the decline in the absolute value of oil revenues) with the sole exception of 1986 taxes still bring in less than 50% and often less than 40 or even 30% of government revenue. See Amirahmadi: 1990, p.165.

20  *Kayhan*, 18/4/82. This was not the first occasion on which such a demand was voiced.

21  See for example *Kayhan*, 25/1 and 4/8/84, as well as *Resalat*, 23/10/85 and 22/2/89.

22  *Ettela'at*, 15/8/91. At this time the rumour was circulating that Ayatollah Karrubi had arranged such a wedding for his son.

23  The participants use the term *jenah*, which can be translated as 'wing' or 'faction'.

24  See for example Menashri: 1992; Sarabi: 1994. Both authors are conscious of the inadequacy of a division into two camps, though they persist in making it.

# Bibliography

'Abdi, 'Abbas (1991) 'Jam'eh-Shenasi-ye Hoquq-e Irani.' *Salam* 9/9/ to 15/10/91.

Abrahamian, Ervand (1993) *Khomeinism: Essays on the Islamic Republic*. Berkeley and London.

Akhavi, Shahrough (1987) 'Elite Factionalism in The Islamic Republic of Iran.' *The Middle East Journal*, No. 2, pp. 181–201.

Algar, Hamed (1980) *Constitution of the Islamic Republic of Iran*. Berkeley.

'Amid Zanjani, 'Abbas 'Ali (1988–1989) *Feqh-e Siyasi*, 3 vols. Tehran.

Amirahmadi, Hooshang (1990) *Revolution and Economic Transition: The Iranian Experience*. New York.

Arjomand, Said Amir (1988) *The Turban for the Crown*. Oxford and New York.

—— (1993) 'Constitution of the Islamic Republic.' *Encyclopaedia Iranica*. vol. VI.

—— (1993) 'Qavanin-e Asasi-ye Iran dar Chaharchub-e Tarikhi va Tatbiqi.' *Negah-e Now*, No. 16, pp. 6–19.

'Arabi, Hosein (1991) *Naqd va Barrasi-ye Qanun-e Jadid-e Kar*. Tehran.

'Askari, Mehdi (1979) *Nezam-e Showra'i*. Tehran.

Azari Qomi, Ahmad (1986) 'Majlesi keh dar Ra's-e Omur Ast.' *Resalat*, 22/6/86 ff.

—— (1987) 'Dar Partow-e Bayan-e Maqam-e Rahbari.' *Resalat*, 2/6/87 ff.

—— (1987) 'Padideh-e Sho'm-e Ehtekar. Gerani va Geranforushi.' *Resalat*, 22/8/87 ff.

—— (1987) 'Nazari bar Feqh-e Siyasi.' *Resalat*, 19/9/87 ff.

—— (1988) 'Hokm-e Hokumati.' *Resalat*, 6/1/88 ff.

—— (1988) 'Eslam-e Nab-e Mohammadi.' *Resalat*, 25/5/88 ff.

—— (1988) 'Velayat-e Motlaqeh-e Faqih.' *Resalat*, 6/8/88 ff.

—— (1989) 'Esteghna-ye Feqh.' *Resalat*, 21/1/89 ff.

—— (1989) 'Maslahat-e Nezam.' *Resalat*, 3/4/89 ff.

—— (1989) 'Velayat-e Motlaqeh va Rahbari-ye Jadid.' *Resalat*, 27/6/89 ff.

—— (1989) 'Velayat-e Motlaqeh bar Hasab-e Nass ya Hasbe.' *Resalat*, 17/7/89 ff.

—— (1989) 'Maslahat-e Nezam va Pasokh be Moshkelat-e An.'*Resalat*, 16/9/89 ff.

—— (1989) 'Eshkalat-e Aghayan va Pasokh-e Ma.' *Resalat*, 3/10/89 ff.

—— (1989) 'Towzih-e Bishtar Piramun-e Masa'el-e Mostahdaseh.' *Resalat*, 21/10/89 ff.

Baher, Hosein (1979) *Nezam-e Showra'i*. Tehran.

Bakhash, Shaul (1986) *The Reign of the Ayatollahs: Iran and the Islamic Revolution*. London.

Bani-Sadr, Abolhasan (1980) *Sad Maqaleh*. USA.

—— (1982) *Khiyanat be Omid*. Paris.

Baghi, 'A. (1983) *Dar Shenakht-e Hezb-e Qa'edin-e Zaman, Mowsum be-Anjoman-e Hojjatiyeh*. Qom.

Binswanger, Karl (1980) 'Das Selbstverständnis der Islamischen Republik Iran im Spiegel ihrer neuen Verfassung.' *Orient*, Nr. 21, pp. 320–30.

Bonyad-e Farhangi-ye Baqer al-'Olum: (1992) 'Nezam-e Amuzeshi-ye Howzeh-e 'Elmiyeh.' *Ettela'at*, 2, 9 and 17/10/92.

Borqe'i, Mohammad (1992) 'Shenakht-e Dini dar Barabar-e Shenakht-e 'Olum-e Tajrobi.' *Kankash*, No. 8, pp. 76–103.

Büttner, F. (1991) 'Zwischen Politisierung und Säkularisierung – Möglichkeiten und Grenzen einer islamischen Integration der Gesellschaft.' In E. Forndran, ed., *Religion und Politik in einer säkularisierten Welt*. Bonn, pp. 137–67.

Chehabi, Houchang (1991) 'Religion and Politics in Iran: How Theocratic is the Islamic Republic?' *Journal of the American Academy of Art and Science*, vol. 120, No. 3, pp. 69–91.
———— (1993) 'Klerus und Staat in der Islamischen Republik Iran.' In *Aus Politik und Zeitgeschichte, Beilage zur Wochenzeitung das Parlament*, B 33/93, 13/8/93, pp. 17–23.

Dezhkam, Taqi (1991) 'Azadi az Didgah-e Emam Khomeini.' *Kayhan*, 3 and 12/6/91.
Dilger, Konrad (1982) 'Die Gewalt des Rechtsgelehrten (walayat al-faqih) im islamischen Recht. Ein Beitrag zur schiitischen Staatslehre in Iran und ihrer Verankerung in der iranischen Verfassung.' *Zeitschrift für Vergleichende Rechtswissenschaft*, Nr. 81, pp. 39–62.

Flanz, Gisbert (1980) 'A Comparative Analysis of the Constitution of the Islamic Republic of Iran.' In A. P. Blaustein and G. H. Flanz, ed., *Constitutions of the World*. New York.

Hadavi Tehrani, Mehdi (1992) 'Daramadi bar Barnameh-rizi-ye Amuzeshi-ye Howzeh-e 'Elmiyeh.' *Kayhan-e Andisheh*, No. 40, pp. 2–5.
Ha'eri, 'Abd al-Hadi (1985) *Tashayyo' va Mashrutiyat dar Iran va Naqsh-e Iraniyan-e Moqim-e 'Eraq*. Tehran.
Ha'eri, Kazem (1985) *Asas-e Hokumat-e Eslami*. Tehran.
Hakim, Mohammad Baqer (1988) 'Jomhuri-ye Eslami-ye Iran va Vizhegiha-ye Hokumat-e Eslami.' *Hokumat dar Eslam*. Contributions to the Third and Fourth Conference of *Islamic Studies*, 2nd edition. Tehran.
Hakimi, Mohammad Reza (1983) 'Afaq-e Fekri-ye Borunhowze'i.' *Howzeh*, No. 1 (pp. 22–46) and 2 (pp. 21–43).
Hamidi, Anvar (n.d.) *Dowreh-e Kamel-e Qanun-e Madani*. Tehran.
Hezb-e Iran (1979) *Nazar-e Tahlili va Enteqadi-ye Hezb-e Iran dar Bareh-e Pishnevis-e Qanun-e Asasi*. Tehran.
Hojjati Ashrafi, Gholam Reza (1983) *Majmu'eh-e Qavanin. Asasi–Madani*. Tehran.
Hojjati Kermani, Mohammad Javad (1992) 'Naqsh-e Zaman dar Feqh.' *Ettela'at*, 21/2/ to 4/3/92.
*Howzeh*: (1984) "Aleman-e Motahattek va Jahelan-e Motanassek.' No. 5, pp. 3–10.
———— (1984a) 'Naqsh-e Howzehha.'
———— (1986/87) 'Arzyabi-ye Mas'uliyat-e Howzeh-e 'Elmiyeh.' No. 14, pp. 25–42.
———— (1986/87a) 'Tarhha va Barnamehha.' No. 18, pp. 45–61.
———— (1987a) 'Feqh va Payeh-rizi-ye Eqtesad-e Salem.' No. 25, pp. 139–46.
———— (1987a) 'Masa'el-e Nezam-e Howzeh.' No. 20, p. and 21,
———— (1987-1988) 'Azadi-ye Tafakkor.' No. 24-30.
———— (1987/88a) 'Fatava-ye Emam. Tahavvoli Digar dar Tarikh-e Feqh-e Shi'a.' No. 23, pp. 21–26.
———— (1988) 'Sokkan-dari-ye Enqelab.' No. 29, pp. 3–20.
———— (1988a) 'Bang-e Rahil.' No. 28, pp. 3–24.
———— (1988b) 'Masa'el-e Mali va Eqtesadi-ye Nezam.' No. 27, pp. 58–74.
———— (1988c) 'Negahi be-Mavane'-e Ehya-ye Feqh.' No. 27, pp. 155–69.
———— (1988d) 'Osul-e Kolli va Shivehha-ye 'Amali-ye Resalat-e Ejtema'i-ye Howzeh.' No. 26, pp. 39–57.
———— (1988e) 'Cheshmdashti az Majles-e Sevvom.' No. 25, pp. 28–36.
———— (1988f) 'Maktab va Maslahat.' No. 28, pp. 139–60.
———— (1989) 'Shaqshaqiyeh.' No. 31, pp. 11–40.
———— (1989a) 'Bazsazi va Resalat-e Howzeh va Daneshgah.' No. 35, pp. 3–30.

——— (1989b) 'Naqsh-e Howzehha dar Tadavom ya Shekast-e Enqelab.' No. 31, pp. 59–73.

——— (1989-1991) 'Azadi-ye 'Aqideh.' No. 31–42.

——— (1990) 'Qebleh-e 'Eshq.' No. 37/38, pp. 3–25.

——— (1991) 'Vaz'iyat-e Mowjud-e Howzehha.' No. 42, pp. 18–26.

——— (1992) 'Fasl-e Shekoftan-e Armanha.' No. 48, pp. 13–34.

——— (1993) 'Eslah-e Howzeh. Az Teori ta 'Amal.' No. 58, pp. 3–16.

Ilzad, Dara (1984) *Chomeini und sein Strafgesetz. Barbarei oder Gerechtigkeit.* Berlin (East).
Iran Research Group (1989) *Iran Year Book.* Bonn.

Jannati, Mohammad Ebrahim (1986a) 'Ra'y-gera'i dar Ejtehad.' *Kayhan-e Andisheh,* No. 9, pp. 9–22.

——— (1987) 'Ejtehad dar Jame'eh-e Eslami.' *Kayhan-e Andisheh,* No. 10, pp. 6–18.

——— (1990) 'Feqh-e Ejtehadi va Eslah-e Howzehha az Didgah-e Emam.' *Kayhan-e Andisheh,* No. 29, pp. 15–38.

——— (1990a) 'Jayigah-e Masaleh-e Morsaleh va Esteslah dar Manabe'-e Ejtehad.' *Kayhan-e Andisheh,* No. 31, pp. 57-73.

Jebheh-e Melli (1979) *Nameh-e Sargoshadeh-e Jebheh-e Melli be Mellat-e Iran dar Bareh-e Enheraf-e Majles-e Khobregan az Osul-e Qanungozari va Tashkil-e Hey'at-e Hakemeh-e Jadid Tavassot-e Qeshr-e Momtaz-e Mazhabi.* Tehran.

Johansen, Baber (1984) 'Das Islamische Recht.' In Ruprecht Kurzrock, ed., *Die Islamische Welt I,* Berlin, pp. 129 –45.

Kadivar, Mohsen (1992) 'Mabani-ye Eslah-e Sakhtar-e Amuzeshi-ye Howzehha-ye 'Elmiyeh.' *Kayhan-e Andisheh,* No. 42, pp. 5–15.

——— (1992a) 'Seyri dar Majmu'eh-e Nazariyat-e Showra-ye Negahban.' *Ayeneh-e Pazhuhesh,* No. 13/14, pp. 81–8.

Katuzian, Naser (1981) *Gozari bar Enqelab-e Iran.* Tehran.

——— (1990) *Moqaddameh-e 'Elm-e Hoquq va Motale'eh dar Nezam-e Hoquqi-ye Iran,* 12th edition. Tehran.

Kauz, Ralph (1992) 'Die Partei der Islamischen Republik.' *Münchener Materialien und Mitteilungen zur Irankunde,* No. 2.

Khalilian, Khalil (1979) *Qanun-e Asasi-ye Jomhuri-ye Eslami-ye Iran.* Tehran.

Khomeini, Ahmad (1989) *Ranjnameh be-Hazrat-e Ayatollah Montazeri.* Tehran.

Khomeini, Ruhollah (1982) *Velayat-e Faqih.* Tehran.

——— (1982a) *Maktubat, Sokhanraniha, Payamha va Fatava-ye Emam Khomeini.* Tehran.

——— (1983) *Estefta'at,* vol. I. Qom.

——— (1984) *Tali'eh-e Enqelab-e Eslami. Mosahebehha-ye Ema Khomeini dar Najaf, Paris va Qom.* Tehran.

——— (1986) *Sho'un va Ekhtiyarat-e Vali-ye Faqih.* Tehran.

——— (1987) *Balagh. Sokhanan-e Mowze'i-ye Emam Khomeini,* vol. III. Tehran.

——— (1987–90) *Tahrir al-Vasila,* 4 vols. Qom.

Kooroshy, Javad (1990) *Wirtschaftsordnung der Islamischen Republik Iran. Anspruch und Wirklichkeit.* Hamburg.

Krüger, Eberhard (1988) 'Zwei Beiträge zum iranischen Parlamentswesen.' In E. Krüger, ed., *Münchener Materialien und Mitteilungen zur Irankunde,* Heft 1. Munich.

Lahiji, 'Abdol Karim (1985) 'Mavared-e Tanaqoz-e Qanun-e Asasi-ye Jomhuri-ye Eslami-ye Iran ba 'Elamiyeh-e Jahani-ye Hoquq-e Bashar.' *Alefba,* No. 5, pp. 19–41.

Lambton, Ann (1964) 'A Reconsideration of the Position of the Marja' al-Taqlid on the Religious Institution.' *Studia Islamica*, No. 20, pp. 115–35.

Liga zur Verteidigung der Menschenrechte im Iran: (1988) Dokumentation über Menschenrechtsverletzungen in der *Islamischen Republik Iran*. Berlin.

—— (1991) *Internationale Berichte über Menschenrechtsverletzungen im Iran*. Berlin.

Löschner, Harald (1971) *Die dogmatischen Grundlagen des schiitischen Rechts*. Berlin.

Madani, Jalal al-Din (1986-1990) *Hoquq-e Asasi dar Jomhuri-ye Eslami-ye Iran*, 6 vols. Tehran.

Mahmasani, Sobhi (1967) *Falsafeh-e Qanungozari dar Eslam*. Tehran.

Majles-e Showra-ye Eslami: (1981) *Ashna'i ba Majles-e Showra-ye Eslami be-Zamimeh-e Karnameh-e Sal-e Avval*. Tehran.

—— (1982) *Negahi be-Majles-e Showra-ye Eslami*. Tehran.

—— (1982a) *Negahi be-Majles-e Showra-ye Eslami*. Tehran.

—— (1984) *Ashna'i ba Majles-e Showra-ye Eslami. Karnameh-e Sal-e 1362*. Tehran.

—— (1985) *Mo'arefi-ye Namayandegan-e Dovvomin Dowreh-e Majles-e Showra-ye Eslami*. Tehran.

—— (1985a) *Karnameh-e Majles-e Showra-ye Eslami, Sal-e Avval, Dowreh-e Dovvom*. Tehran.

—— (1986) *Fehrest-e Mowzu'i-ye Dastur-e Jalasat-e Mozakerat-e Majles-e Showra-ye Eslami, Dowreh-e Avval*. Tehran.

—— (1988) *Majmu'eh-e Qavanin Avvalin Dowreh-e Majles-e Showra-ye Eslami*, 2nd edition. Tehran.

—— (1989) *Mo'arefi-ye Namayandegan-e Majles-e Showra-ye Eslami, Dowreh-e Sevvom*. Tehran.

—— (1990) *Fehrest-e Mowzu'i-ye Dastur-e Jalasat-e Majles-e Showra-ye Eslami, Dowreh-e Dovvom*. Tehran.

—— (1990a) *Majmu'eh-e Qavanin-e Dovvomin Dowreh-e Majles-e Showra-ye Eslami*. Tehran.

—— (1993) *Mo'arefi-ye Namayandegan-e Majles-e Showra-ye Eslami, Dowreh-e Chaharom*. Tehran.

Makarem Shirazi, Naser (1989) *Barrasi-ye Feshordeh'i Piramun-e Tarh-e Hokumat-e Eslami*. Qom.

—— (1992) 'Mafhum-e Daqiq-e Ta'sir-e Zaman va Makan dar Ejtehad.' *Ettela'at*, 13/6/92 ff.

Markaz-e Amar-e Iran (1990) *Salnameh-e Amari 1368*. Tehran.

—— (1992) *Salnameh-e Amari 1370*. Tehran.

Martin, Vanessa (1987) 'Shaikh Fazlallah Nuri and the Iranian Revolution 1905–09.' *Middle Eastern Studies*, vol. 23, No. 1, pp. 39–53.

Mehrpur, Hosein (1992) *Majmu'eh-e Nazariyat-e Showra-ye Negahban*, 3 vols. Tehran.

—— (1992a) 'Majma'-e Tashkhis-e Maslahat-e Nezam va Jayigah-e Qanuni-ye An.' *Salam*, 1 to 29/12/92.

Menashri, David (1990) *Iran: A Decade of War and Revolution*. New York.

Meshkini, 'Ali (1979) *Hokumat-e Jomhuri-ye Eslami*. Tehran.

Middle East Watch: (1993) *Guardians of Thought. Limits on Freedom of Expression in Iran*. New York.

Milani, Mohsen (1992) 'Shi'ism and the State in the Constitution of the Islamic Republic of Iran.' In S. K. Farsoun and M. Mashayekhi, eds, *Iran. Political Culture in the Islamic Republic*, London, pp. 133–59.

Milani, Mohsen (1993) 'The Evolution of the Iranian Presidency: from Bani Sadr to Rafsanjani.' *British Journal of Middle Eastern Studies*, No. 2 pp. 82–9.

Mohammadi Reishahri, Mohammad (1990) *Khaterat-e Siyasi 65–66*. Tehran.

Modarresi Tabataba'i, Hosein (1983) *Zamin dar Feqh-e Eslami*, 2 vols. Tehran.

—— (1985) 'Islamic Legislation and the Majority: A Discussion on the Legal Basis for the Validity of the Majority Opinion in Islamic Legislation.' Summary of a paper presented at the John Olin Center for Inquiry into the Theory and Practice of Democracy, University of Chicago, on May 9, 1985.

Montazeri, Hosein 'Ali (1988) *Ehtekar va Qeimatgozari*. Tehran.

Mohaqqeq Helli, Abu'l-Qasem (1983-1985) *Shara'i' al-Islam*, edited by M. T. Daneshpazhuh, 4 vols. Tehran.

——— (1988–1992) *Mabani-ye Feqhi-ye Hokumat-e Eslami*, 4 vols. Tehran.

Motahhari, Morteza (1974) *Mas'aleh-e Hejab*. Tehran.

——— (1980) *Nezam-e Hoquq-e Zan dar Eslam*. Tehran.

——— (1982) *Barrasi-ye Feqhi-ye Mas'aleh-e Bimeh*. Tehran.

——— (1983) *Eslam va Moqtaziyat-e Zaman*. Tehran.

——— (1985) *Piramun-e Jomhuri-ye Eslami*. Tehran.

——— (no date) *Ashna'i ba 'Olum-e Eslami. Osul-e Feqh.* Qom.

Musavi, 'Ali (1981) *'Oruj-e Azadi dar Velayat-e Faqih*. Tehran.


Na'ini, Mohammad Hosein (1955) *Tanbih al-Umma wa Tanzih al-Milla, ya Hokumat az Nazar-e Eslam*, with commentary and notes by M. Taleqani. Tehran.

Nehzat-e Azadi: (1982) *Asnad-e Nehzat-e Azadi-ye Iran*, vol. I. Tehran.

——— (1983) *Barkhord ba Nehzat va Pasokhha-ye Ma*. Tehran.

——— (1983a) *Asnad-e Nehzat-e Azadi-ye Iran*, vol. XI. Tehran.

——— (1988) *Tafsil va Tahlil-e Velayat-e Motlaqeh-e Faqih*, Tehran.

——— (n.d.) *Moshkelat va Masa'el-e Avvalin Sal-e Enqelab az Zaban-e Mohandes Bazargan*. Tehran.

Nuri, Fazlollah (1983/84) *Rasa'el, 'Elamiyehha, Maktubat, va Ruznameh-e Sheikh-e Shahid Fazlollah Nuri*. Ed. by M. Torkan, 2 vols. Tehran.

Nurizadeh, 'Ali Reza (1986) 'Mehdi Hashemi ya Hasan Sabbah-e Rezhim-e Hakem dar Iran.' *Ruzegar-e Now*, No. 10, pp. 42–55.

Nouraie, Fereshteh (1975) 'The Constitutional Ideas of a Shi'ite Mujtahid: Muhammad Husayn Na'ini.' *Iranian Studies*, vol. VIII, No. 4, pp. 234–47.


Pakdaman, Naser (1990) 'Dowr-e Batel-e Velayat-e Faqih.' *Cheshmandaz*, No. 7, pp. 1–31.

Peiman, Habibollah (1988) *Dar Bareh-e Velayat-e Motlaqeh-e Faqih*. Tehran.

——— (1992) 'Sohbat va Taghyir dar Andisheh-e Dini.' *Kiyan*, No. 5, pp. 26–30.

Rahimi, M. (1978) *Qanun-e Asasi-ye Iran va Osul-e Demokrasi*, 3rd edition. Tehran.

*Resalat:* 24/10/1987 ff., 'Tavana'i-ye Eslam dar Edareh-e Jame'eh-e Emruz va Khala'-e Teorik.'

Ruhani, Mohammad Sadeq (1977) *Nezam-e Hokumat dar Eslam*. Qom.

——— (1978) *al-Masa'el al-Mustahdasa*. Qom.

Rosskopf, Fritz (1990) *Die Entwicklung des Steuersystems im Iran nach der Revolution von 1979*. Berlin.

Graf v. Rotkirch, I. (1977) 'Einführung in das Gesellschaftsrecht, Steuerrecht, Volkaktiensprogramm.' In T. Eggers und J. D. Ostrowski, eds, *Iran-Engagement*. Hamburg.


Sabi, M. (1972) *The Commercial Code of Iran*, Tehran.

Sadr, Mohammad Baqer (1979) *Jomhuri-ye Eslami*. Tehran.

Saffari, Said (1993) 'The Legitimation of the Clergy's Right to Rule in the Iranian Constitution of 1979.' *British Journal of Middle Eastern Studies*, pp. 64-81.

Salehi, 'Abbas (1993). See: *Howzeh*: 1993.

Sanjabi, Karim (1989) *Omid va Na-omidiha*. London.

Salamatian, Ahmad, Chamlou, Simine (1990) 'Les dix années de la Révolution Islamique en Iran.' *Revue Tiers Monde*, t. XXX, no. 123, juillet–septembre 1990, pp. 505–35.

Sarabi, Farzin (1994) 'The Post-Khomeini Era in Iran: The Elections of the Fourth Islamic Majles.' *Middle East Journal*, Vol. 48, No. 1, pp. 89–107.

Sazman-e Mojahedin-e Khalq-e Iran: (1979a) *Bayaniyeh-e Mojahedin-e Khalq-e Iran dar Bareh-e Referandom va Entezarat-e Marhale'i-ye Ma az Jomhuri-ye Eslami*. Tehran.

——— (1979) *Didgahha-ye Mojahedin dar Bareh-e Qanun-e Asasi*. Tehran.

Shabestari, Mohammad Mojtahed (1987–1990) 'Din va 'Aql.' *Kayhan-e Farhangi*, in various issues.

—— (1990a) 'Siyasat az Didgah-e Motafakkeran-e Mosalman dar Qarn-e Akhir.' *Kayhan-e Farhangi*, No. 2, pp. 19–22.

—— (1992) 'Azadi, Esteqlal va Hakemiyat-e Ensan dar Elahiyat-e Eslam.' *Iran-e Farda*, No. 4, pp. 70–1.

Schirazi, Asghar (1991) 'Die neuere Entwicklung der Verfassung in der Islamischen Republik Iran.' In *Verfassung und Recht in Übersee*, Year 24, 2nd Quarter, pp. 105–22.

—— (1991a) 'Hintergründe für die neutrale Haltung der Islamischen Republik Iran im Krieg am persischen Golf.' In N. Mattes, ed., *Wir sind die Herren und ihr unsere Shuhputzer*, Frankfurt am Main, pp. 66–82.

—— (1992) "Oh Gott, lasst die Tyrannen sich gegenseitig bekämpfen' – Iran, Islam und der Golfkrieg.' In F. Ibrahim and M. A. Ferdowsi, eds, *Die Kuweit-Krise und das regionale Umfeld. Hintergründe, Interessen, Ziele*, Berlin, pp. 163–76.

—— (1992a) *Die Widersprüche in der Verfassung der Islamischen Republik vor dem Hintergrund der politischen Auseinandersetzung im nachrevolutionären Iran*, Berlin.

—— (1993) *Islamic Development Policy. The Agrarian Question in Iran*. Boulder, Colorado.

Shakuri, Abu'l-Fazl (1982) *Feqh-e Siyasi-ye Eslam*, 2 vols. Tehran.

Shari'ati, 'Ali (1971) *Fatemeh Fatemeh Ast*. Tehran.

—— (1978) *Zan dar Cheshm va Del-e Mohammad*. Tehran.

Soltani, Yadollah (1981–83) 'Entekhabat az nazar-e Eslam va qanun-e asasi.' *Pasdar-e Eslam*, No. 1–23.

Sorush, 'Abdolkarim (1987) *Tafarroj-e Son'. Gozarha'i dar Maqulat-e Akhlaq, San'at va 'Elm-e Ensani*. Tehran.

—— (1989) 'Mavane'-e Fahm-e Nazariyeh-e Takamol-e Ma'refat-e Dini.' *Kayhan-e Farhangi*, No. 4, pp. 7–14, No. 5, pp. 6–10, No. 9, pp. 7–12.

—— (1989a) 'Jameh-e Tahzib bar Tan-e Ehya'.' *Farhang*, No. 4/5, pp. 1–100.

—— (1990) 'Qabz va Bast-e Teorik-e Shari'at. Nazariyeh-e Takamol-e Dini.' *Kayhan-e Farhangi*, No. 1, pp. 12 18.

—— (1990a) 'Jor'at-e Danestan Dashteh Bash.' *Ayeneh-e Andisheh*, No. 1, pp. 24-41.

—— (1991) *Qabz va Bast-e Te'orik-e Shari'at*. Tehran.

—— (1991a) 'Qabz va Bast dar Mizan-e Naqd va Bahs.' *Kiyan*, No. 2, pp. 5–12.

—— (1992) 'Pasokh be-Naqdnameh-e Sohbat va Taghyir dar Andisheh-e Dini.' *Kiyan*, No. 7, pp. 14–18.

—— (1992) 'Eine religiöse demokratische Regierung?' *Spektrum Iran*, Heft 4, pp. 79-85.

—— (1992a) "Aql va Azadi.' *Kiyan*, No. 5, pp. 13–25.

—— (1993) 'Hokumat-e Demokratik-e Dini.' *Kiyan*, No. 11, pp. 12–15.

—— (1993a) 'Farbehtar az Ide'olozhi.' *Kiyan*, No. 14, pp. 2–20.

Tabataba'i, Mohammad Hosein (1959) 'Zan dar Eslam.' *Maktab-e Tashayyo'*, No 1.

—— (1969) *Eslam va Ehtiyajat-e Vaqe'i-ye Har 'Asr*. Tehran.

Taleqani, Mahmud (1979) *Khotbehha-ye Namaz-e Jom'eh va 'Id-e Fetr*. Ed. Mojahedin-e Khalq. Tehran.

—— (1980) *Partow-i az Qor'an*, vol. III. Tehran.

—— (1983) *Vahdat va Azadi. Majmu'eh-e Panj Sokhanrani*, edited by M. Basteh Negar and M. M. Ja'fari. Tehran.

Tellenbach, S. (1985) *Untersuchungen zur Verfassung der Islamischen Republik Iran vom 15. November 1979*. Berlin.

—— (1990) 'Zur Änderung der Verfassung der Islamischen Republik Iran vom 28. Juli 1989.' *Orient* 31 (1990), pp. 45–65.

Vardasbi, Abu Zarr (1979) *Mahiyat-e Hokumat-e Eslami az Didgah-e Ayatollah Na'ini*. Tehran.

Vezarat-e Dadgostari: (1980) *Majmu'eh-e Qavanin 1358 (1979/1980)* Tehran.
Vezarat-e Ershad-e Eslami: (1983) *Negareshi bar Naqsh-e Matbu'at-e Va-basteh dar Ravand e Enqelab Eslami-ye Iran*, 2 vols., 2nd edition. Tehran.
—— (1985) *Karnameh-e Jomhuri-ye Eslami-ye Iran, Sal-e 1363.* Tehran.
Vezarat-e Keshavarzi: (1979) *Khotut-e Asli-ye Hadafha, Siyasatha va Sazman-e Keshavarzi dar Iran.* Tehran.

Watt, W. Montgomery (1980) *Der Islam*, vol. I.
Welhausen, Julius (1961) *Reste des arabischen Heidentums*, 3. Auflage. Berlin.

Yazdi, Ebrahim (1987) *Barrasi va Tahlil-e Gozaresh-e Komision-e Tower.* Ed. Nehzat-e Azadi. Tehran.

Zarshenas, Shahriyar (1992) *Farhang, Siyasat va Falsafeh.* Tehran.
—— (1992a) 'Azadi, Farhang, Towse'ah.' *Kayhan.*
Zanjani, Abu'l-Fazl (1978) *Nezam-e Ejtema'i-ye Eslam*, 3rd edition. Qom.


## Minutes:

Majles-e Showra-ye Eslami: (1985–89) *Surat-e Mashruh-e Mozakerat-e Majles-e Barrasi-ye Naha'i-ye Qanun-e Asasi-ye Jomhuri-ye Eslami-ye Iran.* Tehran.
—— (1990) *Surat-e Mashruh-e Mozakerat-e Showra-ye Baznegari-ye Qanun-e Asasi-ye Jomhuri-ye Eslami-ye Iran*, 3 vols. Tehran.
—— (1980–94) *Mashruh-e Mozakerat-e Majles-e Eslami.* Tehran.


## Newspapers:

Ayandegan, Kayhan, Khalq-e Mosalman, Azadi, Neda-ye Azadi, Kar, Ettehad-e Chap, Salam, Peygham-e Emruz, Ettela'at, Resalat, Jomhuri-ye Eslami.

# Index

165; politicisation of 142
World Bank 193

Yazdi, Ayatollah Mohammad 36, 38, 77, 95, 108, 190, 214, 235

*Zan-e Ruz* (periodical) 141
Zanjani, Ayatollah Reza 47, 48
Zarshenas, Shahriyar 143, 144
Zavvare'i, Reza 190, 126
Zionism 69
Ziya'i-Niya, 'Abdollah 53